Klaus Schulze

Electronic Music Legend

By Greg Allen

Order this book online at www.trafford.com
or email orders@trafford.com

Most Trafford titles are also available at major online book retailers.

Edited by Alan M. Perlman.
Cover design by Jan R. Kloosterman
Photography by Georg Abts.

Print information available on the last page.

ISBN: 978-1-4251-6050-0 (sc)

Trafford rev. 08/19/2019

www.trafford.com

North America & international
toll-free: 1 888 232 4444 (USA & Canada)
fax: 812 355 4082

Table of Contents

Acknowledgements

Thanks to the following people:

All those who granted me an interview for this book, including Harald Grosskopf, Dennis Rea, Joerg Schaaf, Michael Shrieve, Arthur Brown, Robert Rich, Julia Messenger, Thomas Kagermann, Kitaro, Marian Gold, Steve Roach, and Klaus Schulze.

Thanks also to Jan R. Kloosterman for graphic design help; Matt Howarth for permission to use his reviews of Klaus' music; David Law of Synthmusicdirect.com for support and review fragments from Synthmusicdirect's website; Matt Friedman, The Vintage Synth Explorer, for permission to use pictures and descriptions of synths; Derek Sheplawy, SPV North America for seven promo re-release CDs of titles I already owned; Matthew North, Arthur Brown's assistant for helping coordinate the interview with Arthur.

Additional thanks to Dino Malito for helping set up the interview with Kitaro; Georg Abts, Claus Cordes and Christian Piednoir for photography; Alan Perlman for manuscript editing; my brother-in-law Dave Donaldson for encouraging me to write this book; my wife Jeanette for being supportive and helping me edit and analyze portions of the interviews and graphics; my friend Kevin Urie, another huge Klaus Schulze fan, for suggestions and encouragement.

Last but not least, thanks to Klaus D. Mueller for general information, perspective and reviewing an early manuscript.

Introduction

My intention in writing this book on Klaus Schulze's career and music is to pay tribute to the person I consider the most important in the history of electronic music/synthesizers. That's a big claim. It's my opinion that Klaus Schulze was the central and most important figure in the advancement of electronically created music, specifically at the dawn of the electronic/synthesizer age in music - indeed, the greatest synthesizer based musician since the early 1970s.

I have long thought that when people in the future look at the "classical" music of our time (mid-20th century through early 21st century), they would view Klaus Schulze's music as the classical music of this era, just as we view Beethoven, Bach and Stravinsky as the "classical" musicians of their eras.

To back up that opinion, I will document the state of electronic music at the beginning when Klaus started his career in the early 1970s and then follow Klaus' astonishing progression through a string of ever more creative and emotionally satisfying albums. I will also try to emphasize the ever-reaching, -growing, -changing character of Klaus' music. To the delight of his fans, Klaus has gone through many distinct phases in his career but has always been unafraid to try new things, to open the door to new musical horizons.

Further advancing the argument that Klaus Schulze is the greatest of all the electronic musicians from the period 1970 through 2007 is the combination of the astounding quality of his output with the sheer volume of his released CDs, which number somewhere around 130-140.

Klaus' greatness has been recognized by others:

- Don Robertson: "I know that if you ask many musicians today who the greatest pioneer of the synthesizer was, they would say that it was Walter Carlos (who later changed his name to Wendy). For me, however, the greatest pioneer was the German, Klaus Schulze, whom many people have never heard of, at least in America" [Don Robertson, Nashville, TN, October, 2005 – more on Don Robertson at http://www.risingworld.tv/DonBio.asp].

- "Music Shop/Germany," November 1986 from the booklet of the re-release of Dreams: "What Klaus Schulze is doing right now has a great chance of becoming celebrated classical music in the future."

- At a CD shop in Crystal Lake, IL (USA), about four years ago, I met a guy who was working behind the counter and had a conversation about Klaus Schulze with him. We were talking about an Ash Ra Tempel CD that I wondered about, and the conversation got around to Klaus Schulze. I forget which one of us mentioned it first, but we found that we each had previously thought that Klaus Schulze's music would be the "classical" music of the future. We were both amazed, and I remember him telling me he couldn't wait to tell his friend (to whom I presume he had made this "crazy" assertion in the past) that he had met someone who had the very same opinion.

- See the section entitled "Relationship to Pink Floyd" for material on the mutual admiration of KS and Pink Floyd.

- See the 1975 reference to *Timewind* in the Music section for an accolade: "widely recognized as a masterpiece of electronic music."

- http://www.gepr.net/sa.html#SCHULZE

  "A pioneer who is still blazing new and unfound trails as we speak. It's not easy to find an individual who after making music for over 20 years professionally is still putting out excellent, uncompromising music.

  "For many years Klaus Schulze was one of the most influential European musicians in regards to synthesizers and their role in contemporary music. He is not only famous for his work with the legendary band Tangerine Dream, but also for his many experimental solo projects."

- Klaus D. Mueller (Klaus Schulze's publisher, longtime friend and occasional album producer):

  "Very positive article about Klaus I found in an American magazine, which printed this summer: 'He's the godfather of electronic keyboard music, the synthesizer Messiah incarnate, and along with Brian Eno, one of the most powerful influences, either directly or indirectly, on the world's greatest contemporary musicians. For over 20 years Klaus Schulze has been out in front of the pack and has never looked back.'"

- Klaus received the French Grand Prix International du Disque for Timewind, which in the three years before had gone to Soft Machine, Jimi Hendrix and Pink Floyd.

- http://tmachine.chat.ru/germ/S1.htm SCHULZE:

  "Along with Tangerine Dream, he has been the most important pioneer of electronic music, a genre that they indeed invented during the mid-seventies with their several pioneering albums. Maybe someday these artists will get the attention they deserve. In the meantime, new generations of synthesizer players continue to be influenced by them."

- http://www.syngate.net/008%20manikin/Manikin_Rainhorse_200014.html:

  "Klaus Schulze is the undisputed maestro of electronic music. Since his debut solo album in the early seventies, Schulze has repeatedly forged new ground with synthesizer music, creating several signature styles over the years that many consider to be the templates to judge all others in this genre."

- http://musicforyoureyes.blogspot.com/2007_01_01_archive.html:

  "Klaus Schulze began as a drummer (and what a drummer! Just listen to him on the first Tangerine Dream record or on the first Ash Ra Tempel [record]), but in his solo career, that started in 1972 with *Irrlicht*, he became the wizard of synthesizers, creating his own evocative and grandiose style that made him the main pioneer of popular electronic music."

- http:/www.soundonsound.com, from a February, 1996 interview with KS by Paul Tingen:

  "The reason for the sheer variety of sound sources and processing gear becomes clear only when you discover that this is the playground of one of the world's electronic synthesis pioneers... Since his debut album *Irrlicht* in 1972, he has influenced virtually everybody who has ever worked with synthesizers. To name but a few: '80s keyboard luminaries Vangelis, Kitaro or Jean Michel Jarre, '90s acts such as The Orb or The Grid, and the current new age and ambient house movements."

- July 1984, "Synthetic Pleasure, USA" (from the Official KS Website)

  "Ah, the master has done it again. I firmly believe that Klaus Schulze is as important to electronic music as BACH or MOZART were to classical music."

Discography for Klaus Schulze from the Official Klaus Schulze Website:

http://www.klaus-schulze.com

Solo Albums

- ▷ *Irrlicht* – 1972
- ▷ *Cyborg* – 1973
- ▷ *Blackdance* – 1974
- ▷ *Picture Music* – 1975
- ▷ *Timewind* – 1975
- ▷ *Moondawn – The Original Master* – 1976
- ▷ *Moondawn* – 1976
- ▷ *Body Love* – 1977
- ▷ *Mirage* – 1977
- ▷ *Body Love Vol. 2* – 1977
- ▷ *X* – 1978
- ▷ *Dune* – 1979
- ▷ *...Live...* - 1980
- ▷ *Dig It* – 1980
- ▷ *Trancefer* – 1981
- ▷ *Audentity* – 1983
- ▷ *Dziekuje Poland Live* – 1983
- ▷ *Angst* – 1984
- ▷ *Inter*Face* – 1985
- ▷ *Dreams* – 1986
- ▷ *En=Trance* – 1988
- ▷ *Miditerranean Pads* – 1990
- ▷ *The Dresden Performance* – 1990
- ▷ *Beyond Recall* – 1991
- ▷ *Royal Festival Hall Vol. 1* - 1992
- ▷ *Royal Festival Hall Vol. 2* - 1992
- ▷ *The Dome Event* - 1993
- ▷ *Le Moulin de Daudet* - 1994
- ▷ *Goes Classic (Midi Klassik)* – 1994
- ▷ *Totentag* – 1994
- ▷ *Das Wagner Desaster* – 1994
- ▷ *In Blue* – 1995
- ▷ *Are You Sequenced?* – 1996
- ▷ *Dosburg Online* – 1997
- ▷ *Live @ KlangArt CD1* – 2001
- ▷ *Live @ KlangArt CD2* – 2001
- ▷ *"Andromeda" Promo CD* – 2003
- ▷ *"Ion" Promo CD* – 2004

- ▷ *Moonlake* – 2005
- ▷ *Vanity of Sounds* – 2005
- ▷ *The Crime of Suspense* – 2006
- ▷ *Ballett 1* – 2006
- ▷ *Ballett 2* – 2006
- ▷ *Ballett 3* – 2007
- ▷ *Kontinuum* – 2007

The Wahnfried Albums

- ▷ *Time Actor* – 1979
- ▷ *Tonwelle* – 1981
- ▷ *Megatone* – 1984
- ▷ *Miditation* – 1986
- ▷ Trancelation – 1994
- ▷ *Trance Appeal* – 1996
- ▷ *Drums 'n' Balls (The Gancha Dub)*

The CD Sets

- ▷ *Silver Edition* – 1993
- ▷ *Historic Edition* – 1995
- ▷ *Jubilee Edition* – 1997
- ▷ *The Ultimate Edition*
- ▷ *Contemporary Works I*
- ▷ *Contemporary Works II*

Collaborations with other Artists

- ▷ *Electronic Meditation* (with Tangerine Dream) – 1970
- ▷ *Ash Ra Tempel* (with Ash Ra Tempel) - 1971
- ▷ *Join Inn* (with Ash Ra Tempel) – 1973
- ▷ *Tarot* (with Walter Wegmüller) - 1973
- ▷ *Lord Krishna von Goloka* (with Sergius Golowin) – 1973
- ▷ *The Cosmic Jokers* (with The Cosmic Jokers) – 1974
- ▷ *Planeten Sit In* (with The Cosmic Jokers) – 1974
- ▷ *Galactic Supermarket* (with The Cosmic Jokers) – 1974
- ▷ *Sci Fi Party* (with The Cosmic Jokers) – 1974
- ▷ *Gilles Zeischiff* (with The Cosmic Jokers) – 1974
- ▷ *Go* (with Stomu Yamash'ta) – 1976
- ▷ *Go Live from Paris* (with Stomu Yamash'ta) – 1976
- ▷ *Go Too* (with Stomu Yamash'ta) – 1977
- ▷ *Aphrica* (with Rainer Bloss and Ernst Fuchs) – 1984
- ▷ *Drive Inn* (with Rainer Bloss) – 1984
- ▷ *Transfer Station Blue* (with Michael Shrieve and Kevin Shrieve) – 1984
- ▷ *Babel* (with Andreas Grosser) – 1987
- ▷ *Friendship* (with Ash Ra Tempel) – 2000

- ▷ *Gin Rose at the Royal Festival Hall* (with Ash Ra Tempel) – 2000

The Dark Side of the Moog Series

- ▷ *The Dark Side of the Moog* – 1994
- ▷ *The Dark Side of the Moog 2* – 1994
- ▷ *The Dark Side of the Moog 3* - 1995
- ▷ *The Dark Side of the Moog 4* - 1996
- ▷ *The Dark Side of the Moog 5* - 1996
- ▷ *The Dark Side of the Moog 6* - 1997
- ▷ *The Dark Side of the Moog 7* - 1998
- ▷ *The Dark Side of the Moog 8* - 1999
- ▷ *The Dark Side of the Moog 9* - 2002
- ▷ *The Dark Side of the Moog 10* – 2005

The Samplers

- ▷ *2001* – 1991
- ▷ *The Essential 72-93* – 1994
- ▷ *Trailer* – 1999

The Lone Tracks

- ▷ *Macksy* – 1985
- ▷ *Berlin 1* – 1986
- ▷ *Unikat* – 1989
- ▷ *Face of Mae West* – 1990
- ▷ *Große Gaukler Gottes* – 1994
- ▷ *Vas Insigne Electionis* - 1994
- ▷ *Conquest of Paradise* – 1994
- ▷ *Soirée Académique* - 1996
- ▷ *Les Bruits des Origines* – 1996
- ▷ *Dédié à Hartmut* – 1996
- ▷ *Ooze Away* – 1996
- ▷ *Ein würdiger Abschluß* – 1996
- ▷ *Dreieinhalb Stunden* – 1996
- ▷ *Himmel und Erde* – 1996
- ▷ *Der vierte Kuss* – 1996
- ▷ *The Schulzendorf Groove* – 1998
- ▷ *Manikin Jubilee* – 2002
- ▷ *Schrittmacher* – 2004

Chapter 1 My Feelings about Klaus Schulze's Music

Klaus Schulze is my favorite musical artist, period. Even though I developed a love for such musical styles as 1960s top 40, 1970s progressive rock, 1980s/'90s dance music, reggae music and of course, electronic music – Klaus still tops the list for me.

Why would I rate Klaus Schulze ahead of all the music that I've heard since I was 12 years old?

In the early days the music was new, different, very compelling and could evoke deep emotion within me. It was like discovering an amazing new planet! Klaus Schulze released a string of brilliant albums right at the start of his career, some that could immediately elicit the sentiment as "best album I've ever heard." *Timewind* was one of the first to evoke that kind of feeling within me (others: *Picture Music, Moondawn* and *Mirage*). This was an astonishing album; unlike any I'd ever heard before, using the sweetest sounding synthesizer pads imaginable. It stirred deep emotion and positive feelings in me with its yearning, plaintive sounds.

Moondawn, Klaus' 6th album, was ethereal and soothing, transporting me to another place. *Moondawn* was aesthetically pleasing and caused a warm, yet introspective feeling within me. A mysterious voice reciting a prayer near the start of the album was very different from any beginning to an album I'd yet heard. There was almost a feeling arising from hearing *Timewind* and *Moondawn* that made me feel I was understood in my human pain - that Klaus' music lifted me up and out of that pain into a place where beauty, majesty, and inspiration existed. At its peak, this feeling resulting from listening to Klaus' albums could compare to that inexplicable feeling experienced rarely - when viewing great art or watching a stunning sunset or attending an unforgettable concert.

Mirage, again, was unlike any music I'd ever listened to. The wall of sound in "Velvet Voyage" excited and stimulated me. How could anyone dream up such a unique soundscape that is so different from anything recorded before or since?

This trend of innovation kept going on, with some exceptions, through the rest of the '70s and into the '80s. I had great difficulty obtaining Klaus Schulze albums for a period in the 1980s. Klaus' music in that decade overall surely didn't measure up to the high standards set by the string of innovative albums of the 1970s. However, there is plenty of great music available on the '80s albums. *Audentity* and *En=Trance* represent Klaus' 1980s pinnacle, in my opinion. There is solid material to be found on *Dig It, Dreams, Inter*Face,* and *Trancefer* as well. Those albums tend to have a little less consistency in terms of the strength of the material. Yet each does offer some brilliant music that stands up to Klaus' best work. They represent a listening challenge at first, but repeated listening will be rewarded.

Highlights of Klaus' 1980s output include "FM Delight" and "Velvet System" from *En=Trance,* "Death of an Analogue" and "The Looper isn't a Hooker" from *Dig It,* "Spielglocken" from *Audentity,* "The Real Colours in the Darkness" and "Inter*Face" from *Inter*Face, Transfer Station Blue* with Michael and Kevin Shrieve, "Ludwig II" from *Dziekuje Poland,* and "Dreams" from the album of the same name.

Klaus experienced a resurgence in the 1990s with such works as *Beyond Recall*, *In Blue*, *Royal Festival Hall Vol. 2*, *The Dark Side of the Moog* releases, *Le Moulin de Daudet*, much of the material from the boxed sets and *Dosburg Online*.

Klaus' career has blossomed in a stunning way since 2000, with *The Contemporary Works* sets (The Ballett series being excellent), "But Beautiful" as a bonus track on *Cyborg*, the extended version of "Georg Trakl" on the re-release of *X*, a good but not great album in *Moonlake*, and the final installments in the *Dark Side of the Moog* series. And then I had the pleasant, almost shocking experience of listening to *Kontinuum* for the first time – a superb album, one of Klaus' best in years and probably one of his best ever. Klaus Schulze, nearing 60 (Klaus will probably be 60 when you read this), is still creating, composing and playing at a very high level!

I occasionally feel a little discomfort when listening to a strange sample or a bizarre or frightening passage in Klaus' music. Sometimes I don't know if it's because the passage disturbs me or whether I am disturbed by the fact that the passage ensures that I will probably not be able to share the music with friends and get a positive reaction.

When I bought 10 CDs of *Jubilee Edition* on eBay and listened to "Opera Trance," I experienced this phenomenon when the operatic voice changed pitch and took on a bizarre sound.

This may be an example of what Klaus means when he says that you need ugliness to contrast with beauty so that beauty can be appreciated (see my interview with Klaus later in this book for insight on this subject). And, I think it works, actually. "Opera Trance" is a well recorded, very emotionally rewarding work.

This gets to the bottom of why I feel the way I do about Klaus' music. Klaus' output already ranked as brilliant, with about 50 solo releases. Add the 50+ CDs of unreleased material that was of frequently high quality and his body of work becomes mind blowing!

Not to mention the excellent *Dark Side of the Moog* collaborations with Pete Namlook (and sometimes Bill Laswell). I had never heard any of the CDs from this set, so I read lots of reviews and ordered *Dark Side of the Moog 4, 5, 6* and 7 from Eurock.com. The music is great, and no KS fan should be without at least some of them, depending on their availability.

I also acquired *The Dark Side of the Moog IX* towards the end of writing this book (don't miss my review of that CD!).

With each additional revelation of great Schulze music, I feel more in awe of his genius. The re-releases have very nice covers, artwork, interviews and bonus tracks, so I have probably become a bigger Klaus Schulze fan now than ever before; my appreciation is at its peak. And that feeling is still growing!

This is a rewarding hobby, being a Schulze fan! I want to connect with other fans and to celebrate his music and its rich emotional content. When speaking of emotions while considering Klaus

Schulze's body of work, it's important to remember that Klaus has said many times that his music is created to elicit emotions, just emotions. Throughout my reviews of his music contained in this book, you'll see many references to emotions, ranging from fear in parts of *Irrlicht* to joy and even bliss at times in the most uplifting passages of Klaus' music (of which there are many).

So I unabashedly say: Klaus Schulze is my favorite musical artist of all time! I hope that this book will find its way into the hands of other enthusiasts and enrich their knowledge and appreciation of this man who has thrilled and inspired us all.

Introduction to Klaus D. Mueller

Note: Klaus D. Mueller is Klaus Schulze's good friend, publisher and sometimes CD producer, not his manager, as many think.

From an interview with his friend Archie Patterson (of Eurock.com):

KDM: "I worked with him (notice the "with"), by doing the things he's not able or not willing to do: from bookkeeping, statistics and writing letters, to carrying and maintenance of the instruments. Also making photos, covers, tour management, the stage set-up, the stage lighting... Care of the instruments' I dropped in the early eighties. Officially, and since 1978, I'm his publisher; I "publish" his compositions. And that's my only income. Except if I produce albums, then I get my share from this too.

I gave an older interview the heading: I try to bring order into the chaos. This explains in 8 words my job. If someone wants to know more details about my work then and now, this other interview can be found in the "Miscellaneous" section on the KS website: www.klaus-schulze.com"

Chapter 2 Prevailing social conditions and attitudes in Germany in the late 1960s and early 1970s relevant to the career path of Klaus Schulze

Here is Harald Grosskopf's take on the social conditions and attitudes in Germany, from my interview with him [since I split up Harald's interview according to subject, his first answer may appear out of order]:

GA: I read in an article in the booklet for the re-release of *X* that Klaus indicated you were looking for something different than conventional rock music. Can you talk about that in terms of your motivation at that time to do something different?

HG: I touched on that theme during other answers. Let's get deeper into the matter. From my point of view, music in Germany - I am talking about the young music scene from 1945 until the end of the sixties, was much influenced by psychological and political circumstances. WW2 changed several of the German young generation and their identification with its own cultural musical roots, radically. It separated the society into two big parts. Symbolically seen in that real separation of the country until 1989, the year the wall came down.

On the one hand "the besieged" Nazi generation (in reality rescued!) denied every refreshing cultural "outside" influence and tried hard in keeping their old identification. This was my parents' generation. On the other hand the younger Germans swallowed everything that came from "outside", like modern Anglo-American music (big band jazz, rock 'n roll) and film and denied their own traditions. Tradition = Nazi = we don't want anything to do with that.

A whole country went numb. The old said: "we didn't know anything!" or "we don't wanna hear!" or "it's enough!". The whole German administration, jurisprudence, police and education structures were still dominated by Nazi people.

A change was brought by student riots against this system at the end of the sixties. But that change seems to miss music. Young people still hated their own tradition. Just a handful [of] people started to create their own music, by using most developed technique. Tangerine Dream, Ash Ra Tempel in Berlin, Popol Vuh in Munich, Neu, Kraftwerk (the most successful!!) and Harmonia in Dusseldorf (west). East Germany was "out of business" for a long period.

The following, from an interview with KDM in November of 1994, describes KS's contributions at this point:

"Because it was KS and Edgar who fought hard, who starved, who put their souls into Electronic Music in 1971, 1972, 1973, 1974, 1975, 1976, 1977, 1978...; it was KS with his money who established in 1979 the first label for young electronic musicians: Innovative Communication. It was KS who founded a school to learn synths, from 1978 to '79. It was Klaus who turned on Kitaro (1975) and many others to electronics. It was Edgar and Klaus who made hundreds of concerts for 25 years, and who gave thousands of interviews, showing and explaining to the world about this crazy new music. So, we have indeed some reason to speak, and therefore we say now: 'Merde.'"

Chapter 3 Klaus' Early Instruments

TEISCO organ

Please see the booklet in the *Irrlicht* re-release from Revisited Records for a picture of Klaus with the TEISCO organ, which is the brand that he used in the recording of *Irrlicht*.

"The ARP 2600 enjoyed a 10-year production run. The picture below shows the version that Klaus used, according to KDM."

From www.vintagesynth.com (description and photo):

ARP 2600P

"Later in 1971 came the 2600P V1.0, which featured the same metal case (housing the same electronics as the original models), now enclosed in a much more road-worthy suitcase-style enclosure (similar to the one in the pic).

In 1972, ARP switched out the unreliable (Teledyne) VCO chips for the model 4027 and 4027-1 (National Semiconductor) VCO chips in the 2600P V2.0 and 2600P V3.0, respectively. These new VCO chips sounded weak and nowhere near as good as the originals.

A new duo-phonic keyboard (3620) with LFO was introduced with the 2600P V4.0 in 1974. The 2600P V3.0 and V4.0 models are denoted by the "G-clef" ARP logo and are the most common models out there, with roughly 1700 2600P's produced during 1971-1974.

Unfortunately, further changes to inferior parts were just around the corner. The Model 4012 filter used in all the 2600's through 1976 used a design that was a copy of Moog's patented ladder-filter design. This led to a lawsuit between Moog and ARP, and ARP was forced to design its own filter for their next version"

Moog Modular

A highly distinguished leader – and probably the most famous modern synthesizer designer – was Dr. Robert Moog.

In an interview from April, 1997, which is on the Official Klaus Schulze Website Klaus said, "I was a fan of Pink Floyd in the sixties. And I always loved the Moog sound. It is legendary. I met Robert Moog face to face first during an electronic festival in Austria in 1980. I did the opening concert there, and we were both in the jury to choose which newly invented electronic music instrument gets a prize. Later we phoned, and we met again on a music fair here in Germany."

Dr. Moog began building synthesizers in 1964 with a modular synthesizer; he applied the term "synthesizer" to his new creation in 1967. The 1964 model was the first to use subtractive synthesis and a keyboard. In 1968, the first commercially successful electronic record, *Switched on Bach*, was released by Wendy Carlos (then known as "Walter").

Here is part of a Wikipedia article that describes the impact of *Switched On Bach*:

"It was the first record to popularize music performed on electronic synthesizers, and resulted in a huge increase in interest in them, particularly Moog synthesizers. The album was the first classical album to sell 500,000 copies, and go platinum. Entering Billboard's pop Top 40 charts on March 1, 1969, it climbed quickly to the Top 10; it stayed in the Top 40 for 17 weeks and in the Top 200 for more than a year. In the 1970 Grammy awards, the album took three prizes: Best Classical Album, Best Classical Music Performance, Instrumental Soloist(s) (With or Without Orchestra) and Best Engineered Classical Recording."

Wendy Carlos was the only one creating and releasing albums of any commercial viability using all electronics, until Klaus Schulze began doing so in 1972.

www.vintagesynth.com (description of Moog Modular)

According to the site:

"If you could look up 'Vintage Synthesizer' in the dictionary, you would likely find a picture of some monstrous Moog modular system. These systems are simply racks of modular components, a VCA module, different types of Oscillator modules, VCF filters and other modules. This modular system allows you to build your synth to your needs and liking. These systems require you to use patch cables to route your signal from the keyboard through the modules and out the amp... think you can do it? This is analog synthesis at its finest and rawest. And the sound is legendary Moog sound. Commanding very high prices even today, almost 30 years later, these machines are the property of only the lucky few."

EMS VCS3 - Modular Synthesizer

www.vintagesynth.com (photo)

The VCS3 was only used briefly by Klaus Schulze. It was used on *Cyborg* and *Picture Music*. The following is from my correspondence with Klaus D. Mueller:

"Apart of a very short time in the beginning, Klaus never played the VCS3. Soon after he got this instrument he exchanged it (I think he gave it to Edgar Froese) for the smaller and better-to-carry 'Synthi A' (it looks like a suitcase, if closed)... Also, he never had and he never used the EMS keyboard (that you can buy separately for adding to the VCS3 or the Synthi A)." (See Harald Grosskopf's drawing of Klaus' studio in the coming pages.)

EMS Synthi A

In the words of KDM, "this is what KS used and still uses immensely. [See my interview with Klaus for further explanation on the Synthi A and how he uses it today - GA]"

Klaus in concert with the Synthi A (the Synthi A is on the left).

ARP Odyssey 1972–1974

www.vintagesynth.com (description and photo)

"The ARP Odyssey was and still is a very popular synth because it is a powerful lightweight version of the awesome ARP 2600. It was also ARP's response to the Minimoog and the Odyssey became the most popular synth ARP ever sold!

"The Odyssey is a 2-oscillator analog synth (with duophonic capability) which sounds really nice; the Minimoog has 3 oscillators and is considered fatter. The Odyssey comes well equipped with all the tweakable features you'd expect: resonant low pass filter, ADSR envelopes, sine or square wave LFO and even a sample-and-hold function.

"It also added a few new features such as a high pass filter in series with the low pass, oscillator sync capability and pulse width modulation. It is a very professional and expressive machine that can create nice analog basses, interesting leads and great effects and sweeping sounds or noises!"

The ARP Odyssey is the synthesizer used to create that bubbling, percolating, magical rhythm that is at the heart of "Totem" from *Picture Music*. Again, in the words of KDM, "Yes, Klaus had one of these, with the light colour. Important: Klaus used it with two pedals: one for the important Sample & Hold and one for the filter!"

The Minimoog, the Preeminent Portable Synthesizer of the 1970s

www.vintagesynth.com (description and photo)

The top early portable synthesizer was The Minimoog. The last Minimoogs were produced in 1985 before Moog Music went bankrupt in 1986. From vintagesynth.com: "The Minimoog is responsible for some of the warmest and best analog synth bass, lead and whistle sounds ever. Its control panel can lay flat or propped up perpendicular to the keyboard. It also has a great wood casing. Very rugged. A very versatile synth, useful in all styles of music and easy enough for anybody to operate!"

The Mellotron

The mellotron was made from 1963-1986. The mellotron is included in the instrument listing for Klaus's 10th album, *X*. Regarding the mellotron in the context of Klaus Schulze's work, as related by KDM, "I saw it once in KS' studio. It was white (and rarely used, because it was impractical and instable. When I saw it, it was used just as a table)."

Korg Poly Synthi PS-3300 (used on *X*)

www.vintagesynth.com (description and photo)

"The PS-3300 is a megalithic semi-modular two piece synthesizer system from Korg. It was one of the first truly polyphonic analog synthesizers from the mid '70s! Beautiful wood panels, plenty of knobs and patch-points and a bold Korg sound! The system follows the PS-3100 model.

"The PS-3300 is like having 3 stacked PS-3100s with a built-in mixer module. In addition to a great Korg sound, it features incredible modulation abilities and is still a very useful and coveted synth even today."

Fairlight Computer Music Instrument

www.vintagesynth.com (description and photo)

"The Australian Fairlight Computer Music Instrument (CMI) is a vintage but state-of-the-art Synthesizer/Sampler workstation. An incredible sampler with 28 megabytes or more of memory! One or two full 73 note velocity sensitive keyboards! Complete synthesis and editing of digitally sampled sounds. Three different on-board SMPTE Sequencers and storage to various disk mediums. The processor itself is housed in a 24" module. It was also the first digital sampler to hit the market back in 1979 and has endured throughout the eighties and nineties."

An important observation by KDM shows that Klaus did not use this instrument much at all: "KS was not very happy with that tool and rarely used it, at least not very long. It was just very expensive. When he tried it for the first time in a concert, it didn't work; from that moment on he dropped it. This is the only thing I can say about it."

Harald Grosskopf Sketch of Klaus Schulze's Studio 1976

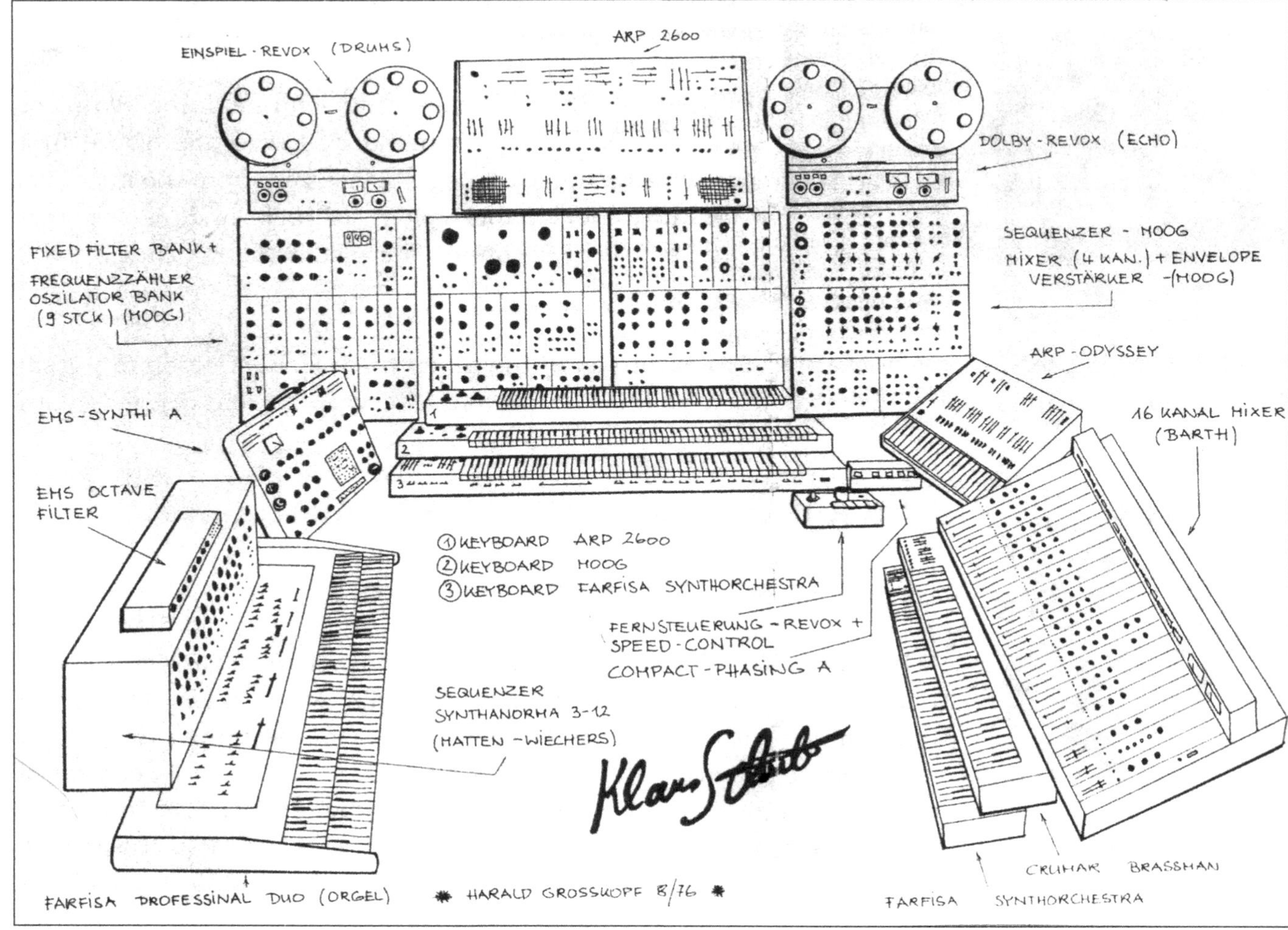

Klaus' studio circa 1976, when *Moondawn* was released, as sketched by Harald Grosskopf (drummer on *Moondawn*) shows some of these early synthesizers.

KDM: "Some other explanations of the German words:
Einspiel-Revox = playback Revox (Revox = a very good tape recording machine)
Verstärker = amplifier
Fernsteuerung = remote control
Frequenzzähler = frequency counter"

Chapter 4 Chronology: Klaus Schulze's Early Life

Certain elements of the chronology below with permission from Jan R. Kloosterman (© *2007 Volkmar Friauf / Jan R. Kloosterman* http://users.bart.nl/~klooster/faq/intro.htm:)

August 4, 1947 – Klaus Schulze was born in Berlin, Germany

Klaus' father was a writer and his mother a ballet dancer. His parents presented him with a classical guitar, wanting him to learn classical music

1952-1958 (approximately) – Klaus took guitar lessons

1963 - Klaus' family lived in Dusseldorf for a few years where Klaus played bass in a small dance band named "Les Barons."

Klaus D. Mueller, on whether Klaus played drums or bass in this band: "I saw a private photo where KS was playing the bass in that beat band, but not the drums."

1967 - Klaus had been dissatisfied playing the Anglo-American rock style of music, so wanting to play a different style of music, he became a member of the band Psy Free. As Klaus put it in the original release of his 10th album *X* and on many other occasions: "I started as a drummer, playing Anglo-American pop music and began soon with my own group Psy Free to search for my own direction."

1968-1969 - Klaus was a member of Psy Free. Other members were Joachim Schumann and Alex Conti (from the band Curly Curve). The band had several gigs at Berlin's Zodiak, Magic Cave, and Silver Apple.

From an interview with *Perfect Sound Forever* by Billy Bob Hargus (May 1997):

PSF: Could you talk about the work you did with Psy Free? Are there any surviving recordings?

KS: No, there were no recordings made. Why should we, or someone else? Psy Free was a trio consisting of guitar, organ and drums. I was the drummer. We did what the name suggests: psychedelic, free music. Not "free jazz" which was in common at this time, but more rock orientated noise. We played in Berlin clubs.

1969 - Joined Tangerine Dream and made one album, *Electronic Meditation*. Before the release of *Electronic Meditation*, Klaus had left Tangerine Dream and founded Ash Ra Tempel with Manuel Göttsching.

In my research I ran across references to Klaus and Manuel co-founding Ash Ra Tempel and some that cited Klaus as having founded Ash Ra Tempel. The references to co-founding seemed more numerous, but I will mention that Klaus said that he had "founded" Ash Ra Tempel and as you will see in the following quote from KDM, he concurs. So the best information that I have, relayed in the first person, is that Klaus founded Ash Ra Tempel rather than co-founded.

KDM: "Manuel and Hartmut were playing blues-rock when KS met them. Klaus had the idea for the trio and for the musical change. So, it's either "KS founded Ash Ra Tempel" (as it is remembered today) or "all three made then...".

Generally it's said that the band was KS' idea. Also, the new name comes from KS (Before, the two were the Steeple Chase Blues Band.)

And if you knew the other two (who are five years younger than KS), you would quickly agree: Klaus is a "maker" -- the one who has the ideas, and is eager to try them out, then and today."

From *Perfect Sound Forever*:

KS: Then I founded Ash Ra Tempel. The two guys, Manuel (Göttsching) and Hartmut (Enke), were playing a kind a fast blues rock when I met them. My fast bass drum style impressed them. From Blues we changed to "Space Rock."

Here is Klaus' memory of recording the album *Electronic Meditation* with Tangerine Dream:

"We recorded and toured *Electronic Meditation*. That for me is the primary electronic album. Edgar played guitar, Schnitzler organ and me drums through loads of effects. We were experimenting with a lot of random stuff and were making up our own sounds. I remember Conrad had this metal cup full of these bits of glass in which he stuck a microphone attached to each machine. I played a lot of different percussive sounds that were then altered by machines. It was just great to be in a band who were open to so much experimentation."

KDM notes that "toured" may be a misunderstanding: "Tangerine Dream was not touring much. Just five or six gigs outside of Berlin are known during the few months as a trio with KS. And what they were playing (and what TD was generally playing at least up into the seventies) was always improvised."

KDM also says that "Primary electronic album" may be a mis-translation: "I only remember KS often saying in interviews that his first album was anything but 'electronic.' He calls *Electronic Meditation* often as 'The first true punk album' but not "electronic."". And of course he's right: there was no 'electronic' involved."

The following, from *Perfect Sound Forever*, is also relevant:

PSF: With Tangerine Dream, how did you come to work with Edgar? What was your, Edgar's and Conrad's idea about the band and its music? What did you think of its later music? With Ash Ra Tempel, how was this band different for you? What was the idea behind it?

KS: There was no "idea" behind it. Please understand that we did it not with today's retrospect view. We just did it. Then. And we had fun doing it. This goes for both bands, TD as well as A.R.T. For Tangerine Dream: One evening their drummer was absent, and I joined instead. And I kept the drum chair for the following eight months or so. During this time, we also recorded the first album. I told the following story very often: at one of our concerts I tried to play some organ tapes that I had recorded and treated in an uncommon fashion. Edgar didn't like that. He wanted just a drummer for his guitar/bass/drums group, and no "funny" experiments. Therefore, I left. Conrad Schnitzler soon followed. Both of us in a friendly way.

KDM notes that "Edgar was a huge fan of Jimi Hendrix."

1970 - Ash Ra Tempel with Manuel Göttsching and Harmut Enke

1971 - After one album with Ash Ra Tempel and some concerts, Klaus decided to go on his own, thus leading to the spectacular solo career that is the reason for this book! Klaus has talked many times about his reason for going solo: in the band context, there was too much discussion; each member had different ideas about which direction the music should take. Klaus has mentioned how the group would sometimes spend more time in discussions about the music than in playing the music. He grew tired of that and wanted to have control over the music he played.

In Klaus' own words:

PSF: What led you to go solo? How did that feel after being in all of these bands?

KS: Thanks, I feel good. I went solo because I could do much better what I wanted to do. I didn't have to ask or discuss things and ideas that are already shaped in my head.

Chapter 5 Klaus' Early Reception at the Start of his Solo Career

Klaus' Early Reception

Wendy Carlos had performed classical music that was previously composed, in *Switched on Bach*, but Klaus had embarked on a new voyage, which included composing strange new music, different from anything that had come before. Here are some comments to me from KDM; they reveal a lot about the conditions in Germany at the outset of Klaus' career and about the adversity Klaus faced as he ventured into uncharted territory.

"In 1972 when KS started, even Edgar Froese was still very much an electric guitar player a la Hendrix (Edgar's great idol then). KS told me the story when they had a gig as supporting group for a new star, Jimi Hendrix, here in Berlin. Edgar was scared: He, with his Hendrix-like playing (but not so good and 'cool') must play before the original!"

"In these years there were no cheap mixers available. Synthesizers were out of reach for young musicians here in Germany (and elsewhere) who just came from school and wanted to make music. Parents of course hated that and didn't support. Multitrack recording was even more difficult and you had to go to (and to pay) a professional studio for that. Ash Ra Tempel once did it, before their first album: A disaster. The studio people and the secretaries hated it. 'Too loud,' of course (as always), 'Too wild, Too long, Too disorganized.'

"Most of these youngsters made rock during this time, but in most cases it was the rock of the day, either Beatles, Stones, or they tried to play like The Grateful Dead etc. (but in all cases it was just lousy copies). Not many sit down and start on their own with simple equipment to invent something of their own. They had their albums at home, from their idols, and wanted to play like them. As in every generation.

"*Irrlicht* was different. It was not the usual pop or rock of the day. But it was released and marketed as a "pop" record (and not like Stockhausen or Subotnick or Ussachevsky etc.).

"And the reactions to *Irrlicht* and *Cyborg* (from the pop/rock front) were: 'he's an idiot,' 'what is this. . . shit?", 'not listenable,' etc. What else?

"The colleagues from Amon Duul, Can, and all the rest, still played with drums, bass, electric guitar, (organ sometimes), and a singer, trying to follow the English-American trend. Sometimes they found their own sound (as CAN) because they simply could not play as good as their idols from the USA or England.

"Best example: Tangerine Dream, who was really into Pink Floyd. Of course they wanted to do the same as Pink Floyd did. But what came out? Something else. And it was successful, at least after'73 and with a good working label. I cannot prove it, but I guess that this happens often in music history: A young man (or group) tries to copy something that he likes from his idol(s), but he is not good enough; instead he 'finds' a new music.

"Who else was (in 1972, 1973, 1974, etc.) in solo "home-recording"?

The discussion continues as follows:

GA: Just Klaus Schulze? Especially *Irrlicht, Cyborg*? *Blackdance/Picture Music*? Does this mean the original recordings of these albums were made at home rather than a recording studio and that was unique to KS?

KDM: Yes, at home. In his living room, sometimes sleeping room. Didn't you know this? Isn't this said in the album's credits? Or in interviews? And if you look at the photos of this era. Of course young KS spoke (then) of "The Klaus Schulze Studio" which in fact consists of a cheap tape recorder (in the beginning not even a "Revox" but a little common "Telefunken" with quarter-tracks and a built-in microphone with which he recorded a string orchestra for *Irrlicht*), the usual little tape-echo machine like electric guitar-players had, and a broken old electric organ. If you look at today's music scene, nearly everyone is doing home-recording. In the press I read that many of the former famous studios close down, also in the USA and of course even more of the small studios close.

"Techno" or "electro" is the big thing, regardless if in fact the music is simply a pop singer like Madonna or really some interesting electronic stuff. This was absolutely not the case in the early seventies. And this is what I tried to say (in my above cited "Who else...")

KDM: Who else (in 1972, 1973 1974 etc.) tried to work with only electronics?

GA: Tangerine Dream and Tomita in 1974, Wendy Carlos, Morton Subotnick and maybe TONTO's Expanding Headband.

KDM: There was this success made by Virgin Records with Tangerine Dream's *Phaedra*. Early '74, this was. And there was this huge worldwide success on the pop market with *Autobahn* by Kraftwerk (end of '74). Before, in 1972, there was a hit called "*Popcorn*," made with just electronics. And in 1969 was of course Carlos' now famous *Bach* album, even praised by Glenn Gould then; a sensation, but not very influential to the normal pop and rock scene. And a man like Subotnik, and many others - "unknown" professors who worked with "electronics" since the fifties, were completely without influence. Their albums were not even released here - or hard to get. There was simply no interest and no market for that kind of "serious" avant garde music. There is still not. There was no general working with electronics or doing home-recording

And there was a producer named Giorgio Moroder with his huge Donna Summer hit in December 1975, based just on a driving sequencer. (He is not even mentioned in a large German "Rock Lexikon").

This is what I always mean and say if someone tells me he writes a book about that time, but he was not born yet and not present. And suddenly some Krautbands are in [his] hindsight "electronic" but in fact they were still playing in that rock vein, until "electronic" was more popular, at the very end of the seventies. Then, the keyboard players of each rock band had suddenly their own Moog or whatever. Sometimes they surrounded themselves with more electronic keyboards than KS had in his heyday! The music was still not "electronic" but pop or rock (nothing wrong with that, only said for the history).

And who was laughed at, by the press, by most of the people, by many of the colleagues?

GA: Klaus Schulze?

KDM: Yes, of course Klaus Schulze. Just one example: when KS was at the local radio to promote his new album *Irrlicht*, the radio people said, "He's nuts." Later, KS told this story in various interviews. And when you listen to *Irrlicht*, and remember 1972, you understand these radio people.

Is *Irrlicht* the usual pop or rock album which you expect from a long-haired hippie and rock drummer around 1972? Just look what was popular in 1972 - Gilbert O'Sullivan, Don McLean's "*American Pie*", Roberta Flack, "*A Horse With No Name*" by America, Bill Withers with "*Lean On Me*", *Chicago V, Concert for Bangla Desh*, Neil Young's *Harvest*, etc.

Best new artist of the year was a group with the name America. Of course, the American and British music successes were always taken over to Germany and Europe. I remember a German group had a recording date in a German studio. To get the right feeling and groove (and inspiration) they were listening over the headphones to the latest hit by Fleetwood Mac. And with this permanent sound they recorded their single, which later was indeed a mild little hit in Germany but it was the biggest thing that this Krautrock group ever made and sold, and of course it reminded stark on this Fleetwood Mac song. Their drummer told me once this story.

These questions lead to: what was the situation for such a musician being noticed? Same as in other countries, I guess. The wider audience did not notice. A few minutes of this music was just rarely on a special radio program, and one or two music magazines noticed it, and that's it.

This happens all the time and again and again. Normally, the artist then changes his style, or he gives up playing and recording music, or he becomes A&R manager in the record industry, or studio manager, or whatever. The leader and keyboard player of the above mentioned Kraut-group is today a very good and prominent critic in Germany's leading daily newspaper, when it comes to cooking, kitchen, food, and restaurants: Juergen Dollase.

For KS, the wider audience still does not notice. He's never on TV (once or twice during 35 years), and rarely played on the radio (only in very rare special programs). For the press he's simply no "sensation" anymore, no new young turk.

KDM: What could he [Klaus Schulze] do about it?

GA: Promotion, play concerts, continue releasing new work, persevere through a strong personal love of the art form and ignore things such as fame, commercialism or acclaim as prime motivators, which is just what I think he did.

KDM: To do "promotion" costs a lot of money. After all, it's never done by the artist himself but by people or companies who believe that it will pay, sooner or later - but... if no one wants to hear the music? KS' record company did promotion, then. Even over-did it, to the result that the German press was just laughing at so much over-the-top promotion: The "Cosmic Bullshit" (as we call it) comes from this time. Many American fans still seem to believe in this "Cosmic" stuff. To "play concerts" you need someone who wants (and is able) to organize such concerts. And you need an audience.

GA: [Other things that might have helped would be] a promoter or publicist and maybe others who came to make this kind of music such as Michael Hoenig, Manuel Göttsching (*A New Age of Earth*) and Brian Eno, even David Bowie with *Low* and *Heroes*. I always felt that Eno and Bowie came later and were, dare I say, copying a form already well established by Klaus Schulze (or at least they were not the real originators of the form).

KDM: You should ask Edgar Froese about this. He was very angry once about Bowie, just because of this. As far as I understood him, Bowie learned from Edgar a few things about "electronic" when he lived in Berlin (Bowie I mean), but he never mentioned Edgar on discs or in interviews.

Besides, Eno or Bowie are part of the British and international record industry, with managers, lawyers, huge and professional labels and publishers backing them. In Germany all this did not exist, and today it exists only to a certain degree, because of historic reasons. Until the '90s it was not even allowed to be a "manager" of an artist. This is because his job would be to "give work" to an artist, and this function was entirely and exclusively in the hands of the Government (of course they were far from being able to do this job). So, every German "manager" of a musician had an illegal status. Therefore, there were no (good) ones.

Once, and for a short time, KS had a professional British manager. He took a lot of money from Klaus. Too much for Klaus' taste.

GA: Now, it seems Eno is far more widely mentioned as a pioneer in electronic music than Klaus Schulze. Example: *All Music Guide* Book has an extensive selection of write-ups on Eno's "landmark" albums but no inclusion of Klaus Schulze in the main section of the book at all.

[Author's note: I'm not trying to downgrade the contributions of Brian Eno or David Bowie. In fact, I enjoy and respect the music of both. My sole point is that they were not originators of the form as Klaus was, in my opinion. And yes, it does bother me when leading musical observers get this issue so completely wrong!]

KDM: I do know that. And I know the reason but to understand this, you should have lived and worked in (and thought about) the music field through all these many years. It would make no sense to tell it, it must have been experienced. Maybe just one thing: Pop music is still the second-largest "industry" in England. In Germany it's nothing.

GA: I believe in Germany at that time the market was poor for Klaus Schulze's new form of music and that German younger audiences were more interested in American rock music.

KDM: This is still the case. Being a "German" singer or musician is just not "cool" for the journalists and then also for the public. Of course we have our bunch of cheap German pop singers for the "underclass". Every day a huge German TV station broadcasts a show with that stupid trash, often disguised as "Volksmusik" ("Folks' music"). For the more educated Germans this is always a reason to make jokes about. I think the image of it is similar to "polka music" which you have in the USA.

The majority of "younger" people do not automatically have... better taste (the listeners to that "Folksmusik" were once young, too!). What the younger people call today hip-hop or whatever, is musically the same trash as the older people's trash. What I can hear from it, it's mostly only a very loud and always the same bass-drum (and no melody or other instrument): boom-boom-boom-boom. This is today's avant garde?

GA: The exciting part is that 30-35 years later he still has a lot to offer in new compositions. I can think of few, if any, rock artists that could be said about, which is not to say that KS has anything to do with rock music.

KDM: Because I was once a great fan of rock music when it was new and later when it was huge, I state now that rock music today is dead. It's only, with a few exceptions, (but is Van Morrison really "rock"?) producing the formula of rock, over and over again. Using the "usual" tools and licks, the technique of rock which was invented many years ago by names such as Pete Townshend, Hendrix, Jeff Beck, Jagger/Richards, the Beatles, of course Chuck Berry, and of course the old blues singers and players.

KS started in the sixties with rock. He was a rock drummer, also played a bit of guitar and bass in his teenage years, with rock or pop groups. Interestingly, (and rarely noticed or mentioned by a journalist) Klaus' idols were not the usual singers and players who came from the blues (Elvis, Chuck Berry, Stones, Beatles, Who, Them...) but more the groups who did something new with the sound, such as the guitar bands Spotnicks, Ventures, Duane Eddy, Johnny and the Hurricanes, even the Shadows. Still, today, KS cannot play a simple blues line on the keyboard (even I can do it!) and he won't.

I try to speak and to write honestly and as good as I understand it. Not many ideological or scientific words or other blah blah but the simple truth as I know it and understand it. By the way, KS is the same. He never (or rarely) pretends to know more (or being a "better" person) than he actually is. He even has a liking for the more "simple things in life", if I may say so. And he shows it. He likes to rave about the latest soccer game, or some cheap TV series, but not to discuss the meaning of a Coltrane solo. And if you start to mention "new age" he suddenly has more important things to do. Maybe a "Formula 1" car race on TV.

Chapter 6 Klaus' Solo Career, 1972-1974

General Comments on the re-issues that were released starting in 2005

First, some general comments on all the re-releases. *Moonlake* and *Kontinuum* are pretty much packaged in the same way as the re-releases as well. The re-releases all come in very nice packaging that opens up to show not only the CD (with simulated record grooves, no less!) but also a 16-page booklet, which is very nice. In each booklet come two interviews with KS. The first is repeated in all the re-issues and more general in content. The second is an interview with KS on the specific CD one has just purchased. Each time I open one of these up, I feel somewhat like a kid on Christmas Eve!

The interviews are conducted by Albrecht Piltz and are very good. Each interview for a specific album finds Klaus usually really opening up and talking in a flow that sounds natural and sometimes humorous. There is lots of really good information in these interviews.

Then there are the bonus tracks which vary in quality from spectacular ("But Beautiful" on *Cyborg*) to at times, unremarkable such as the track at the end of *Ballett 3*. Generally, though, the bonus tracks are a treat and sometimes the bonus track or other alteration means you should buy the re-issue if you're a Klaus Schulze fan (even if you own the original). The aforementioned "But Beautiful" is one example. Here's another, totally unexpected example that made a great album even greater - the expansion of "Georg Trakl" from about 5:20 to around 26 minutes. This expansion transforms "Georg Trakl" into one of the all-time great KS tracks, in my opinion. As I listened to it for the first time, I was thrilled at the sequencing that developed after the expanded segment started.

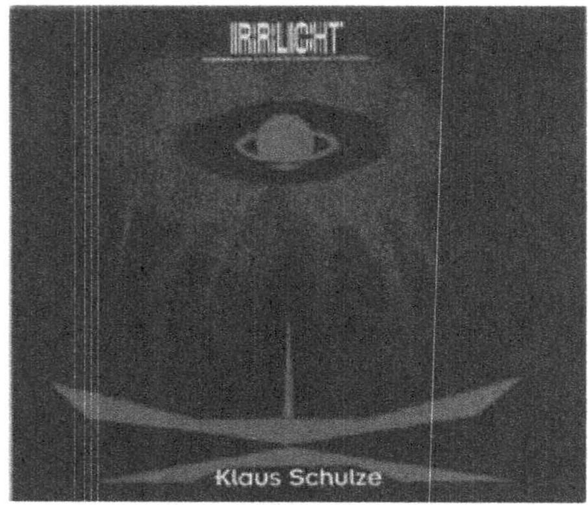

1972 *Irrlicht*

Klaus continued his experiments with organs and tape machines in his sleeping room, which had been furnished as a small studio. After he got a record contract with Rolf-Ulrich Kaiser's record label "Ohr" (then the only label for new German rock music and groups), he recorded his first solo album *Irrlicht*, with the help of Berlin's Colloquium Musica Orchestra in April 1972. Klaus played a broken TEISCO organ and used a broken guitar amplifier. He recorded samples of the orchestra and then patched them into the music, yielding a sound that was quite pleasing (to my ears, at least). It might be possible, without knowing the story of the making of *Irrlicht*, to think that the orchestral passages were produced by an early synthesizer, but this was not the case. Klaus did not acquire his first synthesizer until after *Irrlicht*.

A note on the title: the definition of '*Irrlicht*,' courtesy of KDM, is will-o'-the-wisp, Jack-o-Lantern. In other languages: French: le feu follet; Finnish: virvatuli; Dutch: dwaallicht.

KDM also offers this: "*Irrlicht* is a word from nature. Check Wikipedia or any lexicon: The will-o'-the-wisp or ignis fatuus, or in plural form as ignes fatui ('fool's fire[s]') refers to the ghostly lights sometimes seen at night or twilight that hover over damp ground in still air, often over bogs. It looks like a flickering lamp, and is sometimes said to recede if approached. Much folklore surrounds the legend, but science has offered several potential explanations."

Klaus reflects on *Irrlicht* as printed in an article by KDM in the booklet included with *X*:

"My first solo LP (*Irrlicht*, 1971) was created with the most basic technical means and the help of an orchestra which agreed that I and my new music were crazy. The commercial or artistic success of this album was near zero (see my interview with Klaus for more on this statement). The reaction of the majority of the media was about equal to that of the orchestra."

Reviews of *Irrlicht*

It seems that the consensus of reviews in recent years gives *Irrlicht* a higher standing than given by Klaus in the above statement. First, I'll print some small quotations from reviews on the internet and then I will give my feelings in detail.

Also note [based on comments by KDM]: "KS did not have the benefit of looking at *Irrlicht* after the passage of 30 or so years, as many recent reviewers have. Since he was quoted in the notes for the album *X*, he probably made that statement in about 1978, only 6 years after the release of *Irrlicht*."

From www.vintage.com:

"However, if you're in the right mood, then Schulze's best albums will take you on an unforgettable, dreamy and hypnotic trip, and *Irrlicht* remains among his classic '70s releases."

The above appears to have been written somewhere between 1998 and 2006.

In KDM's words, "To write good about something that has stood the test of time... is very easy (just see fans' websites). It's not so easy to discover the newness and quality in a certain music when it is new, outstanding and even terrifying!"

From www.hippy.com review by Ben Miler:

"Schulze newbies are probably advised to check out one of his mid '70s electronic works like *Timewind* (1975), but this early album certainly is a great album to have to see the origins of one of the masters of electronic music!"

From Joe McGlinchey at http://www.progreviews.com/reviews/display.php?rev=ks-irr (December 3, 2004):

"*Irrlicht* (literally meaning "erring light") is the German equivalent to the British 'Will o' the Wisp'; malevolent lights said to be fairy tale creatures luring people off of well-known paths and into a marshy doom. In any event, rest assured that in purchasing Irrlicht you can distill the essence of what Klaus Schulze in his prime period was bringing to the table."

If you want to look up this review by Joe McGlinchey, I would recommend it. I think his description of this album is one of the best, if not the best, reviews of *Irrlicht* that I've read. Using words, he captures the mysterious, ethereal nature of this LP splendidly.

From Matt P. at the same site as Joe McGlinchey, we get this interpretation:

"Schulze's debut, *Irrlicht*, is my favorite of the early Klaus Schulze records. Thick, resonant, repetitive and sometimes dramatic, *Irrlicht* does indeed out-Zeit Tangerine Dream's infamous double-LP spacefest, which was also released in 1972."

John Bush of www.allmusic.com continues the trend of surprisingly strong reviews for *Irrlicht* with this high praise:

"Klaus Schulze's solo debut is a masterful album featuring some of the most majestic instances of space music ever recorded, all the more remarkable for being recorded without synthesizers. "Satz Gewitter," the first of two tracks and the highlight here ["Satz: Ebene" is actually the first of three movements on the original *Irrlicht* - GA], slowly progresses from oscillator static to a series of glowing organ lines, all informed by Schulze's excellent feel for phase effects. [The 2006 edition features the bonus track 'Dungeon.']

From www.SynthmusicDirect.com:

"Back to the future...that might just be the case. I have to admit, having not played this album for about two decades now I'd forgotten just how good it is with its beautifully haunting organ work and tonal structures over a sea of raw electronics and treated tape recordings.

"Given that Schulze is known best for his massive synth excursions I wouldn't recommend *Irrlicht* as a representative entry level Schulze album, though I might quickly add that it is not an album to be overlooked."

So there we have a sampling of reviews of *Irrlicht*, from the internet.

The first thing I think of when I consider *Irrlicht* is the unique instrument set that Klaus Schulze used to create this album in 1972 before he acquired his first synthesizer. Think about it, Klaus could not afford a synthesizer then, and here are we, his many fans, in the year 2007 valuing it so much that we will pay $18-$20 in U.S. dollars to acquire this CD. And for me, as I would guess is the case for many fans, this isn't the first purchase of *Irrlicht*. My purchase of the re-release of *Irrlicht* was my 4th copy of the first Klaus Schulze solo album.

Remember: Klaus used a broken TEISCO electric organ, recordings of the Colloquium Musica Orchestra and a broken guitar amplifier, a guitar, zither and human voice to record this album. No synthesizers.

Irrlicht is divided into three movements, ""Satz: Ebene"", "Satz: Gewitter" ('energy rise and energy fall') and "Satz: Exil Sils Maria."

I'll take a look at the original three tracks, starting with "Satz: Ebene" and then comment on the bonus track on this re-issue, "Dungeon."

First, "Ebene." This starts the album out with patches of the Colloquium Musica Orchestra welling up into the sound field with a distinct character of echo or fluctuation in the sounds. The orchestra sounds resemble those of a mellotron or other early synthesizer. For years, I thought this was a synthesizer. The real explanation is that Klaus recorded samples of the orchestra and then spliced them into the composition. The orchestral sounds are both haunting and beautiful at once. The orchestral passages yield to a droning sound which swells, relents and then swells again. The shape of the drone changes but begins to dominate around the 2:30 mark. There appear to be a least two, maybe more layers of this droning, perhaps created by a guitar. The drone and another sound wrestle and from that emerges a series of cascading, achingly beautiful orchestral passages.

Around the 6:00 mark, there emerges a human voice which appears to have been treated further adding to the surreal, mystical, ethereal feeling. This voice is fascinating. I played it a few times to see if I could determine what it was saying but no luck. Placed in the context of 1972, this music is mind boggling. How can something this capable of evoking strong emotions and feelings of aesthetic beauty be created with a collection of items that just happened to be on hand and were even in disrepair?

At 9:38 of the first movement, the organ makes its first dramatic and overpowering entry and comes in brief rushes. This is followed by a repetitive, sequencer-like passage and again the overpowering organ (sounding like a church organ).

The organ takes over for the next several minutes; Klaus plays with a sound like a frightening wind on a scary Halloween night lurking in the background.

It was always my impression that this pumping organ section went on too long but as I listen, I get into it more – perhaps because of increased volume. For about 6 minutes, organ and haunting wind-like sounds combine to form the soundscape. Klaus begins to play the organ in a much more frantic, almost manic way, with one note bursts of sound. The organ keeps wildly pumping, rising, almost assaulting until suddenly it disappears and then returns. Quiet, meditative sounds take over as "Satz: Ebene" ends.

The second movement, "Gewitter" ('energy rise – energy collapse') comes as a relief. Thunder-like sound starts Gewitter. The organ still plays but much lighter than before. Several jolting crashing sounds disturb the momentary peace and lead to a drone. Strange sounds emerge, building and then tailing away. The music becomes almost trance-like at the 5:00 mark.

As the movement ends, the sound is nearly inaudible.

At the beginning of movement three, "Exil Sils Maria," sounds are of a low volume and remind me of perhaps a scary film track; yet emotion is being stirred by this passage of music. I feel alternating fear and comfort.

The music is strange. It has taken on a more bizarre, disturbing feel, with surges of industrial sounds mixed with an oscillating drone in the background. There are at times scary sounds, haunting and strange.

A siren sounds with hints of the Colloquium Musica Orchestra. A sense of beauty is returning again as the song takes on a more musical feel. The organ is sharing space with some semi-droning sounds and it feels that the music is gradually progressing.

Listening to this track is like being lost in a forest and experiencing many feelings of fear and then joy as hope – about finding one's way out – comes and goes.

"Dungeon," the bonus track, starts with a fluctuating, bass-like sound and then a deep drone and suddenly, the Colloquium Musica Orchestra – (or is this the Colloquium Musica Orchestra, because this is no longer part of the original *Irrlicht*?). A beautiful twittering synth sound ala "Bayreuth Return" (from *Timewind*, 1975) drones and a Minimoog solo joins in. All the while a steady, loud drone dominates in the background.

The combination of the two droning synths sounds great! A sound similar to Manuel Göttsching's slashing guitars on *In Blue* joins in. There are several intermingling layers. A guitar-like sound emerges, possibly the Minimoog. There are always several layers in this song, but each is continuously evolving.

This reminds me of the complexity and adventurousness and slowly unfolding quality of "Velvet Voyage," a wall of ever changing and evolving, cohesive sounds. Deep bass pedals, Moog solos, string pads and drone.

Like many Klaus Schulze albums, *Irrlicht* has periods of rapturous beauty. Often, I feel a sense of awe, especially in the first ten minutes of "Ebene." Other times, it feels scary, like walking in the woods in the dark. There is some brilliant music here. And I think it's consistent with most Klaus Schulze albums where periods of astonishing, even shocking beauty emerge out of other periods that may not be as compelling.

I think this is a very worthwhile album. "Exil Sils Maria" probably has the most challenging parts and ultimately, periods that I don't enjoy.

The thing that amazes me the most is that Klaus, with primitive equipment, was able to turn out an album like this! Who else was recording samples of orchestras and interspersing them in their works to such stunningly beautiful effect? Who else could take an old TEISCO organ, a broken guitar amp, guitar, etc. and compose something this creative and totally unprecedented for 1972? It's not only unparalleled for 1972 -- but can you think of any other album like this in the history of all recorded music?

I have often thought that part of the greatness of KS, is his ability to constantly explore new musical horizons, ever reaching – never afraid to try something daring and new. The albums released in the last 10 years have shown that but actually, in retrospect, all the evidence needed of that creativity, reaching, experimenting, trying new things and daring to fail was present right here in *Irrlicht*.

I think Klaus underrates his own album in the case of *Irrlicht* (granted from a disadvantageous perspective in 1978). It's not the best Schulze album – but it has moments that can compare with some of the best!

1973 *Cyborg*

From an article by KDM in the booklet included with *X*:

KS: In February of 1973 I played my first "Big" concert, in Paris. The reaction of the audience had to be called enthusiastic. This was my breakthrough - at least in France.

In 1973, Klaus Schulze released the double album *Cyborg*, where he started working with an EMS VCS3 synthesizer.

In February 1973, Klaus had his first solo concerts. At the same time, he recorded *Cyborg*, his second album. Rolf-Ulrich Kaiser had a concept of "cosmic music" in mind, so he promoted his artists (Tangerine Dream, Ash Ra Tempel, Klaus Schulze and some others) as the "Cosmic Couriers". Some sessions where most of the "Ohr" musicians played were released as "Cosmic Jokers" albums.

KDM notes: "By the way: the words 'cosmic music' came from Edgar. Later he was excusing for the mis-use and heavy over-use by Kaiser."

But Klaus and the other artists were not satisfied with the "Ohr" label [KDM: "in fact, with Herr Kaiser']. Record sales were not as expected. But KDM says "that was not the reason (even if it's always a reason but not here). KS or Edgar didn't expect to sell millions of copies of *Irrlicht* or *Electronic Meditation*. They are not idiots.... And the musicians disliked Kaiser's demand to take some pills before playing. While they sued Kaiser to get out of the contract in 1973, Klaus recorded *Picture Music*, which could only be released in 1975 because of the lawsuit."

Press reviews

This comes from Archie Patterson, writing for the *All Music Guide* and was printed on http://www.answers.com/topic/Cyborg-germany-bonus-track

Archie Patterson is the man behind Eurock.com, which has long sold progressive music.

"From the early days of electronic experimentation in the pop field, Klaus Schulze's second solo album still stands as one of the most powerful examples of ambient pulse music ever conceived. The dense layers of rhythm and synthetic tone colors melt into a seamless, flowing soundscape of melody, motion and spatial effects. *Cyborg* is a monumental double-album of cosmic music. [The 2006 Revisited Records edition contains a bonus track, the 50-minute "But Beautiful," in addition to improved packaging.] (Archie Patterson, *All Music Guide*)."

Reviewed by Mark Kadzielawa on 10/22/2006 at http://www.dailyvault.com/toc.php5?review=4547

"Whether winding through difficult soundscapes, moments of beauty or harsh electronica befitting the cold, robotic album title, Schulze proves here why he is considered a founding father of both new age music and electronic music.

"These four 24-minute songs aren't just challenging, disturbing and different. They are spaced-out overtures for the mind. *Cyborg* presents an innovative sound that's worth checking out for the musically adventurous."

The following bits of a review of *Cyborg* come from http://www.synthmusicdirect.com, a website that has many reviews of Klaus Schulze albums which are probably the highest quality set of reviews that I encountered. They are the best written and the most well thought out, objective and informative reviews -- and they're entertaining as well.

According to B22, an industry figure who, according to David Law, prefers to remain anonymous, "First there's the *Cyborg* album, probably the most alien sounding album Schulze ever made. Its time to dig out your winter woollies with this one as it's a cold, cold-sounding album which flows indistinctly from one movement to another lacking some of the ethereal warmth... As for the bonus track – well I'd say that you'd have a 'live' albums worth of material there, the content is superb and see's a very busy Mr. Schulze on top form in the glory days of the seventies."

My review of *Cyborg*:

In sections of *Cyborg*, I felt some warmth emerge suddenly and unexpectedly from the coldness. The one thing that has stood out in my repeated listens (in May of 2007) is that the 50 plus minute bonus track is stunning! It's on a par with some of Klaus' best work, and it does sound like it's from a different time period (it is, having come from the 1977 concert in Brussels at St. Michael Cathedral).

Track one, "Synphära," starts out with a wavering minor key drone, joined by a thinned out organ sound. This evolves into a full church organ sound a la *Irrlicht*.

For several minutes, the organ solos; then suddenly a sound enters that reminds me of the bubbling synth sound on *Picture Music*'s "Totem" (but not nearly as nice). Klaus continues to take chances and experiment with every sound imaginable! That in itself starts to create a feeling of respect, if not awe. The poor man's "Totem" sound continues to slither and slash around through the musical landscape as the organ continues, undisturbed.

A slippery sounding, high pitched synth sound begins oscillating in the background. This sound is used extensively in "Synphära." I don't think it's the most pleasant sound but it does add that element of creativity and interest which attracted me to Klaus' music in the first place. The organ thins as if an accordion sound has melded with it; the sound swells briefly and then dies.

"Conphara" starts with a drone. It quickly evolves into a drone with a beat, a slow and methodical beat. Several layers enter in rapid succession. The sounds are all changing except for the beat in the background. This section is challenging but sounds interesting. Suddenly, the gorgeous sounds of the Colloquium Musica Orchestra enter with plaintive cries and passages which are startling in their beauty, causing me to experience chills.

The magnificent, repeated surges of the orchestra seem more gorgeous because of the way they were set up by the preceding section. We're almost in *Timewind* territory in terms of beauty and ability to stir emotions. A flute-like sound appears. Over the flute-like sounds come synth pads that alternate in pitch and leave me almost breathless as three different octaves are used in rapid succession.

"Conphara" is a brilliant piece of music in both conception and execution! I think about the fact that Klaus was only 26 when he performed this and wonder what it is about youth that lends itself to such stunning works of creativity.

The third movement, "Chromengel," is difficult. My impression is that the early synth pads sound a little reminiscent of early Tangerine Dream, a la *Phaedra* or *Rubycon*, which is good. The bad news is that the wild sounds overlapping the synth pads (the synth pads grow more understated as time goes on) are not very pleasing. This is a dark and strange piece of music overall.

Even the synths that I gave credit for sounding reminiscent of *Phaedra* begin to sound dark. And even though the spacy sounds shimmering through the music are of a higher octave, they sound strangely unappealing, almost annoying. And they get more and more prominent and shrill.

This seems to be a very experimental piece of music which just never found its stride.

"Neuronengesang," the fourth song, starts with some of the same kind of drones as the first movement of *Irrlicht*, but in abbreviated bursts. Some plaintive string synth pads play, and more drones evolve into a synth pad.

Several more varied and interesting sounds flicker onto the scene, vacillate and then leave. At about the 4:00 mark, most of what remains is a steady background drone with surging drone-like sounds coming in on a regular basis. "Neuronengesang" bears the mark of the *Irrlicht-Cyborg* time-frame. It's definitely more pleasing than "Chromengel" and is not nearly as dark and chilling (even disturbing). This is experimental music that has a surprising amount of maturity behind it.

The drone in the background almost sounds like a low volume bagpipe player holding a note for a very long time. A persistent patting sound comes from the left speaker, as if something were in there, pounding on the wall of the speaker.

The last offering of the new *Cyborg* is "But Beautiful," which starts in similar fashion to other songs in the *Irrlicht-Cyborg* canon.

Soon, a choir–like sound arises to remind me of "Velvet Voyage" from *Mirage*. This sound continues and becomes the dominant sound in the composition for awhile. Also present are string pads that remind me a lot of *Body Love*. *Moondawn*-like textures surface and then a unique but very nice sounding sequenced pattern comes in. This feels like a brilliant composition, one of pure genius! "But Beautiful" combines some of the best of *Body Love*, *Moondawn* and a little *Mirage* – even *Timewind*. The sequencer patterns in the background are brilliant, some of the best I've ever heard from Klaus, and indeed, combined with long *Moondawn*-like passages (with the occasional *Body Love*-like Minimoog sounds), it's a very delicious musical recipe.

At the 21:00 mark, the sequencer tempo and Minimoog sounds quicken for several minutes to a frantic pace. At this point, the soundscape is less appealing than before.

Subtly, the whole thing shifts as the sequencer pattern is scrambled, a new sound introduced into the background. However, the pace is still frantic. Some background explosions and pads add interest again. A sound like bubbling water emerges, and eerie, higher-octave synth pads come through, leading to the familiar sound of the Colloquium Musica Orchestra.

Choirs join in, and the soundscape is now filled with a wide variety of ever changing sounds, as if Klaus was throwing hints of all the high points of his first eight albums at us in very short bursts. At the 36:00 mark, things have evolved to some very interesting dueling sequencer patterns and are soon joined by luscious synth pads evoking *Moondawn* and/or *Timewind*.

The way that "But Beautiful" can evolve in such imperceptible, gradual ways is amazing. This feels like an all time great in the history of synthesizer music! There are a few minor 'dropouts' in the recording but nothing to mar it, in my opinion.

Summary of *Cyborg*

Even though this is not of the quality of Klaus' classics of the mid to late '70s, it shows Klaus at a young age squeezing some very pleasing electronic music out of a collection of equipment that was very primitive compared to what was to come. The quality overall is a little uneven, but the level of creativity, adventure and daring is striking.

1974 *Blackdance*

Blackdance featured Ernst Walter Siemon singing music mostly composed by Verdi, on the track "Voices of Syn." Klaus had recorded the operatic singing a few years before *Blackdance*. He had met Siemon in 1970 while recording with Tangerine Dream. The album also features Klaus playing a 12-string guitar. Additionally, he played congas and tabla. From my perspective, the singing and the 12-string guitar used on "Ways of Changes" both add a lot to *Blackdance*.

Blackdance reviews:

http://www.vintageprog.com/sss.htm:

""Ways of Changes" opened in a promising way with a moody and mystical synth that soon was joined by an acoustic guitar...... But personally I don't think it works very well. The track seems pointless and fails to create any engaging atmosphere... Some Velvet Phasing...works good... [T]he 23-minute "Voices of Syn"... is the most boring track Schulze ever did in the '70s... *Blackdance* is a failed experiment, and is for Schulze-completists only. "

From http://www.intuitivemusic.com/klaus-schulze-biography:

"*Blackdance* (1974) featured the vocal collaboration of Ernst Walter Siemon and was the first Klaus Schulze album oriented primarily to synthesizers, featuring an EMS Synthi A, an ARP Odyssey, and ARP 2600."

http://www.allmusic.com:

"This is more atmospheric than most of his albums. That gives it a nice appeal and a cool change of pace." Jim Brenholts, *All Music Guide*

http://www.starbase1.co.uk/review12.htm:

"Some Velvet Phasing...very sad and very beautiful...'Voices of Syn'...begins with an unaccompanied operatic male voice, and he does not sound very happy about his lot in life."

My take on *Blackdance*:

I think no matter what it sounds like today, *Blackdance* rates highly just because of the memories it provides and the landmark that it was. As the third Klaus Schulze album released, it was the first post-*Irrlicht*/*Cyborg* release and therefore represented a new dawn in the musical form that Klaus Schulze was creating. *Blackdance* didn't sound like *Irrlicht* or *Cyborg* at all. Even though Klaus has had second thoughts about the inclusion of the 12 string-guitar, I love it – and it is recorded with stunning clarity.

The charm of *Blackdance* begins with the opening strains and an instrument that sounds like a cross between an accordion and a bagpipe. This is a truly unique, endearing sound that is joined by some of the crispest and cleanest sounding 12-string guitar that you will ever hear. *Blackdance* had me hooked with this amazing beginning.

The exotic lead synth sound plays a compelling melody, followed by a deep bass synth and increased intensity from the 12-string guitar. The first four minutes of *Blackdance* are brilliant. The congas and tabla, played by Klaus, add a driving beat to the first song, "Ways of Changes." The recording quality is very good.

For a while the song stays in essentially the same framework, but the lead synth line and other factors have enough changes along the way to keep it interesting. A long drone on the organ holds things together. “Ways of Changes” now actually sounds better than ever before to me because of the driving force and the clarity of the percussion played by KS. The last four minutes of the song are a little less interesting than the rest.

“Some Velvet Phasing” is next. The song has an experimental air, fairly slow and perhaps a little melancholy - although it still sounds good. The song is consistent with the often interestingly surprising nature of a Schulze album track during the ’70s; it doesn’t change much – but it doesn’t need to, in my opinion.

“Voices of Syn” is next, with the wonderful vocal introduction by Ernst Walter Siemon, recorded by Klaus three years earlier and used on *Blackdance* in 1973. Every creative trick in the book has been used – the lead sound of “Ways of Changes,” the 12-string guitar, the congas and tablas played by Klaus himself, the near melancholy of “Some Velvet Phasing” and now this wonderfully mysterious intro to ‘Voices of Syn.”

About six minutes into the track, Siemon fades, and driving percussion takes over on top of winding and bending synth patterns. “Voices of Syn” goes on for quite a long time in virtually the same groove and sound. It is, however, a sound that is consistent with the mood of the album, which could be called a bit dark. At around 14:00, there is a break, with a little piano and a drone, and then the piece picks right back up with the percussive foundation.

The sound of *Blackdance* was a one-time occurrence in the Klaus Schulze catalog. *Blackdance* is an album that I hold close to my heart; it was a big part of the reason why I was irrevocably pulled in as a Klaus Schulze fan.

The first bonus track is called “Foreplay.” It starts out with a rising bass line followed by a crashing sound, something like thunder. There are searing, soaring synth lines, thunderclaps, then choirs come charging in and become an integral part of the track. The choirs sound like they could come from one of the *Body Love* albums. The first time I listened to this track, it didn’t make an impression on me. However, the next time I listened to *Blackdance* while working on the album cover graphics, it blew me away!

Last is “Synthies Have (no) Balls.” The final track starts out nicely, with some fairly higher register synth pads and crashes of sound similar to those used in “Foreplay.” There is a dreamy, ethereal beauty to the synth pads. At around 6:00, a drum begins to lay down a methodical rhythm. This is a wild, untamed beast of a song! The pace slows as if someone was putting a hand on a record, slowing it down. It regains momentum just at the end. Overall, “Synthies Have (no) Balls” is a pretty good track.

As for *Blackdance*, it’s a treasure in the Klaus Schulze collection - perhaps without the “it” of some of his other albums, but still a unique Schulze album and one that I have deep feelings for.

Chapter 7 Klaus' Solo Career and Collaborations, 1975–1979

1975 *Picture Music*

This album was held up for legal reasons until 1975 although recorded in August, 1973, before *Blackdance.*

From http://tmachine.chat.ru/germ/S1.htm:

"On *Picture Music,* he introduced rhythm and drums into his music - no big surprise really, as he started his musical career as a drummer! Also his keyboard arsenal was extended with ARP Odyssey and ARP 2600 synthesizers. The spacy sounds he achieved with these instruments helped to increase his (well-earned) reputation as a synthesizer wizard."

From Dave Connolly at http://www.allmusic.com:

"Though recorded in August 1973 (shortly after *Cyborg*), *Picture Music* was not released until January 1975... The sum effect of 'Totem' is frankly underwhelming"... " *Picture Music* is more percussive and limited in scope and effect than the work of Tangerine Dream, a vantage point from which many may be approaching Schulze's work."

From Matt P at http://www.progreviews.com/reviews/display.php?rev=ks-pm

"Recorded in 1973 but not released until two years later, Klaus Schulze's *Picture Music* must be considered one of the more groundbreaking electronic albums of the 1970s... With a skittery, sequenced bounce programmed throughout the piece, 'Totem' sounds startlingly contemporary. Percolating as it does for 24 minutes... *Picture Music* does not seem to have quite as high a reputation as a few of Schulze's other '70s albums, but I think it is excellent and I would rank it as an essential purchase for fans of the genre" (January 18, 2007).

Here are the 2005 comments from Rev. Keith A. Gordon at http://www.mondoGordo.com/play501.html:

"Schulze had his eyes on the stars with *Picture Music.* Predicting Brian Eno's ambitious experimentation in ambient music by a half-decade...The album opens with the almost twenty-four minute piece 'Totem'... Fragments of rhythm and melody swirl in and out of the piece, lost beneath bubbling electronics... [T]his [is an] important and often overlooked entry in the canon of electronic music."

From Tobias Fishcher at http://www.tokafi.com/newsitems/cdfeatureklausschulzepicturemusic/view

"The drummer in Schulze slowly found his way back into the music with *Blackdance* and *Picture Music*. This becomes clearest on Side B of the original record, the 23-minute long 'Mental Door'... Still, the first composition here, 'Totem', is even better: A three dimensional musical vision full of truth and madness. A fragile pattern of bell-tones is the rhythmical pulse, which guides the listener through swathes of harmonic fog and constantly evolving motifs."

From http://www.vintageprog.com/sss.htm:

"The opener 'Totem' is a pleasant cosmic journey of pulsating electronic rhythms with a very spacy synthesizer on top... 'Mental Door' starts with a floating, spacy and relaxed part that turns into some energetic and powerful improvisations on the Moog. At the end the whole track slows down to a very relaxing and beautiful part with great atmosphere."

From http://www.side-line.com/reviews_comments.php?id=9745_0_17_0_C:

"The opening track 'Totem' being a nearly 24-minute tour-de-force consisting of a hypnotic bubbling sequencer rhythm and cosmic synth leads,... 'Mental Door' takes off as a continuation of 'Totem' but quickly shifts... Note that there is some distortion audible on 'Totem' that originally was not there, an error or on purpose?" (BVI:7) BVI

From B22 http://www.synthmusicdirect.com:

"Never before or since have I come across an extended piece like 'Totem' where a single sound can so easily carry the whole composition... The whole soundscape created works perfectly, the sounds gel brilliantly. The only thing that tells us that this music wasn't made just last week is the use of the rather dated sounding Farfisa organ... [regarding 'Mental Door':]... Ah, the tiny patter of drums arrive, building like the solo to a thunderous thrashing of the kit to a point at which it sounds like Klaus is testing it to destruction!!!... [T]his REALLY was a seminal LP, a daring one off. A classic, you betcha!!!"

My opinions of *Picture Music*

Picture Music is one of my all-time favorite Klaus Schulze albums! I was spellbound with the lead track "Totem" and its bubbling, percolating rhythmic beat from the first time I heard it. This main, driving rhythm in *Picture Music* is created with the ARP Odyssey. It's amazing that I still have that same feeling when I listen to it to this day. This foundation sound for 'Totem' is perhaps the most unusual synth sound ever conceived and recorded. It is both addictive and relaxing and yet stimulating as well. "Totem" was my reason for liking *Picture Music* for most of my time as a Klaus Schulze fan (about 35 years). "'Mental Door" didn't move me much. Still, *Picture Music* was elevated, for me, solely on the strength of "Totem."

I was very excited to hear that the re-release would have a 33-minute bonus track, very similar to "Totem." "Totem" starts out with some light chiming sounds, a little contorting synth sound and then, the main beat, which plays at a hurried pace, almost as if it is sequenced (but it is not). My new interview with him has Klaus' explanation of how he created this repetitive, addicting sound on the ARP Odyssey.

Also notable is that once this beat starts up and throughout the time it continues its hypnotic syncopation, there are often floating, dreamy synth pads that sound exquisite. These pads convey a passionate, plaintive feeling; they clearly evoke emotions in me as they intertwine with the mystical beat. The beat itself is accompanied by a sort of bubbling, stabbing higher pitched synth sound that goes along with it at the same pace.

At about the 12:00 mark of "Totem," the pace quickens and a lead synth plays its melody over the accelerated beat. Around the 19:00 mark, the trademark beat disappears and the final four minutes have layers of synths weaving a rewarding tapestry of stimulating, yet serene sounds.

After acquiring the re-release of "Totem," I have a better appreciation for "Mental Door." For one thing, it's very different hearing "Mental Door" as a virtual continuation of "Totem" on CD as compared to hearing it as a very separate entity on LP. On CD, it becomes quickly apparent that the first six minutes or so of "Mental Door" continue the texture and mood of the serene ending of "Totem."

"Mental Door" is contemplative for the first seven minutes or so and is gorgeous music. At around the 5:30 mark, it even gives me a feeling of being in church and hearing the organ playing as communion is starting.

After the 7:00 mark "Mental Door" kicks up the pace and combines a twisting synth line with drums and becomes almost frantic for several minutes. The payoff comes when this almost droning yet frantic section, lasting around 10 minutes, ends in a beautiful musical climax, dropping stunningly into a majestic sounding synth pad combined with some very crisp, clean and exotic percussion which darts back and forth between the speakers. The stereo effect is startling. The effect of this moment in the album is so wonderful that it's hard to put into words. It's one of the grandest passages in any Schulze album.

The music from this point forward is simply brilliant. It was almost as if Klaus had intentionally lulled us to sleep with the repetitive, not so dazzling, ten minutes of frantic drumming and frenzied synth just to have this finishing passage experienced as lovely and striking. In that context, the splendid "Totem" combined with the first seven minutes of "Mental Door" and the exquisite ending to "Mental Door" are enough for a truly great album.

Following the beauty of the last several minutes of "Mental Door" comes "C'est Pas La Meme Chose," which is very similar to "Totem" but feels not the slightest bit redundant. Of course, I could listen to this groove for an hour and not be the least bit bored.

The beat that drives both songs is bubbly, percolating, robust and surrounded simultaneously by darting, reflecting synth jabs. Behind that, I can hear some quieter, yet beautiful synth pads, at times two at once, separated in the stereo spectrum. The more I listen to this and pay close attention to it, the more awed I become. This composition is a pure and absolute delight!

Closing my eyes, I feel emotion welling up as I listen to the progress of this track. Subtle synth blurbs, distinctly in the background, sporadically add yet another reason to be wowed by this track. An occasional chime-like sound enters the sound field, attacks and decays in a second. A chime-like sequenced pattern takes over from the awe-inspiring synth pad.

The synth pad takes over again. A misty, somewhat muffled vibraphone-like sound enters. "Crystal Lake"-like chimes begin and are sequenced for a short time, lending an unexpected, yet fulfilling feeling of wonder. Suddenly, there is a faint hint of a human voice in the background, speaking slowly, very slowly as the whole composition slows.

Finally, a Minimoog-like sound enters and oscillates as it slowly decays, followed by more warm-sounding synth pads that are as beautiful as the warmest cello sound I can imagine. This is just an absolutely brilliant composition! The layering of astounding sounding synth textures continues, one on top of the other.

I think *Picture Music* is a vastly underrated album in the Klaus Schulze canon. It is, in my opinion, one of the best. The reason I am such a big Klaus Schulze fan lies in the fact that I can easily envision several other Schulze compositions carrying me away as this one has. I just can't fathom why this has not become a legendary piece of music.

In the first ten minutes of "Totem" on the re-release, there are some spots where the sound peaks and a momentary twinge of clipping or distortion can be heard. This may vary on your system and your pressing of the CD.

Picture Music is a masterpiece, standing tall as an epic achievement early in the splendid career of Klaus Schulze. This is astounding, considering it was recorded in 1973 with the comparatively primitive equipment of the time, in sharp contrast to the technology that would become available to him in the coming years!

1975 *Timewind*

(The second half is "wind," as in "the wind was blowing," not "wind," as in "wind your watch").

Timewind is an improvised album which has been widely recognized as a masterpiece of electronic music. In the fall of 1975, after the release of *Timewind*, Klaus moved from Berlin to the countryside in Northern Germany.

He says: "After the release of my album *Timewind* in fall 1975, I moved from Berlin to the countryside in northern Germany. *Timewind* was awarded - and I say that with some pride - an international prize, which in the three years before had gone to Soft Machine, Jimi Hendrix and Pink Floyd."

Klaus also mentions in the re-release booklet how this prize lead to more earnings in France. Schools, libraries and universities would have to purchase two or three copies. This resulted in 20,000 to 30,000 overnight orders of *Timewind* and some much needed income for Klaus, which allowed him to rent a real studio for the recording of *Moondawn*.

From B22 http://www.synthmusicdirect.com:

"*Timewind* was the recording that announced to the world that Klaus Schulze had arrived with this his first international release, relative album chart success, plus a piece of musical kudos in the form of the 'Grand Prix du Disque International' award for the recording!!! *Timewind* marked a watershed moment, doing for electronica what Pink Floyd's *Dark Side of the Moon* had done for prog rock... So there you have it. [I]f you're looking for a musical experience that touches your sonic nirvana providing music that really does seem like it comes from another planet, *Timewind* is the answer. It's a 31-year-old recording now that still doesn't sound like it's dated at all!!!"

From http://www.vintageprog.com/sss.htm:

"'Bayreuth Return' is one of his most hypnotic tracks ever... This track will have an almost trance-like effect on you if you're in the right mood... *Timewind* was easily Schulze's best and most consistent release to this point."

From Heather Mackenzie at http://www.progreviews.com/reviews/display.php?rev=ks-time:

"[W]ith this release, *Timewind*, he was starting his series of multi-layered, 30-minute-long architectural synthesizer epics" (October 23, 2003).

Joe McGlinchey adds: "I find it to be not quite as interesting as, say, Tangerine Dream's *Phaedra*. But if you like that kind of music, you should certainly be into this, no sweat" (August 2, 2000)

From Mike DeGagne, *All Music Guide*, at http://www.allmusic.com:

"The first 30 minutes involve icy pulsations and lengthy tonal flights that unnoticeably converge into each other... *Timewind* serves as splendid mood music, and the ears are forever kept busy following Schulze's electronic wandering."

My impressions of *Timewind*:

This is possibly the one Klaus Schulze album that had the biggest impact on me when it was released. The classical sound, the emotive playing and the general excellence of both sides of the LP made it more evident than ever that Klaus Schulze's music was special, something very different from the pop and rock that I grew up on. The sweet sound of the synthesizers and the super-clean recording make *Timewind* even better. There was a feeling that I was in on something that was on the cutting edge, more sophisticated than what I had listened to previously.

"Bayreuth Return" (recorded in the two hours between 10 p.m. and midnight) is cued up, so I'm ready to take this journey once more.....

A sharp wind-like sound, twittering sounds and the warm synth pad of *Timewind* all are on display in the first thirty seconds. The twittering sounds and the richly textured synth pads dominate. A synth bass line comes in, kicking the pace up. The synth pads still play at their own pace. Of all the Schulze albums, these evolving, changing, layered synth pads are more central than perhaps any other album.

This piece and this album are all about the emotion inducing style in which the synthesizer pads drift and change. It's the composition and the playing. This is possibly the most unified sound within a single Klaus Schulze album. Up to this point, there had been nothing like it. I can imagine the joy Klaus must have felt in composing and playing this music. Deep, clean sounding synth pads join with the higher, sweet sounding pads to give a very rewarding feeling.

Each time there is a shift in the synth pads, it seems the piece is building in intensity. There is also a sequencer pattern present in the background. Some of the synthesizer pads lead into deep, rich bass lines.

As "Bayreuth Return" moves toward the 20:00 mark, it is gaining energy - an unmistakable build-up is taking place. Sequencer, bass line, and thick, expressive pads which are becoming more melodic carry it forward. A long-held synth pad occurs just past 20:00. There are 18 seconds of an uninterrupted pad with no change at all, which then gives way to another long pad. The sequencer gains in ferocity and multiple pads reach up to meet it, then they all back off, yielding to the twittering and softer playing.

I sense Klaus is totally into it and feeling great passion and emotion as he plays and the track evolves. With this piece, Klaus had taken a new art form which he largely created and elevated it to a powerful new level.

"Wahnfried 1883" (side 2 of the original LP) starts with middle register, very richly textured synth pads, laid over a droning organ. This song begins with an even more symphonic feel than "Bayreuth Return", perhaps due to the absence of the latter's ubiquitous twittering sounds. These first several minutes are exquisite. The uncluttered feel, the absolute purity of the playing for the first several minutes feels like it defines classic Schulze. Arguably, this is the best playing ever done on a synthesizer by anybody at any time. Even though there are some twittering sounds that develop, the composition consists largely of sweeping synth passages of uplifting grandeur.

That this album won the French Grand Prix International du Disque is no surprise. I consider *Timewind* to be a masterpiece of the recorded music of the last 50-75 years. As the last ten minutes evolve, the front line of synth sounds begin to break into fragments and oscillate, even echo. At least one synth line below this continues to hold a solid texture. A general feeling of raw intensity develops - a cacophony. There is a sense of mystery about where this is leading. It's even a little unsettling, especially when compared with the purity and inspiring simplicity of the first two-thirds of "Wahnfried 1883."

"Wahnfried 1883" concludes the original *Timewind.*

The bonus tracks take up a whole second CD. "Echoes of Time" is the first; it's the first of two variations of "Bayreuth Return" on the bonus CD. As such, it bears great similarities to "Bayreuth Return", especially after the track gets going. The first five minutes seem to bear only a small similarity to "Bayreuth Return". Most of the song sounds nearly identical to the "real" "Bayreuth Return".

Klaus had performed it three times for 30-45 minutes and then started it over again, as he reports in the booklet that comes with the re-release. This version is about eight minutes longer than the "Bayreuth Return" that made it on to the classic *Timewind.* Strangely enough, I think it would still qualify as a classic piece of music, had it been released (not possible due to LP constrictions).

"Solar Wind" is the second variation on "Bayreuth Return" but clocks in at a much shorter 12:35. It starts with pronounced wind sounds and brash twittering sounds, followed by some droning sounds and then slow industrial type sounds. For over four minutes, it sounds little like "Bayreuth Return". Then the synth pads come in and return this track to the familiar "Bayreuth Return" sound. This track sounds quite a bit less similar to "Bayreuth Return" than does "Echoes of Time." "Solar Wind" is more like a practice sketch and as such is interesting but does not hold up on its own as do "Bayreuth Return" and "Echoes of Time."

"Windy Times" was recorded as a "little remake" of *Timewind,* according to KS in the re-release booklet, in the year 2000, and was included in the promotion CD for *Contemporary Works I.* It starts out with a heavy sequencer sound that changes in interesting ways a few times in the first minute. A couple more sequenced patterns, higher in pitch, join in, and we are in the midst of a pleasant track. Synth pads are added, and "Windy Times" is in top form by 1:30 or so. It is a short yet appealing song.

Klaus playing in Paris May 9, 1977

1975 Guenther Schickert "Home Tapes" made with Klaus Schulze

These home tapes have shown up on Myspace and are in fact the first thing you hear when you enter the page. It sounds like a poor man's "Bayreuth Return", not bad at all. This was a private session that was done in Klaus Schulze's house.

Far East Family Band

As Klaus says in the *X* booklet:

"In Hamburg I met the Japanese group Far East Family Band. In August 1975 I was invited to come to Tokyo to do the mixing of their first LP ("*Nipponjin*" on [the] Vertigo [label]). It is an outstanding group which in style and quality can easily be compared to Pink Floyd.

"Too bad that the record company failed in promoting this group sufficiently. I have received several requests from people interested in this album, which seems to be developing into a much wanted rarity."

An article in http://tmachine.chat.ru/germ/S1.htm offers this about Far East Family Band:

"In August 1975 he mixed *Nipponjin* by Far East Family Band, a Japanese progressive rock band that included two keyboard players that later went solo: Akiro Ito and Masanori Takahashi, the latter better known as Kitaro. Only months later (November to December) he was to produce their next album *Parallel World*. Both albums are well worth acquiring, particularly for fans of the early seventies style of Pink Floyd."

From Ben Miler at http://www.hippy.com/review-409.html

"Just when I thought I knew Far East Family Band through albums like *Nipponjin* (1975) and *Tenkujin* (1977), they gave us *Parallel World*, which is their third album. Like their previous album, Klaus Schulze was given a hand (in the mixing department), only this time around his influence is even stronger. The three guys handling the synthesizers here (Fumio Miyashita, Akira Ito, and Masanori Takahashi aka. Kitaro, the famous New Age star of the 1980s and 1990s) are given an even bigger role here."

Here's Miler again:

"It's no doubt that *Parallel World* is not only the best album Far East Family Band ever did, it's one of the all time great electronic and prog rock albums. This is truly a recommended album to those who enjoy prog and the Schulze-end of electronic music."

More on the middle '70s: Kitaro Interview with Greg Allen

GA: When Klaus Schulze produced *Nipponjin* and *Parallel World* for the Far East Family Band, had you used synthesizers previously?

K: Yes, at the time he produced our music, I already had a few synths for the recordings at Manor Studio in the UK. I brought 3 KORG synths. During the recording with Klaus, I was trying to play my synth and he was very interested in the operation of it. It wasn't my first recording, at the time I already had some experience with synths for a couple of years.

GA: What are the specifics about how and where you met Klaus Schulze? Did you call him to invite him to produce *Nipponjin*?

K: Klaus' music was very interesting in the '70s, was a very new kind of music.

GA: Klaus has mentioned in an interview, that you said to his friend in Quebec (October 5, 1994), that you still thank Klaus for your initiation to synthesizers. How specifically did Klaus help you in your initiation to synthesizers?

K: Klaus's music is Klaus's music and Kitaro's music is Kitaro's music. We had a great time learning from each other. During the '70s, the synthesizer inspired our creative imaginations in a powerful way.

GA: Klaus also said, I do like what I hear in Kitaro's music. Assuming that you had read that, how did that make you feel to hear such praise?

K: I still continue to create new synth sounds and I think Klaus is doing the same. We have each created our own individual sounds. I look forward to hearing Klaus' new sounds and music.

GA: Klaus also mentioned that he met Stomu Yamash'ta during the recording sessions for the Far East Family Band. What relationship did Stomu have with the band?

K: Tsutomu Yamashita created his own world and movement. The Far East Family Band had a good friendship with Tsutomu. During our stay in the UK, he invited us to his London home.

GA: How did working with Klaus Schulze influence your career as Kitaro?

K: Both of us work towards different directions but we create music in a similar way. I love Klaus' music.

GA: Along the same line, did listening to any of Klaus Schulze's albums in the 1970s have an influence on your solo career?

K: Klaus' solo albums. Also Tangerine Dream's album. It was fun!!!!!

GA: Was the Far East Family Band influenced by Pink Floyd? Their sound has been compared to Pink Floyd on many occasions.

K: We were so interested by the Pink Floyd sound. But the Far East Family Band was working to create a sound that was more spiritual and religious in our time.

GA: Have you kept up with the music of Klaus since you left the Far East Family Band and started your solo career?

K: I always had an interest in Klaus' music work.

GA: Did you have any more contact with Klaus once you started your solo career?

K: I haven't had any contact with him since then, but some day I like to see him again, also I'd like to hear his new music. His music gave me so much inspiration.

The following is a little note to Klaus from Kitaro, directly quoted from this interview:

Dear Klaus, it was a great time at Manor Studio, also in Tokyo, Japan. I hope we can meet somewhere and some time. Please keep good, your health and creativity.

Best regards,

Kitaro

1976 *Moondawn*

On the recording of the re-release:

Excerpt from an interview:

GA: I know they're not remastered but I could swear that when I listened to the re-release of *Moondawn*, the clarity of the sounds were just so sparkling, much more than my old copy.

KDM: It depends maybe on your old copy? The sound is the same as on the old Brain LP and as on the old Manikin-CD. Except maybe that we made it "louder", means: close to 0 dB, but I don't remember any such doing, and it was probably not necessary. I just checked: The Manikin-CD is minus 0.22 dB, so there was nothing left to "make louder."

From http://www.amazings.com/articles/article0048.html

"The new LP by Klaus Schulze, *Moondawn*, presents a new evolutive step with a greater musicality."

From http://www.vintageprog.com/sss.htm:

"*Moondawn* is for most people one of Schulze's seminal and definitive albums...Another important feature on this album was the inclusion of Harald Grosskopf on drums...Highly recommended."

From B22 at http://www.synthmusicdirect.com:

Moondawn has arrived on the re-issue roster and again we are confronted with another slice of real classic Schulze, realizing as I write that this recording is now exactly 30 years of age!!!... A major feature of his music now being the seamless transitions from spacy nothingness into all out speaker pounding sequencing, (joined here by Harald Grosskopf on drums to further fill out the percussive ends of things)... On to the 21-minute bonus track for this re-issue... still a fascinating listen and one which I think you Berlin School sequencer nuts may actually prefer to the original mix as those sequencers are manipulated, added delays causing psycho-acoustic timing tricks on the ear. An essential purchase? Ask a Schulze fan."

From Jim Brenholts, *All Music Guide*, at http://www.allmusic.com:

"Klaus Schulze is one of the most legendary electronic musicians of all time. He is also one of the best and most original. *Moondawn* is one of the true classics of the genre."

My review of *Moondawn*

(followed by part of my new interview with Harald Grosskopf covering *Moondawn* and a few other things): *Moondawn* is one of the all-time Klaus Schulze classics.

I remember at the time of *Moondawn* and sometime after, struggling with the presence of drums in it. This was probably because I really enjoyed Klaus' all synth style as I had grown accustomed to it. And also the fact that the ethereal style established on both sides of *Moondawn* was seductive, yet meditative, a spacy quality that seemed like it could go on for the whole album and never get boring.

Of course, in later albums and over a period of time, drums and percussion would become much more commonplace in KS' music and sound very, very good at times. So, after 31 years since the release of *Moondawn*, I have a different context in which to hear it. And the music is still fresh and intriguing, so I can bring that "beginner's mind" to my perception of it.

The initial sparkling chime-like sounds are very, very clear on this edition, followed, of course, by The Lord's Prayer in Arabic. This was mysterious in 1976 when I heard it and added to the allure of the album. It still does. The beginning strains of synthesizer pads are heavenly sounding and very long and drawn out before chord changes are made. Bells chime in the background as well as the more diffuse sparking, twinkling sound that started the song. As I listen to it, I'm sometimes taken back to 1976. The feeling I felt then was that it seemed with these new sounds in "Floating" that Klaus was taking us on a tour of something new, intriguing and delightful.

Drumming and a hypnotic sequencer pattern take over at around 8:00 and sound great. Klaus uses only top notch sound elements in *Moondawn*. A twittering sound floats through but it's unlike any of the other twittering sounds used in previous KS music. The warm, intoxicating long synth pads rejoin, and I experience musical bliss, spellbound by the layers of wonderful sound and absorbed in the overall composition. A minor key synth enters in the background to add even more to the aural pleasure. The sequencer moves through an enchanting chord shift.

In listening to "Floating," it's obvious what drew me to Klaus Schulze's music originally. There is an undeniable feeling, from listening to *Moondawn*, that this is the work of a musical genius. There simply was nothing else to compare this to in 1976. Every album Klaus released was a tour de force through previously unimaginable sonic territory.

To my ears, as "Floating" continues, the sound quality on the re-issue is superb. I know that no remastering was done, but somehow this just sounds clearer to me. I rate the recording as excellent (only one or two stray clicks), especially for 31-year-old-tapes.

The music builds to a crescendo with drumming and cymbals adding to its drive. By the 21:00 mark, the music has become like a runaway train, intensified greatly from its earlier pace. At this point I suppose you could almost get up and dance! The piece still has the sequenced characteristic and Harald's drumming fits in well, as do the Moog synth lead sounds, which are actually in the background.

"Mindphaser," the second side on the original LP, starts out, of course, with the sound of waves. To this day, this sounds incredibly realistic for a synthesizer. The opening pads layered on top of the ocean waves are sublime. A thundering is heard in the background. A very intoxicating mood is being created by this opening. Occasional chord changes and three layers of synths are present, one a deeper droning pad, another of a higher pitch, with a bit thinner sound playing the lead but still drifting and changing.

As more and more layers are introduced, I'm almost at a loss for words.... awestruck by the grandeur of this music. As swells of warm, luscious synth pads arise, I close my eyes and experience myself close to getting chills and then feel strong emotion and tears welling up – this music is moving me.

The buildup towards the stark entrance of Harald's drums has begun.

A sudden crash accompanies the entrance of the drums, which sound quite clear. From here on, the music takes on a completely different feel. Harald's drums are still complemented by the lead synth that was present before and then replaced by a lead with a lower octave with both playing expressively together. Gone is any hint of the peacefulness of the opening 13 or so minutes.

From this point, "Mindphaser" is basically Harald laying down the beat and Klaus soloing intensely around that beat with a variety of synth sounds and twitters. The finish slows down for maybe 45 seconds.

The bonus track is "Floating Sequence." It starts out somewhat like "Floating," but the sequencer is present sooner and with a weaker pulse. The overall recording seems to be at a lower volume level than the two tracks from the original *Moondawn*. In time, "Floating Sequence" builds in intensity.

"Floating Sequence" seems very similar to "Floating" but with enough variations to make it interesting. It settles in to sequenced synth and drums, creating a really nice, hypnotic effect. The pace becomes just as frantic as the last part of "Mindphaser," but in my opinion, everything holds together better; drums, sequencer and lead synth twitters all move forward cohesively in harmony. "Floating Sequence" fits in so well with the rest of the material that it actually adds to what is already a classic album.

Moondawn is a potentially very moving album (depending on one's mood and level of concentration) and a brilliant masterpiece from Klaus Schulze and Harald Grosskopf. I still struggle a little with the last part of "Mindphaser," but I can see how it is a contrast to the earlier part of the song and the culmination of a musical idea.

Bottom line on *Moondawn*: a brilliant masterpiece of its age, full of musical creativity and heavenly sounds. An album that holds up as well or even better than when it was released 31 years ago.

Harald Grosskopf Interview with Greg Allen, May 2007 (mostly relating to *Moondawn*):

GA: When did you first start drumming? At what age?

HG: 1965, aged 15.

GA: Did you take drum lessons? If so, how many years did you take lessons?

HG: I had a few lessons by one of the drummers that later took my place in my rock band Wallenstein, after I had quit in 1974. That was before I was looking to join in with Klaus Schulze and later Ashra. I found those drum lessons quite boring and lost respect completely, when I suggested to that teaching dude to improvise afterwards. He, later became a drumming teacher at the local music school, but was not able to put out real music, by switching the brain off for a while. After that I never tried again.

GA: Was your start with drumming due to your parents encouraging or more something you wanted to do (your idea totally)?

HG: My parents weren't too keen about me, knocking on everything, with everything I could reach, aged 11 years. On the other hand, they were quite tolerant and did not do anything to bring me away from my idea of becoming a musician. Yes, it was my own decision. It all began when I bought this small tape machine by Phillips, looking like a small ghetto blaster. We used to copy Beatles LP's by recording it with the onboard microphone.

During those numerous "recording sessions", I accompanied the backbeat by knocking on the table. That could be heard on the tape. In summertime we use to take my Phillips recorder into the local public swimming pool to listen to the music. One time a dude, the bass player of a local band, asked who did that percussive knocking on the recording. I expected a critical statement and did not answer. But the guy said that he liked it. The one who did it should become a drummer. This statement of more than 40 years ago, made me become a drummer until today.

GA: Where did you live in the 1970s during your time with Ashra, Wallenstein and Klaus Schulze?

HG: I was born in a little town named Sarstedt, a few miles southwards of Hannover in central Germany, not too far from where Klaus is living since the mid seventies. There was that US singer Peter Sarstedt, who had a world hit in the sixties. Anyway, I went to kindergarten and school there with Rudolf Schenker of the Scorpions. He was born in Sarstedt Too. I joined the Scorpions for a few weeks in 1966. In 1970 one member of a band called Blitzkrieg cast me and took me to a town named Moenchengladbach, 30 miles north of Cologne in western Germany. Blitzkrieg later changed its name into Wallenstein.

GA: Would this be the correct chronology: 1-Wallenstein 2-Ashra 3-Klaus Schulze? Did you play with Ashra before working with Klaus from 1976-1980 and then after that time as well?

HG: Yes, that's the chronological line up. I played on an Ashra record titled: *Ash Ra Tempel starring Rosi.* That was Manuel's former girl friend. We just had some e-mails across the ocean. Since 1981 she is living in New York. That is more than half of her life now. Never again, with Klaus after 1980. Ashra, with that line up, had a long break until 1997. We were invited to tour Japan. I brought my new music colleague Steve Baltes into the band. He "refreshed" the Ashra sound with technoid sounding parts. He sampled old Ashra material and made loops out of the stuff. We 3 improvised on top of it. It sounded like Ashra but much more up to date. After the Japan tour we issued two live albums quite well and had a few more gigs. The last one was in 2002

GA: When did you first meet Klaus Schulze? What year and under what circumstances?

HG: That must have been around 1971/72. Wallenstein recorded an album. When we had arrived Klaus, Manuel, Hartmut (Enke) just had finished their last album before Klaus left the group to start his solo career. I liked the uncomplicated, friendly characters.

I had problems with Klaus' first record. I was more into melodic things and in the meantime more a rock musician. Later, during some of those famous Cosmic Courier Sessions, Klaus just had bought a big Moog from Popol Vuh, my refusal sight about his music changed and got quite enthusiastic when I, back home again, heard *Blackdance* the first time. I was very impressed by the melodic sequences and strong rhythms. It grooved. My band Wallenstein didn't.

About the same time I got hold of Manuel's LP, *Invention for Electric Guitars.* Completely different but very catchy. I could not stay any longer with Wallenstein after that experience, sat down and wrote two letters. Both were answered. Manuel visited me personally. K.D.M. (Klaus Dieter Mueller) invited me to see Klaus in Hambühren, the place where they both just had moved after leaving Berlin

GA: Were you and Klaus more casual acquaintances before 1976 and *Moondawn* or friends even before *Moondawn*?

HG: Until *Moondawn* I had only a few casual meetings with Klaus. I really liked him. He was and I guess still is, a very earth bound character, that never left out any party. In those days, a great womanizer. He always was able to create an atmosphere of trust and fun. The mixture I deadly needed, because I was so frustrated with the music I was involved with, in the meantime.

GA: How did your partnership for the work on *Moondawn* form? Did you approach Klaus or did he call you about working and/or recording together? Could you describe how it happened that you decided to collaborate?

HG: It was a quite curious situation that lead to our cooperation. When I visited Klaus & Klaus at their new home near Hannover with my old metallic green VW Beetle, I had to wait half a day, because Klaus used to sleep until 3 or 4 pm most of the time, because he worked on music during night times. A lot of Berliners did. Berlin was special. No time limits for pubs and clubs. People used to live during nights. When I lived in Berlin I did that too. Anyway, Klaus had a little studio in his cellar where he kept his big Moog. I told him that I liked *Blackdance* very much because of its drive. He switched the Moog on and started the sequencer. I never had heard that synonym before in my life and later had to explain for years to other musicians what a sequencer was.

From the first moment on I heard the sequencer doing its job I was thrilled by the groove that "dead" machine produced. Better than anything I had experienced with real musicians. Something forced me to accompany that powerful music and I looked around for something to drum on. The only thing I could get hold of was a plastic cascet. Klaus turned around, he was sitting facing his back towards me, and smiled, when he heard my drumming. After the "session" ended he said, "We must do the next album together!" It took a few months before I heard from him again. I did not have a telephone in 1973/74. He telegrammed: Be on XXXX in Frankfurt at Panne Paulsen Studio.

GA: The recording was done in Frankfurt. What was the reason for recording in Frankfurt? Where did you both live at the time?

HG: I lived in Moenchengladbach, 60 miles north of Cologne in the west of Germany. Klaus in Hambühren, 15 miles north of Hannover, which is in the middle of Germany, 200 miles away from each other. For Americans, this is maybe nothing. Here quite a distance.

When I arrived at the studio, my first impression was: What a tiny little studio thing! My expectations were disappointed. The studios in Cologne I had worked in before were much, much bigger. Eberhard Panne, one of the owners, a very friendly man with a straight image, told me that Klaus will not be here today, he will arrive tomorrow. Disaster, I thought.

Later I felt very comfortable in that place. Eberhard Panne was a very professional sound engineer, and his partner, Mr. Paulsen, an electronic engineer and great technician, had built most of the equipment, from speaker cabinets, mixing console to the recording machine, himself. The building was a former cinema. The big audience screen room was used by a local carnival club and a restaurant. Klaus used the screen room for recording the orchestra parts on *X*.

GA: Could you describe for me how *Moondawn* took shape? Did Klaus have a pretty good idea of what he wanted it to sound like? Was it composed already when you got together or did it come out of you and Klaus maybe jamming and experimenting?

HG: I was used to rehearsing music for a month before recording. Klaus' way of working was totally different. His way of producing was dependent, and driven by, emotions and improvisation. Like me, he could not read, nor write music in these days. Until late afternoon nothing happened. He slept until 3 PM. I was bored half the day and read books. Then "breakfast". Klaus was very tall and skinny these days, because he did not eat well. From my point of view it took ages before the big Moog was able to put out a note. The "thing" was very sensitive in keeping its tuning. Leaving a door open for 5 minutes made its oscillators go up and down. It was some sort of a long ritual to control the horse.

After a couple of days he asked me to accompany him on an improvisation. I went into the drum cabin, from where I could not see Klaus. After 5 minutes the music stopped and we talked about what went wrong. After a few sentences we felt that we had the same ideas about it. Klaus said, "Let's do it again". After 25 minutes, without any "mistake" or uncomfortable feelings, *Moondawn* was born. I left the drum cabin and we hugged each other, full of joy and peace. Eberhard Panne, father of two children, was impressed. He liked the music very much and was a great, most patient supporter, even late at night and he had to work recently, for a big radio station, during daytimes .

GA: How did the fact that you were both drummers (Klaus, by then, a former drummer) affect your musical working relationship, if at all?

HG: Klaus said that he wasn't any more able to drum in those days. Before I experienced him as a very original drummer. Like Keith Moon for example. Standard wasn't his thing. He played a very fast bass drum. It seemed his right foot was the driving drumming force. We never drummed together.

GA: Had you been following Klaus's solo musical career before this from the time of *Irrlicht* through *Timewind*? If so, how did that affect your feelings going into the time you got together for *Moondawn*?

HG: We met at the Dirks studio and when I heard *Irrlicht* the first time, it didn't touch me at all. I found it very strange and intellectual. *Timewind* was different. It had more structures I could follow. But as I said before, *Blackdance* was a milestone that changed my mind and feelings about his music.

GA: How long did it take to complete *Moondawn*?

HG: In just a few days. There is not much editing apart from that Arabian prayer. *Moondawn* was a perfect sketch, a classic first take.

GA: How did you and Klaus feel about it once you completed it?

HG: We were very happy!

GA: Was there a feeling of great excitement or were you surprised at the reception of the album?

HG: I was sure that it would become some sort of a hit.

GA: What kind of reaction did *Moondawn* get, once released?

HG: In Germany a lot of skepticism, mostly bad press. In foreign countries, like France and England, overwhelming reactions.

GA: What was your general sense at the time, based maybe on reviews or record sales?

HG: I had this feeling that most of the musicians I was surrounded by, didn't like EM at all. Cold machine music. Just switching knobs. I was very sick of rock music and musicians that convulsively tried to imitate Anglo-American rock musician's attitudes; instead I was trying to create something original.

GA: Did you do one or more concert tours around the time of making *Moondawn* and the two *Body Love* albums? If so, were they all across Europe or limited in scope. Where was the best reception by the concert crowds? What stories or memories could you relate from concerts you played in at that time? Did you have to learn any of Klaus' material from pre-*Moondawn* to play in concert?

HG: Telling the truth, I was very disappointed that Klaus made, apart from two exceptions, all his tourings in the time, still by himself. I never found out why. Together, we played one gig at the 1976 Meta Music festival in Berlin and one at a festival in Essen, on the 26th of February, 1977 that was fucked up by the sound engineer. A most horrible monitoring wasted my feeling. I remember that Klaus was like me, pretty pissed off.

The Meta festival was cool. Rosie Mueller, Manuel's girlfriend in those days, told us after the gig, that she had spotted Bowie among the crowd. Which was not too unusual, because the White Duke used to live in Berlin during these days and was interested in EM and had good contacts to Tangerine Dream.

[KDM: "Harald's performance at the Meta Music festival in Berlin is heard [live] on the Klaus Schulze album, ...*Live*..."]

The Go Sessions with Stomu Yamash'ta

From the Official KS Website:

Q: What was it like working with Stomu Yamash'ta?

KS: That was fantastic, Stomu comes from the classical field of music, and he has a very sensible way of composing. For me it was never a problem to catch up with other artists, be it classical, with *Go*, or whatever. To work with Stomu was an honour, because I rate him very highly, along with my friend Michael Shrieve who played on some of my own records afterwards. Through the ISLAND Records connection I got to know Arthur Brown. A great singer and person. Many things happened because of *Go*, not on the actual record, but all the combinations, happenings around were very positive. (Because of my producing records of the Japanese Far East Family Band I got the contact to Stomu). Stomu is a great composer, but sadly he stopped composing, as far as I know. He should do it again.

From http://www.intuitivemusic.com/klaus-schulze-biography:

"In 1976, Schulze got involved in one of the most interesting projects from the '70s, the album by the Japanese percussionist Stomu Yamash'ta *Go*, along with other prime figures of the music scene like Steve Winwood, Al DiMeola, Pat Thrall, Rosko Gee, Michael Shrieve and Michael Quartermain. That same year Schulze also released the albums *Moondawn* and *Body Love*, using for the first time his Moog modular system, and he also started touring Europe extensively."

This description of his time with the *Go* project is taken from the booklet included with the 1978 LP release on Brain of *X*:

"During the recording sessions with the Far East Family Band, I met Stomu Yamash'ta, who was looking for a synthesizer player for a recording project. Between January and March of 1976 I joined Stomu, Steve Winwood, Mike Shrieve and several others in English studios. There wasn't enough time to fuse these solo performers into one group. The result of this period is the LP *Go* (on Island). Then we gave two sold out concerts: Royal Albert Hall in London and Palais des Sports, Paris. This second concert will be released on LP (Island – *Go - Live from Paris*)."

Review from http://www.allmusic.com

The next paragraph contains part of a review of the studio album *Go* from *The All Music Guide* online. By the way, I'm happy to see all these Klaus Schulze reviews online, as I had bought the *All Music Guide* to Rock, the cover of which says "The definitive guide to Rock, Pop and Soul." This purchase was in book form. I was very disappointed to see other groups such as Can and Brian Eno get very thorough coverage with a main section and numerous reviews of albums, and yet Klaus Schulze was nowhere to be found in the main section of the book. I refer especially to the Eno inclusion and reviews of many of his "electronic music" classics. Where's the founding father??? Despite that, AMG has a pretty nice set of reviews for KS on its site, even if some of them are fairly short and to the point. And the book is overall a very nice acquisition.

"*Go* (1976) is a concept album in the truest sense of the term, fusing pop/rock with tinges of jazz and elements of classical all connected by a central motif of space travel.".....” Each side of the original LP contains a complete suite of interconnected and continuous music. The haunting and brooding "Crossing the Line" is reminiscent of prog-rockers Alan Parsons Project or pretentious Pink Floyd [read: anything past *Meddle* (1971)].".....” It scored considerably well with audiences in 1976, reaching number 60 on the Pop Album chart."

http://www.allmusic.com

These review snippets are from a review, by Lindsay Planer, of *Go - Live From Paris* (from *The All Music Guide* online):

"The stage show was recorded at the Palais Des Sports in Paris, France on June 12, 1976 and the recital setting allows for considerably longer and more exploratory interaction amongst Stomu Yamash'ta (percussion/piano), Steve Winwood (vocals/keyboards) and Michael Shrieve (drums). They are joined by legendary jazz axeman Al DiMeola (guitar) as well as Tangerine Dream and Ash Ra Tempel veteran Klaus Schulze (synthesizer) — all of whom had contributed to *Go*... On the whole the material on *Go* sounds like a blueprint for the exceptional and inspired outing found here."

From http://calyx.club.fr/bands/related.html

"The all-star international line-up featured such luminaries as Steve Winwood, Klaus Schulze, ex-Santana drummer Michael Shrieve and fusion guitar virtuoso Al DiMeola, but the resulting efforts *Go Live From Paris* (1976) and *Go Too* (1977) met with mixed reactions from the critics. After that, not much was heard from Yamash'ta, apart from a few more new-age oriented, synthesizer-based efforts in the eighties, notably *Sea & Sky* (1983)."

My capsule reviews of *Go* and *Go - Live From Paris* (this is a set of all three *Go* albums together on two CDs so the sequence may be out of order compared to what you are used to):

1976 *Go*

Go starts out with spacy sounds that could be coming from Klaus' synthesizer. Since Stomu plays synthesizers also, it's hard to know when it's KS playing. Steve Winwood sings a lot on *Go*, and to me that makes it sound a little like a Steve Winwood solo album. I like Steve Winwood; it's just that a lead singer tends to obscure those in this supergroup. If Klaus' name weren't on the cover, I probably wouldn't guess that KS was involved.

A synth passage just into the second song sounds starkly like early Tangerine Dream, almost as if it was lifted out of *Phaedra*. A passage that begins around the

9:00 mark, featuring Steve Winwood singing, isn't very impressive. The music has a tendency to shift drastically in styles suddenly and often on *Go*, even though there are only two track markers on the CD. There are moments of occasional beauty, but it's not the most cohesive album I've ever heard.

My impression of *Go* – mediocre at best.

1976 *Go – Live From Paris*

Go – Live From Paris starts out in a very spacy way, as did *Go*. The beginning bears a slight resemblance to parts of "Velvet Voyage" (even though this was recorded before *Mirage*). The first four minutes sound somewhat Schulze-ish, and then there is a shift to a jazzy sound that is superior, at least to my ears, to anything on *Go*. The tracks on *Go – Live From Paris* are all the same tracks as on the studio album but somehow they sound a lot better. The drumming is superb.

Quite noteworthy is the fact that when Klaus Schulze is introduced to the crowd, he gets the loudest ovation up to that time by far – it's quite rousing and impressive. Michael Shrieve's ovation is pretty close after that also.

Go – Live from Paris is vastly superior to the studio album, in my opinion, the live setting drawing out very inspired performances. The recording also sounds much better! How often can you say that a live recording sounds better than the studio? The last few minutes are the most recognizable Schulze on either *Go* or *Go – Live from Paris*.

My impression of *Go – Live from Paris* – superb!

1977 *Go Too*

Paul Kohler writes, in *All Music Guide* online:

"represents a collage of sounds and textures.... difficult to describe"

My impressions of *Go Too*:

Unlike *Go* and *Go – Live from Paris, Go Too* is divided into eight distinct songs. The first song starts out with spacy effects and some loud drum crashes and ends in an almost King Crimson-ish way. "Seen You Before" is jazz-funk with lead female vocals of a somewhat ethereal quality.

The third song, "Madness," sounds like a throwaway, although I could see it sounding much better on repeated listens.

"Mysteries of Love" is quite a lovely song, slow paced and slightly bluesy.

"Wheels of Fortune" is blues-rock and unimpressive to me, although I like the ending (blues-rock is generally not my cup of tea).

"Beauty" is a stellar song, very pretty.

"You and Me" is the penultimate song on *Go Too.* I'd rate it pretty good but not great.

Last is Ecliptic and I think I detect the presence of our hero KS in this album, finally! And yes, the beginning is very good, better than any other song on *Go Too.* Unfortunately the song only lasts 2:25!

Noteworthy on *Go Too* are the outros and intros between songs; these are quite good.

That's it on the *Go* project. *Go – Live from Paris* is easily the highlight.

Klaus playing at Go Live in Paris.

1977 *Body Love* (Soundtrack)

From KS in the *X* re-release booklet:

"In fall 1976 I was offered to compose the music for a movie by Lasse Braun. My initial skepticism vanished once I met Lasse. A very pleasant 'freak' and a great project. (LPs: *Body Love* and *Body Love Vol. 2*)."

Harald Grosskopf Interview with Greg Allen (more on *Body Love* and *Body Love Vol. 2*)

GA: You also played on *Body Love* and *Body Love Vol. 2*. How long a break was there between the finishing of *Moondawn* and the beginning of recording *Body Love*?

HG: I can't remember and have to take a look on the credits. I am surprised. Just one year. *Moondawn* was 1976. *Body Love* 1977. My memory says 3 or 4 years.

GA: Did Klaus ask you to be involved in the *Body Love* project after he had met Lasse Braun and decided to do the soundtrack or did you both know, even as making *Moondawn* ended, that you would collaborate again on the next album?

HG: As far as I remember, I was living for 6 months in Hambühren with Klaus & Klaus.

During that time we went to Dusseldorf to meet a porno producer that had produced a porno movie in which the director had used *Moondawn* and *Blackdance* underlaying the film shootings. That dude wanted to have individually made compositions in that specific style on his film material.

GA: Did you meet Lasse Braun soon after Klaus did?

HG: No. Together with him once or twice.

GA: Did you have any input into the composition of *Body Love*?

HG: Yes indeed! My specific way of drumming.

GA: Klaus talked about having initial reservations about doing a porno soundtrack -- which were overcome by seeing the movie and meeting Lasse Braun.

HG: Those reservations were wiped out fast by the salary that was promised and paid to Klaus.

GA: Was it the same for you? Did you have any reservations about working on a porno soundtrack, or was it more of the case that Klaus had laid the groundwork and it was just like any other music project from there?

HG: I was a child of the seventies. Free sex for free people and my reservations were quite limited. During the production it became fast boring to see the sex sequences over and over again. After a while you start counting pimples on the actors' butts.

GA: Did you meet Lasse Braun also?

HG: Yes, an old, curious Italian hippie, accompanied by two Thai sex slaves. I was not impressed.

GA: Did you see the film before or after recording the music?

HG: Before, during, during, during, during, during. But never ever again.

GA: Did you have any feelings at the time, once the film was released about how the music and the film worked together?

HG: Music can neither be real pornographic or anything else and can be everything at the same time. It's feeling, a creation in the listener [himself]. It's relative. Klaus' fans were different consumers than the clientele that went to see such movies. So one thing did not have anything to do with the other. It didn't bother me at all. We all have seen porno movies before, liked some of them and got excited. Didn't we? So what?

GA: How did *Body Love Vol. 2* come to be?

HG: No idea.

GA: Was it due to an overflow of good music from the same sessions as *Body Love*?

HG: Could be.

GA: How long did you work with Klaus on these two albums?

HG: It was a bit like in the movie business. Waiting for a long time and suddenly it happens. Sometimes I slept in my drum cabin when Klaus woke me up asking whether I would like to join in. I surprised the crew by being present like a starting Porsche, two minutes after they had woken me up.

GA: When you were making the music, did you know exactly what was going to be used for *Body Love* and what was going to be used for *Body Love Vol. 2*?

HG: No!

Harald as a young drummer.

My review of *Body Love*:

Just minutes after reviewing *Body Love Vol. 2* with ""Stardancer II", I begin my review of *Body Love* starting with "Stardancer". This will be a chance to compare the two songs back-to-back with concentrated listening.

As I note in my comments on "Stardancer II", the beginnings are virtually identical except for the textures of the drum crashes and the fact that "Stardancer II" uses minor key synth pads. The drum crashes are probably more tumultuous in this version. The sequencer seems to creep in with a stronger pulse on this version as well.

The heart of "Stardancer" is essentially the same as "Stardancer II", perhaps with more choirs. My feelings about "Stardancer" have run the gamut from feeling that the sequencer formed a really nice groove to thinking that the song was diminished by the extensive twangy sound of the lead synth. I think "Stardancer" is probably a stronger song than "Stardancer II" due to some interesting chord changes and more interesting activity around the lead synth (I'm guessing Minimoog).

Second up is "Blanche," who, I recall from liner notes, was Klaus' French girlfriend at the time. It starts with soft piano and lush synth pads and some swirling sparkling chime like sounds. This is accompanied by the yearning sound of female choir voices. This is a gorgeous piece of music that tugs at my emotional heartstrings and brings me to the edge of tears; tears of joy and tears of yearning for that missing feeling of warmth and love that seemed to leave sometime during childhood (but is restored to a great extent when listening to Klaus' music!). Klaus plays this song with pure passion and emotion.

Last of the songs on the original *Body Love* is "P.T.O." It starts with stunningly exquisite synth pads, followed by majestic, grand sounding choirs. The portion of *Body Love* starting with "Blanche" right on through "P.T.O." is achingly beautiful music.

A seductive sequencer bubbles up from the pads and choirs around the 4:00 mark. The sequencer percolates as the dominant instrument until another wonderful sounding, higher register sequencer joins and takes over the lead. Choirs, Minimoog and an occasional patter from Harald's drums accompany the strongly pulsing sequencer, which takes over "P.T.O." for several glorious minutes. An occasional minor key Minimoog surge adds to the overall pleasure of listening to "P.T.O." At around 22:00, a few sparkling notes precede a change to a more pad-oriented, lush and moving section of music. This is pure sonic bliss.

The original three songs of *Body Love* constitute a superb album.

The bonus track is named "Lasse Braun" after the director of the *Body Love* film. It starts with a resonating bouncy synth sound that plays pretty much on its own for the first two minutes. A few crystalline sounds float through. Long, floating pads finally join the mix at about 3:45; soon joined by drumming (perhaps tablas). At around 13:00, the drumming takes on a brisker pace, sounding somewhat like the drumming in "Ways of Changes" from *Blackdance*.

There are some unique, nice twittering sounds which surface from time to time, but the last several minutes see Klaus soloing on the Minimoog. Overall, "Lasse Braun" is not a bad song but nothing really special either. The positive is that it continues some of the themes heard earlier in *Body Love*. The negative is that it doesn't elevate the overall quality level of *Body Love*. That seems to be what frequently happens with bonus tracks.

A couple of examples I can think of where the quality of the original album was diminished by bonus tracks are *What's Going On* by Marvin Gaye and *All Things Must Pass* by George Harrison. I think the listener who never heard the album in its heyday and is exposed to it with the bonus tracks is likely deprived of the sense of awe that the owners of the original albums felt.

All that said, I believe that KDM has made many great choices for bonus tracks that have enhanced the original CD (see *Angst* or *Cyborg*) and a few with bonus tracks that were not so great. Even though I think "Lasse Braun" is the weakest track on the *Body Love* re-release, overall the bonus tracks have been a great plus in this re-release series.

1977 *Mirage*

From the *X* booklet (translated):

KS: After this tour I released my eighth album, which was a commercial risk. As I promised on the cover of *Moondawn*, I am opening a new door on this album. No memory-loaded melodies or rhythmic power sequences, more a threatening silence, the presentation of a mood. Nevertheless my most advanced album: *Mirage*.

From B22 at http://www.synthmusicdirect.com:

"[*Mirage*] was seen as a coming of age album for Schulze...[It] was produced to international critical acclaim...'Velvet Voyage' kicks off brilliantly with its rather disturbing chords and atmospherics...Eventually a sequence emerges, taking a hold from the drifting blizzard of synths and FX. The Moog's mono voice calls out working its magic, but is ultimately overwhelmed by the power of Schulze's huge synthesizer soundscape...

"The epic 'Crystal Lake' drifts into play at 29:15...with its repetitive merry little music box style beginnings...I'm sure it's a CD many of you would fall over themselves to get their hands on given that the track 'Velvet Voyage' has also been altered for this release!!!...However, buyer be warned - this is a CD that is strewn [with] the audio artifacts...clicks predominantly, and an added slight digital distortion in the higher register...which should and could have been dealt with on this, the ultimate version of such a classic album...[I]t's those technical flaws which sink this, an otherwise mesmerizing album."

Author's note on the *Mirage* re-issue: The original re-issue did have the problems mentioned in the review above. However, SPV re-pressed the CD with the artifacts cleaned up. I personally sent my original copy back and got the new and improved version. To my ears (that is, pretty much audiophile ears), the new *Mirage* sounded like all the problems had been corrected, and I was happy. I would think that any *Mirage* re-releases purchased now would be of the re-pressed version.

Here's an e-mail exchange with Klaus D. Mueller on the recording quality of the *Mirage* re-issue:

GA: I personally dealt with the label here in the states and they told me that SPV was producing a new version that corrected the flaws. I sent in the defective one and sure enough, the new one was perfect!

KDM: Yes, Greg, the record company made immediately a new master, and they even sent everyone this new version if they had sent them back the "wrong" early version. Funny was to see that some journalists in German music magazines were even praising the "very good" sound of *Mirage* in their reviews. Probably they have never listened to the CD, but just copied the propaganda from the label? One German review even mentioned the "double CD" *Mirage* and gave it the maximum "stars"!

From Jim Brenholts at http://www.allmusic.com:

"*Mirage* is one of Klaus Schulze's best albums. It is certainly among the eeriest e-music sets ever... This is vital space music."

From http://www.vintageprog.com/sss.htm:

"*Mirage* was the most low-key work of Schulze's best albums, and remains my favourite by him... Most of the album was instead based in slow, sweeping, mystical and dreamy soundscapes that conjured up images of snow-covered forests and icy winter-landscapes... [It's] one of the best electronic progressive albums ever made. Essential."

My impressions of *Mirage*:

I remember buying this album, finding it in the import bin at Finder's Records in Bowling Green, Ohio. I paid at most $8.99 for it -- a steep price, but by then a new Klaus Schulze album was an automatic buy. And an exciting one. I remember listening to it the first time and being surrounded by a wall of majestic, slowly changing sound that was unlike anything I had ever heard before.

I said that about *Picture Music*, and that is also true – but this album was really different!

I'm reviewing the original "Velvet Voyage" here. I'll make some comments on the alternate version that appears on the re-issue afterward. "Velvet Voyage" starts off innocently enough with some echoing chime-like sounds. Then an eerie portion begins with the first spooky sounding synths gliding into the mix. More surges and layers of eerie sounding synths join in. It can be a little unnerving at first, as Klaus is going "way out there."

Reassuring synth pads join in, some higher-register and some a little lower. Voices can be heard in the background. I can't tell what they are saying, but they sound intriguing for their creativity and serve to remind that this is so far an eerie piece of music! Gradually a wall of choir-like sound builds up in the background and seems to drift on for most of the rest of the song, evolving only slowly.

Behind the choirs are glorious synth pads playing somewhat mournful music that can also tap into my emotions and evoke a feeling of joy. The composition shifts from eerie to a comfortable and occasionally exhilarating feel.

The twittering sounds that Klaus has used appear sporadically. Eventually, a hypnotic, pulsing, bell-like sequencer begins to play. This sequencer stays in the background for most of the rest of "Velvet Voyage". The music at this point sounds awe inspiring!

There is a sense of childlike wonder at this soundscape that has built and shows no sign of letting up. Time stands still – it could be hours, days or years that this song has been playing and will continue to play.

The middle period of "Velvet Voyage" just continues reliably, confidently and reassuringly. Over a period of time, it seems that the Moog-like synth sound that is playing, the bass synth sound and the methodical sequencer have become more dominant over the choirs. They alternate in soloing at the forefront of the mix but the alternation is subtle. "Velvet Voyage" is a challenging and at times exciting piece of music.

The New "Velvet Voyage"

In the first few minutes, there isn't a lot to distinguish between the older and newer versions. This one starts out perhaps with a little less frightening sounds in the first couple of minutes. The "wall of sound" choir effect seems much less prominent, although in the first six minutes, one can also hear some sporadic choir effect. This version seems like a shallower version, one that has not found its voice yet. The voices heard in the background of the original "Velvet Voyage" are either totally missing or so sparse in the mix as to make comparatively no impact.

This version doesn't have the confidence and conviction of the original. At the 11:00 mark, I feel that this version is not even close to it. The sequenced sound that starts and stays in the mix for a long time (as in the original), comes in around the 12:00 mark, then becomes mixed with chime-like bells. The chimes sound like those at the beginning of "Crystal Lake" and could be considered one area where the new version outdoes the old. If you focus on those bell-like sounds, the listening experience can be sustained for a quite while.

These bell-like sounds begin to dominate the mix of the new “Velvet Voyage” and can be appreciated as they carve out a nice mental groove. That’s why it’s good to have both versions. If you can only have one, though, it should be the original.

Everything that is great about the original “Velvet Voyage” is implied at times, but the new version is not close in quality.

Now on to “Crystal Lake”, the second epic track, which is happily the same on both versions of *Mirage*. The original “Velvet Voyage” combined with “Crystal Lake” made for an absolutely magnificent album.

“Crystal Lake” starts immediately with a moderate tempo sequencer with a chime-like bell sound. These start softly but soon begin to rise in volume.

The whole mix has a very pleasing sound, the chime-bells are playing a repeating melody, and soon deep bass joins in. Each time the bass joins in, the music shifts direction a little.

If one pictures a human playing the xylophone instead of a sequencer, it seems that person would be quite tired by now due to the pace! Some drifting, floating synth pads in the background add to the grandeur of “Crystal Lake” and continue from around the 8:00 mark.

Around 11 minutes the song takes on an even more majestic feel. The song has progressed beautifully, and every new sound and layer has added to its magic. Around 12:40, the bass signals a change. Relentlessly, the bell-chimes play on. They have not paused since the track began!

Long, resonating bass chords mix with slowly decaying synth pads to form a whole new feel to the piece - not less grand, perhaps even more so. The tinkling of lots of bells can be heard in the background – but very different from before. More like a diffuse spray of chime-like electronics, like snow falling to the ground.

The whole soundscape remains in a subdued mode but with a lower-register synth playing a somewhat plaintive tune in the background. This is just a nice mellow space which reminds me more of the beauty of the last parts of “Totem and “Mental Door” on *Picture Music.*

Suddenly the pace picks up and the steady, pulsing sequence starts to play boldly and much more quickly than earlier.

“Crystal Lake” is a great piece of music; for many years it has ranked very high on my list of individual KS album tracks.

The bonus track on the *Mirage* re-issue is “In Cosa Crede Chi None Crede?” It starts with thin, organ like sounds. The sound seems like a bit of a throwback, but my impression at the 4:00 mark is that it is quite nice. The booklet states that it’s the complete version of a piece used for a Dutch movie (where only the first 5 minutes were used).

A steady sequencer plays as a synth solo plays along. The recording is a bit rough in spots, but the song is strong enough to obscure that. Some deeper bass synth sounds join in, very reminiscent of what we just heard on "Crystal Lake".

This is a very nice bonus track. It feels like an upper echelon Schulze track. It's clearly better than a lot of tracks that were included on regular Schulze releases. This could have strengthened albums like *Dreams* or *Inter*Face* instantly.

A whole lot of the material that was in the vaults and got released in the boxed sets could have been used in the '80s – and then the phrase "the difficult '80s" would never have been used! Just a thought. No matter, this track only serves to point out that before the boxed sets, we KS fans were not being exposed to a lot of his best music, because it was stored away. I'm very glad that it's been released and that I'm able to own this material now.

1977 *Body Love Vol. 2*

From James Mason at http://www.allmusic.com:

"*Body Love, Vol. 2* does not differ greatly from the rest of Schulze's body of work from around this time, similar to contemporary albums *Moondawn* and *X*. This album is as recommended as any other of his albums from this phase of his career."

My review of *Body Love Vol. 2*:

I'm reviewing the LP on the Brain label since the re-release was not available at the time of this writing. The only track on Side One is "Nowhere – Now Here," clocking in at just over 29:00.

The track starts out with a minor pad surrounded by phaser-like sounds and twitters. The mood is very contemplative right from the start. The minor-key drone is the one constant for several minutes as Klaus' lead pad plays and the other sounds swirl about.

A plodding sequencer sound begins the first hint at rhythm, and then Harald's drums come in at around the 5:00 mark. Just after the drums begin, very lush choir sounds enter to give the overall sound an almost regal feeling. "Nowhere – Now Here" is filled with sounds and patterns that produce strong emotions in the listener.

Just seven or eight minutes into the track, the sound is powerful, inspiring, dynamic. This may be better than anything that's on the original *Body Love* album. Klaus plays some mind blowing minor-key synth lead that rises majestically above the rest of the soundscape.

The overall equation is typical KS: building a lot of musical tension. At about the 15:00 mark, bell-like sequencer sounds add a sparkling, moving feeling.

The same compositional genius that I've experienced in reviewing close to 80 CDs was apparent even at this early stage of Klaus' career. The wonder of it is how so many sounds mesh together so perfectly to form a mesmerizing, magical, even miraculous soundscape. It's in evidence in so many of Schulze's albums through the years, and when it all comes together as it does here, it's just plain exhilarating. "Awe" is the only word to properly describe my feelings.

"Nowhere – Now Here" is an overall excellent side of music – totally worthy of fitting in to the Klaus Schulze "classic period" (at least his first classic period; more on that later!).

First up on Side 2 is "Stardancer II" which starts in similar fashion to "Stardancer" from *Body Love*. Minor key synth pads that go along with the early choirs set it apart from the original "Stardancer". The differences between the two songs are subtle but noticeable.

The drum crashes early on have a little crisper sound in "Stardancer II." The middle section consists of sequencer and Minimoog style lead. For much of this sequencer and Minimoog section, the song does seem to be somewhat repetitive and less interesting than many Schulze songs. There is an almost complete absence of pads for several minutes.

The third and last song is "Moogetique," which features some "Velvet Voyage"-like textures at the outset. The tempo and mood have changed completely from "Stardancer II. Some of the ensuing sounds are slow and reminiscent of the *Irrlicht/Cyborg* period.

Even though there is a somewhat eerie quality, there is also a certain beauty derived from reverberating, dancing chime-like sounds, falling like autumn leaves on the edges of the sound stage. Pads are layered, and there is definitely a resemblance to "Velvet Voyage" that can't be missed. It's noteworthy that this song was released after *Mirage*. It sounds like it was recorded right about the same time.

All in all, "Moogetique" is classic Schulze of the '70s – an enjoyable song.

1977 Concert at London Planetarium

From *Perfect Sound Forever* in May, 1997 (http://www.furious.com/PERFECT/kschulze.html):

"...In 1977, you did shows at the London Planetarium. Do you feel this is an ideal atmosphere for your music?

KS: It was the very first time that a concert was given in a planetarium! I don't know if a planetarium is the ideal place for each and every music. I care for a good sound. And some concert places have a good sound, some have not. A planetarium with its hemisphere shape is difficult to play, if I remember well (?). There are echoes and shattering from all sides, if you play too loud. But in fact, I don't exactly remember what it was like, then, twenty years ago, in London.

Klaus D. Mueller has these recollections about the concert at The London Planetarium, "The London Planetarium was to promote the newly released Schulze album, the first for (British) Island Records. It was the first live concert in a planetarium. Later, many copycats (of the music of KS or TD) played planetariums all over the world. It became a kind of fashion among them. Once I was invited to visit such a concert from two copycats, here in Berlin. It was awful. I mean the music. It hurt, so bad it was. And boring. What a luck that there were only seven visitors in the concert at the planetarium (which can be filled with a few hundred paying guests). They even made a repeating concert the next day – without getting more visitors. Funny that these amateurs don't give up. They still do 'their' music, after fifteen years. It's like Dixieland in the field of jazz. (The last sentence I said very often, because it brings the matter to the point.)"

Paris - 16 novembre 1978

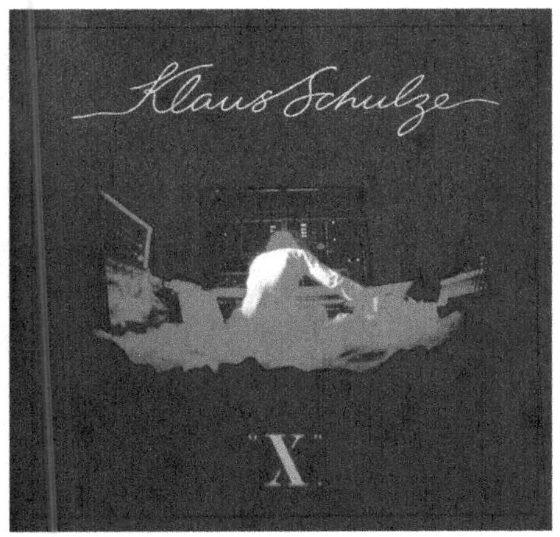

1978 *X*

From the Harald Grosskopf interview with Greg Allen:

GA: The period from *Moondawn* through *X* was an incredibly productive period (both at the time and looking back now, in my opinion).

HG: The money Klaus had scored via the Lasse Brown connection, including the film score *Barracuda*, made *X* become real and "bigger" than everything he did before. The porno people didn't know that they were featuring a new album of Klaus'.

GA: What was your feeling during this period when these classics were being made? Did you have the feeling then that some very special music had been made by you and Klaus (and Wolfgang Tiepold)?

HG: My involvement and participation was quite small on *X*. I had the feeling that Wolfgang Tiepold did most of the work. He arranged what Klaus had improvised on his Moog. He wrote for the orchestra and conducted it. I prefer *Blackdance* and *Moondawn* until now.

GA: Indeed that these albums would be called classics in Klaus' discography, especially *Moondawn* and *X*?

HG: *Moondawn*, Yes! *X* sounds classic. But new?

GA: How did having an orchestra affect your role in *X* and how was it different from the previous three albums in terms of the process you went through in making the album?

HG: It didn't affect me. I wasn't impressed.

GA: I'm interested in the feelings of the orchestra about playing in a project with Klaus Schulze, who was doing a very new kind of music with mostly electronics and synthesizers. Did you get any sense of that? Did they seem excited about the project?

HG: I guess they were hired [as] musicians that did [their] job like any other."

GA: A major portion or all of the recording for these four albums was done in Frankfurt. What was the reason for choosing this location?

HG: This positive, professional, almost familiar atmosphere. And it was much cheaper than in the big studios.

From Mike DeGagne at http://www.allmusic.com

"[I]t's the provocative electronic music within the names that makes this one of his best albums... A true pioneer at his craft, Schulze's *X* is one of the more definitive albums of his career, since its length and instrumental combinations make for a multifaceted electronic piece."

Who is Georg Trakl? Klaus Schulze explains in an interview on his Official Website, "Georg Trakl is Austrian, was born in 1887, and died 1914 as an ambulance man in World War I, because of a voluntary overdose of drugs. He is remembered because of his expressionistic lyric. I love him because of these poems."

Wolfgang Tiepold today (2007) is a busy member of the Frankfurt Radio Symphony Orchestra; he is also freelancing as a jazz cellist.

My impressions of *X*:

I always called this "Ten" but when I talked to Klaus on the phone, he pronounced it "Ex" like the letter X, so that is the correct pronunciation, which I will adopt. I owned *X* for years on a double chromium dioxide cassette that I bought in Ann Arbor, Michigan. And I wore it out. I remember one day being at work, putting the cassette in my jam box and the pad on the cassette had fallen off. I was quite unhappy at the prospect of losing my access to one half of *X*, so I asked my co-worker, Rob, if he could fix it. Somehow, he got that pad back in there and *X* was playable again, to my great relief!

Now I have the re-release on CD and access to the much longer "Georg Trakl" (a great addition) and "Objet D'Louis," which although a marginal recording, audio-wise, is a wonderful document of Klaus' most "classical" sounding composition ever, Ludwig II von Bayern (this coming from someone who's not really a fan of classical music). Ludwig II von Bayern is one of my all time favorite tracks so I was happy to learn of "Objet D'Louis"' inclusion on the re-release. I liked the prospect of an orchestra playing it just as an orchestral piece, although it seems there is still some synthesizer early in the mix.

On CD 1, *X* starts out with "Friedrich Nietzsche," which begins with sparse, swirling synth, quickly joined by male choir sounds, which gradually increase in volume. Sequenced synth starts in the background, joined by drums, cymbals and lead solo synth. Sweeping, gorgeous sounding synth pads enter the mix. When the drums come in, they enter in an accelerated way, with short, rapid strokes. They fit in nicely with all the other sounds that shape the overall feel of the song. Staccato, piano-like sounds enter sporadically adding a unique flavor to the pacing.

Between Harald's drumming and the background sequencer, the unusual rhythm for the song is established. There is a certain confidence and assuredness about this song – as if this were a piece of music that was destined to be made.

"Georg Trakl" has an interesting history in terms of its use as a track on Klaus Schulze LPs or CDs. The original piece, running 5:20, was used on the original release of *X*. Later, the complete long version was used on Disk #47 of *The Ultimate Edition*, clocking in at 27:55. And, of course, on the re-release of *X*, we get the much expanded version at 26:04. The first time I heard this expanded version, it blew my mind. The expansion performed a miracle with this song, changing it from just another track to one of the all time great Schulze songs. In fact, "Georg Trakl" received the #2 ranking of all time Schulze tracks in the 2000 KS Circle Readers' Poll.

This is from an e-mail exchange I had with KDM about this song's history:

GA: Is "Discover Trakl" from *The Ultimate Edition* related in any way to the additional 21 minutes of "Georg Trakl" from the re-issued *X*?

KDM: The version of "Georg Trakl" on the re-release of *X* is 26:04, which is a bit shorter than the version (27:55) on *The Ultimate Edition*. On re-release *X* the last 90 seconds had to be cut because the CD is full. The (original) Brain *X* versions (LP and CD) contained only the very first approximately 5:20 of the "Georg Trakl" track.

GA: I think that expansion on *X* turned "Georg Trakl" into one of KS' best tracks ever!

KDM: KS was thinking differently in 1978. He said that at about 5:20 "everything is already said," and therefore he only released this short faded-out version in 1978. [See my interview with Klaus for his viewpoint on this!]

Here's my review of "Georg Trakl". The song starts in a mellow way with a synthesized bass sequence pattern along with solo synth. The classic KS synth pad floats in, lasting about 17 seconds on the same note. The volume increases as the piece begins to accelerate early, around 2:30.

At close to 6:00, a new, delightful sequencer pattern joins in, played in a higher register. This pattern is strong and confident and sounds great on top of the previously established mix. Then a bit past 7:00, another sequencer pattern joins, and the first one shifts direction, creating a sequencer heaven! And it comes as such a thrill because I love beautifully layered synth sequencer patterns and because this part of the track was previously unheard. What a discovery!!!

"Trakl" now has a bouncy, fun character. One sequencer line drops out, leaving another to shine. All the while Klaus plays synth pad notes that continually evolve. Chord changes in the sequencer patterns along with Harald's drumming lead to an increased force and drive to the song.

More sequencer patterns join, as the song continues in a strong rhythm, accentuated in an astonishing way by chord changes and multiple sequencer lines. At around 14:00, the song has taken off to its highest energy level yet.

"Trakl" can only be described as sonic bliss, one of the best synthesizer/sequencer-based songs ever recorded and possibly the very best. The recording is far superior to the other great contender in

Michael Hoenig's classic *Departure From the Northern Wasteland.* This expanded version of "Georg Trakl" is a complete and total revelation and so much more valued for its surprise factor.

Third is "Frank Herbert." It starts out with a brisk middle register sequencer pattern combined with choir sounds that are toward the "male" side. The song comes right at you from the start, unlike most Schulze tracks, which take a while to build momentum. Harald Grosskopf uses similar drumming patterns to "Nietzsche" and to a certain extent "Trakl."

The sequencer is a bit hypnotic and yet aggressive, forming a very comfortable groove and serving as a great focal point, allowing the rest of the instrumentation to shine. The song has a somewhat ethereal feel, even though it's largely beat driven, accentuated by choirs around the 9:00 mark.

Fourth on CD 1 is "Friedemann Bach," an 18-minute track. It starts with somewhat tentative synth pad surges that are close to eerie. Drum hits fall into the mix at a slow pace. The sound of violin enters (real?). A long drum roll yields to a strange synth noise. The piece still has a slightly uncomfortable feel.

Arising from that discomfort is a reassuring sequencer pattern in a middle register that increases in intensity around the 9:00 mark. This sequencer alternates as the stronger element, for the rest of the track, with a soundscape consisting of drums, eerie sounds, unsettling minor-key synth splashes and, toward the end, myriad synth and string sounds swirling and darting about the sonic landscape

CD 2 starts with the celebrated "Ludwig II von Bayern."

The beginning doesn't really hint at what is to come, just huge waves of synths and synth noises, some rumbling and then a tentative, yet methodical sequencer pattern.

Very deep cello adds to the upsurge in feeling and very plaintive, yearning strings play a compelling tune. Already, around 2:30, the harbinger of greatness is present.

The deep cellos stroke confidently, followed by higher pitched strings. The quality of the sound recording is magnificent. The first occurrence of the classical sounding strings playing boldly arrives at close to the 4:00 mark. The strident strings play a song of joy and delight, rising emotion, and indescribable beauty. I've never heard a string passage this confident, joyful and awe inspiring. For the next few minutes, the music continues in this invigorating mode.

Choirs emerge as the song turns a bit darker, slowing more and more. Beauty is still present at the 9:00 mark, but a major change is taking place.

Another exquisite sweeping string section plays before the song goes into the famous (or infamous) tape loop. I guess I'd have to say I always thought it marred the song because it seemed to drag on so long without much change. The upside is that when the tape loop ends, there is more stunning orchestral music to be experienced.

Having written so many of these reviews, I feel like I'm more in touch with how Klaus structures his songs and how he uses certain sections to set up other ones. One theory could be that this loop was "monotonous" and a little long merely to set up the brilliance to come. That theory might seem to be contradicted, however, by the fact that the "Ludwig II" version on *Dziekuje Poland '83* has interesting melodies playing during the "tape loop." And that the version in the Jubilee Edition also has a very melodic section playing over the loop.

The loop continues, not varying much at all for several minutes, until grandiose strings sweep into Ludwig in a stirring fashion. Sequencer patterns return, followed by the boldly surging string section that is the signature sound element in this song. Drums and sequencer dominate for about five minutes, with the strings returning to close the track.

"Heinrich Von Kleist" finishes the original album (not counting the extra "Trakl"). According to an essay by David M. Cline on the Official Klaus Schulze Website, "Heinrich Von Kleist" was chosen over the last 20-plus minutes of "Georg Trakl" when the decisions were made as to what music to include on the original version of *X*. Dr. Cline indicates that the consensus is that the expanded "Trakl" would have been preferred, considering that it ranked #2 in the 2000 poll alluded to above. He also indicates that he prefers the choice that was made, high praise for "Von Kleist."

"Heinrich Von Kleist" features swirling strings overlaying contrasting, droning synth pads in a minor key.

The droning synth pads exist as a backdrop for the string soloing, but for the first several minutes, the pads are the highlight for me. Soon, the pads and the strings meld for a pleasing effect. Some bizarre "shots" of synth noises go blasting into the sound spectrum from time to time.

This piece of music is very unhurried, a bit mysterious. Choirs enter around the 11:00 mark, a bit of a relief for a piece of music that seems to be meandering. A wide variety of unusual sounds – some quite crisp in sound quality – float in and out of the sound field. At about the 15:00 mark, all that remains is a parade of unusual sounds.

Expect any passers-by to comment to you on the "weird" nature of the music you are listening to if they are within earshot during this period, lasting a little over two minutes. However, if they walk in just seconds later and hear the heavenly choirs, they might ask "what is that gorgeous music you are listening to?" This choir passage is one of the best in any KS album, powerful in its unrestrained expression.

As the beautiful synth and string playing emerge after the 20:00 mark, it seems the wait was worth it for this piece of music to reveal itself thoroughly. Slow, sporadic drumming joins the choirs in the later parts of the song.

The beauty of these last several minutes of "Von Kleist" is hard to put into words. Maybe it's because I've used every superlative in my vocabulary already! This is a sensational end to *X*, a supremely creative musical masterpiece.

The bonus track is the orchestral version of "Ludwig II," entitled "Objet D'Louis" for this edition of *X*. A complete orchestra was used, and the concert was broadcast live on the radio. The first couple of minutes sound like they could have been created by electronic instruments. At close to 3:00, the stirring string section plays. This is not a state of the art recording, but to hear this played by a full orchestra is a real treat.

The tape loop plays for around four minutes in this version, but there is a bit more activity in the background here since another melody line plays for most of the loop. There is only about a minute and a half where the repetition of the strings playing the original loop is front and center, so it doesn't come across as monotonous.

X has finished playing. It's a real tour de force in music and one of the top Schulze albums ever!

On Synthesizer School

Klaus in a 1994 interview said that "It was me who founded a school to learn synths, from 1978 to 79."

From a KS interview posted on Official Website, September 1993:

"Yes, my Synthesizer School. I did this from 1978 to 1980, after working for some years on analogue synths. About '78 were many people around who were interested in learning about my instruments, the synthesizers. Regular schools taught only piano or violin or vocals, whatever, but not these exotic new tools. In nearly every interview from 1973 until the late seventies I had to answer the usual 'Please Klaus, tell me, what is a synthesizer' question. There was a big gap for people who wanted to learn about this type of music. Okay, I said to myself, I will start a school. I employed one teacher, and he and myself, we both split the job. But I had so many other things to do, I gave it up after these two years. I never really wanted to do other things beside my music. Only if I have spare time, it's okay, and as long as it doesn't become bigger than my music."

1979 *Dune*

From Arthur Brown's assistant, Matthew North [in response to my saying that I thought Arthur would really have a lot to add to the book]:

"...So do I. I'm actively trying to get as many of Arthur's memoirs down as possible, and I'm always keen to know myself about things like the KS years; for the record I do know that one day Arthur would like to perform again with him.

He also told me that they never rehearsed and on their first gig in Paris around 1978, Arthur got lost inside the venue and the gig had started while he was trying to get to the front!!!!!"

Here's my review of *Dune* with Klaus Schulze, Arthur Brown and Wolfgang Tiepold (cello). This has never been one of my most played Schulze CDs or even a favorite, although I've always liked "The Shadows of Ignorance" with Arthur Brown more. The last time I listened to *Dune*, however, I felt quite fascinated with the title track, "Dune." Klaus mentions in the accompanying booklet how he was heavily into the science fiction trilogy by Frank Herbert and how he would "read all three volumes, over and over, like an endless loop."

The play button has been pressed and *Dune* is in progress.

I hear glassy sounding synth sculptures and choir sounds that sound like a mixed male and female choir. The beginning of "Dune" is a potpourri of sounds, male choirs, female choirs, some string, alien synth sounds and plucked synth sounds.

This seems, at best, a challenging piece of music for the first five minutes or more, because it involves a hodgepodge of sounds all thrown into the mix but has no feeling of continuity or any semblance of a developing song.

Wolfgang's cello does appear around the 6:00 mark, though, offering a sign of "normalcy" and the hope of some impending continuity that will allow a feeling of connection to the music.

After the 7:00 mark, a thin sounding synthesizer melody is played by Klaus, and, with Wolfgang's cello, there is a trace of song structure.

In the next few minutes, I begin to feel moved emotionally by the music of "Dune" for the first time. The music has a rising feeling of grandeur and seems to promise more. There are periods where the music feels a little flat, intertwined with periods where it sweeps upward into very emotionally charged passages. The track has done something impressive: it allowed me to plunge so deeply into a state of awareness of my emotions that I lost track of time. I looked up and "Dune" was past the 19:00 mark.

I'm struck by how KS produced such an advanced composition at such an early age. That could be said about several of his albums in the 1970s, but this composition is both a very challenging piece of music and very gratifying.

"Shadows of Ignorance" is next, starting with Wolfgang's cello. With Arthur Brown singing on this track, expect a steady, moderately paced groove for him to sing with. That seems to be the rule, though it became apparent after "Dune," when Arthur had performed more with Klaus.

Wolfgang's cello and a bit of vocoder begin, before a beat emerges, likely sequenced but sounding like sequencer and percussion both. It's a hypnotic beat and features Wolfgang's cello and Klaus' synth working together before Arthur's entrance.

Arthur enters with a poetic recitation around 8:30. Klaus has described how he and Arthur sat around together and came up with the lyrics, Arthur adding a few puns. Arthur shifts from a reading to singing that is light in quality but not without emotion. His singing seems to blend well with the beat, but more importantly, the other emotion producing elements such as choirs, strings and synthesizer.

The lyrics to the song (as printed in the re-release booklet) seem to go well with the instrumentals and Arthur's singing performance is very good.

The original *Dune* ends with the conclusion of "Shadows of Ignorance."

The bonus track, "Le Mans," is part of a very long concert performance on the Dune Tour in 1979. The way the song starts, it seems obvious that it's in the middle of a track.

An instant beat, with rather thin sounding, persistent percussion, is present along with inconsequential sounding synth soloing. The impetus of the beat and soloing seem to lend more substance to "Le Mans" as it reaches the 4:00 mark. Even so, at 6:00, the song has the feeling of an improvised jam with the beat being accompanied by a variety of synthesizer "noises." As I listen to this, I have a hard time with the music – specifically, the barrage of bizarre synth noises that accompany and sometimes overpower the steady beat.

The song takes a turn around 12:00, with the same beat playing alongside KS' synth pads, producing a dramatically better feeling. "Le Mans" sounds more and more mellow as it passes the 16:00 mark. The combination of sounds is vastly more pleasing than in the first ten minutes of the song.

My experience of the music has evolved from "insubstantial" in the first half to "very interesting." "Le Mans" seems like a decidedly mixed bag, quality-wise, but I feel open to the possibility that it can sound much better with repeated listens.

My interview with Arthur Brown follows. I sent Arthur a list of questions. When I got the interview back, I found it very fascinating reading. After reading it, I decided to do away with the Q&A for most of it, because I think it's unnecessary and Arthur's writing about his time and work with Klaus reads better without the format getting in the way.

Arthur Brown Interview with Greg Allen

AB: I seem to remember meeting Klaus in the office of Graham Lawson in London. As I recall, he was managing a project with Stomu Yamash'ta and *Go*, in which Klaus was involved.

That would have been just before I went to live in Burundi in Africa for six months. During this period I was intent upon furthering the experiments with drum-machine and synthesizer I had been involved in - particularly with Kingdom Come. I tried to get something going with David Voorhaus (White Noise) and he was playing with the first Fairlight to come to England. We didn't get much going before I left for Africa.

When I returned, there was a telegram for me which had been floating from address to address while I was away. It was from Klaus, inviting me to sing with him at a gig in the Paris Hippodrome - a huge inflated venue, in Paris, France.

I was living in Sherborne house, Gloucestershire at the time I got the telegram. Soon, I was en route. It took longer than anticipated to get there. I arrived to find the crowd rammed against the sides of the building. It took ages to get through. Finally, I got in just in time to leap on stage. Klaus said later this was one of the highlights of his career. And for me it was a glorious challenge to be singing with a master of his form. The crowd loved it. It was this gig and the response that encouraged Klaus to invite me to do a full European concert tour with just him and myself. Klaus was as usual going out on a limb - pushing into new ground.

It was the first time he had had a vocalist on one of his tours. Most of the responses were over the top. On several gigs, the crowd was still applauding after we had changed clothes, cooled off and begun driving away in the car!

One word about Klaus here. He is one of the small number of German people that I have met who understands English humour. So he could be very funny. He loved to play cards with the roadies. He was an avid chess player who could easily defeat the chess computer - and myself! I traveled with him in his Cadillac with the company of his manager.

There was some friction on the tour between Klaus and me - but hey, two dominant personalities aren't going to get along all the time. Klaus had definite ideas for his performance, which involved the gravitas of the music. So, I wasn't to make the audience laugh, I wasn't to dance, and I wasn't to use any Turkish-style vocal runs. Well, I was used to running my own show, so it took a little for me to accept these strictures. However, Klaus had a definite idea of what he stood for and what he wanted to communicate - and it was his tour - so that's the way it was. I did not always accept the limitations with good grace, but I think the tour was a success. A live album was released from it. Klaus, of course, had me improvise the melodies and lyrics on *Dune* - and this was the basis of the tour. Klaus wore white and sat with his back to the audience, looking into a vast mirror on the back of the stage. I stood at the front, unmoving, in a black still-suit modeled on those described in Frank Herbert's novel.

Klaus' sound, for me, reached areas others only dreamed of. He was totally different [from] Wendy Carlos or Jean Michel Jarre. Had he had more interest in going out to far flung audiences, he might have been truly enormous. He was one of the artists who decided to take the business reins himself, and start his own record company. In the end this became a burden to him, and it dragged him down - so that others who had remained in the normal commercial practice overtook him.

Well done, Klaus, say I, for one. You tried to cross another frontier. You got across and had some success before it went wrong. I myself was a beneficiary of your adventurousness - with the album *Faster Than The Speed of Light* that I recorded with Vincent Crane on Klaus' Label. It was not what Klaus had hoped for, nor what I expected. Vincent Crane, having been through the synthesizer class that Klaus was presenting, decided he didn't like synthesizers! So, the electronic album that Klaus thought he was going to get turned into one with the Frankfurt Philharmonic Orchestra. It was a really good album, but not what Klaus or I had started off thinking would be produced.

While I was staying with Klaus, in Hambühren, where he had his studio in the house, we would jam together. He hit on the idea of coming up with themes and some chords and rhythm, telling me the basic theme. For instance he would say I have this vision of someone who is an actor who uses time as his language. From this I began, and the piece "Time Actor" came out in two takes. The first one had probably 90% of the finished item. Then, on the second pass, having listened to it a couple of times, the finishing touches were added.

Klaus was a good host in his house. I remember he used to breakfast on peach juice and cream cake! As a generous host, he offered me whatever stimulants I cared for. By the time of the tour, I had been living in a meditation community where drugs were not regarded as helpful - so Klaus met a changed person.

GA: Had you met Wolfgang Tiepold before Dune or known of him?

AB: I had not met Wolfgang Tiepold before the record, as far as I remember.

GA: The *Avec Arthur* CD from *Jubilee Edition* mentions that you sang in French. It appears that was in Brussels. Had you sung in French much before that or since? Do you speak more than English and French, any other languages?

AB: I had not sung in French before the tour. I speak French reasonably well. I speak very little German. I speak a tiny bit of Spanish and I speak Texan.

GA: Have you seen or talked to Klaus much in recent years?

AB: I haven't spoken to Klaus for many years - partly, I suppose, because I went to live in Texas for 16 years. I should like to do something more with him. I'm not sure if what I did with him was actually what he wanted. But I love his sounds and the grandeur of his vision. Beyond that, he was for me the inventor of electro dance music.

He belonged to that whole larger-than-life cultured classical artist tradition. But he took it into new territory.

He asked me to sing in a style that was unfamiliar to me. I was steeped in the soul-blues-jazz tradition. He wanted me to reach outside of that. This meant that I was indeed introduced to a new audience. They either loved it or hated it. Klaus was always a gambler, God bless him.

1979 *Time Actor* (Richard Wahnfried)

From www.allmusic.com:

"The music is pure Berlin school electronica. Nobody does that better than Schulze. Because of Brown's unique contribution, this disc has no peer."

1979 Work with Earthstar

KDM adds: "...and with many others, mostly for the IC label which KS (and Michael Haentjes) had founded at the end of 1978. "

From the writings of David M. Cline (see Official Website for David's essays on Klaus Schulze's music):

"After the 1979 tour, the *...Live...* album is released, and KS remains very busy with other production work for his IC label and for other artists such as Earthstar."

My interview with Dennis Rea follows on the next page.

Dennis Rea Interview with Greg Allen

Here is my interview with Dennis Rea who recorded with Earthstar in 1979 (Craig is Craig Wuest, who was the founder of the Earthstar project):

GA: At the time that Craig was corresponding with Klaus Schulze and before that (when you were aware of how big a fan he was of KS), what were your impressions of Klaus Schulze? Were you a fan as well?

DR: My introduction to the German electronic music movement of the 1970s came through a chance purchase of Tangerine Dream's *Phaedra* when it was first released, basically because I found the name intriguing. (I later attended TD's first North American concert, in NYC.) Around the same time, my hometown friend and fellow musician Craig Wuest began delving heavily into the Krautrock/Kosmische Musik genre, and it was Craig who introduced me to Klaus Schulze's music. This would have been around the time that LPs such as *Timewind*, *Blackdance*, and *Moondawn* came out. I liked what I heard, having already acquired a taste for electronic music through exposure to pioneers such as John Cage, Karlheinz Stockhausen, and Morton Subotnick. I followed Schulze's music fairly closely until he entered his "digital" period, though as a guitarist my tastes naturally tended more toward guitar music.

Dennis had this response when asked about the location of Hambühren:

DR: Hambühren is in the Niedersachsen region of northern Germany - West Germany at the time. It's near Celle, a very attractive small city that is among the few in Germany that were left relatively unscathed by the war. The closest large city is Hannover.

GA: When you went to Hambühren, did you know then that you were going to be recording in Klaus Schulze's studio with Craig's Earthstar? Were there specific plans for the music you were going to record? Was it finishing *French Skyline* and doing all of *Atomkraft*?

DR: I went to Hambühren specifically to record an Earthstar record at Schulze's studio. Rewinding a bit, Craig had relocated to Germany from Utica, New York, about a year earlier than the rest of us arrived. He'd been carrying on a correspondence with Schulze, who encouraged him to try his luck in Germany, where audiences were much more receptive to the type of music Craig was exploring, than they were in the States. So Craig set out for Europe, turned up at Schulze's door, and found himself warmly welcomed. It was around this time that Schulze was launching the IC label.

They wanted to release work by complementary artists.

At this point Craig had already released one Earthstar LP, *Salterbarty Tales*, back in the U.S. in 1978. (One of the tracks on *ST* was reissued in slightly enhanced form on *French Skyline*.) It should be mentioned that Earthstar was entirely Craig's concept, fleshed out with contributions from guest musicians from his hometown and later from Europe. Craig began recording the tracks that would eventually be released as *French Skyline*, traveling around Germany to various illustrious studios of the time such as Studio Panne-Paulsen in Frankfurt and Dieter Dierks' studio in Köln, where he availed himself of numerous state-of-the-art electronic keyboards. (Schulze's IC studio had not yet been completed at the time.) In an interesting footnote to this story, some of the Earthstar tracks were recorded on a recycled Popol Vuh master tape.

Craig made a deal with Hamburg-based Sky Records to release the tapes, as well as two future Earthstar LPs (*Atomkraft* and *For Humans Only*). The decision was a no-brainer for Sky - the recordings had already been completed at no cost to the label, and the fact that the record had been produced by Klaus Schulze lent instant cachet to a release by an otherwise unknown artist.

Craig remained in Hambühren. Schulze welcomed Craig to make use of his new IC studio in Winsen, not far from Hambühren. It was at this point that Craig invited three hometown friends - me, drummer/vibraphonist Daniel Zongrone, and flautist Tim Finnegan - to join him in Germany and work on the next Earthstar record. The understanding was that this was to be more of a collaborative effort than a Craig-plus-guests scenario. But since we were all moving down divergent musical paths at that juncture (I was in the midst of an ECM infatuation myself), the band developed a rather split personality and the sessions yielded such a potpourri of different musical styles - everything from Mike-Oldfield-inspired instrumentals with a string section to progressive pop tunes with vocals - that we failed to produce a cohesive album in the end. A couple of the tracks ended up on *Atomkraft*, but the bulk of the session has never been released to this day, probably for good reason. The remainder of *Atomkraft* was filled out by various tracks Craig had been working on during this period, including one to which I contributed guitar loops.

GA: How do you account for *French Skyline* being mentioned as a Synthesizer Classic, when I read your own view of it is quite a bit less than that? I read one reviewer who stated that for those wanting one extra Klaus Schulze album from the '70s, *French Skyline* could be it. It was also said that at times it sounded more like Klaus Schulze than Klaus Schulze himself!

DR: I do think it's a good record, but hardly a classic. For one thing, for the very reasons you cite here, it was somewhat derivative of the work of Schulze and others. I also think there was an unfortunate tendency to add everything plus the kitchen sink to the mix, making for an overly dense sonic experience. And some of the then-fashionable keyboard sounds haven't aged well either. But hey, we were awfully young at the time, about 22 years old as I recall.

GA: Is it true that Klaus Schulze produced *French Skyline*? If so, did that necessitate frequent contact during the recording process? Or did you only get there after *French Skyline* was complete and in time for *Atomkraft*?

DR: See above. I personally was not involved in the recording of *French Skyline*, but Schulze indeed produced the record.

GA: When you first met Klaus Schulze, what was your feeling? Did it seem like you were meeting someone who was an established star? Did it feel like he was an important artist in his neck of the woods or was there more a feeling of anonymity?

DR: As longtime admirers of European progressive music who'd been feeling rather isolated in a fairly hostile American environment, we were all a bit awestruck at brushing up against a titan of the genre. The situation was so improbable from our perspective that I felt like pinching myself at first to make certain that it wasn't a cruel hoax. We weren't so naive as to think that Klaus Schulze was a household name in Germany or anywhere else for that matter, but the fact that he'd been a founding member of Tangerine Dream, had released so many records, and was continually touring throughout Europe was a good indicator of his stature as a musician. In sleepy rural Hambühren he didn't seem to be well-known at all, which is no doubt the way he liked it and one of the reasons he moved there from Berlin.

GA: Was his recording studio in or attached to his home like it appears to be now from the KS website photos? What kind of equipment was there? Did Craig have his own synthesizers by that time, or did he use some of KS' equipment?

DR: Schulze had a small recording studio in his home but apparently used it only for his own projects. The studio where we recorded was down the road in Winsen, behind a small restaurant where we would fortify ourselves with beer and boiled potatoes between sessions. Not being a technological fetishist, I have little recollection of the equipment it contained; my memories are chiefly of a very large recording room and a glassed-in mixing booth where Schulze's full-time engineer was installed. As for keyboards, Craig did have his own synthesizer and Elka 'string machine', but he made liberal use of whatever else happened to be around.

GA: Where did you stay for the six months? Was this in a countryside setting (consistent with the description of his current studio)?

DR: We all lived in a small farmhouse in the hamlet of Ovelgonne, a few kilometers from Hambühren.

We were typically impoverished twenty-something musicians and lived on next to nothing. We rode bicycles to the studio and hitchhiked whenever we needed to go further afield. We even had to ration hot water for twice-weekly showers, leading one band member to suggest that if it continued, we'd have to consider renaming the band 'Dirtstar.'

GA: Did you have any other musical interaction with KS other than his production? Was he only involved in producing *French Skyline* or was he also around and interested while *Atomkraft* was being crafted? Was he involved in shaping the music in any way, making suggestions, etc.?

DR: Although I don't believe he was officially credited as producer of any of the material that ended up on *Atomkraft* (or the unreleased tracks), Klaus generally acted in that capacity during the sessions. He wasn't really involved in the creative aspect of the music apart from the actual studio session. I do have a fond memory of mixing down two of my own tunes with Klaus at his home studio; they reminded him of King Crimson, as I recall. Honestly, I think Klaus was a bit disappointed with the results of the Earthstar session in Winsen - he would have liked something more electronic and less "prog" - but it didn't really concern him, as it wasn't destined to be released on his label anyway.

GA: When did you first take guitar lessons and for how long? I read that KS took eight years of guitar lessons so you had that in common with him. Did you talk with him about the craft of playing guitar?

DR: See my Expose interview at http://www.dennisrea.com/expose.html. Klaus and I never really talked about guitar playing that I can remember.

GA: Have you followed Klaus Schulze's career since the time you left after six months?

DR: I followed his output up to the time he adopted digital synthesizers - which happened while Earthstar was in Germany, in fact. While we were in the studio, a technician from Bell Labs in Princeton, New Jersey, showed up and gave Schulze one of the very first digital synthesizer prototypes. Bell Labs were apparently laying ten of these prototypes on various keyboard luminaries such as Jan Hammer, Keith Emerson, and Rick Wakeman, hoping that they'd be so excited by the possibilities that they'd enthusiastically endorse the instruments to the public.

Personally, with few exceptions, my own enthusiasm for electronic music dwindled with the advent of the digital era. The sound quality of digital instruments simply doesn't grab me, and as a musician who's invested a great deal of time and effort in physically mastering my instrument, I have a hard time considering knob-twiddlers and laptop-tweakers genuine musicians. I was briefly encouraged at the rise of so-called electronica in the early '90s, but in my opinion most of it is basically disco with a different name.

GA: What did you think of *French Skyline* when it was finished and you heard it, pleased, disappointed? Is that different than what you feel years later, looking back?

DR: Like I said, I wasn't involved in the making of that record, apart from the fact that it included a slightly reworked version of a tune I'd played on *Salterbarty Tales*. Back then I was very proud of the guitar solo I'd put down on that tune, so naturally I was ecstatic that it gained wider exposure. In general, though, I was very impressed with what Craig had managed to pull off in Germany. But as I mentioned earlier, it was definitely a product of its time, and not all of its aspects have worn well. The same is true, of course, of a lot of other records from that or any other period.

GA: Do you still enjoy making music now as much as ever? What has been the highpoint of your career as a musician?

DR: Big question. Absolutely. I feel that I'm currently in the most productive period of my musical life to date, with numerous recordings and live projects underway. As far as a "high point" of my musical career, I'd have to say it was stumbling into the opportunity to perform creative music widely in China at a pivotal point in that country's modern history.

GA: What was the role of the birotron and how did it come to be a tool used on *French Skyline*? How did it differ from the mellotron? Was it used in *Atomkraft*?

DR: I was never really clear as to the difference between a birotron and a mellotron. I guess both could be considered primitive samplers of a sort. All I know is that Schulze owned one and let Craig use it, I don't remember on which tracks.

GA: Any other impressions of the time in Germany and being around KS? Had Craig and KS become friends by then?

DR: My impression was that they enjoyed very cordial relations. For a time Craig was pretty much a part of the family. And one would think that Klaus would have to appreciate Craig's enthusiasm for his (Schulze's) music.

From a separate interview with Dennis Rea (by Jeff Melton in *Exposé*, issue No. 23, December 2001):

"In retrospect I've come to appreciate that Earthstar was perhaps the only American group to participate, however peripherally, in Germany's 'Kosmische Musik' scene during its heyday. Thinking that our records were laughably obscure, I was astonished to discover that at least one of the Earthstar titles, *French Skyline*, was reissued two years ago on CD and hailed as a "synthesizer music classic." But I can't really agree with that assessment - although the records do have their moments, there are sections that are excruciating for me to listen to at this distance. And Earthstar was truly one of the most awful band names ever."

Here are review snippets about *French Skyline*:

(1) "A re-issue from the Sky label in 1979, this is the long-awaited appearance of what has become a synthesizer music classic. Earthstar was basically Craig Wuest, who on the band's first, very limited edition album *Salterbarty Tales* played a lot of acoustic piano and a few simple synth parts.

"For French Skyline, however, the band decamped to France via Klaus Schulze's studio in Hambühren, and as a result the American influence is overlaid with a very large dose of Teutonic romanticism" (© 1999 Mark Jenkins, E-Mix magazine).

(2) "This is a re-release from an LP of 1979. Of course the thing which attracts the eye most is the name of Klaus Schulze on the cover: he was in the production-seat. Well, he did that more in those days (especially on the IC-albums), but this music also sounds so much like his that evil tongues even thought it was him playing. The cover says an American guy named Craig Wuest plays all the synths (and a lot of them!). He came to Germany to make electronic music and with his group Earthstar he made several albums during the period at the end of the seventies/early eighties and this one is the best. The music on the first track, 'Latin Sirens Face the Wall,' divided into three parts, is very Schulze throughout" (© 1999 Paul Rijkens).

(3) KDM: By the way: Schulze or IC has produced 20-30 different albums during this time, 1979-'82. Three albums were NOT released on IC but on another label; besides Earthstar it was Scala 3 and W. Bock.

Here's my take on *French Skyline.* I had never heard this album before. I got a copy from Dennis Rea and am listening to it for the first time (I listened to it twice before finalizing the review).

It starts with heavy choir effects and an increasingly rapidly pulsating synth in the background. The synth moves more toward the front and the choir recedes for a while. Abrasive crashing sounds slash through the mix.

The synth picks up more vigor and reminds me of the energetic beat on "Spielglocken" from *Audentity.* Three layers combine: the pulsating beat of the synth, the choirs and background synth pads.

This is evocative of Klaus Schulze in one way: it is one continuous track. I think it does build more quickly than a typical KS track, though. Once into the third track, the mix is very dense with all kinds of sounds flying about the soundspace.

In the next track, the mix does start to be filled with too many sounds, it seems, leading to an occasional moment of distortion. The section of music fades with a pleasant synth sound receding, then dying. A wind picks up, some whistles enter. There is just a hint of a "Velvet- Voyage"-like element in the background.

So is *French Skyline* a classic? Is it the extra Schulze album of the seventies? No to both questions. My impression is that the composer of the music had many ideas in his head and felt compelled to use just a few too many. There are some pleasant passages, some exciting ideas but too often they suffer from a reduced impact because of a mix that holds too many other instruments. The layers, the changing sounds entering and leaving the sonic landscape – all evoke comparisons with Klaus Schulze but yet are not comparable in quality to his work.

Chapter 8 Klaus' Solo Career and Collaborations, 1980–1984

1980 ...*Live*... (Live)

My review of the ...*Live*... release:

The CD starts out with thunderous applause and rousing clapping lasting over 1:20; it sounds like a crowd calling for an encore. The first song is called "Bellistique," clocking in at a little over 21 minutes. It begins with a classic sequencer line, a second synth, and a cowbell-like sound. The sequencer rhythms flow and change in quite interesting ways – the song takes little time to build. At around 4:00, some *Body Love*-era soloing arrives front and center, overlaying the sequencer and percussion. The intensity builds quickly, and the track is at full force by 5:30. This is a throwback to the days when KS' music was so forward and futuristic sounding.

The pace subsides after a time, leaving just the experience of space music. "Bellistique" comes to a virtual standstill and changes completely (at the 16:00 mark) to some stringlike bursts followed by long dreamy synth pads with hints of choirs. The music becomes nearly emotionally overpowering until the song ends.

The second track is called "Sense," a 51-minute piece of music. It gained 20 minutes in this re-issue version vs. the original release. It starts off in an almost *Moondawn*-ish way with choirs and waves splashing - very similar to "Mindphaser". Eerie sounds, thunderclaps, budding sequencer and waves occupy the next few minutes.

During the first seven minutes, I hear traces of "Velvet Voyage"-like sound and even some synth pads remindful of *Timewind*. This is an excellent track sounding like the best of Klaus Schulze in the mid '70s. The peaceful, sublime feeling continues, embracing the richest and most atmospheric elements of Klaus' '70s sound.

At about 12 minutes, a strong, rhythmic sequencer presence has taken over the track along with drums, played by Harald Grosskopf. After a fairly hypnotic period, the sequencer rhythms increase in power, with additional energy provided by droning synths, drums and cymbals. The intensity continues to swell as the song passes the 17:00 mark.

The musical tension formed by this ever rising energy level continues unabated. Percussive elements in the song are played with increasing clarity and force. Sequencer continues to supply an ever building, steady, yet relentless feel to the track. Intense synth soloing is a part of the mix.

At around 27:00, irregular and heavy drumming combines with gurgling, bubbling, wildly swirling synth sounds, creating a "musical disturbance" that yields to two sequencers, one at a high pitch and the other lower, taking the track forward. This sound is extremely intoxicating, right up there with the best sequencer sounds KS has played. A heavenly synth pad emerges from the persistent sequencers to enhance the exotic atmosphere. This is about as good as it gets! The track just continues to build in energy, led all the way by strong, extraordinarily beautiful and compelling sequencers.

As the sequencers fade, past the 40:00 mark, long classic Schulze synth pads, with some muted sequencing still present, take over until the end. "Sense" is an absolutely wonderful treat, an incredibly satisfying musical peak!

CD 2 starts with "Heart." The first tones do sound like a beating heart, as they consist of pumping bass and are surrounded by Klaus' trademark evolving synth pads with some chords held for a long time. For the first six minutes, classic Schulze synth pads dominate. Klaus solos with the long pads as the track continues in a sparse, almost quiet, soundscape past the 10:00 mark.

A cowbell, a sequencer line, and a thumping drum all contribute to a rapidly accelerating pace. All remnants of quiet are gone. The track is now very beat-oriented with multiple synth melodies surrounding the now methodical rhythm – still accompanied by the cowbell, which is used throughout the album.

For the rest of the track, the cowbell-like percussion is the highlight, forming an irregular, yet compelling beat.

"Dymagic," featuring Arthur Brown, wraps up the original album. The song starts with very slow, methodical drumming, mixed again with the sound of cowbell as a prominent percussive element. Around 2:45, Arthur enters with a sustained note. The methodical, even slow, groove forms a good background for his unhurried vocals. The beat is slow, yet gripping and approaching hypnotic.

Arthur's vocals sound slow and a bit weaker at first but as the song goes on, they take on more power and eventually have an awe inspiring quality which is both confident and forceful. This change actually happens rather dramatically around the 9:00 mark and from there, Arthur's singing takes on a burning passion and a commanding power. The backbeat is unchanging – the focus is on Arthur Brown's singing and synth pads and soloing.

"Dymagic" develops a very nice feel. Arthur's voice takes on a boominess due to the recording technology. Again, the music is good enough to overcome the recording quality shortcomings.

An extremely high energy burst takes place around 26:00 and then suddenly quiets. Arthur sings in a much more sedate voice, which, frankly, sounds better. It's as if the acoustics support the vocals better, perhaps, when he backs away from the microphone a bit. From 26:00 on, the audio quality seems less a factor.

Overall, "Dymagic" is a success.

The bonus track is "Le Mans au premier." As KS states in the re-issue booklet, "This is from a concert at Abbaye de l'Epau near Le Mans in France on November 10, 1979." The song starts off in a bit of an eerie fashion, slow and a little spooky. Long-held synth pads with occasional soloing form a section of the song with gathering energy. The ubiquitous cowbell arises from these long synth pads. A lot of intense sound builds around this beat. This driving rhythm carries the song toward its conclusion.

1980 *Dig It* (CD + DVD on the Revisited Records Re-release)

From B22 at http://www.synthmusicdirect.com/:

"Opinions remain diverse amongst fans and critics alike over the 1980 release *Dig It*. Klaus took a different approach to make what is ultimately a typical Schulze album. Was it merely a technological exercise (big issue being made of the fact that this was an entirely digital recording), or was it Klaus heading for a more contemporary style, pundits having spent more time speculating over the album than it actually took to record the darn thing!!! To the fan - love it or hate it - there have only been good Schulze albums, albeit some stronger than others. The music from the original LP had become more muscular than cosmic, which may have upset many."

Here's my review of *Dig It*, Klaus' first digitally recorded album. I'll give my impressions of the CD and then the DVD. "Death of an Analogue" is a methodically paced, hypnotic song, played on the G.D.S. computer plus drums. Klaus sings through a vocoder to give the song an even more mystical sound. This vocoder based singing is a major plus, and Klaus' voice has a lilting quality that keeps pace perfectly with the beat. I love the pacing of this song!

The drumming is excellent, especially the very clear sounding tom-toms (my guess). There is also string-like synth playing behind the relentless beat. "Death of an Analogue" is a superb, even spectacular song – one which I never get tired of listening to.

"Weird Caravan" uses a tape loop from the group IDEAL. Bass and drums are from the IDEAL loop. Klaus plays synth over the loop. For me, this isn't one of the better KS songs. It's not bad but it doesn't produce any good feelings for me; it just kind of plods along, in stark contrast to the quality of "Death of an Analogue."

"The Looper Isn't a Hooker" starts out with drumming and sweeping synth sounds; it sounds like a kick drum and then maybe some toms. A deep bassy synth pad enters. This is a stunning beginning to the song. This initial minute or so is great for showing off your stereo system.

The higher sounding drums, which I assume are toms, sound superb on *Dig It* and are used liberally. They compare to the sound achieved by Michael Shrieve on *Transfer Station Blue* (which he describes in his interview in this book).

Did I mention that *Dig It* is a stunning recording in terms of sonics? It is. "The Looper Isn't a Hooker" gels very nicely and is again a return to a high level of musical quality after the letdown of "Weird Caravan." Klaus' synth playing carries the pace of the song along well and the drums are interjected liberally, coming through in stunning clarity.

The fourth song, "Synthasy," is a long one, starting with swirling synth sounds, a few twinkling bells and myriad sharp, crisp drum beats. After three minutes, things are pretty quiet. Drums and gradually increasing sound of a droning synth signal the beginning of accelerating intensity. The sound comes to a mini crescendo and then continues in an understated way. Some intense, pounding tympani comes and goes from the soundscape.

A quivering, higher pitched synth has been playing in the lead for a while. The intensity of "Synthasy" is clearly building at the 12:00 mark, including liberal sprinklings of ultra-clean-sounding drums.

Organ riffs play as an addition to the soundscape.

The sound of a human voice enters in a near whisper. It's a treated voice and is virtually unintelligible but sounds nice in the background. This voice becomes an unlikely focal point for a while; it seems that all the other sounds are choreographed around this "vocal."

The high pitched, quivering synth is the most unlikely lead synth you'll ever hear, especially for as long a stretch as it has lasted. Klaus pulls it off though as it doesn't sound inappropriate. The mix sounds good all the way through. This is yet another one-of-a-kind song from Klaus Schulze. We're out on the cutting edge as we listen to this music.

"Synthasy" is a nice song, engaging and sounding distinct enough to keep one involved for the duration.

The bonus track is called "Esoteric Goody" and runs over 28 minutes. It starts with several minutes that sound like they could have been conceived around the time of *Irrlicht* or *Cyborg* and then evolves at around the 14:00 mark into a song that sounds distinctly like it could have come out of the *Body Love* sessions. This is a strange combination all in one piece of music.

At around 17:45, it becomes slow and spacy again, yet more accessible. "Esoteric Goody" finishes with spaced-out electronics - about the way it started. Overall, not a special track in my opinion – and it doesn't sound much like it came from the *Dig It* recording sessions, even though it did.

1980 Ars Electronica in Linz, Austria

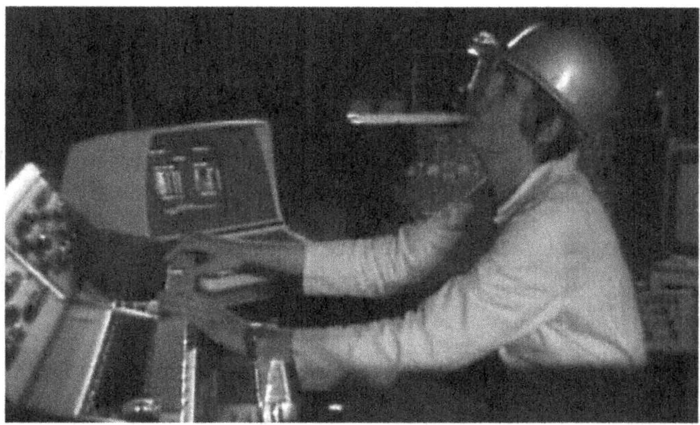

Now on to the Ars Electronica DVD included with *Dig It*. I wasn't so impressed by it the first time I watched it, possibly due to my expectations of seeing Klaus in a typical concert setting, manipulating his synths and seeing his face. In fact, I was quite disappointed in it. When I saw the YouTube *For Barry Graves* video, I thought that to be much, much better. That was exciting, but alas, unavailable for purchase for KS fans.

Now that I've actually seen some real Klaus Schulze concert footage that show his face and shows him working with the synths and playing some great music (*For Barry Graves*), perhaps my expectations won't be so high and I may be able to accept this Ars Electronica video for what it is. I'll go into it with an open mind.

As I suspected, watching the video was a totally different experience for me. It also helped to read Klaus' explanation of the concert, where I found that KS likes metallic sounds and this was the reason why the live sounds of the steel workers at work were used as "instruments" in the concert. I also learned how the sounds were conveyed from the factory to the concert hall and in fact that speakers were set up all over the town of Linz so that anyone in the whole town could experience the concert.

I enjoyed it much more this time and got into the music more. There was still the soundtrack from *X* playing and it didn't look like KS was playing that. It may have just been pre-programmed as another instrument. The first time I watched the DVD, I thought that the music from *X* was just put into the soundtrack of the DVD without regard for what KS was playing.

These questions regarding Ars Electronica (the event depicted in the *Dig It* DVD) were asked in an interview around 1980 (on the Official KS Website www.klaus-schulze.com):

Q: Klaus, you played in Linz lately, at the Ars Electronica. What are your impressions?

KS: Too many to speak about everything. I did the opening concert of this festival. It was a huge event, with TV, live broadcast from a steel factory, a true multi media spectacle. Hardly to be repeated, although I have offers. But the costs were immense; the Linz promoters spoke about 400,000 DM ($250,000) expenses for just my evening.

Q: Did you use in Linz the new toy, the G.D.S. computer?

KS: Yes, but not entirely. Also I had a percussion player with me, who will join me again in Brussels on my next concert. He played four or five huge gongs, two tympanis and a lot more.

IC Record Label and IDEAL

"After his college years, Haentjes became a music teacher and freelance writer for music magazines. In 1979, he teamed up with Klaus Schulze, a former member of the synth-rock group Tangerine Dream, and co-founded the IC record label, which specialized in electronic music. The label was licensed by the German subsidiary of the major label WEA" KDM: "I was against it!"

The biggest success on the IC label came with the issuance of the album *Ideal* by the group IDEAL in 1980. Klaus ended up giving away the IC label in 1983 and had nothing more to do with it.

From David M. Cline in 1998: "As if this wasn't enough, KS begins his synthesizer school and of course sets up the IC label. Furthermore, he helps in the production of multiple artists on the IC label."

From a 1994 interview with Klaus Schulze: "It was me with my money who established in 1979 the first label for young electronic musicians: Innovative Communication (and gave it completely away in 1983)"

From interview of KS on the Official Klaus Schulze Website:

Q: Some questions about *Dig It*. It's the first LP that was done exclusively with the G.D.S.

KS: Not exclusively. For instance, I used some percussion. And I used a tape loop from the group IDEAL. But I also did some percussion sounds with the G.D.S. itself.

From KS interview on Official Website:

KS: I founded IC in late 1978 because at this time there was no other label interested in "electronic music," and I wanted to promote this music, that I had "invented nearly single-handed" (as one English magazine wrote). But all the "electronic" albums on IC did not sell, except my own albums and one rock album: *Ideal* (700,000 copies sold in Germany. I wasn't the discoverer and producer; it was my friend KDM who managed IC until late 1981).

Then, in 1983 I went on a very long concert tour all over Europe. When I came back I had to realize that IC was not in a very good shape - all the...money that we had because of the huge *Ideal* success, was gone. I was very upset. And I gave the whole company away; to the man who was responsible for the IC disaster (no one else wanted it). This was in summer 1983. Since that time I have nothing to do with IC and with the shit that happens on this label [the quotation comes from an American journalist].

From the May 1997 interview of Klaus by Billy Bob Hargus in *Perfect Sound Forever*:

PSF: You started Innovative Communications and Inteam to control your own music. Did you find the problems with these companies taught you anything about the music business?

KS: Sorry to take away your naive believings: I did not start IC and Inteam to have control over my music. I had control before and after. A look at my discography shows this, because my albums were still with another company when I started IC and after. I never had many problems to do my music and to give it to a record company.

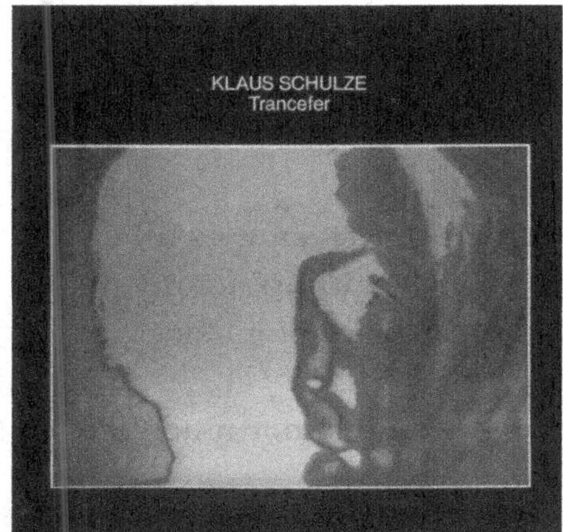

1981 *Trancefer*

From B22 at http://www.synthmusicdirect.com/:

"All told, *Trancefer* is a pretty underrated album that sees the eclectic trio working well together, producing some astoundingly good music between them, which never for one moment loses direction. In places it almost seems like a blueprint of what was to come on the next legendary release; those same three players again all taking part in that recording. Critics have said time and again that *Trancefer* was just another harsh, cold and teutonic/industrial strength album from Schulze. Doubtless these would be the same reviewers that preferred their mellotronic choirs and swashes of analogue strings, but that wasn't where Klaus was heading back in the early eighties with his all new digital approach."

My review of the *Trancefer* re-issue:

The lineup for *Trancefer* includes Klaus Schulze, Michael Shrieve and Wolfgang Tiepold on cello. Klaus and Michael Shrieve met during their participation in the *Go* project.

First up are the two original tracks from *Trancefer*. "A Few Minutes After Trancefer" is the first song. It starts with a few surges of synth and sequencing with a little twang combined with synth pads. Wolfgang's cello comes in at about the 3:30 mark.

A melody line played on synth energizes the song somewhat. Sequencer is still the prominent element, with somewhat subdued percussion.

A choir-like sound surges, then Michael Shrieve's percussion becomes prominent, playing a repeating rhythm with the usual crystal clear sound associated with his playing. Michael's drumming has supplanted the sequencer as the focal point. At one point he breaks from the repeating rhythm and attacks the drums without interruption before returning to the former pattern.

The tempo of "A Few Minutes After Trancefer" is fairly methodical. Klaus lends some variation to the piece with evolving synth pads as Wolfgang plays cello intermittently. All elements are back in the mix around 13:00 and the song takes on more melody lines – it's less robotic and more expressive as it heads toward the end. Most of the expressiveness is coming from the cello and the long synth pads.

"A Few Minutes After Trancefer" is fairly enjoyable but not a standout track in the KS catalogue.

The second track, "Silent Running," starts with a subdued yet slightly haunting sounding synth soon joined by a synth pad that emerges gradually. The track intensifies with a thick, swelling, rich synth pad along with some choppy cello and intermittent drum hits from Michael. As usual, the striking of the drums is recorded with the utmost clarity, making it sound very attractive.

The cello begins to repeat a stronger pattern. A weeping violin plays. The haunting sound that began the track re-enters the mix occasionally. At this point, "Silent Running" is a lot more interesting than "A Few Minutes After Trancefer." The recording on "Silent Running" seems better than on "A Few Minutes...."

Klaus holds one synth pad note for what seems like forever in the middle of the song as all of the other instruments continue to spin and swirl energetically about it. "Silent Running" totally defies categorization in a genre, but it's an interesting, compelling and even great piece of music.

The total combined running time of the two songs comprising the original LP is not much longer then some single Schulze tracks at a little over 37 minutes.

The bonus tracks are "A Few Minutes After Trancefer" and "Silent Running"! The recording method on "A Few Minutes..." is 33 1/3 halfspeed, and the mix is supposed to be a little different. "Silent Running" is recorded at 45 rpm and also with a little different mix.

The 33 1/3 halfspeed version of "A Few Minutes After Trancefer" is up first. I detect a change in the sequencer pattern: it seems separated into two different components as opposed to the single twangy sound I described the first time around. An organ-like synth surge that I don't recall hearing in the first version enters the song early on.

A violin-like sound has entered about a minute before Wolfgang's cello first appeared in Version 1. A sparkling sequencer at around 4:00 is another deviation from the first version. I can almost hear the bow on the strings as Wolfgang plays the cello boldly. His playing seems more interesting in this version than the former.

I've noticed enough differences by the 6:00 mark to make me think that this version of "A Few Minutes After Trancefer" is superior to the 1981 original - owing largely to the new mix, which varies more than just a little from the original. This version does seem crisper and more energetic, which may have some relation to the halfspeed approach.

Contrary to what I had thought, there is value to owning this CD with bonus tracks that are the same titles as the original songs. I'll really be surprised if the second version of "Silent Running" exceeds the first due to my high praise of the first version. There is potential for my opinion of *Trancefer* to be elevated significantly from where it was pre-review.

Next is the 45 rpm version of "Silent Running." A few clicks and pops in the recording may be intended as part of the music. This version is much slower to develop than the first. A synth pad holds one note at the outset of the track for a very long time. This version of "Silent Running" seems much more subdued than the original, as of the 6:00 mark. The strings seem to dominate more than in the first version, and the recording quality favors Michael's percussion work less than on the first version. The sound of echoing human whistling represents another departure from the original version.

It seems that the first version of "Silent Running" was better than the 45 rpm version. Overall, *Trancefer* is quite interesting in its current format. There is now one strong version of each of the two tracks.

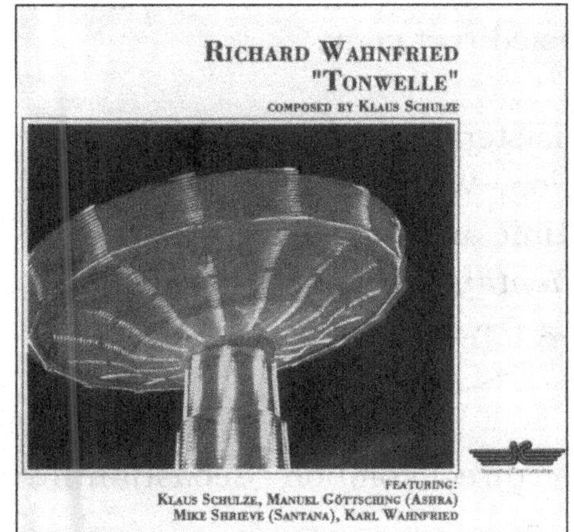

1981 *Tonwelle* (Richard Wahnfried)

From http://www.ambientvisions.com/1102002.htm:

"As listeners would expect, there is a strong rock and roll emphasis on this disc. Michael's percussion is absolutely frenetic. Klaus's electronics are dreamy and expansive. Manuel's and Karl's guitars smoke. Harald's guitar rocks hard."

From www.allmusic.com:

"Amphetamine sequencers, metallic synth chords, merciless drum machines, monster guitar riffing, palpitating basslines, and vocals on 'Angry Young Boys' (sung by Arthur Brown of "Fire" fame) make this an endurance test for all but the most die-hard heavy rock aficionados" (© Backroads Music/Heartbeats).

1982 *Ideal* goes platinum

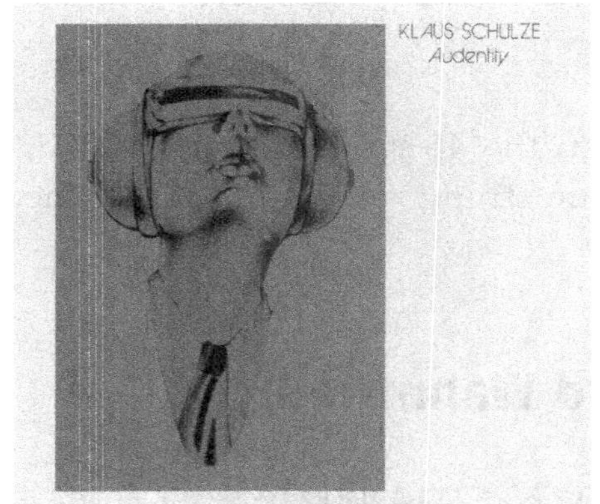

1983 *Audentity*

From Dave Connolly at http://www.allmusic.com:

"Both the three-part suite on side one and the side-long "Spielglocken" are interesting, compelling electronic pieces."

From B22 http://www.synthmusicdirect.com:

"Though it suffers several inconsistencies this is a powerhouse of musical artistry and invention. With the other musicians heavily involved [in] the pieces the quality throughout shows itself time and time again. The bonus track, recorded largely on the fly, doesn't really add anything to *Audentity*; it's just too long winded. Then again, better to have than have not!!! Better a diamond with a flaw than a pebble without.... or something along those lines."

Two different views (both from the same review on www.synthmusicdirect.com) on "Sebastian Im Traum," from *Audentity*:

From B22 http://www.synthmusicdirect.com:

"'Sebastian Im Traum' (28.21) has to be one of the strangest tracks ever from Schulze...Obscure, abstract or avant garde, call it what you will, it's all these things and more. Schulze holds the piece together for about 20 minutes before it starts to lose its cohesion. With a track of such great length that never really finds its true direction, I think it's fair to say that after all these years, it's not the easiest listen in the world."

David Law of Synthmusicdirect.com says that "the track 'Sebastian Im Traum' [is] my number one cut from that album...There is no doubt that, as B22 mentions, 'Seb...' is one of Klaus' more left field outings. For the most part it is just downright weird...This is Klaus at his most inventive and the playing from Wolfgang Tiepold is inspired. B22 mentions that he is not sure if it was ever intended as a serious piece. I would say it most certainly was - probably one of his most serious. I would also disagree that the track starts to fall apart at the 20:00 mark. I have listened to it again, all the way through, another couple of times before writing this but to me it just continues on from this point in a similar intriguing/disturbing way right until the end"

My impressions of *Audentity*:

It's time to review one of the stalwarts of Klaus Schulze's catalogue.

The first song is "Cellistica," which starts with piano and what sounds like the plucking of strings on a stringed instrument. This plucked string sound even resonates back and forth between the speakers. It may be Wolfgang on the cello, with some audio editing tricks applied. There is a lot of varied activity right at the outset. The recording quality is outstanding!

Klaus plays a lead synth solo while Wolfgang plays an expressive cello. A synthesized beat enters, sounding not unlike a drum. Synth pads, synth lead, synthesized drums and the cello form the sound. The drum sounds have an exaggerated stereo effect.

The guests on *Audentity* are the aforementioned Wolfgang Tiepold, Michael Shrieve playing Simmons percussion and EEH computer, and Rainer Bloss on Glockenspiel and "Sounds."

Close to the 9:00 mark, the trademark recurring theme of "Cellistica" plays for the first time. This melody repeats for about the next three minutes. The rhythm accelerates with a sequencer running at the same time as the patterned drums.

The recording is just mind blowing. The back of the cover indicates that the recording was done by "Funky Ebby" and the mixing by Klaus Schulze and Funky Ebby.

Wolfgang's cello sounds exquisite over the drum patterns, sequencer and droning synth pad. It's quite nice to have the real thing involved even though the synthesized instruments are recorded so well that they also sound very good. Wolfgang adds so much to every Schulze album that he plays on. The cello plays in a mournful way for a few minutes as "Cellistica" heads for the home stretch.

Around the 20:00 mark a new drum pattern enters, played more briskly, giving the song a surge of adrenaline.

"Spielglocken" is next and starts with sequencer combined with a repeating percussion sound. At 2:40, the song is building momentum and a feeling of urgency. There is a definite tension in the music. This is alleviated somewhat by a sudden shift to a drum pattern (which has an exaggerated stereo effect) and a rapid fire sequencer pattern.

Glockenspiel, cello, long synth pads and the above mentioned drum pattern play as the intensity continues to build at the 9:00 mark. Swirling synths plus various noises enter and retreat as the sequencer and drum machine dominate. "Spielglocken" features a driving rhythm that is one of the most intense on any KS song.

Glockenspiel provides a twinkling, sparkling accentuation. A sequencer pattern that sounds like a repeating plucked string joins the fray and the pace quickens even more, if that is possible. This is one of the ultimate KS rhythm tracks ever, with a pulsing, driving, uncompromising beat that is hypnotic. Several layers play at once, joined briefly by a higher range sequencer on a couple of occasions; adding even more flavor to the sonic recipe. "Spielglocken" is a powerhouse song that is just plain fun!

The third song on CD 1 is "Sebastian im Traum." The song starts in a minor key and sounds at times almost *Irrlicht*-esque in the first minute. An opening and closing door is followed by a violin playing in a rather unusual way. A massive surge in the music takes place and then relents. The sound effect used to simulate the opening and closing door is extremely realistic.

Twin violins play in a mysterious way as another crushing wave of sound gathers steam. The door opens and closes, crossing the stereo spectrum. The violins play on with no real direction. The feel of "Sebastian im Traum" is dark. The sound quality is nothing short of stunning on the various effects, strings, and sounds that comprise this track. I've never heard this level of audio quality on a Schulze album (even though the typical KS recording is quite good).

The tumultuous surges in sound repeat intermittently, several times in all. Glockenspiel enters around the 11:00 mark, and each note seems to echo. This brings a little bit of a "friendly" quality to a bizarre composition. "Sebastian" is not bizarre in an unnerving way, however. Violins wail, are plucked and echo. Human voices enter and cackle and laugh in a strange way.

"Sebastian" never develops any melody nor really sounds like a song in any conventional sense. It's still interesting to sit and listen to. And it has one thing going for it that is a very high priority for me, and that's a great audio quality. It sounds absolutely nothing like either of the first two tracks.

CD 2 starts with "Tango-Saty." The order of the songs was altered for this release to accommodate the whole bonus track. "Tango Saty" opens with a catchy synthesizer melody that repeats many times. Drums sounding like bongos are played by Michael Shrieve. The song has a beat and a catchy melody and is over soon after it starts. “Tango-Saty” is an unusually short song for Klaus Schulze but it’s a good one.

“Amourage” starts with light piano and some synth sounds that remind me of sounds used in the song “Popcorn” by Hot Butter. A synth sound resembling a flute rises and fades along with the entrance of string sounds and gently played piano. There is a sense of yearning conveyed and yet the song could be described as pretty.

“Opheylissem” rounds out the original contingent of songs from *Audentity* with 55 minutes of bonus track yet to come. It’s immediately bouncy with bongo-like drums being played in irregular patterns. A somewhat muted sequencer plays with synth pads in the background.

The drums may be the highlight of the track, although a bright, sparkly sequencer adds quite a bit to the sound. “Opheylissem” is a nice little song.

The original soundtrack to the 1983 Australian film *Next of Kin* is called “Gem” here and has five track markers. “Gem” starts with metallic synth sounds that resonate but give little indication of melody for the first few minutes. This is quite an unusual track and sounds a bit like a sound demo for a new synth.

The second subtitle of “Gem” is “Tiptoe on the Misty Mountain Tops”; it adds sequencer to the metallic sounds before letting the sequencer soar alone for a short time, in a very good sounding pattern. The metallic, industrial sounds return to share the stage with the sequencer. A second, higher pitched sequencer enters unobtrusively. After a while, the synth sounds moderate from the industrial sound to something closer to what we’ve heard from Klaus before. Combined with the driving sequencer pattern, it makes for an overall nice track.

The third part of “Gem” is “Sink or Swim.” It represents a continuation of the same sequencer pattern from “Tiptoe on the Misty Mountain Tops” with surrounding synth pads and some more industrial sounds. There is a bit of incongruity here for me as the sequencer patterns at times combine brilliantly producing an exhilarating feeling. Yet the industrial sounds are a bit harsh at times. The hypnotic sequencer pattern is among the best KS has used, especially because of its relentlessness and overall length of time that it stays in motion.

“At the Angle of an Angel” is the fourth part of “Gem” and there is no break. The driving rhythm continues unabated. There are upwards of 45 straight minutes of addictive sequencer combined with Klaus soloing using a variety of synth sounds. That’s “Gem” in a nutshell.

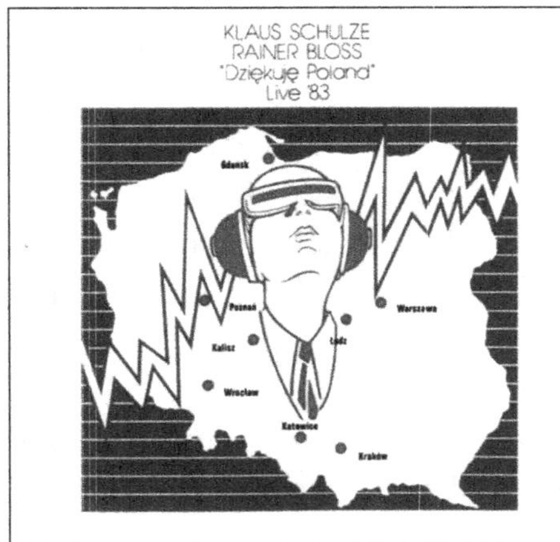

1983 *Dziekuje Poland Live* 1983

From B22 http://www.synthmusicdirect.com:

"...the foundations of most all the *Dziekuje* pieces being made up from many of the main sequences and rhythms of *Audentity*. The combined talents of Messrs Schulze and Bloss providing us with pretty much a completely different take on the studio album set...Again this is a recording that displays music that is amongst some of Schulze's most powerful and vibrant that pounds the listener into submission with a huge wall of sound coming from both synths and samplers. Though it is readily identifiable in places as chunks of the *Audentity* album, I have to say that sonically it has more in common with *Angst*, its hard abrasive edge overriding much of the warmth that Bloss's piano playing tries to inject into the set...Do you really need me to tell you that this is a 'must have' purchase?"

My review of *Dziekuje Poland Live 1983*:

Katowice is the location for the first portion of music in Poland.

Klaus opens with some warm synth pads, slashing strings sound briefly leading to piano playing and choirs. Another, imposing synth string blast propels the acceleration of the music with piano and synth matching each other in intensity. There is yet another synth string explosion, again signaling a shift in the music.

One more crescendo sounds and right into Spielglocken we go! This has the driving beat of *Audentity*'s studio version but seems to have more synth pads accompanying it. The additional string work makes it sound quite interesting. The driving beat is not as strong as on the studio version but it is still intense and fun.

The string crescendos are brought in suddenly, even to the point of being startling but in a pleasant way. Some chime/bell like sounds enter the mix. Slash! The bells are gone, and a new pad joins along, playing at a moderate pace. The driving beat is relentless.

It's easy to tell that Rainer and Klaus are playing for all they're worth. There are lots of pleasing and sudden changes here, highlighted by the sound of a synthesized but remarkably realistic sounding flute.

The driving rhythm is fronted by varying instruments. A lead instrument of a higher pitch attacks sharply and crisply - one of the highlights of this track. That sound fades, replaced by several other sounds that accompany the seemingly endless driving beat.

A series of wild synth string crashes ensue, preceded and followed by synth pads. The side ends with the closing melody of "Cellistica" sans rhythm, strings only, sounding very good (the synthesized strings sound close to an orchestra). With repeated listens, I like this track more and more.

Track 2, from the Warsaw concert, starts out with a minor-key piano lead dueting with piano in a higher key. It almost sounds like ragtime, scrambled by several sudden, intense synth bursts and leveling out into warm, dreamy synth pads together with the piano. A hint of rhythm begins and increases rapidly. This driving rhythm carries the song for several minutes....a very fast, almost trance-like pace.

The relentless beat gets obscured by Klaus with a Minimoog solo, which at times does resemble a guitar solo. As Klaus' Minimoog solo progresses, the strength of the beat gathers more and more energy, and the track has taken on a searing intensity. This is splendid music! The groove is hypnotic, with the KS trademark string-like bursts entering just when you least expect them.

"Warsaw" is a very intense and raw track, yet enjoyable.

The first bonus track is next, "The Midas Hip Hop Touch." The first thing I notice about it is that the recording is superior – of studio quality. The track starts with drumbeats in both the left and right channel, at differing paces. Chanting and hypnotic drumbeat carry the track through. I've never heard Klaus do this kind of music before. Altogether, not so impressive, although repeated listenings could change that.

The first track of CD 2 is "Ludwig II Von Bayern" from *X* played in a concert in Lodz. It starts with a high pitched church organ. Some twangy synth plays just before the strings that lead up to the tape loop. Again, it's astounding how close the synths sound to the real strings of the studio album.

The tape loop section of "Ludwig II" comes fairly quickly. It's spiced up here, which is a real treat for anyone that thought the original tape loop went on too long. Playing with the loop are a nice sounding sequenced rhythm and piano. The loop plays on, but many other interesting sounds reduce or eliminate the chance of boredom.

There is bold, almost grandiose piano playing at times. The piano really takes complete charge of the track. A deep synth pad seems ready to break up the loop and does, yielding to the bold, grand string playing that is the highlight of "Ludwig." The strings take on a plaintive quality, backed by a hypnotic beat as in the studio version. There are some changes to the studio version, all tasteful and all keeping this rendition of "Ludwig II" on the same high plane as the original.

The musical selections that were chosen for this live album could hardly have been better!

We arrive in Gdansk for the next piece. It starts out very quietly and features a church organ sound early. Loud, thick, twittering sounds and a steady, almost funky beat ensue, with a lot of unusual synth effects thrown in for the next few minutes. After that, a lead synth contorts and aside from the steady beat, it takes on a jam feel. "Gdansk" sounds pretty interesting, with a wide variety of sounds that all add something. "Gdansk" ends with deep bass and some higher sweet sounding string pads.

There are five plus minutes devoted to thank you. Klaus speaks amidst loud twittering synths, which are lowered in volume so he can be better heard. He gives credit to all the people involved, many people. A soaring synth comes in as Klaus repeatedly says thank you. At the end Klaus introduces his band in a whimsical moment: Mr. Yamaha, Mr. Minimoog, Mr. Fairlight, Mr. GDS, Mr. EMS.

The CD 2 bonus track is from the last concert of the tour, in Gdansk, named "Dzien dobry!," clocking in at 35:58. This is said by Klaus (speaking on the CD) to be "Spielglocken". This is a very different interpretation than the one on "Katowice". The syncopated "Spielglocken" beat starts at around the 6:00 mark with swirling string sounds surrounding it in multiple layers. The beat sounds like it is recorded better than the beat on "Katowice." This is certainly a nice version of "Spielglocken," with the synth pad orchestrations lending a nice touch and the beat having more punch than the Katowice version.

Summary: For a live album, it's quite good, although perhaps the only track that stands up to the original is "Ludwig II." The first interpretation of "Spielglocken" (Katowice) is energetic but loses out to the studio version based on sonic quality at least. The second bonus track, "Dzien dobry!", sounds better. Intensity, even if it is raw, characterizes all four original songs from *Dziekuje Poland '83.*

If the recording quality doesn't bother you (it's not bad) and you enjoy an intense, raw, live performance then this is a good one, especially due to the song selections. I'm finding that the more I listen to this album, the more I like it.

1984 *Angst*

From B22 http://www.synthmusicdirect.com:

"*Angst*, an album that's everything and nothing. An album which I always regarded as the Schulze equivalent of TD's *Thief* with its abrasive, rocky edge. Yes, a soundtrack first and foremost, but at its heart a thoroughly focused Schulzian recording. *Angst* from 1984 stands out as an essential part of the Schulze back catalogue due to its power, diversity, (and on a technical level) it's novel and extremely evident use of sampling throughout, a technology that Klaus was exploiting to the full, implemented so effectively on this recording."

My interpretation of *Angst*:

I've always had a hard time getting into this CD, except for "Pain." Let's give it a fresh listen, though.

The first track, "Freeze," starts out with the bell-chime sound used often by Klaus, playing at a slow pace. A filtered, hazy sounding synth takes the background. Klaus wrote the music for this "crazy movie" (about a man released from jail who goes wild and kills a bunch of people in a residential area) after reading the script.

The movie was said to be shot based on Klaus' music and featured very little dialogue. "Freeze" was used in the film *Manhunter*, directed by *Miami Vice* director Michael Mann. This information about the movie and its relationship to the soundtrack comes from KS' interview in the booklet for *Angst*. The first track merely sets a mood. It's nothing special to listen to as a piece of music.

"Pain" follows "Freeze" and starts out in much more interesting fashion with a progressing sequencer combined with drums. This has always been the one song on *Angst* that I enjoyed. Lead synth pops in occasionally and continues to elicit that eerie, murder-movie kind of sound. Unlike "Freeze," it stands on its own as a quality listen. The drumming and sequencer sound good, unlike the high pitched, wailing, eerie sounding synth. The movie probably needed it though. A shift in the direction of "Pain" around 7:30 adds interest. "Pain," as a song, rates as average to slightly above average.

"Memory" is next, beginning with bells, flutes and a pulsating, irregular sequencer mixed with a little piano. The track is moderately paced. This song comes across as a decidedly mediocre piece of music at best.

The fourth song, "Surrender," starts out with emphatic drumming and is fairly well recorded. Classic minor-key Schulze synth creeps into the music; at first hardly decipherable and then increasing in volume a bit. The ingredients are present for a strong Schulze track. The synths are in two layers now, one a deeper sound and the second sounding like the hazy, foggy synth that appeared in *En=Trance* at times. The drumming pattern is quite irregular but not bad. The highlight is the synth work, playing off the drums. Again, to be honest, the song is nothing special.

The final track of the original *Angst* album is "Beyond." A *Moondawn*-like synth opens, giving hope that this might be a stronger song. Very well recorded tom-tom sounds then enter the mix for a more positive effect. This is easily the best track, combining the clean sounding percussion of *Transfer Station Blue* with classic Schulze synth sounds evocative of the 1970s and specifically *Moondawn*. The best song was saved for last.

Overall, the original *Angst* is one of KS' weaker efforts, in my opinion. "Beyond" really gives me pause, however, because it is quite good.

The re-release has a potential huge advantage over the original release of *Angst* and that is the presence of a 31:40 bonus track named "Silent Survivor" (so named by KS because it survived silently in the KS archives for 20 years or so). If it's good, it could change my overall evaluation of *Angst*. The bonus track is almost as long as the whole original album.

"Silent Survivor" starts with choir sounds, which are somewhat dark, combined with droning synth. A thumping sound, like a heartbeat, starts behind the alternately surging and fading choir effects. A sequenced pattern starts out quite suddenly at about 4:30 and goes through occasional chord changes. It all sounds quite nice.

A much more frantic, scrambled sequenced sound starts a couple of minutes later. It sounds rather disturbing at first because it's so "messy" sounding compared to the rest of the track, but as I listen to "Silent Survivor" more, the whole still sounds fascinating. The slow "heartbeat sound" has evolved into or been replaced by a more rhythmic sequencer line that at times sounds like percussion. The pace has accelerated to close to trance level. "Silent Survivor" takes on a very hypnotic flavor, with sequencers and percussion combining in a very seductive way.

Everything breaks down to just the heartbeat sound and some lingering synth effects. The rhythm is rebuilt totally by the 21:00 mark and sounds just as pleasing as the first time - though in a totally different way. About a minute of the music towards the end sounds like a throwback to the most bizarre parts of *Irrlicht* before concluding in a more harmonious way.

"Silent Survivor" is a very, very fine piece of music!

It could easily have been one of the best songs on several released albums such as *Dreams*, *Inter*Face* and even *Dig It* (although I always reserve #1 ranking there for *Death of an Analogue*). It's probably the best song on this *Angst* re-release and elevates the album greatly.

The original *Angst* suffers from the fact that three of the five tracks are nondescript and a fourth, "Pain," is just slightly above average. The arrangement of the new *Angst* allows it to finish with about 42 minutes of consecutive very good to excellent music. *Angst* is now a worthwhile buy, whereas it wasn't before.

1984 *Aphrica*

This album was deleted soon after it was released because the record company forgot to make a contract with Ernst Fuchs, who along with Rainer Bloss and Klaus Schulze, participated in the making of the album. The album seems to have received a thumbs-down from those who have commented on it. I've never heard it.

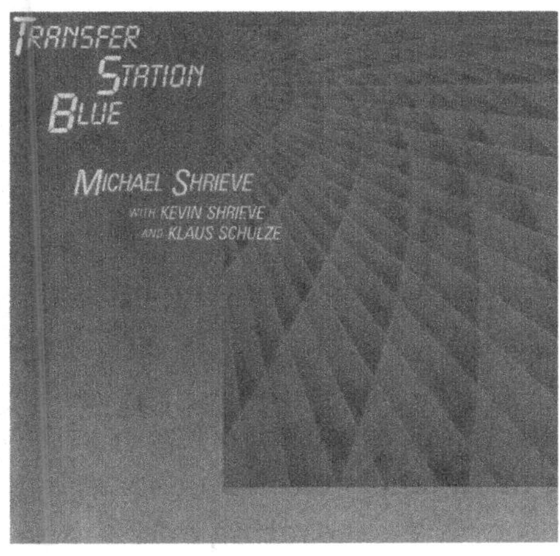

1984 *Transfer Station Blue* (with Michael Shrieve and Kevin Shrieve)

Pre-listen comments:

This is one of my favorite albums that Klaus has been involved in. The pairing of Klaus' synthesizer and Michael Shrieve's stunning percussion work makes for a dramatic combination. Additionally, the recording of the percussion is astonishing.

I like the inscription on the back of the CD cover:

"Effortlessly, across an Empire,
through a channel propelled.
An extremely pleasurable motion.
On line, like the drums and electronics of
American percussionist Michael Shrieve;
Ultra smooth, like the synthesizers
of Germany's Klaus Schulze;
suffused in translucent blue,
like the guitars of Kevin Shrieve....
Just up ahead. "TRANSFER STATION BLUE"."

Combine this poetic writing with the attractive blue cover and the presence of two musical giants and the stage is set for something special! Listen...

At the start of "Communique: 'Approach Spiral'" Michael Shrieve's percussion comes out of the speakers with great stereo separation and stunning clarity. This CD was one of the CDs I used when I was shopping for quality bookshelf speakers. The high end could not be better recorded. Klaus joins Michael with some synth pads, which are a little hazy in the background. The percussion sounds absolutely fabulous. It's played using cowbell, a fact I discovered only through my interview with Michael. Michael adds timbales to the mix, which sound very much like they could be played by a sequencer (see Michael's interview after this review).

Both the percussion by Michael and the sequencer and/or timbales, move at a fairly brisk pace. The second track, "Nucleotide" starts with reverberating synth sounds from Klaus and some dreamy pads playing in the background. This is followed by a crashing sound, another synth pad and another crash. Klaus is front and center with some creative synth sounds/noises. This is a short yet pleasant track, a bridge between two sensational compositions.

The title track, "Transfer Station Blue", starts with eerie synth pads from Klaus and a voice processed with vocorder. A brisk, alluring sequencer from Klaus combined with excellent, bubbling percussion from Michael lead to a very thrilling musical passage!

Shortly before 3:00, Kevin's guitar comes in with drums and takes over the soundscape. Michael backs him with an occasional crisp percussion phrase and Klaus with a pad or two, but the focus is clearly on the guitar solo. After this guitar segment, the track turns sensational again with the timbales, Michael's percussion and some exquisite, velvety synth pads from Klaus.

Kevin's guitar re-enters at about 9:00, playing much the same tune as earlier. His playing has just a little bit of a jazzy tinge to it.

The CD finishes with "View from the Window." It starts with spacy electronics and then Kevin playing a slower, quite expressive guitar passage. There are some nearly melancholy electronics playing and Klaus is offering a sprinkling of chime sounds that sound like they are separating and falling to the ground. From there, Kevin's guitar continues, with KS adding plaintive synth sounds in the background. The final track is pleasant and mellow. I like the playing of Kevin's guitar better on this final track than on the title track. It drives the mood of the song, which is subdued, yet imbued with emotion.

Transfer Station Blue is a very good to excellent album, offering several thrilling moments.

My interview with Michael, beginning on the next page, covers *Transfer Station Blue* as well as other areas of Michael's work with Klaus.

Michael Shrieve Interview with Greg Allen

GA: You and Klaus met during the *Go* Project, right?

MS: Yes, we met during the *Go* project with Stomu Yamash'ta. In fact, I'd never heard of Klaus before then and Stomu had told me about him. I believe I probably got one of his CDs before going and was very interested in the music. It was something that was really different for me. And then seeing him and his setup and hearing what he did, I was blown away. I'd never encountered somebody like him, even though I had worked in the past with Patrick Gleason, who had a whole wall of EMU synths. Patrick's was a different type of music as well, although he was a master of what he did.

I was drawn toward Stomu Yamash'ta because of his avant-garde approach to music and the same is true with Klaus Schulze. I learned from Stomu that if you want to do interesting things with interesting people, then you should first do interesting things! Stomu was a real Renaissance man. He was always surrounded by fascinating people. I had wanted to do a percussion album with him, but it ended up as more of a pop album.

GA: Klaus was pretty much playing music that was totally unique at that time, in the early to mid-seventies, it seems like.

MS: Yes.

GA: Except for maybe a little bit of Tangerine Dream but...

MS: Yes, exactly.

GA: I got a picture, when Klaus sent me the pictures for the book and it looks like he had a big Moog setup - like a big wall there at the concert in Paris.

MS: Yes, he had a big wall with a lot of equipment.

GA: How about the encore you played with Klaus, just the two of you, *Live in Paris*.

MS: I really enjoyed doing that a lot! I used electronic percussion, the Impakt drums, which were invented by a guy named Steve Lamme' from Portland. Klaus was playing very spacy electronics and I was playing the Impakt with pedals, echoes and reverbs. It was a wonderful moment. Maybe we should have done more of that during our collaborations, although we did some of that on *Transfer Station Blue*.

GA: You described about how you were already attracted to his music and it was different than things you had heard before. What was it specifically that lead to the mutual connection between you and Klaus during the *Go* project which led to you collaborating after that?

Klaus and Michael during the recording of Transfer Station Blue in 1984.

MS: Well, in an overall sense it was the general sound of what he was doing, which was something that I hadn't encountered. I was familiar with Tomita, and I was familiar with some serious synthesists, but Klaus was doing something that was different. I think a part of it that attracted me to him was his use of sequencers and the rhythmic aspect of that. And that it propelled the music forward. There was a pulse to it that I related to as a drummer.

GA: So, your drumming and the sequencer rhythms would kind of coordinate with each other?

MS: Well, on *Go* it wasn't quite like that. He was used in a way that was somewhat ambient or he would do something by himself in the live performances that was him doing a piece of his live show in the context of *Go*.

Then there were some other records I heard that he had done including *X*. I began to buy more of his records and really loved it! I think *X* really got me going just because of the sequencers, but I wasn't crazy about the drums that were on his recordings.

GA: You know it's funny, I felt the same way at first, because on his first few albums it was just floating synthesizer music and that was what I was used to. And I think maybe *Moondawn* was the first one where he used drums. Now, he's used so much percussion on his music since then that it's something that's enhanced it, I think.

MS: I think what it was, was that somewhere between *Moondawn* and *X* - I loved the music so much and then when the drums came in, it ruined it for me. And I called him up and I said, "I love everything except the drums. Can we do something together? I wanted to try playing to some of those fast sequencers, you know, and the pulse of that. And that's initially how it started, where I just proposed, "Why don't we try doing something together?" This was because I loved the music so much, but when the drums came in, it spoiled it for me. Now nothing against the drummer, it was what Klaus wanted and it was appropriate for that but I felt that it needed a different kind of groove, really.

GA: So you kind of envisioned a different style...

MS: Yes, even what we ended up doing, at least like for instance on *Transfer Station Blue*, on my record that he played on - we tried a lot of different things. The thing that worked best was just kind of cowbell and timbales that ended up on that main track.

GA: The first track.

MS: Yes

GA: Where your percussion is so clear sounding.

Michael, drumming with Santana, at Woodstock.

MS: Yes, it's so sharp and I think that we ended up going with that because it filled a lot of space within the music in terms of frequency. There wasn't a bass drum or a snare drum. It was cowbell that was being played but it sounded very much like it could have been part of a sequence. The pulse of the sequencer - in fact I went right with one of the sequences which just made it like a cowbell rhythm. Then, I essentially just filled in the timbales where it felt appropriate. I was really into it and I felt the groove of that. I would try to play fills that would either answer a phrase of Klaus' or introduce and bring in a phrase that Klaus was doing. So, it was very much a supplementary role, even though the whole thing was pulsing really hard.

And then on some of the other records like *Audentity* and some of the other albums, I did play drums and there was more a different kind of groove happening there on *Audentity*, because I still - I really wanted to get that stuff in there somewhere.

GA: Was it the Simmons drum machine on *Audentity*?

MS: Yes, didn't I play regular drums as well?

GA: I think so.

MS: And I tried to keep that groove going because I still had wanted to play drum grooves with him but yes, we did use the Simmons as well. Some of that *Audentity* material is some of my favorite stuff.

GA: Did you go to Hambühren to Klaus' studio in the forest?

MS: Yes, I was very impressed with the vast array of electronics and instruments.

GA: Did you go there with the intention of recording a whole album?

MS: We did go to Hambühren to record an album but we weren't sure how it would sound. I brought my brother Kevin along too. That was a great experience. He really loved Klaus' music and can still recall in great detail what went on in the sessions.

At his studio, it was amazing to see the big wall of electronics and to hear these incredibly lush synthesizer pads coming from them. The sound was amazing. He has a great sounding setup in his studio.

GA: What, if anything, did you learn from working with Klaus Schulze that you took with you as your career went forward?

MS: Just the seriousness and commitment that he had toward the music.

GA: What is unique about him that makes him such a special musician?

MS: The single mindedness that he brings because he has worked alone so much. He is so self contained, and has a definite vision about his music. He's one of a kind!

With respect to how Klaus and Michael usually worked together (with the exception of *Transfer Station Blue*), Michael provided this description via e-mail:

"Most of the Richard Wahnfried material that I played was done just with me and Klaus and then Klaus would add people as he saw fit. The whole idea was for him to work under a pseudonym, so that he could experiment with different music and people outside the 'Klaus' name. Much of it was recorded at different times, and he would later put them on different CD's that he released, like *Audentity* or *Drive Inn* or whatever. We didn't really do most of those CD's as specific CD's, if you know what I mean. They would just come out later with these various pieces on them, some of which I had played on, and some not."

1984 *Drive Inn* (with Rainer Bloss)

This quote came at the start of a review if *Drive Inn* (also used in the Introduction to this book): From a July 1984 interview with Klaus attributed to "Synthetic Pleasure", USA on the Official KS Website: "Ah, the master has done it again. I firmly believe that Klaus Schulze is as important to electronic music as BACH or MOZART were to classical music."

Matt Howarth summed it up as "High energy. Pretty good".

From Jim Brenholts at http://www.allmusic.com/cg/amg.dll?p=amg&sql=10:kifrxqugld0e:

"It features heavy synth washes and catchy hooks, but it has no depth. The performance is superficial and formulaic."

The Official Website of KS chimes in with this about *Drive Inn*, "Easy listening but sounds quite nice."

My review of *Drive Inn*

(I'm reviewing a vinyl copy obtained on eBay):

Side A contains four songs, all short by Schulze standards. The title track is first and wastes no time building up, starting with a sequenced beat surrounded by piano, chimes and the occasional synth wash. Also present are trademark KS string "bursts" signaling a change in direction. "Drive Inn" is a fun tune and seems like a good cruising tune for the car.

"Sightseeing" is second, starting with flute, a steady thumping beat and synth pads. Sound flares up all around the central beat, including a steady piano, soaring synth, Minimoog and briskly played percussion. This track sounds light and breezy at times but is overall a track that cooks.

The third song is 'Truckin'", starting with sequencer, sharp crashing sounds and the smoothest synth pads of the album so far. The sequencer doesn't change much throughout the song. It's a nice mixture of sounds, all appealing. It's not complex but fun nonetheless.

The last track on Side A is "Highway." It starts like the others, at a fairly high energy level from the first notes. The formula is sequencer, swirling synth pads and percussion. There are a few moments of deep bass.

I like Side A – in fact, I'm surprised how much I like it. *Drive Inn* doesn't seem like it's one of the better reviewed Schulze albums out there. I really couldn't find much written about it on the internet in terms of reviews. Now I wish I had a CD copy!

On to Side B with three songs – "Racing," "Road Clear," and "Drive Out" – that last just over 20 minutes combined. It feels strange to be reviewing an album that has a total playing time shorter than some of the individual KS tracks I've been reviewing "Racing" begins with exciting percussion, and it sounds fairly close to "Communique: 'Approach Spiral'" from *Transfer Station Blue.*

Percussion is courtesy of Michael Garvens. The recording on this track is brilliant! Interesting and unusual vocals "work it out" behind the percussion. Very stimulating sequencer patterns join in the mix toward the end, spicing things up even further. This is an absolutely scintillating track. I don't think I've ever heard anyone rave about "Racing" as a Schulze classic (possibly because it's a collaborative effort or because *Drive Inn* is an underrated album) – but I'm raving now!

"Road Clear" begins with a synth burst, then a hypnotic, almost Kraftwerk-like sequenced rhythm. KS plays hazy synth pads in the background, while Rainer plays interesting and enjoyable piano runs. The basic rhythm is quite seductive and even more creative. Standout percussion adds to a feeling of increasing admiration for this song and *Drive Inn* as an album. It's hard to say which is more interesting here, the propulsive rhythm or the soloing around it! As "Road Clear" progresses, Rainer's outstanding piano work plays a greater role. Klaus contributes a little Minimoog soloing as the track winds toward the 8:00 mark.

Drive Inn ends with "Drive Out," which starts with the same synth burst as the song "Drive Inn." It also features the same hypnotic rhythm as "Drive Inn" and actually sounds very similar.

My conclusion: *Drive Inn* is a very strong album that frankly surprised me a lot!

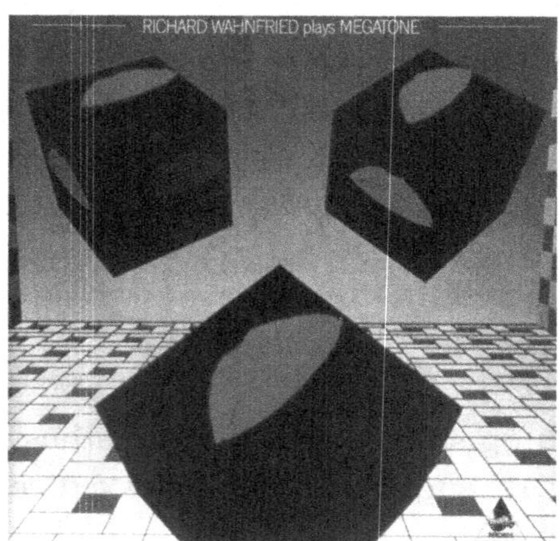

1984 *Megatone* (Richard Wahnfried)

Allmusic.com rates *Megatone* two stars out of five, with no review included.

Chapter 9 Klaus' Solo Career and Collaborations 1985-1989

1985 *Inter*Face*

From B22 at http://www.synthmusicdirect.com/:

"Both fans and reviewers alike having remained divided over this particular album in the past, I guess I'm pretty much walking on broken glass here with this write-up...Now here's where it gets a bit confusing - apparently when track two, 'Colours in the Darkness,' was put onto the original album back in 1985 the wrong version was stamped onto the album, not the version that Schulze had originally intended. So with this definitive version he has amended this rather sizable gaffe by including the correct version as one of the two bonus tracks...that's great news."...[T]he bonus tracks are well placed, making for an excellent addition and as a result a much stronger album. I wonder how differently the music press may have treated *Inter*Face* if the correct tracks had gone onto the original vinyl back in '85."

From David Law at http://www.synthmusicdirect.com/:

"Finally we have the title track (24:49). Great bubbly cosmic start, then a couple of delightful sequences are introduced, one high register and the other of the bass variety. The lead line plays over the top. This is by far my favourite track on the album."

A review of *Inter*Face*, prior to the re-release by Matt Howarth:

"Klaus Schulze: *Inter*Face* (CD on Manikin Records, Postfach 450274, D-12172 Berlin, Germany).

"Unavailable for some time, this classic Schulze album from 1985 has been reissued on CD by Mario Schönwälder at Manikin Records. Ah, you say, there are lots of old Schulze albums, each full of wonderfully epic layered synthesizer music. What makes this one special?

"This album marked an evolution in Schulze's electronic style, injecting more pep to his majestic swells and E-perc rhythms. The keyboards became less rushed, taking time to weave tender melodies. Ah, but the music is still rich with drama and hypnotic splendor. And the best reason in favor of this 49-minute CD is the music itself: especially outstanding compositions, gripping harmonics applied to energetic trances.

This is not a part of history you can afford to overlook."

From J. Munnshe at http://www.amazings.com/reviews/review0330.html:

"The music varies between Electronic Pop and Space Sequencer Music. 'On the Edge,' 'Colours in the Darkness,' and 'The Beat Planante' are near to synth-Pop. 'Inter*Face', the long theme that gives its title to the album, enters within the realm of Space Music."

My review of *Inter*Face*

I agree with B22 above that the exclusion of the proper version of "Colours in the Darkness" was a significant oversight. The real version is far superior to the one on the original album. Placing "The Real Colours in the Darkness" directly after a very strong title track leads to approximately 37 consecutive minutes of excellent music.

*Inter*Face* opens with "On the Edge." The first strains sound like Klaus' music, but after several seconds, the sound turns very light, almost like elevator music with drums joining in. A bass line adds a little more interest. This sounds odd for a Klaus Schulze track. Some reverberating chimes add some interest.

Percussion spices things up some, and piano joins in. The beat and lightness of the instrumentals just don't sound like anything I'd expect from KS. I hate to say it but this doesn't feel like one of KS' better songs, although it seems like a song where repeated listens might help.

And I have to keep in mind that KS has never really been obligated to make his music in any certain style. That's a big part of the Schulze catalogue's appeal in 2007 – that it contains the work of a musician who follows his heart musically and is never defined by a strict style.

"Colours in the Darkness" is next; the infamous "mistake" song placed on the original LP instead of the desired version, which has now become a bonus track. At first this song sounds as weak or weaker than "On the Edge." Again, it doesn't sound at all like a Schulze track. Around the 2:00 mark, some very clean percussion and a shift in the song direction help out. At about 5:00, I'm feeling better about the song. It's still lighter and breezier than the normal KS composition, but it does have a decent beat and some interesting sounds. As the song winds down, I feel better about it and think maybe with repeated listens, it'll sound worthy of the Klaus Schulze name.

"The Beat Planante" starts out in the same very light sounding way as the first two songs (a somewhat unsubstantial sound). A synth pad drifting in the background sounds more like Schulze, but the rest of the song sounds like someone else. "The Beat Planante" is an overall weak song for Klaus Schulze. I think the whole fate of this album rests with the possibility of "The Real Colours in the Darkness" and the title track being the salvation for the album. Rarely, if ever, has a Klaus Schulze album had three consecutive tracks of such overall weakness. As the reviews above mentioned, opinions on *Inter*Face* are sharply divided, and the difference between Matt Howarth's review and mine illustrates that fact pretty well. However, there is more to come.

The title track "Inter*Face" starts out in a very different vein than the first three tracks. There is some bubbling, some twittering and then the emergence of a sequencer line. A droning synth with a foggy sound occupies background space. Some of the sounds are reminiscent of *Body Love*. Sparkling chimes float about. This sounds more like a typical Schulze track, with interesting sounds layered and evolving changes occurring on a gradual basis. At about 5:30, it starts to really get good, with the entrance of tympani and choirs.

The pace becomes somewhat methodical. This song is far superior to the first three, in my opinion. The chime sounds begin to become sequenced. "Inter*Face" uses some very sudden and interesting chord changes to shift the direction of the song from time to time. At about 15:20, the sound starts to really intensify into a very ethereal, mystical, and pleasing sound that compares with some of Klaus' best. Overall, the title track is a very good song that could hold its own on any Klaus Schulze album. With this song, the balance tips in the direction of more than half the album being good.

The first bonus track is "The Real Colours in the Darkness", which was apparently supposed to be on the original release. By the 1:00 mark, the track takes on a classic Klaus Schulze feel, very stimulating, tapping into that place where strong emotions are felt. The song is in a minor key, unlike Track 2 (Colours in the Darkness). There is an otherworldly sound that inexplicably lifts my spirit and stirs positive, if brooding, emotions. Klaus uses a slowly changing background synth to set the mood. This song is excellent – by far the highlight of the album, even though the title track was also strong. Choir effects around the 7:30 mark elevate the track even further. It's in territory where it can compare to the all-time classic Klaus Schulze songs.

The second bonus track and final song is "Nichtarische Arie" which contains drumming that sounds like that on the first few tracks – rather weak. It almost sounds like Tracks 1, 2, 3 and 6 were recorded in the same session and Tracks 4 and 5 (the best ones) were recorded in another. For the first few minutes, "Nichtarische Arie" sounds similar to "On the Edge" and "The Beat Planante." At about 5:30, there are vocals, but the identity of the singer is a mystery - KDM says in the liner notes that he is sure it's not Klaus singing. I think the singing helps the song. At around 7:30, some very crisp, very well recorded percussion that sounds more like Michael Shrieve enters the mix, offering a real plus to "Nichtarische Arie." As the song ends, it seems as if the initial impression I had has changed to a more favorable one. That's typical of this enigmatic album!

This album presents me with a conundrum. It contains two tracks which are "typical" Schulze songs and others that are quite challenging because they're in a very different style from anything KS has ever put down on vinyl or CD.

Klaus mentions in the liner notes that Michael Shrieve was on the road when *Inter*Face* was recorded; so he had the fellow from the neighborhood, Ulli Schober handle the percussion. I wonder how much better this album would have been if Michael Shrieve had participated instead?

Poznan.

Poznan.

1986 *Dreams*

From B22 at http://www.synthmusicdirect.com:

"On this occasion recording was accomplished with assistance of some of his musical friends, but it's still very much a Schulze album all the way. This is a CD release of variety and inventiveness which also has me thinking that Schulze raised his game a little on this one."...All is looking well for Klaus over the first quarter hour of this very classy piece of music, but then disaster strikes - oh no – vocals!!!!! Things probably wouldn't have been so bad if there were more structure to the lyric and maybe having used a singer that could sing!! This whole episode deteriorates rapidly into something sounding rather like a very bad night of drunken karaoke down the pub – truly awful. Klaus' music is excellent, but virtually drowned out by this aimless warbling; end the track right now!!!... As for *Dreams* the album, at nearly twenty years of age I think it still all sounds pretty fresh. With a large slice of bonus track thrown in too, it makes for an impressive CD package. For me it's certainly an album of highs and lows, very entertaining and benefits from repeated playing, but oh those vocals on Track 5 – where's Simon Cowell, I think I need a second opinion."

From Dave Connolly, *All Music Guide*, at http://www.allmusic.com:

"*Dreams* is another modest triumph. The cover art seems to promise Zen 'n' EM, while in fact the title track may be the most disturbing piece Schulze has written... Unfortunately, the nearly half-hour "Klaustrophony" unravels midway through when Ian Wilkinson (uncredited on the Magnum America reissue) engages in a half-sung dialogue... *Miditerranean Pads*, for example, transitioned better from song to song, but *Dreams* is at least its musical equal. Just be careful not to let the cover art cloud your perceptions; most of this music bears no connection to Oriental or Zen themes."

My impressions of *Dreams*:

Dreams was released when I was reaching a dead end in trying to obtain Klaus Schulze CDs. They had always been available in Toledo in the '70s and on into the '80s. Then, suddenly, there was a period where the local record shops were telling me that they couldn't get the current Klaus Schulze album, even as an import. Thank goodness, the re-release series has changed all that, and I have a deluxe version of *Dreams* to review, with "Constellation Andromeda" as the bonus track.

I've listened to it multiple times since buying it, and it's kind of a mystery album. I tend to look at it as a second-tier Klaus Schulze album. That said, there is some intriguing music on *Dreams*, and it seems like one of those albums that I could grow to like more as I listen to it repeatedly. Of course, there is the controversial vocal by Ian Wilkinson on "Klaustrophony". I have mixed feelings about it.

At my last job, I was always talking up Klaus Schulze's music to the younger guys (a generation younger). I would play Klaus Schulze CDs at my desk through the computer speakers. When Ian's singing came on, I cringed because I felt others would hear it and generalize, "So that's the music that this guy you call a legend makes!"

On the other hand, if I just listen myself, I have mixed emotions about the singing. In some ways it sounds expressive, and other times I feel it detracts from very good instrumentals behind it.

"A Classical Move" starts Dreams and enters with an immediate crescendo followed by some classic KS synth pads that sound quite good. After a bit of nice playing, a very attractive sequencer pattern comes in. It's a pattern with a fairly bass-laden sound. Another crescendo launches a new phase to the music and reminds me very much of the technique employed on "Velvet System" from *En=trance*. In fact, the unique clanging keys of "FM Delight" are hinted at as well.

Another crescendo launches a phase where drums become the primary backbeat, although the sequencer is still going in the background a la *En=Trance*. For the first time I am seeing the connection between *Dreams* and *En=Trance*. I think I had read a review where that connection was made, but I didn't see it. Now I do, and in fact, it's obvious, especially in the way a new phrase or section is delineated by a sound burst.

An appealing section of "A Classical Move" reveals strings which start to sound like a violin. The sequencer remains in the background as Klaus plays a more staccato type synth lead. At 8:23, a rousing crescendo blasts into the mix and in the new section a flute-like sound emerges. The track dies, but not totally. There is a segue to "Five to Four," the second track, without a stop in the music.

"Five to Four" starts with Klaus' synths sounding a bit oriental (see the aesthetically very pleasing cover to *Dreams*!). The sounds are somewhat halting, introducing new layers one at a time. First choir voices, then a piano run followed by a layer that sounds like a harpsichord.

The effect of the layering is pleasing, similar to humans singing in rounds. Klaus gets off some good piano runs to go with the chiming synth and all the other layers here.

"Five to Four" blends into the title track, "Dreams," the highlight of the album. It starts out slowly, with hints of "Velvet Voyage" and even the droning sound that starts "Satz: Ebene" of *Irrlicht*. Heavenly sounding, stirring choirs emerge, causing me to feel a hint of the chills!

The soundscape becomes dominated by multiple choir effects while a steady background drone and a bassy lead synth play slowly. A drumbeat comes in at a little over 5:00, and the overall sound level soars like a seagull flying majestically through a blue sky.

"Dreams" fades into "Flexible," the fourth track. A brass sound enters, trading off with a short, repeating bell-like sound. Drums lead the track slowly, along with a hint of a choir. So far, this track is not as impressive as the first three. Suddenly, out of nowhere, the pace quickens; dramatically and spellbinding Hawaiian-like guitars enter. As this lovely section of music ends, the music blends into "Klaustrophony," the last track on the original *Dreams*.

This song starts out with "Crystal Lake"-like sequenced chimes. Two layers develop fairly quickly, first the chimes, then a xylophone-like sequencer that adds excitement when combined with the chimes. A muffled, distant sounding human voice can be heard deep in the mix.

Powerful, fluctuating choir sounds give "Klaustrophony" an unusual centerpiece.

Drums enter with a methodical beat. A guitar-like sound enters, sounding similar to that in "Gringo Nero" from *Beyond Recall*.

Just past the 15:00 mark Ian's voice enters, changing the track – for better or worse. On the positive side, it seems that his voice fits with the pace of the instrumental and is expressive. On the downside, it's a very unusual voice that is not really "singing" in any traditional sense. He almost sounds like Vincent Price reciting a haunting horror poem.

Klaus is laying down a very nice instrumental cushion for Ian's voice.

As I understand it, the bonus track, "Constellation Andromeda" was originally a demo track for the Alesis Andromeda analogue synthesizer (as the accompanying booklet says, 300 copies were given out at The Frankfurt Music Fair).

The bonus track starts with multiple sequencer patterns which emerge quickly, and it's in mid-track form in no time.

At about the 7:00 mark, sequenced drum-like sounds enter and quicken - as does the whole track, building in intensity.

There is a lot of sequencing over drawn-out pads. The drum pattern starts to really intensify as does the lead synth pattern, playing notes very rapidly. This is one of the less attractive sequencer sounds on a Schulze track, in my opinion; it limits the appeal of "Constellation Andromeda."

Dreams is a nice CD to look at, with wonderful cover artwork that looks like a Japanese watercolor. I enjoyed *Dreams* probably a little more this time than previous listens. I had a definite feeling that the album was better than I'd realized during the first three songs.

The title track is very good, and it seems the album might be stronger if the song "Dreams" were longer. The CD does have a certain intrigue, which makes the prospect of repeated listens attractive.

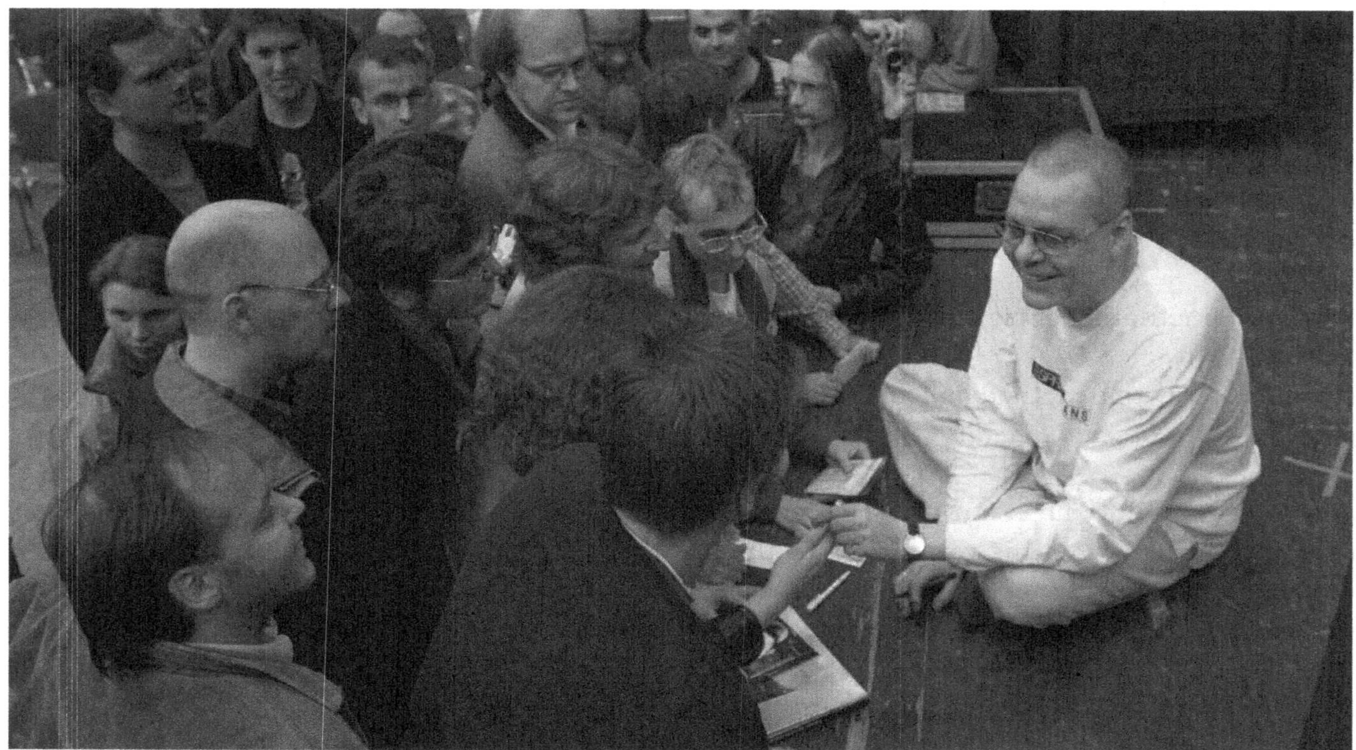

Klaus signs autographs after a concert.

1986 *Miditation* (Richard Wahnfried)

From Jim Brenholts at www.allmusic.com:

"....two long-form compositions, each over 25 minutes in length, lean more toward the atmospheric side of e-music. Samples, a sitar, and a choir complete the soundscape. This CD is one of the best Wahnfried discs."

1987 *Babel* (with Andreas Grosser)

As I sit and listen to *Babel* – I'm reviewing the LP -- one thing strikes me: This is a much underrated album in the Klaus Schulze catalogue. I always liked it a lot and played it quite a bit when it first came out. Andreas Grosser's piano and Klaus' flowing synths make for a great combination. The whole first side of the LP has a feeling of slowly and majestically building. The melodies of Andreas' piano playing are catchy and have a certain elusive quality that can make a piece of music feel just right. I'm feeling a sense of not only comfort but delight in the music. There are six titles listed for Side 1, but it's simply one continuous track.

There are three main layers of music in Track 1 – Andreas' methodical piano, Klaus' velvety synth pads and some lead synth to complement Andreas' piano playing. There is a sense of magnificence that accompanies this side of music. Toward the end of Side 1, some very nice sounding, crisp percussion is introduced.

Side 2 starts in a spellbinding fashion with a slowly building synth pad and Andreas' ominous, methodical, yet beautiful piano (in a minor key) re-entering. The synth pads played by Klaus are very long and sensuous - layered to introduce even more sonic wonder. The shifts in the synth pads are gorgeous, and there is a hint of choir in the background. The choir sound becomes the dominant sound for a while. In time, there are higher and lower pitched multiple choir sounds with a subdued piano.

Klaus' synth pads return, sounding nearly like a string section in an orchestra. There is a very plaintive, yearning and almost mournful quality to the music. The longer the sustained brilliance of the music continues, the more I think that this album deserves a place high on the list of Klaus' works (remembering Andreas, of course).

Listening to this music definitely brings back memories of the very high regard I held for this album in the late '80s. Some minor-key choir sounds increase in power, adding an even more intense feel to the music. The piece takes on an elegance. As Klaus' synth pads return, I'm reminded a little of "Ludwig II von Bayern," probably because of the way the synths resemble strings, but also because this piece has the feel of a classic to it.

The song slows to a near stop as various clanging sounds resonate. This must be the sound of workers as they build. The female choir sounds return before striking sounds, as if on an anvil, are heard. Choirs flood the landscape and then die as the sounds of work being done are all that remains.

The cover artwork is fascinating, showing the Tower of Babel from different viewpoints as well as a village, countryside and a river; all giving a medieval feel. The front cover is an exact replication of "The Tower of Babel" by Pieter Brueghel the Elder (1563).

See http://en.wikipedia.org/wiki/Tower_of_Babel for more on the Tower of Babel. There are other paintings of The Tower of Babel, some quite different from the one on the cover of *Babel* since no one knows what the original in the Book of Genesis was supposed to look like.

Wikipedia mentions a picture of the construction of the Tower of Babel used in the Maciejowski Bible. I think it's interesting, because my review mentioned the striking sounds as if on an anvil and this picture shows the same interpretation. It also heaps even more glory on the album, because I think more than any other album I can think of, Klaus and Andreas were able to convey the sense of the subject of their album – the progress, struggle, awe, grandeur, and labor all associated with the building of the tower – using only instrumentals. My final thoughts on *Babel* are that it's a really excellent album, although it may be the kind of album that you have to be in the right mood for.

1987 Elisa Monte Dance School Video

The Elisa Monte Dance School is in New York. The following is a brief excerpt from the "Company" heading on their Home Page:

"ELISA MONTE DANCE was founded in 1981 on the conviction of bridging cultural barriers through the universal language of dance. From its earliest recognition on the world stage as 'best company' at the International Dance Festival of Paris in 1982 to its tremendously successful touring to over 35 nations worldwide, Elisa Monte Dance has lived that conviction for over two decades."

If you go to http:/www.elisamontedance.org and click on the link labeled, "Check it out in our Repertory Section!", you can either watch the whole video or set the timing slider to 3:12, where the dancing to *Audentity* begins.

1988 *En=Trance*

From Jim Brenholts, *All Music Guide*, at http://www.allmusic.com:

"... Schulze uses deep atmospheres, symphonic synths, and experimental sci-fi sounds to create these trance-inducing soundscapes..."

From B22 at http://www.synthmusicdirect.com:

"[*En=Trance*].... was applauded on its release as a return to the classic Schulze of old!!...[With] Track 3, 'FM Delight' (17.28)... we've either gone back ten years to the Schulze of the seventies or I've accidentally put the wrong CD in, only to find we're now listening to one of Jean Michel Jarre's more airy, pastoral moments... Entertaining, fascinating, another little gem from the archives. Another excellent album."

My impressions of *En=Trance*:

This is probably my favorite Klaus Schulze album of the 1980s. I remember driving around the suburbs of Detroit, being totally intrigued by "FM Delight" and its fascinating sound - a slashing, clanging, forcefully repeated sound throughout the work. It sounds like a rapid pounding of the keys on the keyboard, yet with a sound that is more electronic and unique than the sound of a piano. This sound made "FM Delight" compelling to me in much the same way the pulsating, bubbly sound in "Totem" made that so alluring. I also remember feeling that "Velvet System" was a great song, with sudden major changes and lots of excitement.

I'm reviewing the original *En=Trance* on Magnum. (Late note: I received the comp re-issue from SPV after writing this. Since the music is the same, I added comments on the re-release packaging and bonus track at the end of the review. The sound quality may have a little more "life" in the re-issue.)

The title track "En=Trance" starts with long droning synth sounds, followed by a higher pitched grandiose sounding series of synths announcing the track as if something major is about to begin. This intro lasts at least three minutes and is very slow and drawn out.

Once the synth jabs have finished their pulsing, twisting attack and retreat from the soundscape, a sequenced rhythm starts and is soon surrounded by some dreamy, almost sleepy, synth pads. The sequenced pattern continues for quite awhile.

As is often the case in a Schulze CD, after a period of seemingly endless repetition, the music accelerates, and the pads take on a more urgent, passionate quality. This is another example of Klaus lulling us, seemingly for the thrill of the major change about to come. In the last four minutes, the lead synth pads stretch out, at times sounding choir-like. Some of the pads sound very breathy. "En=Trance" trails off suddenly. It's an interesting song but not a knock-your-socks-off track.

"A-Numerique" starts with more sleepy, breathy synth drones with a hint of choir, a sudden cymbal crash before the entire song quite abruptly shifts to a sequenced pattern in the background, a lead synth and an occasional bass line entering and retreating.

The song moves at a fairly slow pace but with a compelling sequenced rhythm and interesting lead synth layers on top. Still, I sense that the track will pick up momentum in time.

Klaus plays a hazy chime-like solo pattern, as very high pitched chime-like solos of greater clarity play along. These two sounds are intriguing enough to merit their own little slice of the song, along with the backing of a bass line joined with piano-like sounds.

The whole piece arrives at a breakdown using only bass and a lead synth. Arising out of the breakdown is a more urgent playing of the keys with sporadic and dramatic groups of drum hits that are very pronounced in their stereo separation.

The drum attacks come suddenly and dramatically and are pleasing to hear. They come in bursts of three, four and even more at times. They begin to alternate between speakers, one outburst on the left, and the next on the right. The stereo separation is like a brilliant musical idea of its own. After the 15:00 mark, the entire piece shifts dramatically again growing to a massive buildup of synths and drums as the track ends.

Next is "FM Delight," one of my favorite Schulze songs ever!

It starts with lush, lengthy synth pads which have a hint of that hazy, dreamy quality from the title track. It's a simply gorgeous beginning to a great song! Immediately, "FM Delight" has a sense of urgency and beauty not heard in the entire CD to this point. One senses right from the first chords that this is a special song. Expectations build as two layers of synths dance provocatively and sensuously with each other.

At about 4:00 a more active lead line joins in, adding to a building sense of excitement! I've listened to "FM Delight" countless times, yet I sense and feel the excitement deep inside me and I'm filled with anticipation as syncopated percussion and choir-like sounds join in the background.

Soon the signature sound of "FM Delight" begins when slashing and clanging piano-like sounds join the mix in repeating phrases. I emphasize "piano-like" because yet again, Klaus Schulze has created a one-of-a-kind, immensely pleasing, spellbinding sound that becomes the highlight of the track.

"FM Delight" has a majestic yet mysterious feel. This is simply classic stuff; another in a long line of masterpieces that borrows almost nothing from the large group of other Schulze masterpieces.

Finally we come to "Velvet System," phasing in with more somewhat dreamy synth and joined almost immediately by a wonderful sounding lead synth melody. Percussion follows soon after, and we have a three layered sound - suddenly, almost alarmingly interrupted by a loud burst of female choir sound, after which the music quickens. This, again, is very powerful and exciting music!

With the lead synths still producing lush textures, a drum based backing emerges, and the music continues with increasingly strong rhythm and repeated exhilarating choir bursts that signal a change in the music via chord changes. I can't overemphasize how much these sudden, stark choir eruptions add to this piece of music, elevating it to a very high level!

The backbeat now comes in staccato percussive bursts. "Velvet System" has entered a simply delightful higher plane, and it's thrilling!

Where did this album come from? Following a series of releases that were not as strong (such as *Inter*Face* and *Dreams*), this album knocks me out with its sumptuous creativity and rapturous sonic pleasure.

"Velvet System" is a brilliant piece of music!

En=Trance succeeds so well because it is its own distinct musical composition with no frame of reference in the Schulze catalog, and it is well stocked with enthralling surprises, especially in the last two tracks of the four piece CD. Score another stunning success for Klaus Schulze!

SPV sent me a complimentary copy of *En=Trance* to review for this book since I already owned it and had not originally planned on buying the re-release. A few comments about the re-issue. The packaging is simply gorgeous. The colors on the front cover are brilliant. I find the combination to be really pleasing, including the pinkish red that shows in the window, the opening doorway and Klaus' name. When you open the cover, you find even more brilliant color.

Klaus' story about starting and finishing the album in three weeks, after taking a break from working with Alphaville, is also very interesting. The packaging is excellent, far better then the Magnum version I have owned up to this point. The re-release features the bonus track, "Elvish Sequencer." As explained by Klaus, this has nothing to do with Elvis Presley, as Klaus was generally not a fan of Elvis' music.

The bonus track sounds spectacular from the start. There are sparkling sounds and dazzling layered sequencer patterns. "Elvish Sequencer" has an absolutely brilliant beginning. The sequenced patterns play very quickly, are very bright and clear, and have several chord shifts that give this a magical, captivating sound. The audio quality is superb.

The sequenced sounds gradually evolve into a quivering, almost metallic sound, somewhat akin at times to feedback. This settles into a twittering sound with some resonating synth. A variety of unusual sounds end the piece. It's short by Klaus Schulze standards but nothing short of brilliant. As a whole, then, with "Elvish Sequencer" as a bonus, a great album becomes even greater. *En=trance*, in my mind, rates as one of the top prizes in the entire Schulze catalog.

Work with Alphaville

From http://www.intuitivemusic.com/klaus-schulze-biography:

"In 1988, while visiting a technician friend, Schulze met the synth pop band Alphaville at their Lunapark studio and after two hours with the band he decided to repeat his experience as a producer for the band's album 'Breathtaking Blue'" (1989).

From http://www.iol.ie/~carrollm/av/klausint.htm

"[Schulze's] first meeting with Alphaville came about by coincidence. A friend of his, a studio technician, had something to do at the band's Lunapark Studio and Klaus accompanied him. The two hours with the band there turned into a year-and-a-half that he spent in Berlin instead of in his own remote studio in the woods near the small town of Celle."

Please see the above web link for more in depth coverage of what Klaus has to say about his time with Alphaville.

KDM says: "Klaus did not spend a year-and-a-half in Berlin. The full recording time - from the first note played, to the final master - had indeed this length, but KS was of course not always present – just a weekend here and a few days there, again and again, during these circa 18 months."

From http://www.specialradio.net/alphaville/inter.shtml:

SR: Alphaville have once worked with Klaus Schulze. He's quite popular in Russia. Could you tell us what he's like, how does it feel to work with him? And what are the differences when you work in the studio with Klaus or any other artist?

Marian Gold (That's Marian with Klaus in the picture in the coming pages): Since we produced Alphaville's third album "The Breathtaking Blue" together in 1988, Klaus has been a close friend of mine. He is a very unwinded, meditative person, a man with a great sense of humour and besides his competence and unique musical experience he brings in tranquility and "space" into a production, which gives you the chance to explore musical areas you've never been before.

Marian Gold Interview with Greg Allen

GA: Marian, can you describe the circumstances of your first meeting Klaus Schulze? I've read that a studio technician who was a friend of Klaus' was coming to Lunapark and Klaus came along. Can you describe that meeting and how Klaus and the members of Alphaville connected at that time?

MG: Bernhard and me met Klaus during a recording session in our studio in Berlin in 1987. The technician you mentioned above had been coming in order to present a couple of Neumann microphones to us and due to that occasion he brought Klaus along. Klaus is a very friendly and open person and it took only half an hour of conversation between the three of us until he got completely involved in our running production. It was one of those magical moments when you meet someone for the first time and immediately find out that he's on the same wavelength. Hence it suggested itself that we asked him first of all to produce our next album half a year later. And luckily he agreed.

GA: Did you know right away that this person with the studio technician was Klaus Schulze, the electronic music pioneer?

MG: We had been forewarned that he would come around. We were very excited and curious what kind of person he would be.

GA: Had you been a fan of Klaus before that or known his music?

MG: Definitely yes. One of my favourite albums is *Mirage*. Another great one is *Go*, his collaboration with Stomu Yamash'ta. Records like *Mirage* opened a door for me and inspired me to become a musician myself.

GA: How did this initial meeting turn into a strong musical connection and end up in Alphaville and Klaus Schulze working for up to a year and a half on *The Breathtaking Blue*? Can you describe the process?

MG: As I said, after our first meeting it stood to reason that he would be the first we'd ask to work with us. We imagined the whole production for *TBB* as a combination of writing and producing in one go. We did not intend to follow the usual process of composing demos then choosing the most suitable stuff from that material. We wanted to achieve a floating, synergetic trim of the production. We would write a song then arrange and mix it up to its final state. Then we would write the next song and so on. In a way each song of *TBB* became a kind of micro-album by that. Klaus was perfect for this task. He had the curiosity, he liked surprises ...and he was patient enough.

GA: Can you tell me why you and Klaus have had such a good rapport musically and even personally? Is there something about Klaus and his creativity or approach to music that drew you towards him in a musical sense?

MG: First of all he is a great man and a visionary musician. He has a deep and encouraging trust in one's capabilities. He's as cool as a cucumber, in the studio he's always the calming influence. He's open for new ideas anytime, even if that means a complete change of direction. His immense musical experience is a treasure for every production. Besides that I like his curiosity and playfulness.

GA: During that year and a half, how often did Klaus visit Alphaville's Lunapark studio? Did he devote as much time working with Alphaville as on his own work during this time?

MG: He was with us most of the times. In between he went back to his own studio for six weeks and quickly recorded an album of his own, I think it was *En=Trance*, a double-album, naturally. And after that he returned and continued working with us as if nothing had happened. How cool is that?

GA: How did the recording of "Duel" come to be on the Wahnfried *Trancelation* album? Can you describe the history of the song? Did it appear both on an Alphaville album and the *Trancelation* album?

MG: We released it a few years after *Trancelation* on our own album *Dreamscapes*. One day in '93 Klaus played me a tape and asked if I could contribute some vocals to it. It is always a challenge to sing along with his music. It meanders on and on, without any specific cues; it is very transcendental. Actually, concerning "Duel", in my opinion it would have worked nicely without vocals. I had that story in mind about a serial killer who finally gets killed by one of his assumed victims who turns out to be an even more vicious killer. It took some time to find a structure that allowed me to sing the story onto the music, but in the end it all worked out fine.

GA: Can you describe the sense of fun that you and Klaus had together working on *The Breathtaking Blue* and how Klaus helped to shape the album? Can you describe a little about how he and Alphaville worked together and blended each other's creativity to come up with the final product?

MG: Working with Klaus is like being on an expedition into unknown territory. His unusual and inventive perspective on music opens doors to new and astonishing areas. Once, we got stuck with one of the songs for *TBB*, and he made some suggestions that turned the music completely upside down, but in a wonderful way. It was like a magic touch. We then ended up with two new songs instead of one: a proper pop-song "Mysteries Of Love" and "For A Million", which for us was music of a new dimension. In all our previous collaborations Klaus was always very suggestive, but he would never insist on his ideas or feel offended if one wouldn't follow his propositions. I think that is the reason he can work so successfully with artists from even oppos[ing] directions.

GA: How long was it until you worked with Klaus after *The Breathtaking Blue* was finished?

MG: We met from time to time and talked about several projects. We became friends, which ironically may be the reason that we never really got the impulse to work with each other during the '90s. That changed in the new millennium. "The Opium Den" from 2000 was our first proper collaboration since "Duel." From then on we recorded music in a relative regular mode (once or twice a year). From 2001 on we called the entire venture Sputnik Roadhouse. Two pieces thereof were released on Alphaville's *CrazyShow* in 2003, the title track and "Opium Den," both in highly shortened editions. Meanwhile the project to me seems like a never-ending story. Whenever we feel we have enough material for a complete album, another idea ambles by and keeps us carrying on. God only knows when it will ever see the light of its release.

GA: *The Breathtaking Blue* was released in 1989, *Trancelation* in 1994 and the Sputnik Roadhouse segment for the crime movie in 2001. Can you describe how your working relationship developed with Klaus between those dates? What kind of projects did you do?

MG: For me the production of "Opium Den" was like a paradigm shift. I was blown away by the epic power of the music. I had never dared to hope I would be involved in something like that. It changed my approach to singing and to writing lyrics completely. So much space compared to the narrow design of pop-music! And Klaus' music has changed too since then, all is new for both of us. Erstwhile Klaus would record some of his music and I'd sing on it, doing my best to get along.

Marian and Klaus

Now we choose certain segments from his stuff, which serve me as ideal modules to sing on. It is like catching beautiful fish out of the enormous ocean of Klaus' music. We then dispose these segments in an order we like and blend it sometimes randomly, sometimes systematically with the remaining musical parts. In a third step Klaus improvises with his synths on the resulting arrangements and does the mix almost simultaneously. The whole course takes between three or four nights per musical piece. We always work at night, starting at dusk. It always feels like taking off for a flight into the unknown. What will happen tonight? To me it's a very poetic, mysterious way of producing music.

GA: Can you also describe how you and Klaus became good friends? What makes for the good chemistry between the two of you?

MG: We are opposite polarities. Klaus is a very calm and relaxed worker, I am often excited and impatient, less the sanguine type. But that doesn't lead to tensions at all; on the contrary, it seems to me a perfect match.

GA: Can you describe how it developed that the group of musicians with you, Klaus, Florian, F.J. Krüger, Toni Nissl came to be involved in this movie?

MG: In Spring 2001 FJ, who sadly passed away last April, asked me if I was interested to sing "Those Were The Days" for a TV-production. After a few drinks in Krüger's fave bar we came up with the idea to involve some more musicians into the project, just for fun. Wouldn't it be a nice occasion to meet each other and dress up in funny clothes and stupid hairdos (almost like in the eighties), a bit like a kids' birthday party? I rang up Klaus, he called Florian, and FJ contacted Tony and that was that. For a moment it looked like we would do some more music after the TV shoot and possibly... merge [it all] into Sputnik Roadhouse. But that remained a crazy idea since we were all involved in too many other projects at the time.

GA: When I watched the video, I thought your voice sounded somewhat like Brian Ferry. Was he an influence for you or someone who you admired?

MG: Oh yes, as a teen I was deeply impressed by the music and the style of the glam rock-era, especially by Bowie, Cockney Rebel, Japan and Roxy. Today I can still sing most of their songs by heart. So it wasn't an accident I sounded a bit like Bryan Ferry. I went into the studio and did the song in one take. I thought I was just doing a "pilot" vocal and they would give me some more tracks to sing on after they had set up the recording channel properly. But everybody seemed to be happy with the take, and it turned out to be the shortest vocal session of my entire career.

GA: Can you describe what it is like to go to and work in Klaus Schulze's studio in Hambühren?

MG: The studio is located in his house in a deep forest in the middle of nowhere. Be sure that when you work there you are far away from everything. You are on a different planet.

GA: Thanks again, Marian!

MG: All the best to you and to your project, Greg.

1989 *The Dresden Concert* (before 6800 fans, music to be released the following year).

This concert resulted in Klaus' 1990 release of *The Dresden Performance.*

Chapter 10 Klaus' Solo Career and Collaborations, 1990–1994

1990 *Miditerranean Pads*

From B22 http://www.synthmusicdirect.com:

"If it's a profound musical statement or a mind opening slice of classic Schulze you're after then look elsewhere as here Klaus treads his own tried and tested path albeit one with drums which incidentally I didn't find to be that misplaced or intrusive. If you liked *En=Trance* then go for this album immediately. Many will find a true crowd pleaser in the title track, which is just inspired. Strangely Klaus makes comment of his interest in exotic percussion sounds in the sleeve notes, though oddly doesn't appear to have used much if any of them on the album"

From Dave Connolly at http://www.allmusic.com:

"Listening to this record with half an ear isn't half as much fun as giving it your full attention, so don't expect to just pop the disc in while you wash the dishes and be magically transported. Better to set aside even half an hour and get lost in one of the longer tracks. *Miditerranean Pads* reveals a mastery of the electronic form; if you've found some of Schulze's earlier work too abstract, you might want to re-approach him from this angle."

From http://www.tokafi.com/newsitems/andthentherewerethree/view:

"Finally, *Miditerranean Pads* opens the door to the sampling-phase of Schulze. Just a little too complacent and too relaxed for its own good, this is the only of these four albums you will need to buy if you're a completist."

The following is Matt Howarth's review by of the original version of *Miditerranean Pads* (not the re-release):

"Klaus Schulze: *Miditerranean Pads* (CD on Magnum Music in Germany).

"One learns early in life that only the worst puns are any good. No one remembers a tasteful jape. Those of you familiar with Schulze's long and respected career are used to these things--the awful puns, the awesome music--by now. These people will view this release as the next in a long line of intensely gratifying experiences. Schulze's mastery of electronically induced sounds is, in itself, enough to make one gasp; his abilities to arrange these sounds into melodies make one sigh. Inhale, exhale...the cycle, once complete, endlessly repeats.

"But what about those ignorant of Schulze's music? You people are in for such an eye and ear-opener, it will be like an ape discovering how to use its thumbs. You will hear intricately slippery tempos snaking through the soft but exotic synth-percussion, predominated by neo-computerized bongos, and back-dropped by a mountainous choir of atmospheric keyboard drones and generated orchestral strains. This music is majestic and dreamy, just this side of trancelike repetition. It is evocative of vast fields of sighing grass and lazy waters, carrying in its rhythmic thread all the inspirational gist of the best of all possible sunrises."

My review of *Miditerranean Pads*:

The album leads off with "Decent Changes", which sounds startlingly similar to the first twenty-plus minutes of "Dresden two". The same laid-back pace and subdued percussion are present from the very start.

"Decent Changes", a 32-minute track, disappointed me the first time I heard it (upon buying the re-issue). I was surprised at the lack of remarkable percussion sounds since, based on what I had read, I was expecting such sounds from *Miditerranean Pads*. After listening to "Decent Changes" the first time, I wondered how the album could recover from a 32-minute track being rather listless and mediocre. Since then, the other music on *Miditerranean Pads* has made me sit up and take notice, so this is the track that keeps the album from being outstanding for me.

I think Dave Connolly's point about giving full attention to the music on *Miditerranean Pads* is valid. First, I've discovered that doing these reviews has brought me a new understanding of many Schulze pieces and a much greater appreciation for how he structures his compositions.

I've heard a lot that I never heard before and become more in awe of KS' body of work than I was before - a testimony to the depth and sophistication of his compositions.

In giving "Decent Changes" another chance to impress, I'm noticing a lot of activity with the piano and with synthesized strings that adds intricacy to the piece. "Decent Changes" also contains passages of fairly passionate and intense "string" playing.

"Decent Changes" breaks around the 13:00 mark to focus on the percussive elements, which are not recorded with the same clarity as on other KS albums (notably *Drums 'n' Balls* and Michael Shrieve's *Transfer Station Blue*). This is a song with a slow tempo throughout.

Bouncy piano enters around the 22:00 mark. The very laid back base of "Decent Changes" could be considered like the tape loop in Ludwig, and the interesting elements such as this springy piano, the occasionally emotion provoking strings and various percussive elements could be analogous to the additional elements in the Ludwig "tape loop" from *Jubilee Edition* and *Dziekuje Poland Live '83*.

As I listen to "Decent Changes" again, I'm starting to like it a bit more, but I'm almost positive it will never become one of my favorite Schulze pieces.

The title track immediately makes an impact with very moving choir sounds backed by what sounds like an organ. Strings sweep in along with staccato piano and simulated female voices (it turns out this is a sample of Klaus' wife that Klaus played on the keyboard, as we learn from the re-issue booklet). The pace is fairly slow here also, but I feel a lot more passion and emotion than in "Decent Changes".

Very crisp, high-register piano becomes the centerpiece, backed by choirs, adding a lot of flavor to the composition before and after the 5:00 mark. Male choir and lush violin-like string sounds form a stirring transition and continue to keep the track on a very high musical plane.

Klaus is simulating several sounds, including one close to a saxophone. The song "Miditerranean Pads" is a very moving song that clicks for me in such a way that I feel it's yet another Schulze classic. It's an exquisite piece of music!

"Percussion Planante" is the third and final song of the re-issued *Miditerranean Pads*, and it comes out of the gate with very brisk rhythm and crisp percussion. The song is immediately likeable. In fact it has bowled me over with its energy and creativity.

Piano comes into the mix, yet another of KS' interesting and surprising changes. Coming on the heels of the energetic, almost stunning beginning, it causes a feeling of intensifying awe and joy and has me very excited for the rest of the song.

"Percussion Planante" swells and soars as it reaches the 5:00 mark, and there is not a bit of doubt that this is a fantastic track!

Lively piano and percussion combined with strings continue to be absolutely flabbergasting in the way they come together to form a piece of music that is devastatingly, nearly overwhelmingly beautiful.

The recording quality of "Percussion Planante" is very good. The percussion reminds me of some of the emotionally provocative percussion on *Drums 'n' Balls*.

Sometimes, everything just comes together in a composition to the point where sheer magic is the result. "Percussion Planante" is one of those tracks.

As I listen to it (caught up in the emotion of a great piece of music), I feel that "Percussion Planante" could rate as one of the top 10 Schulze tracks – I like it that much.

Overall, *Miditerranean Pads* is an enigmatic piece of work, ranging from mediocre to superb. If I could experience "Decent Changes" in the same way I've experienced the latter two songs, I would rate *Miditerranean Pads* a top-tier Schulze album.

1990 *The Dresden Performance* (live)

The first thing that comes to my mind before listening to *The Dresden Performance* for commentary/review is that the first song of 44 minutes or so is fantastic and that the rest of it has been hard for me to get into. However, sometimes repeated, fresh listens can lend a new perspective, so this will be interesting.

The concert took place on August 5, 1989 (in an open air setting) in the former East Germany just before the wall came down in (late 1989) and Germany was reunited (in 1990). Five pieces were prepared for the performance but due to time restrictions, only two "Dresden one" and "Dresden two" were actually performed live that night. The three remaining pieces were recorded later in the studio for inclusion on this album. [This paragraph based on liner notes to the *Dresden Performance* CD]

It should be noted that, according to KS, the liner notes also give a misleading impression about why the concert was aborted when they say, "due to last minute restrictions imposed by the police only the main pieces ('Dresden one' and 'two') were performed live to the 6,800 strong audience."

Klaus had this to say in a September, 1980 interview, which can be seen on his Official Website:

Q: In 1989 you gave a concert in Dresden and you had some trouble with the authorities who wouldn't let you do the complete concert.

KS: I read that too, in the liner notes to the CD release, and I was flabbergasted. None of it is true. During the two days of my stay in Dresden I did not see one of these "authorities," and of course no real person stopped my concert, but it was the normal circumstances of an open air concert: When I had finished my second long piece of music, it was already midnight, and it was getting moist and cold. Most of the six thousand and eight hundred visitors were just dressed for a warm summer day. Also, they had to catch the last busses and trains. Those were the natural reasons I couldn't do any encores. They are in studio versions of the "actual" Dresden CDs.

My review of the *The Dresden Performance*:

The first track on CD 1 is "Dresden one", a 44-minute piece of music. The other two cuts are "Dresden three" and "Dresden five," both studio versions.

"Dresden one" starts slowly with multiple hazy sounding synths, a drone and then after two minutes, a stark change - a steady beat surrounded by lovely, melodic "string" synth pads.

Percussion works its way into the mix around the 8:00 mark. The track has a very active and seductive character by this point. The tempo of the song is very purposeful and confident. The effect of the "strings" involved in the first ten minutes can't be overstated. These are distinctive sounding strings in the KS oeuvre and very effective. A chord change occurs around the 12:00 mark and the pronounced beat instantly takes on significantly greater intensity with the introduction of "piano" and swirling "string" sounds. Everything works beautifully on "Dresden one", from bass to strings to piano to drumming and complementary percussion. The major highlights are the pulsating rhythm and the beautiful string pads.

The recording quality on "Dresden one" is very good, especially for a live recording. Percussion adds a special character to the track.

"Dresden one" is a superb composition and performance (as well as a smashing opener for the concert!), ranking among the elite Schulze tracks. It seems KS has more combined minutes of elite caliber music than most musicians have of music, period!

"Dresden three" is the second track on CD 1, starting with passionate choirs, twinkling bells and a little piano. The mix becomes gradually more dense and energetic as the first few minutes unfold with inconspicuous synth pads also present. Bells and piano intermingle in a duet for a while before sweeping strings and choirs re-join. After the upbeat tempo of "Dresden one," "Dresden three" has a more floating, dreamy, angelic quality.

"Dresden five" starts slowly with various sound effects from unique human voices to clanging percussion mixed with a very tentative, warbling synth. Rhythm enters just past 2:30, featuring bass, a harpsichord-like sound, drums and synth pads that sound closest to a violin. The rhythm is slightly bouncy, yet restrained.

There is a period of a very slowed pace and predominant percussion from around the 14:00 mark to the end.

The strength of "Dresden five" lies in its ability to evoke a mood – to stir an emotional reaction. It doesn't blow me away in any particular way but the whole seems to exceed the parts. It's not a piece that can be analytically described; it can only be felt.

CD 2 starts out with "Dresden two" (live), which clocks in at just over 47 minutes. Haunting sounds, similar to a mystery thriller soundtrack, take up a little over the first minute. A beat comes in just after one minute with droning synth/choir and percussive additions.

A trademark burst of sound leads the way to a more robust section with the same elements intensified and a violin-like synth pad playing passionately. The pacing and percussion remind me of "Decent Changes" from *Miditerranean Pads*. In fact, the songs sound virtually identical, for quite a long period.

The percussion, while consistently present is subdued and not recorded nearly as crisply as the percussion in several other Schulze albums (again, like "Decent Changes"). For example, this percussion pales in its sonic characteristics in comparison to *Drums 'n' Balls* or *Transfer Station Blue*.

That's probably intentional, though, to shape the mood of the piece.

"Dresden two" shifts to predominantly percussion around the 27:00 mark, sounding clearer than before. To me, this is more interesting and gratifying to listen to - at least I'm glad this section is included.

A choir burst signals a change to a more active and dense soundscape, featuring prominent sweeping string synth pads. It seems that "Dresden two" is growing on me as it winds its way to the 47:00 mark. There have been just enough changes to keep it from getting monotonous.

A full scale choir burst, similar to those in *En=Trance* surfaces at around 42 minutes. The tempo of the track remains laid back, though, as it has throughout. "Dresden two" ends with a massive flare up of synth noise, totally unlike the rest of the track.

"Dresden two" is a pleasant enough piece of music but I find it challenging in a similar way to "Decent Changes" on *Miditerranean Pads*. It's possible that with additional listening to these songs, I might "get it" and experience them in a different way. For now, they are middle-of-the-road Schulze tracks to me.

Last up on *The Dresden Performance* is "Dresden four," a 22-minute track which starts with a pleasing sounding dramatic surge of synth, followed by piano and heavenly sounding choirs. This is in stark contrast to "Dresden two," and I immediately feel excitement in listening to it.

The strings feature two layers, one brisk and strident; the other has a grand, sweeping quality. The string playing gives the piece a feeling of expansiveness, fascination and even greatness. It's a very moving piece of music, in keeping with the best of KS as far as producing emotions and a sense of wonder.

"Dresden four" is one piece of music that had not caught my ear in years past but definitely distinguishes itself as a standout Schulze track, I would say the best on the *Dresden Performance*, deserving of mention as an upper-tier Schulze track.

Dresden Performance definitely contains some very good music. Some of it is among Klaus' best music. Other parts are intriguing but I didn't experience them as knockout pieces. This is yet another album that has potential for growth with repeated listens.

1991 *Beyond Recall*

From Jim Brenholts, *All Music Guide,* at http://www.allmusic.com:

"Schulze had fun making this CD, and he invites listeners to share the fun."

Here's Matt Howarth's review of the original version of *Beyond Recall* (CD on Venture/Virgin in Germany):

"This CD is quick and energetic, full of electronic percussion and toe-tapping rhythms. Comprised of intricate melodies born out of cyclic repetition, the music has a strong tempo, yet still drifts along with its blend of synthesized instruments: cello, some very exotic percussion, keyboards, and even guitar for a lengthy passage in the first song. That heavenly big room quality possessed by Schulze's music is dominant like rhythmic velvet."

(© Matt Howarth, reprinted from www.soniccuriosity.com with permission.)

My impressions of *Beyond Recall*:

The album begins with an exotic feeling, featuring choirs, crisp percussion and acoustic guitar. The clarity of the audio recording is striking from the start. "Gringo Nero" triples in intensity, and surging synth lines are joined by bird-like sounds in the background. Samples of voices dart in and out. The guitar takes center stage with the choir sounds, which haven't relented. "Gringo Nero" feels special in these first several minutes.

There is a grandiose and dramatic flair as the track builds intensity with very interesting sound combinations.

Shrieks are followed by a near total change in the sound. The backing synths change from choir to a much lower-register synth pad sound. A lilting pace is still present as bird-like samples enter and leave.

The song surges relentlessly forward. The guitar plays more melodically, but then suddenly, we hear high pitched birdlike sounds, and the track is thrown into chaos - a sampled female voice, a choking sound, a female crying "more, more" and the ubiquitous "ya mean that's it" play in rapid-fire fashion. There is moaning in the same ecstatic fashion, then a repeating sound of seagulls.

Klaus is basically using samples as his prime instruments, and for all the criticism, it seems like a very imaginative concept. The fact is, it works. This is KS' first foray into heavy sampling and it is somewhat mind boggling and surely innovative. "Gringo Nero" is a spectacular song, and sampling plays a big part in it, seamlessly integrated with the conventional instruments to create a wondrous tapestry of sound.

This sounds like one of the best recorded albums I've ever heard. A brass-like instrument plays expressively, then yields to choir, percussion and acoustic guitar. There is unquestionably some of the best percussion on any KS album. Despite any possible reservations about bizarre samples, lets face it - this is gorgeous music, boldly creative and stunningly recorded. "Gringo Nero" just jumps out at you from the start, announcing its magnificence suddenly and continuing to delight.

How can this track be topped or even matched? There are four more songs to give it a try. Toward the end, there is a sudden shift, launching "ya mean that's it," crickets, and a barrage of samples. That's it!

The second track, "Trancess," starts out with soft choir effects, male this time, and some boldly played piano. A cello-like sound is integrated into the early mix, followed by a gentle flute-like sound. An operatic female voice sings briefly.

At about the 4:00 mark, very clear and prominent percussion takes center stage. The track is notable for strident synth string patterns that join with melodic string sounds to give the song its definition. Despite all the other instruments involved, I think it is the strings that make the track. The song ends with strings, piano and an oboe-like sound.

I reviewed this song once and gave it a mediocre rating at best. The second time around, I appreciated it much, much more. Sometimes, you have to be in the right mood. This time I have experienced it as near brilliant.

The third song, "Brave Old Sequence," starts out with emphatic chime/bell sounds playing briskly. There are some nice chord changes and more crisp percussion (one of the many highlights of *Beyond Recall*).

The song has a sequenced feel at about the 3:00 mark. "Brave Old Sequence" comes out of the gate decisively and with a startling, almost overwhelming sonic landscape. Choir sounds add to the very tasty mix of sound elements in the first half of the song. Stunning percussion is a major factor in the appeal of this track.

The sound palette of "Brave Old Sequence," combined with the confident and appealing composition, makes for an extraordinary listen!

The fourth song, "The Big Fall," opens with a flute and sounds of water flowing, perhaps birds in the background. This is a remarkable beginning, evoking feelings of being in a forest brimming with life.

There is a sublime synthesizer passage that reinforces this early feeling of being in a magical, enchanted surrounding. At the 3:00 mark, the song is full of mystery, subtle changes, sampled voices, and the sound of brass.

There is a little lull during this period but not for long as multiple piano lines are joined by rich oboe textures.

This sets up a little "jam" with piano and oboe playing off each other. "The Big Fall" is another strong song.

On to the last song of *Beyond Recall*, "Airlights," which starts very boldly with a wide array of strange sampled sounds and rumbling bass. In the first minute, a few of the samples from "Gringo Nero" have reappeared.

Harp-like sounds accompanied by choir appear and linger in dazzling stereo separation and thrill for a few minutes. Oboe-like sound returns very clearly and moves from right speaker to left, back and forth. The sound of oboe plays a fairly prominent role in *Beyond Recall*, even if it is synthesized. It sounds very good, just the same.

Once in a while there is a bizarre or even ugly sound. I think it's very possible that Klaus does this on purpose to make the beautiful passages stand out more. I have been influenced in my interpretation of KS quite a bit by reading his quote about the fact that beauty is not discernable without ugliness to contrast it with. Once the breathy oboe stops, a dramatic, powerful piano enters, played very, very boldly and creating a very pleasing sound spectrum. All else is secondary as this wonderful sounding piano plays.

A drastic shift occurs at almost the 10:00 mark. The power of these dramatic and sudden shifts in Klaus' compositions adds a feeling of being thrilled, intrigued, stimulated – a feeling near joy that is usually followed by something very different but equally stimulating. I really like the timing of the entry of many of the samples in this album.

Wow! Samples enter frantically at 12:45 – a wild array of samples ensues, screeches and animal noises – before "Airlights" ends.

For me, *Beyond Recall* is a very good album. It has always been one of my favorites. I did appreciate it more during my second listening, which occurred as I edited the initial review.

Whether this should have been the only album where Klaus used many of these samples is open to debate. Schulze fans didn't know it when this was released, but several of these samples were going to be used repeatedly in three live albums to come. I think it's challenging and potentially liberating to be open fully to the possibility that the use of samples is another step in the genius of Schulze. It's a step that can open a whole new way of hearing music; a mind-expanding concept, which, once embraced, can lead to amazing new experiences of richness in listening to KS' work.

I think of the two *Royal Festival Hall* CDs, combined with *Beyond Recall* and *The Dome Event* as being like a boxed set. My feel for that set from past listens is that there is plenty of great music in the four CD set, with *Beyond Recall* setting the pace.

1991 *2001*

2001 is a sampling of Schulze's unique electronic music, spanning his career from 1972 to 1990. KDM says: "It is not a greatest hits album, but a collection of four to seven minute excerpts from 15 classic Schulze works."

From Matt Howarth (reviewing the CD on Brain Records; Germany):

"Simply put: [*2001* is] a Klaus Schulze sampler featuring tracks spanning nearly two decades of his solo music. Electronic mastery at its best – from the dense and somber early material to the fanciful and mighty recent works – Schulze is the unsurpassed king of electronic music. The pieces are tightly mixed together into a seamless 77 minutes of the highest quality.

"A decent introduction to Schulze's music should you happen to be unfamiliar with his long and splendid career."

(© Matt Howarth, reprinted from www.soniccuriosity.com with permission.)

1992 *Royal Festival Hall Vol. 1*

From Mike DeGagne at http://www.allmusic.com:

"This music is extremely trying...Although the music doesn't produce its chilling results in an instant, the smoothness and overall mechanical feel emerge halfway through, and the synthesizer begins to slowly warm the ears."

My review of *Royal Festival Hall Vol. 1*:

Royal Festival Hall Vol. 2 has long been one of my favorite Schulze albums. It will be interesting to do one more comparison test to see if *Vol. 1* has the firepower to come close to *Vol. 2*.

The 44-minute "Yen" is the first of two compositions on *Vol. 1*.

The concert starts out with sounds evocative of spaceships, hints of choir, crickets chirping, all manner of voices, whistling – a potpourri of samples with some musical undertones. Since I've had a lot of experience listening to a mixture of KS' seemingly random and bizarre sounds used to create music – and I've even grown fascinated by the idea of making music in this unconventional way – I appreciate these first several minutes of *Vol. 1* very much.

The first time the samples evolve toward a more conventional musical framework is at the 8:00 mark. This change feels intoxicatingly delicious to me because it reinforces the enjoyment of the music-by-samples section which led to it. This is the first exhilarating moment of "Yen."

A flute soars above the beautiful sonic landscape as the tempo stays soft and restrained. Sampled voices and percussion play along with a light beat. The "Minimoog as electric guitar" unmistakably makes its presence felt around the 14:00 mark. At close to 17:00, the flute returns above very subtle but gorgeous synth pads.

Sampled voices and choir surges lead the track up to the 24:00 mark, when a signature Schulze "sound crash" signals a change – not toward a more vibrant section of music, but to an even softer soundscape, featuring more percussion and throaty growling samples. I would call the next several minutes a "diverse sounds jam session."

After a musical breakdown, a particularly subtle and poignant section of music emerges.

Around 39:00, there is a reprise of the flute playing on top of gorgeous synth pads, which evolves into another period of myriad samples forming the music.

That's "Yen," a track with a lot of interesting facets and at least one exhilarating moment.

I had a thought while listening to this music from the "samples period", that although it was controversial among the fans, it may represent Schulze in his greatest period of genius.

The second and final creation of *Royal Festival Hall Vol. 1* is "Silence and Sequence," a 25:00 piece of music. It starts with a crash, a sampled voice exclaiming "Yea!," several more crashes – a general hodge podge of unusual sounds combined in a way that only KS can. Voices, bells and a creeping minor key synthesizer emerge in a subtle, yet beautifully transcendent way. There is a quiet majesty to the music that follows. This is one of the more elegant transitions that I've heard in a Schulze composition. If you want to check out specifically what I'm referring to, try listening to "Silence and Sequence" from about 2:30 through 7:00 and see if you agree with me!

After 7:00, bass, choirs, screeching birds and synth replace the delectable sound of the previous four minutes.

Just short of 12:00, a dramatic change takes place, with a surge in the volume paired with stark percussion. A fast sequencer takes over fairly quickly, changes chords, and pairs with various complementary synth notes and bass sounds to form a magnificently compelling period of "Silence and Sequence." Drums join in to reinforce the beat. A period of electrifying sound creation follows, yielding again to the near frenzied sequencer.

The period after 12:00 is as charged and adrenaline producing, as the first 12 minutes were wonderfully peaceful. Several chord shifts and changes in instrumental palettes invigorate this section with a fascinating contour.

The final several minutes are more low key, with sustained choirs, sultry female voices, birds and long, continuous synth chords.

Royal Festival Hall Vol. 1 is a fine and stimulating album with lots of interesting effects and textures. Perhaps most of all, this CD shows a level of creativity that is eye opening

1992 *Royal Festival Hall Vol. 2*

From Mike DeGagne at http://www.allmusic.com:

"Attentive listening will decipher detailed contrasts in Schulze's artistry, even though his playing might not seem all that spectacular at first. Background rhythms and faint goings-on beneath the main notes make his electronic music both absorbing and, at times, mysterious."

My take on *Royal Festival Hall Vol. 2*:

This album has always been a favorite of mine, probably because KS takes myriad disparate sounds and samples and combines them in a way that makes for an electrifying listening experience. I think he does this more effectively here than on *Beyond Recall*, *Royal Festival Hall Vol. 1* or *The Dome Event*. Let's see if that impression holds up!

The first song is "Ancient Ambience" (44:55), which starts out with breathy synths, crickets chirping, a subtle synth pad, the sound of a shrieking bird, a woman's voice, water splashing and other various samples too numerous to describe in real time! The feeling at the beginning is one of being outdoors. The startling recording combined with the vibrancy of the samples leads to a feeling of wonder and awe. The listener is transported immediately into a magical, mystical world. Here, Klaus is playing nearly 100% with samples as his instruments – a remarkable achievement.

"Thunderclaps" lead to a more restrained sound -- but one with a great deal of gravitas. The mood set by the first six minutes of "Ancient Ambience" is enchanting!

A male voice sings out a refrain repeatedly with choirs in the background. During these repeated phrases, a tension builds, dramatically released by a loud drum crash followed by the sudden emergence of a delightful sounding sequencer. There are repeated drum crashes which lead to chord changes in the sequencer and choirs.

"Ancient Ambience" takes what was begun in "*Beyond Recall*" and raises it to an even more polished and mind boggling level. Myriad sudden changes produce a feeling that there is a simply astonishing quality of greatness to this creation. Erotic sounding gasps and groans occasionally surface.
It seems that I have to be in the right mood for "Ancient Ambience" and the rest of this album, but when I am, it all falls into place and it's a breathtaking experience.

Increasing percussion, subtly beautiful sequencer, a quickening pace and the occasional erotic female cry of "More!" or "Ohhh!" are featured over the next few minutes. By 19:00, the pace has quickened, mostly via brisker percussion playing and a faster sequencer. A female voice cries out "More," and the feel of the piece subtly changes. An erotic female gasp of "Ohh!" leads to a downshift in the music, some bongo or tom-tom drumming and then a buildup again with a lovely higher pitched sequencer backed by lively "strings".

A dramatic and beautiful shift takes place, punctuated by bass, female samples and long synth pads. This section can give me the chills. The pace stays a bit slower and tentative for a while.

Suddenly, an operatic sounding voice sings out unexpectedly, joined by more erotic cries.

The song becomes a little unfocused for a while around 32-33:00, sounding almost like a "Sebastian im Traum" interlude. The breakout from this period features prolonged stuttering bass, drumming, and synth pads of sheer beauty. It's another gradual buildup, though, a heightening of tension that promises another experience of exquisite release! It comes about with another female exclamation of "More!" and then a launch into a Minimoog solo.

The second song, "Anchorage," a shorter piece at 11:03, starts with a very sensuous oboe, which sounds a bit brassy after awhile, giving "Anchorage" a very beautiful start. A rhythmic sequencer, a few more erotic gasps, and a twinkling sequencer appear with "strings" in the background. A lilting, cello-like sound adds some building energy before more brief but ecstatic female gasps are heard. Some forest animal shrieks and groans are thrown in for good measure. Around 10:00 I detect a sequencer pattern, interjected subtly, that sounds like it's straight out of *X*.

"Variation on *b.f.*" starts with a crescendo, then sweeping strings, followed by another crescendo and then some brightly played piano along with a piano-like lower sequencer pattern, stunning cello sounds, choirs and a playfully surging bass line. This song is startlingly powerful from the beginning and doesn't let up.

Of note is that "Variation" is not a live track but was recorded at Moldau Musikstudio (Klaus' studio) by KS. It does sound a little sharper than the other two tracks, and it's simply stunning! Female samples, sounding a bit operatic, are part of the mix, contrasted with alternating "mixed" choirs and "male" choirs. The piano line is buoyant and free, even joyful! There is a flowing feeling of ease, of lightness and of grandeur in this piece. It ends with cello-like sounds.

If I had to choose, I would say that *Royal Festival Hall Vol. 2* is my favorite of the time period, which includes *Beyond Recall*, both *Royal Festival Hall* volumes and *The Dome Event*. It's a very interesting and quite spectacular album.

1993 *The Dome Event*

From Jim Brenholts at http:\\www.allmusic.com:

"This disc features his signature heavy sequences, some very gentle acoustics, and deep atmospheres. Strange vocal samples take the set over the top. This is a good CD".

Here's Matt Howarth's review of the CD (on Virgin Venture Records in the UK):

"This is another live release (with one studio inclusion to fill the disc out to 74 minutes) recorded in May 1991 at the Cologne Cathedral. Schulze is in typical form – meaning utterly in control and masterful in his sonic sculpture. Another mandatory item for the heavy handed electronic music shelf. And it also features cover art and booklet design by Dave McKean (in fact, his cover for "The Dome Event" – a decidedly interesting computer graphic turn for this collage/painter – is very cool too)."

(© Matt Howarth, reprinted from www.soniccuriosity.com with permission.)

My impressions of *The Dome Event*:

"The Dome Event," the title track, is broken down into three movements ('Andante,' 'Allegro' and 'Presto') encompassing over 63 minutes. The CD starts slowly and then introduces myriad vocal samples ("More!" and "Ya mean that's it?" among them), lots of swirling electronics and percussion. The first five minutes or so sound good but don't form anything resembling a song up to that point. The recording is very good.

Once into the second movement, 'Allegro,' at close to the 7:00 mark, "The Dome Event" begins to sound like a song, featuring *Beyond Recall*-style guitar (played slowly this time), drumming, and a synthesized flute-like sound. The pace stays slow so that "string" and vocal solos can weave in and out.

Passionate string and cello action surfaces at around 14:00. This is another album that I found less interesting the first time and now am enjoying it more as I hear it again.

As "The Dome Event" pushes past 20:00, there are some lush orchestrations playing over the consistently plodding backbeat of the track.

Crystal clear drumming and vocal samples both become more active as the track approaches 25:00. The "plucked guitar" sounds increase in frequency and rapidity as the piece approaches 30:00.

A quite interesting period develops when the rhythm drops out and voices and choirs take over, complemented by guitar/harp-like sounds - even sounding a little like the *Dark Side of the Moog* series in the way the voices are used.

Vocal samples take center stage at close to 46:00. After a couple of minutes, sensuous synth pads add luster to the overall sound. Soon, there is a huge surge, and twinkling bell sounds spray liberally in both stereo channels. For the last several minutes there have been lots of interesting sounds and stimulating changes in the music. It all causes a warm feeling to evolve; "The Dome Event" is an excellent track.

A more thumping, yet delightful sequencer pattern enters with drumming and a little Minimoog at about 51:00. This combination of sounds is one of the best yet in the long title track. With the greater propulsion to the rhythm and increased intensity in the accompanying sounds, the song has undergone a metamorphosis from its long held plodding pace.

The Minimoog, as is often the case, sounds like an intense guitar solo by a virtuoso guitarist. It's accompanied down the stretch by relentless drumming and a quickened sequencer pattern. Vibrant bell-chime sounds enter late in the track and continue along with the drumming and choirs.

The Dome Event seems to be an album that can benefit quite a bit from repeated listens. It might not sound as exciting as *Beyond Recall* or *Royal Festival Hall Vol. 2* on first listen but once it "clicks", this track and album have a lot to offer. This long track is definitely different from the previously mentioned albums, though it retains some small similarity, mostly in the vocal samples.

"After Eleven" was recorded in the studio at Moldau Musikstudio in 1992 (the Dome Event took place on May 11th of 1991). It starts with light bass and assorted male and female sound samples. The track becomes very lively, with quickening bass, fast drumming and brisk piano.

Other highlights are the use of a rapid sequencer with fast paced cowbell and reverberating drum crashes echoing from one stereo speaker to the other with violin in the background.

The Dome Event is a pretty good album. It may be a matter of taste as to whether one enjoys it more than the *Royal Festival Hall* pair. My preference is *Royal Festival Hall Vol. 2* but *The Dome Event* is a very good CD -- and another that seems to benefit from repeated listens.

1993 *Silver Edition*

In an interview on the Official Website, Klaus spoke about both the *Historic* and *Silver Editions*:

"*Silver Edition* and *Historic Edition* were the ideas of my long-time partner, publisher and friend, Klaus D. Mueller (KDM). He likes to do crazy things. He has hundreds of my older and newer tapes, and he brought some order into this huge collection. When he listened in 1993 to some newer DATs with unreleased music from 1992/93, he realized that most of it is very good, and so he prepared the first set of five CDs. I urged him to make it ten CDs! In addition to the new music, he put two CDs with old concert recordings into the set. *Silver Edition* (released 1993) was a success, so KDM decided to do a second 10 CD set, with just historic music by me, mostly from the seventies. This set was again a great artistic success. The people – fans as well as journalists – loved it."

1994 Klaus Schulze's Working Hours

In an interview posted on the Official KS Website, when asked about releasing four albums in 1994, Klaus stated, "Music is my profession and my passion. I work every day, or, more correct: every night. And as every self-employed tax payer, I work not just 35 or 40 hours a week, but 80 to 120 hours. And if I have the chance to release a lot of music, I'll take it."

1994 Klaus Meets Royalty

KDM: "During our short *Tourne'e* at the end of May '94, with concert in Lille, Paris, and Rome, Klaus was invited by the Belgian King Albert, and spent an enjoyable evening at King Albert's Palais, with a few other guests of honour. Klaus Schulze had made a soundtrack for a Belgium movie about a French classical author. The people associated with the film and some other "cultural people" were invited and also Klaus.

"By the way; I remember that we (KS and I) were also once (late seventies) invited to a Chancellor Party, which means: We visited Germany's then 'King', The Chancellor Helmuth Schmidt, along with hundreds of other German artists. All this is based on my short reports about it, see 'Biography' in the Official KS Website. I was present, I even had to buy KS a white shirt and a cravat (but I didn't go to the actual party.)

"Two days after in Paris, Klaus was invited by the French President Francois Mitterrand to be his guest at the Palais de l'Eysee among many other people. The movie referred to above [was] about the French classical author, in fact a very famous French writer, Alphonse Daudet, that every French schoolkid knows."

[Note: In fact the next album to be reviewed, *Le Moulin De Daudet*, is the soundtrack for the movie KDM just mentioned]

1994 *Le Moulin De Daudet*

From B22 http://www.synthmusicdirect.com:

"*Le Moulin De Daudet* is everything you might expect a Schulze album to be, with perhaps an extra dynamic thrown in here or there to suit the visuals. OK, no great long extended pieces here, but given that this is a soundtrack I think that's perfectly acceptable. Overall, the production job on the CD is astoundingly good. The recording's clarity is excellent, due in no small part to the simple fact that most all of the musical cues recorded here were done in a single take, which is even more astounding."

A brief comment from Matt Howarth, on the version prior to the re-release (CD on Virgin Records in France).

"This movie soundtrack is another not easily found disc. Pity. It's refreshing to hear Schulze apply his epic mastery to shorter pieces. His drama is not diminished here, but condensed to hard brilliant diamond."

(© Matt Howarth, reprinted from www.soniccuriosity.com with permission.)

My review of *Le Moulin De Daudet:*

My pre-review impressions based on previous listenings are that even though it is a soundtrack and the songs are shorter than the usual KS songs, it sounds very good and is a strong album musically. I recall the recording being brilliant, which adds to the experience of listening to it a lot.

"The Beginning/The Delgates" starts with a sound which is vaguely like a human voice, followed by some startlingly clear percussive sounds, a slow synth pad, choir effects and a little soloing. Synth pad and choir effects combine, then suddenly, a voice cries out "Hah!" and very realistic string-like playing ensues, some sounding like cello.

"Mother Sadness" starts out with plaintive, almost mournful flute sounds. The re-release booklet credits Klaus with "electronics," so all these sounds that come close to the acoustic version are synthesized, possibly sampled. Cello and twinkling bells both sound very realistic in this song. The flute comes pretty close also. The cello moves back and forth between the left and right speaker.

The soundtrack continues with choir effects, synthesized strings and stunningly recorded percussive sounds. I can't recall a KS album with a more sparkling recording than this one, although many have been very good to excellent.

This is a very enjoyable album to listen to, with Klaus' usual variety of instruments and changes in song direction. The heavy use of strings gives it a bit of a classical feel but will probably appeal to most KS fans even if they are not classical music fans (like me).

"Friday's Departure" starts out with a similar oboe sound to the one in *Beyond Recall* and *Royal Festival Hall Vol. 2.* The pause between tracks calls attention to the shortness of this song.

The album is largely comprised of Klaus Schulze synthesizing orchestral instruments and at the risk of repeating myself, the clarity and realism are astonishing! I'm wondering, as I listen, if there is a way that I can see this movie. I'd like to see how the 21 passages on this CD are integrated into it.

Track 11, "Landscape/Way to the Old People," combines a pensive yet intermittently optimistic quality in the same song. "Old People's Piano" follows, with bright and at times very forceful, piano, backed by strings.

An almost operatic female voice backed by male choir voices leads off "Exodus," the 14th track. It's noteworthy that a lot of the sounds involving "stringed instruments" are so realistic sounding that the plucking of the strings can readily be detected.

"Le Petit Dauphin I" has human voices, dramatic strings, choir bursts, reverberating drum beat and harpsichord.

"Le Petit Dauphin II" starts out with drumming and then launches into a much more dramatic period with bold strings, near frantic drumming and percussion.

The next two tracks are "church sequences." "First Church Sequence" contains a minor-key synthesized male choir. "Second Church Sequence & Organ" is the longest song at 6:56. The end of "First Church Sequence" contains children's voices followed by one man talking (at the start of "Second Church Sequence & Organ"), chimes followed by dramatic choir, then bold strings. There is a gap of total silence, about six seconds, followed by extraordinarily realistic string sounds. At close to 6:00, a church organ plays with great strength and flair.

"Paradise and Inferno" has some passionate voices in the background, followed by loud explosions, intense choir, a wailing or crying in the distance. I wonder what is going on in the movie as this part of the soundtrack plays. It's a very tumultuous passage.

"Finale" starts in a more restrained fashion, with an oboe-like sound and children speaking. Then the children speak suddenly, loudly and forcefully, as if they were not paid attention to on their first utterance.

The bonus track, "The Ion Perspective," is also recorded spectacularly and was formerly a Promo CD given out by Alesis at the Frankfurt Music Fair in 2004. KS tells in the booklet how up to $160 had allegedly been paid for the Promo CD by fans on internet auctions. So issuing it here puts a stop to that, as it's obvious Klaus doesn't appreciate his fans getting gouged on price. Not that "The Ion Perspective" isn't good – it's just not worth $160!

The track has a rhythm propelled by a very strong and rapid bass line. It's a very attractive pattern, probably sequenced, with floating brass sounds in the background. Drumming offsets the sequenced pattern at times. This strikes me as one of the better bonus tracks in the re-release series. There is also a human voice which sounds a little like it was run through a vocoder.

All in all, *Le Moulin De Daudet*, as re-issued, is an exciting album, spectacularly recorded. It's an album that beckons from my stack of many Schulze CDs no matter my mood because it has such a great combination of audio quality and great music. It's in the top tier of Schulze albums.

1994 *Goes Classic (MIDI Klassik)*

From an interview at http://www.furious.com/PERFECT/kschulze.html:

PSF: In 1992, you were recording synthesizer interpretations of some 'classical' music on *Goes Classic* with pieces by Schubert, Brahms, Grieg, and Beethoven. How have these composers influenced your work? You included your own piece on *Goes Classic* also -- do you see yourself carrying on a tradition or being a part of a tradition then?

KS: We are all part of a tradition, at least we depend on the past. How else? These composers did not "influence" my work, at least not more than the Beatles or any other musician's work that I know and heard once. Of course I like the works of these old composers, as many people do, partly since hundreds of years. But the recording I did just because it was fun to do it.

From the Official KS Website:

Q: Although your music is far from the traditional classical idiom, you did use classical elements in an innovative manner. What's the philosophy behind it?

KS: I did re-works of some compositions by Brahms, Beethoven, Smetana, Schubert, Grieg and von Weber, because it was fun to do. It brought me joy, satisfaction. As simple as that. Doing music is also a handicraft. And doing a variety of music is more fun than doing always the same. This album had the title *MIDI Klassik*; the record company changed it into a more saleable title: *Klaus Schulze Goes Classic*. To me, it's still *MIDI Klassik*.

Of course, I love and revere the music of the said composers and many others, no doubt about it. I'll maybe do a second *MIDI Klassik* album.

Many lovers of my music will not agree with the statement that my music is "far from the traditional classical idiom" - they will say the opposite.

1994 *Totentag*

KDM's remarks on *Totentag*:

"It took a long time to conceive and produce it: Already ten years ago, KS planned to do his opera, but for some reason or another it was never realized. Now it's completed. The long awaited 104-minute opus is called *Totentag*.

"As very often with Klaus Schulze, it's another daring step. Others may repeat all over again the old-fashioned 'electronic' music, once invented by Klaus Schulze in the early seventies; the inventor himself goes beyond."

From Andras Sumegi at http://www.gepr.net/sa.html#SCHULZE:

"*Totentag* is an opera written and performed by Schulze with German singers. The libretto is about the suicide of Georg Trakl (Austrian poet) in 1914, in Krakow, in a psychiatric clinic. Music in the style of Wagner."

But KDM disagrees: "The opera is not 'about the suicide', but about Trakl's whole life. Much more can be found in the thick booklet of *Totentag*. Or just its titles."

From Jim Brenholts at http://www.allmusic.com:

"*Totentag* is the first and only electronic opera... [T]he vocals, in German, can be a bit overwhelming — they take away from the superb music."

1994 *Das Wagner Desaster – Live*

From B22 at http://www.synthmusicdirect.com:

"With a total playing time of over two and a half hours this album does appear to be one of truly Wagnerian proportions -- or is it???... Recorded live in both Paris and Rome back in 1994 (with the exception of the bonus track, recorded in Spain 1991), the album has a studio feel about it given the quality of the recordings presented here... What we do have is a record of Klaus doing what he does so very well together with that innate ability to use repetition, but not in a repetitive way. The various-mixes idea works for me, though I am a little put out by Klaus's remark in the liner notes that one should throw away the disc they're not so keen on, which to me gives the impression that the music seems of little merit or value to its creator. Shame on you, Klaus."

From Jim Brenholts, *All Music Guide*, at http://www.allmusic.com:

"The source material for each show is the same, but the mixes are different. CD 1 is 'The Wild Mix,' and CD 2 is 'The Soft Mix.' The music is pure Schulze. It is classic Berlin school electronica by a master practitioner of the style."

Here is Matt Howarth's short review of the original (non re-release) version (double CD on ZYX Records in Germany):

"This is a double CD, over two hours of thrilling music from a pair of 1994 Schulze concerts -- but this time he's added a twist. This time Schulze has done several mixes of the music from his awesome concerts in Paris and Rome. The results are remarkably dissimilar. Very tasty stuff."

(© Matt Howarth, reprinted from www.soniccuriosity.com with permission.)

My review of *Das Wagner Desaster*:

This album was recorded Live on May 31, 1994 in the baroque styled opera house, Teatro Valle in Rome and on May 27, 1994 in Paris' Le Cigale. The two CDs represent a "Wild Mix" and a "Soft Mix". The wild mix was done by André Zenou and the soft mix by Klaus Schulze.

"Wagner" leads off CD 1. It starts out with ominous sounding minor-key synth pads and then multiple explosions and crescendos. Sampled voices sounding somewhat operatic, then like monks chanting, are a part of the mix. The recording right away reminds me of the *Beyond Recall*, *Royal Festival Hall* and *Dome Event* recordings simply because a wide array of unconventional sounds, samples and noises are all put together to form a musical composition.

From a tumultuous start, the song settles, at around 4:30, into a softer, laid back posture. Some of the sounds are synthesized (or sampled) brass that sounds quite good. My immediate impression is that this is strong material.

There is a certain freedom in acknowledging that, sure, in this period KS used quite unconventional sounds and lots of samples (some bizarre sounding) – and made joyous music out of it. So what if other people think it's weird? For me, they just don't get it. Who else but Klaus Schulze could pull this off? It's pure genius, in my opinion. Once I free myself from demanding that this period of music be even close to conventional and allow myself to marvel at the way this cornucopia of sounds is somehow melded into enchanting music – at that point, there is a freedom to just thoroughly enjoy it!

"Wagner" fits right into that category, with lots of unusual sounds and some great rhythms. It's one of the better Schulze songs you'll ever hear. There is so much going on that it's impossible to describe. The middle section is filled with sequencer patterns and excellent sounding "strings". As soon as one gets used to a sound in this song, more sounds have been mixed in, the tempo has changed, voices have joined (perhaps slowed down, speeded up, changed to deep bass "male" or higher "female"). The recording is quite good, especially for music recorded live.

The Minimoog starts to cut loose a bit after the 20:00 mark. It takes on a shrieking, piercing quality and then becomes somewhat melodic, sounding like guitar soloing, as is often the case when KS plays a Minimoog solo. An assault of unusual sounds and voices joins with the Minimoog. It's a bit daring, in a way risking the whole song on some very adventurous experimentation. Even if the Minimoog at times sounds as if it might shatter your eardrums, you have to love this last section for its daring quality! "Wagner" ("Wild Mix") is brilliant!

Next is "Nietzsche," another 28+ minutes song, like "Wagner." It starts somewhat similarly but a little more calmly; this part is most notable for string sounds that sound like real violin, layered on top of synth pads. There are the same intermittent sudden thrusts of voices, drum crashes and string bursts. Some of the sonic crashes are a bit jolting, filled with upheaval, consisting of voices, synths, drums, and who knows what else!

This is classic! Sonic crashes alternate with loud operatic voices back and forth, setting up a rousing period of cacophonous sound. Suddenly, out of nowhere, a bassy sequencer takes over and everything has shifted. Voices sing opera and KS' occasionally used "Doo doo doo" voices. The combining and manipulation of the voice samples is terrific!

Some of the operatic style voices and the way they are combined over several minutes come across very well, somewhat similar to "Opera Trance" from *Jubilee Edition*. Subsequent string playing sounds like an orchestral string section, all stroking their instruments triumphantly, in unison. This produces a majestic sound, strengthening "Nietzsche."

"Entfremdung," a wild-mix encore in Paris, is next. It starts out slowly, and then a sequencer and drum pattern come ripping in, only to be stopped for some voices, and then blasts ahead again.

There follows a great sounding period of music that feels like a symphony orchestra performance. This riveting period of "being at the symphony" is interrupted by an operatic voice, a wild crash and then a four on the floor beat - accompanied by flute sounds that flutter all over the stereo spectrum with uninhibited abandon. The beat is at true trance speed in this section, maybe 145 beats per minute. This is an aggressive, confident and authoritative song, employing a stunning array of sound elements in less than ten minutes and sounding cohesive at the same time. In the last 90 seconds, there are some explosive periods of sound. Holy smokes!

"Versöhnung" (soft mix, encore in Rome) rounds out CD 1. Let's see what a soft mix sounds like after three wild mixes. If an early crescendo is any indication, not much different! After that, it sounds like maybe, just maybe, it will be softer as long synth pads, restrained voice samples, solo violin (all Klaus), and some softer female-like choir sounds form the soundscape for a while.

In comes the beat, lurching forward at the 4:00 mark with a synth solo, percussive sounds, and sampled voice.

CD 2 starts with "Liebe," which I presume is the soft-mix equivalent to "Wagner" from the first disk.

The opening consists of reverberating drum sounds -- crashes less violent than in "Wagner" -- and female operatic voices. A Gregorian-chant-like period follows, joined by male operatic voice. Also present is the bizarre sounding speeded-up operatic voice like the one that occasionally appears in "Opera Trance" (or "Vat Was Dat"). There is no question, after four minutes, that the mix is softer. A lot of the notes and vocal samples seem to be slowed down.

A beat comes in peacefully in the form of a mid-to low-octave sequencer, with sampled voices quite active in both channels. The voices sing "da da da" for a while and then are joined by some "doo doo doos." The bouncy beat has a nice feel and becomes accelerated toward eleven minutes by a fast paced high register sequencer. Strings play stridently, following along quite elegantly with the bass sequencer pattern; melding together in a very satisfying way. Voices join in at the same pace, and everything is totally integrated at this point, forming a grand, sweeping and yes, majestic, driving tune!

The main sequencer sound is special and makes "Liebe" sparkle! As usual in Schulze compositions, the sequencers add a glorious flair to the music. I can't think of any other artist that could create a song that creates such a comfortable yet stimulatingly exultant space for the listener. My mind boggles at the composition and execution of this music!

The track approaches the finishing section with rousing sampled voices and fast, emphatic percussive sounds (in a 3-D type sonic effect).

This is just an excellent track, that's all there is to it! It races to the finish with a mid-range sequencer pattern combined with higher sequencer. This is a top 10% Schulze track.

Second on Disk 2 is "Hass," which equates to "Nietzsche." It starts with vocal samples, drums, synth pads and some pretty intense crescendos early on (for a "soft mix"). Violin or cello-like sounds add a delicious flavor to the song, soon supplanted by more operatic-style vocal samples and then a series of blasting crescendos.

As in "Nietzsche," there is a sudden shift to sequencer, which feels very gratifying. The switch to the invigorating sequencer sound combined with the stimulating music that preceded it, creates a surge of adrenaline that soon results in a mounting musical tension. Sequencer and pads hold forth for a bit, the vocals are gone.

After a while, around 10:00, the sampled voices begin, led by a male operatic voice and the "doo doo" chorus. This continues for several minutes. Some of the voices in the left channel sound alive and very near, with a presence that I've rarely heard in these sampled operatic voices – something magical happens for a brief time.

A soaring, driving rhythm, orchestrated by multiple sequencers, joining one at a time, combined with strings, takes hold at around 20:00. The strings fly into the mix, both strikingly passionate and robust, elevating the track to an unrestrained, ambitiously soaring spirit. Spirited, racing sequencer takes over again and is joined by some incredible sounding propulsive strings.

The bonus track, "Encore Sevilla," was recorded during a tour in Spain, in October of 1991. Applause is heard at the outset, the first sign of a live audience. Klaus explains to the audience that the piece was composed especially for Spain.

The sound coming out of the speakers consists of synth pads but with a strength and quality that makes it seem like a test for the speakers. The chords are majestically rising and very moving. It's a great section of "strings"!

The song melds seamlessly into female sounds of ecstasy including, "More!", coming straight out of the *Beyond Recall* vocabulary. It could be said that this music is easily more erotic and sounds much more like a porno soundtrack than *Body Love* and *Body Love Vol. 2.* This song is loaded with more moans and groans than *Beyond Recall* or any of the live albums around that time.

There is a little of a Spanish flavor present with a hint of a flamenco guitar. The recording of this track is a little boomy, the only audio flaw on either disk that indicates that any of *Das Wagner Desaster* is live.

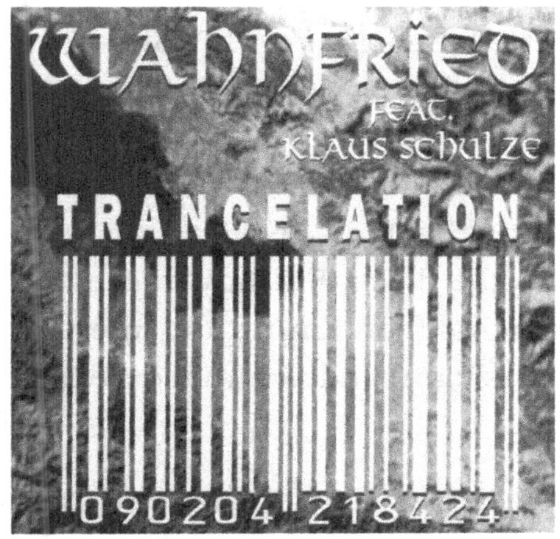

1994 *Trancelation* (Wahnfried)

From http://www.ambientvisions.com/1102002.htm:

"[I]t is a fairly frenetic set. Klaus' signature Berlin school sequences surround a frantic rhythm track. While many of the Wahnfried projects have rock and roll overtones, this project is steeped in avant-garde and funk. There are some very weird samples and some cosmic computer noises"

According to Jim Brenholts at www.allmusic.com, "This is not one of Schulze's particularly strong efforts. It is, in fact, just an average release."

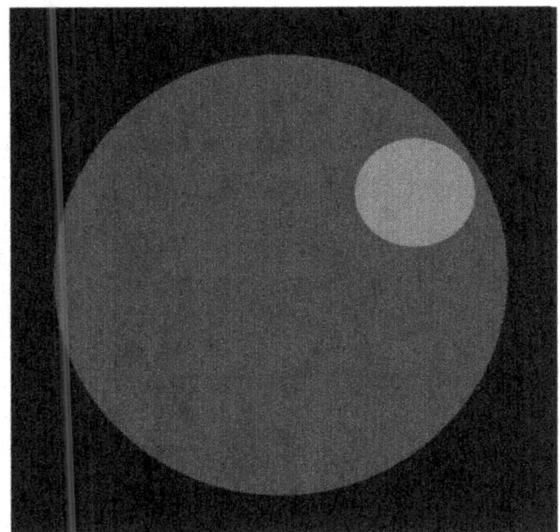

1994 *The Dark Side of the Moog*

This is the first in a 10-CD series featuring Klaus, Pete Namlook, occasionally Bill Laswell. This edition features Klaus and Pete Namlook only.

I have five of the CDs of *The Dark Side of the Moog 4, 5, 6, 7* and *9*. I got four of those from Archie Patterson at Eurock.com at a very reasonable price, probably in 2005. The quality of the music is excellent!

From David Law at http://www.synthmusicdirect.com/mooglaw.cfm:

"So this is where it all began, the first volume of what is currently a nine CD series...We start the first part of 'Wish you Were There' with some lovely deep analogue sounds which after a couple of minutes give way to discordant strings and cosmic twitters. It reminded me a little of some of the stranger moments from 'Sebastian Im Traum'... For the second part... all very strange indeed!... Normality is resumed just as we are about to enter the third part and float on the back of rather pleasant pads which continue through most of this section...Just before the sixth index point another more bass laden sequence comes in along with little melodic flourishes. We seem to be in much more Schulzian territory again... These continue well past the eighth index point forming a very relaxing tranquil atmosphere. When a sequence comes back in it is an excellent one which motors along quite nicely."

Keith Farley at http://www.allmusic.com says it's "similar to Schulze classics *Timewind* or *Moondawn*".

I hope the above review fragments give you some of the flavor of the first *Dark Side of the Moog* release. On the other hand, the following quote comes from a brief review, by Matt Howarth, of the first two releases of *The Dark Side of the Moog Series* (both CDs on Fax Records in Germany)

"These two CDs are a pair of collaborations between Schulze and Pete Namlook—yowl. Two creative geniuses working together--what a surprise! No... the real aorta clencher is how dreadfully boring these two CDs are.

"Okay, I'll try and be objective. The music is generally atonal wandering. Each disc is about an hour long, but things don't start to get interesting until over halfway into the discs. Frankly, these two CDs strike me more as tributes to experimental sounds and textures than containing any interesting application of said sounds and textures (something that both musicians individually excel at). Pity they forgot to add a melody..."

(© Matt Howarth, reprinted from www.soniccuriosity.com with permission.)

1994 *The Dark Side of the Moog 2* (with Pete Namlook)

From David Law at http://www.synthmusicdirect.com/moog2aw.cfm:

"For the most part this is spooky atmospheric stuff... The animal noises increase to include many different types of beasties. It's rather dark sinister stuff. By the time of the fifth index point splashes of echoing electronics have been added... Then just before the ninth section it's all change and a bass beat comes in, little melodies dancing over the top. It's infectious body moving stuff!"

John Bush at http://www.allmusic.com writes that "the music is beatless space music (minus the tremendous feelings of depth on most of Schulze's works)."

1994 *Klaus Schulze: The Essential 72-93*

This is a double CD with edited versions of many of Klaus Schulze's classic tracks from 1972-1993. The reviews and comments that I've heard about the album have been good. It would probably make a worthwhile introduction to KS if anybody is interested in checking out his music and has missed all of it up to this point (e.g., somebody born in the 1980s).

1994 *"Conquest of Paradise"*

This is a review by Matt Howarth of the CD single (CD EP on ZYX Records in Germany).

"This is a CD single (a rather short one too, at 8:30). Two brief versions by Schulze of this Vangelis tune. Schulze duplicates Vangelis' sound perfectly rather than lending his own sound to the melody."

(© Matt Howarth, reprinted from www.soniccuriosity.com with permission.)

Chapter 11 Klaus' Solo Career and Collaborations 1995–1999

1995 *In Blue*

Below is an interview at http://www.ashra.com/press/in9606.htm (MG is Manuel Göttsching):

Q: You worked with Klaus Schulze on his *In Blue* album. How did this happen?

MG: Klaus phoned me in December 1994 and asked me to join. I said yes, and one week later I popped in his studio, and we played two days.

On the original *In Blue* CD (the double CD on ZYX Records in Germany), from Matt Howarth:

"This is a double CD and happens to be one his best releases ever. Schulze's first real studio album in years, it's rich with power and electronic drama. It's really long too, clocking in at over 2½ hours. And there's a special guest appearance by Manuel Göttsching (from Ash Ra Tempel) on one disc, adding his space guitar mastery to Schulze's glimmering keyboard sweeps."

(© Matt Howarth, reprinted from www.soniccuriosity.com with permission.)

From B22 http://www.synthmusicdirect.com:

"I take it Klaus had been listening in on Dave Law's rants about CD's total playing times when this set was put together, now featuring as it does three and a half hours of music!!! Klaus also mentions in the sleeve notes that the original recordings were not remastered by himself or that anyone else down the production chain should have been tampering with his music, which is good news indeed after all the little glitches and imbalances of the first batch of re-issues... The album, sounding thoroughly modern, certainly has classic Schulze stamped all over it, the epic tracks presented here having a rather grandiose, but ambient feel to them... Careful placing of these [sequencer pattern] building blocks providing us with over two and a half hours of thrilling music... which puts a foot equally into both ambient and upbeat territories... "Out of the Blue 2" (live) (32:20) seems like an inappropriate title for this piece as it's not remotely like anything from the original *In Blue* album set."

Jim Brenholts, *All Music Guide* at http://www.allmusic.com, writes: "[t]hat means that these three long-form compositions are full of sequences, dense atmospheres, and drawn-out synth washes."

My impressions of *In Blue*:

I'm reviewing the re-issue (3 disks).

The first CD is all one song named, "Into the Blue" (78:25). It has five subtitles, which all have track markers. I'll refer to the subtitle names as I review CD 1, *Into the Blue.*

The first subtitle is 'Into the Blue' (15:24, the title subtitle, if you will). It starts with windy sounds and a bit of deep rumbling bass, along with slow pads. Some bluesy guitar-like synthesized notes play at around the 5:00 mark. Funny, I never made the connection between *In Blue* and the blues but there it is: plenty of understated blues guitar-like sounds over a period of several minutes. The lead synth takes on a somewhat plaintive sound close to ten minutes.

Choirs sound for the first time at over 12:00 with alternation between female sounding choir and male choir and a tenor voice mixed in at times. When the voices narrow down to the one tenor voice, a lot of feeling is added to 'Into the Blue.'

With the start of 'Blowin' the Blues Away' (the same title as a jazz song by Horace Silver from the 1960s) (20:05), "Into the Blue"'s second subtitle, the sound changes altogether, using energetic percussion which brings the music to life, far surpassing what has gone before. The song gathers a head of steam and boldly asserts itself with crystal clear percussion, harp-like sounds and bass laden sequencer-style synth.

The recording quality sounds very stunning in this section! The stereo separation is also pretty spectacular at this point. Occasionally, a synthesized "horn" sounds a note. Some other synthesized brass also comes and goes.

'Blowin' the Blues Away' is highlighted by the fantastic percussion and lilting tempo.

The brass sounds become much more a part of the song after 14:00. Synthesized brass soloing dominates for a period. I find myself drumming with my thumb, making myself more aware of the rhythm and, more significantly, the power of the song. I had never felt how much energy and even emotion these synthesized brass sounds brought to this song.

"Blue"'s third subtitle, 'Blue Moods' (4:29), sees the tempo slow radically. A powerful blast of strings enters the mix, reverberating and making a positive impact. Toward the end of this short track, there appear hints of an upturn in the tempo.

'Wild and Blue' (35:35), the fourth subtitle, begins with an explosion of sound, giving quick birth to a solid sounding sequencer and ushering new life into CD 1, "Into the Blue". Multiple sequencers play, but they move back and forth in the stereo spectrum so fluidly that it's hard to identify two single sequencer patterns.

The sounds are staggered as well, adding to the indistinguishable aspect of the individual sequencers. Bold and clear "strings" carve a smooth, yet impactful swath through the mix. They sound vibrant, as if a whole string section in an orchestra were coming together at once.

A startlingly good sounding sequencer enters at a brisk pace, complementing the multiple sequenced sounds already present.

At close to the 10:00 mark, 'Wild and Blue' acquires a riveting intensity. The tension in the music makes it seem that there is still something being held back. Breathy sounding brass enters, absolutely dominating the sound spectrum in huge bursts and resonating dramatically.

Klaus' penchant for creating musical tension was never more apparent than in 'Wild and Blue.' There has been a constant tension, hinting at the possibility of 'Wild and Blue' cutting completely loose and reaching a musical climax! The emergence of very fast, higher pitched sequencers exacerbates the building tension.

At close to 16:00, a huge sonic blast takes place, and *Beyond Recall*-style "guitar" plucking takes center stage. This musical surge evokes the technique used in *En=Trance*, pointing to a dramatic change in the music. That change consists of the tempo slowing significantly, as Klaus employs another of his favorite compositional techniques in building the music up, backing it down and rebuilding it all over again.

The rebuilding isn't subtle but is launched into with a trademark KS sound blast and, voila, we have a fast paced track again, very quickly. A lively sequencer re-enters. I just love the sound of sequencers, and I never get tired of their entry into a Klaus Schulze song - especially since they take so many different forms in terms of the speed, shape and tonal quality of the sound. 'Wild and Blue' is replete with a dazzling array of scintillating sequencer sounds! I love it!

There is also something about the lovely colors of blue on the CD cover and the "Blue" names to the tracks that seems to add to the experience of the re-issued *In Blue*.

The fifth and final subtitle, 'Out of the Blue' (2:52), takes the tempo back down.

"Into the Blue" fades away, peacefully. It's a really nice listening experience!

CD 2 features two tracks: "Return of the Tempel," with Manuel Göttsching on guitar, and "Serenade in Blue." "Return" lasts over 44 minutes; "Serenade," over 34 minutes. Both have subtitled tracks.

First up is "Return of the Tempel" (44:38). I'll review it using the subtitle names.

'Midnight Blue' (9:46) starts in a fairly tame vein, sounding like a warm-up period for an orchestra. Light guitar playing features both Manuel's electric and acoustic guitar. The next few minutes see a rewarding development of that guitar playing. Manuel's guitar is clear and echoes about the soundcsape from left to right and back. An occasional "crowd cheering" sound interjects into the guitar work. As that "cheering" sound alternates with the multiple guitars, it seems to increase at times in intensity.

At the start of "Return of the Tempel"'s second subtitle, also named 'Return of the Tempel' (28:42), everything changes completely, with Klaus suddenly introducing an attractive sequencer as Manuel starts to play some impassioned, extended notes on guitar.

Three minutes into the piece, Klaus changes things up again, with more vibrant sequencers and a vivid "flute" taking over from Manuel's electrifying guitar work.

Manuel's guitar returns, combined with a steady beat past the 10:00 mark. This passage includes an extended period of Manuel playing in a relaxed style.

Klaus chimes in with synthesized brass that becomes pretty forceful at times. The mix is quite active with myriad sounds accompanying the brisk beat during this middle period of 'Return of the Tempel.'

At 14:00, very brisk and delightful sequencers enter the mix, playing with speed and stimulating chord changes that no human hands could generate. Here, we're treated to an extended period of sequencer "heaven"!

As the sequencers forge majestically onward, Manuel's guitars join, playing with intensity not yet heard up to this point. There is a hint of a psychedelic feel to Manuel's guitar playing. As it continues, it becomes no-holds-barred, with searing intensity. All the while Klaus' beat and sequencers keep up a fast pace that supports Manuel's riveting guitar onslaught.

A shift leaves just the sequencers playing – a treat, followed by reintroduction of the guitars, but in the former mellow mode. The sequencers play on in a very authoritative, bold passage. There is no doubt that "Return of the Tempel" is the musical peak in this second of three CDs of *In Blue*. It's a pretty spectacular piece of music!

"Return of the Tempel"'s third subtitle, 'Blue Spirits' (4:30), starts in a mellow way with restrained acoustic guitar, electric guitar and slow synth pads mixed with occasional "synth as cello". It's a nice song.

The final subtitle, 'True Blue' (1:40), starts with surging synthesizers that sound somewhat like sirens. It ends with pulsating percussive sounds.

This ends "Return of the Tempel".

"Serenade in Blue" is the second major piece of music on CD 2, with four subtitles.

"Serenade in Blue"'s first subtitle, 'Aubade' (6:16), starts gently, with slow synth pads, minimalist guitar, and choir. More activity gradually enters, in the form of quite dramatic percussive sounds. Crystal clear reverberating acoustic guitar adds to the percussion, as the combined highlight of the track.

The second subtitle, 'Kind of Blue' (the same title as the classic jazz song and album by Miles Davis) (18:06), immediately ramps up the pace with bouncy sequencer and lively flute. Striking percussion and astoundingly clear acoustic guitar-like sounds surround the flute for a while.

'Kind of Blue' returns quickly to a very slowly developing pace that seems like it will intensify. The tempo has been restrained for about 30 minutes, reminiscent of "Return of the Tempel."

A classic Schulze sound burst starts "Serenade in Blue"'s third subtitle, 'Blue Hour' (4:01), followed by quickening percussive sounds. The ubiquitous choir surges are still present. There is a distinct sense of an increasing energy level.

The final subtitle, 'Serenade' (5:56), features a heavy dose of the very nice percussion that has been the highlight of "Serenade in Blue."

There is a lot of good music on *In Blue*. That said, it feels like there is something missing. It just doesn't make the same impact on me as the top drawer Schulze albums. It's a pretty good album with some scintillating sections. It may be that the lethargic pacing of "Serenade in Blue" and the non-impact of the bonus CD have kept me from appreciating it as much as I could.

My other theory is that I have high expectations of *In Blue* based on all the consistently high praise it's received from others. The re-release was my first copy of *In Blue*.

The bonus CD has three tracks, the first named "Musique Abstract (Live)." The track starts out with applause and Klaus speaking to the crowd. The music starts with *Dark Side of the Moog*-like human voices behind sparse instrumentation. A nice sequencer plays, but it's obscured by drums, voices and many other sounds, so it doesn't carry the same weight as a normal KS sequencer.

The second bonus track, "Return of the Tempel 2 (Live)" (13:51), starts with decidedly pleasurable sounding, moving, minor key synth that stretches into a near drone at times. Wah-wah guitar playing is joined by choirs. For the second track in a row, I'm reminded of the *Dark Side of the Moog* series, although this song is much more reminiscent of *DSOTM* than "Musique Abstract (Live)".

The beginnings of an attractive yet very unusual sounding sequencer pattern emerge; the rhythm gradually picks up and morphs into a delightful sequencer/rhythm pattern. This sequencer grows appealingly as the song pushes toward its too-short running time of 13:51. The song has just reached a very nice groove which would sound good for a much longer period – but poof, it ends.

"Out of the Blue (Live)" is the third and final bonus track on the expanded re-release of *In Blue*. It sounds like a live version of material from *Audentity* (very good music), which sounds a little out of place on *In Blue*.

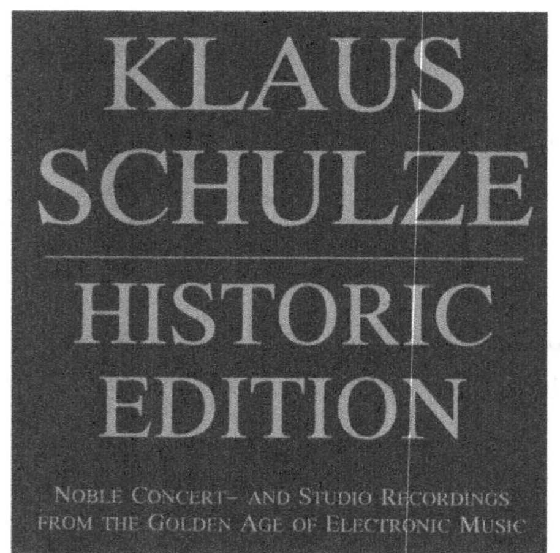

1995 *Historic Edition*

Historic Edition contains previously unreleased works from Klaus' golden period, the 1970s. The concert listing in Appendix B notes that several concert performances from the 1970s through 1981 are included. There is some soundtrack material, "Havlandet," from 1985. The *Historic Edition* was a limited edition of 2000 copies, which has long since been sold out.

Approximately half of the material is gleaned from concerts.

See Appendix A (Concerts) and Appendix B (Soundtracks) to determine the source events for much of the material on *Historic Edition*.

1995 *The Dark Side of the Moog 3* (with Pete Namlook)

From David Law at http://www.synthmusicdirect.com:

"Metallic drones shimmer through the ether. Things become spookier and spookier as we continue on our cosmic trip. Strange sounds can be heard, like lost souls floating through space, occasionally their strange utterances being almost recognizable. The pads deepen and things become increasingly sinister, like some of the more eerie parts off TD's *Atem* or *Zeit*. It's fantastically atmospheric stuff... Little cosmic bleeps and effects are looped to form quite a syncopated yet strangely melodic pulsating brew. It's all fiendishly complicated and there is some excellent stereo separation so it is brilliant listened to with earphones... Immediately an impressive deep sequence comes in and fairly storms along. A bass rhythm is added and things become even more exciting! A lovely very tuneful lead line joins it and I found myself playing air keyboard and tapping my feet like a crazy thing. Absolutely fantastic!"

From Brannan Lane at http://www.allmusic.com:

"It is outside the norm for Schulze and Namlook in that the sequences are low key. This is dark, atmospheric minimalism at its best. The entire series is essential."

1996 *Are You Sequenced?*

From B22 at http://www.synthmusicdirect.com:

"Ah, who said analogue was dead? Schulze himself I think, but here he gives that classic analogue sound a bit of a makeover mixing the old and the new pretty much to perfection. He conforms to his usual standards with a fair tonnage of sequencing and drifting strings."..... "Disc one is an album that sees Schulze in blistering form with a heavily sequenced set. Its tracks are all crossfaded into one another with some precision to produce one long 80-minute piece of audio that does most everything that one may ever expect from Schulze... So to [sum it] up – the *Are You Sequenced?* live set CD is an absolute stunner... As for the Disc 2 recording... In all fairness I didn't find it to be the easiest of listens due in no small part to the many repeated sections and lack of any meaningful structure, though for the better part of it's duration I found it strangely engaging."

From http://www.discogs.com/release/73318:

"Schulze fanatics seem to believe that this was a successful attempt by Klaus to make a 'techno' or 'trance' influenced record; on his website's 'beginner's guide to Klaus Schulze,' this album is described as 'a groovy modern style bestseller,' and it's frequently mentioned as the CD that could get the generation brought up with the electronic dance music of the '90s into his stuff. This, unfortunately, reflects the '70s e-music generation's poor grasp of techno and electronic dance music."

My impressions of *Are You Sequenced?*:

As Klaus says in the re-release booklet, the title is a reference to the Hendrix album "Are You Experienced". It's now a two-CD set with the 2nd CD different from the former release's 2nd CD, which involved remixes by the dance music group Snap! ("Rhythm is a Dancer").

Are You Sequenced? starts with a variety of noises and then slides into a very bright sounding sequencer pattern playing with great clarity. Warm synth pads join in. Even though there are eleven tracks listed on the back cover, the CD is one long piece.

The beat first comes in at the 2nd track marker; it's another four-on-the-floor beat which also ushers in some additional synth mini-explosions. Some of the pads take on an increasingly passionate sound, as does the bouncy, splashy sequencer pattern.

The sound stays basically the same for several minutes, with the beat thumping reliably behind the fluty, brass synth sound.

I had thought of this CD as laid back in pace before this listening, but now it seems quite intense and the steady beat, with its repetition, is a consistent pleasure.

Reverberating synth explosions take place, and the whole track intensifies even more. The sequencer pattern has evolved to a brisk pace that complements the beat very well. *Are You Sequenced?* begs to be cranked up, and that's exactly what I did (with headphones so my wife can hear the TV!). This is a great groove!

The four-on-the-floor drops out, and the sequencer handles beat responsibilities for a while. Soaring synth pads, sounding almost like an orchestra string section are very powerful, touching my emotions. The string pad washes are exotic and celestial.

Lots of phaser-like synth sounds are shot into the mix, adding to the intensity, which is at a "throw caution to the wind" level by now. It appears we're hearing a Minimoog solo, which grows intense; twisting, turning and churning through the soundscape and cutting it to shreds! The track is called "Moogie Baby Goes Solo."

"Moogie Baby" yields to minor key synth pads, sounding like a cellist. The playing is very moving over the first four minutes or so.

Out of this temporarily moving symphony arises a discordant mix of sounds, obviously building toward a forward moving pace again. What's happening along the way is fascinating, though, because it is such a hodgepodge.

Another astonishing album by Klaus Schulze! He is a master innovator, composer and player – a creative musician like no other. It's obvious that Klaus' music rewards repeated and careful, attentive listenings. There is usually a deep reservoir of musical pleasure to tap into although one might not experience a lot of it in the first few listens. *Are You Sequenced?* – magnificent!

The bonus disk is reviewed in *The Jubilee Edition* (just after CD 5), as it is actually a part of a three-CD *Trance Opera* in its original conception.

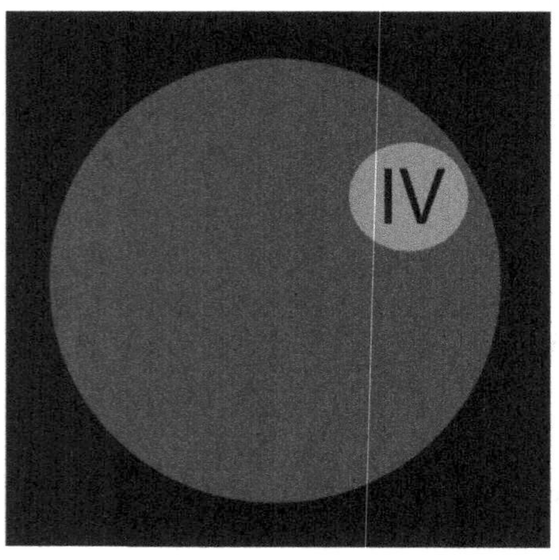

1996 *The Dark Side of the Moog 4* (with Pete Namlook and Bill Laswell)

From David Law at http://www.synthmusicdirect.com/moog4aw.cfm:

"The first part consists of dark orchestral sounding atmospherics with throbbing out-of-this-world bass pulses...The second part makes use of a fast sequence with the pulses coming more often... Track 7 consists of a big deep reverberating gong, which is added to in Track 8 by a heavy dance beat."

From Jim Brenholts at http://www.allmusic.com:

"Schulze, Namlook, and Laswell are e-music legends and it is always exciting when they collaborate. This disc is no exception."

Here's a short review from Matt Howarth (CD on Fax Records in Germany):

"Here's the peak, an outburst of dynamic creativity and top notch electronics. There are a few ambient passages, but the music is mainly on the hyper-tempo side in the style of Schulze's work from the early 1980s.

This time - surprise! - Bill Laswell is added to the collaboration with wondrous results. The pieces with his presence fairly leap from the CD and dance about with electronic frenzy."

(© Matt Howarth, reprinted from www.soniccuriosity.com with permission.)

My review of *The Dark Side of the Moog 4*:

This was my test CD when I went out shopping for speakers. I had actually bought a pair of nice speakers and a subwoofer, and everything sounded great. It wasn't until I played *The Dark Side of the Moog 4* that my new speakers showed any weakness. In the deep bass-filled parts of this CD, with the volume up quite a bit, those speakers started to crumble and vibrate badly. So I went in search of speakers that could stand up to the more intense parts of this CD. Many a demo room simply shook and rattled from multiple areas as speakers were tested with this CD!

As I was testing some big standing speakers in an audio room, I played a passage that has a very slow, deep, droning, bass filled sound similar to a throaty human voice (Track 3 of *DSOTM 4*). I was up by the speakers, listening for any rattling. A younger guy, who worked at the store, came in and asked me what I was doing. I told him I was listening to this passage of music on this CD to see how the speakers handle it and his reply to me was, "that's music?" Needless to say, I was a little agitated at that remark. But...some people just don't get it.

The Dark Side of the Moog 4 has one title, "Three Pipers at the Gates of Dawn," that is subdivided into nine parts.

Bill Laswell appears on Parts 1-3, 5 and 8 along with Pete Namlook and Klaus Schulze.

The CD starts with very moderately long synth pads, higher register string pads and percussion, combined with booming drums. The initial pace is very slow, showing off a lot of sounds, some echoing. A human voice sample is remindful of music by The Orb. The strings have a somewhat eerie sound.

As the second part starts, a rapid sequencer rhythm enters, surrounded by various synth sounds, sampled voices, and percussive elements. The recording quality is exceptional! The energy level is quickened but still somewhat reserved. The Moog mimics guitar in the background, boosting the energy level.

Part 2 takes on a little more of a trance feel, with a quickened beat (possibly) synthesized drums. There are various expressions of the Moog Synthesizer, adding to the track with their stunning sonic clarity and unusual character. This track reminds me a little of *Are You Sequenced?* with its relentless beat.

Part 2 claims over one third of the total running time of the CD. After the 17:00 mark, it shifts to simultaneous multiple sequencer patterns sounding amazingly good, followed by some powerful Moog synth sounds pounding the speakers. The driving rhythm is off to the races, faster than ever. The Moog synth sounds in this section are fun to listen to and have a powerful force and clarity.

Part 3 starts with muffled human voices and a few synth sounds that sound like the beginning phrases of *Irrlicht*. Here is where a really deep bass sound starts to develop. It sounds like a deep groaning voice but just oozes bass. Human voices in the background are a little more distinguishable. The groan turns at times almost into a singing voice but not quite.

Part 4 takes over with an eerie, solemn sounding, very slowly floating synth sound. The sound evolves to a place of greater warmth in a higher register. Gently drifting sounds arrive and Part 4 is over.

Part 5 takes off with a bold sequencer pattern and banging noises in the background. The sequencer line is very, very clear and resplendent in its stereo separation. A pounding, four-on-the-floor, trance-type beat comes in, followed by drums. The highlight is still the snappy, bright sounding Moog synth sounds that are racing along with the rest of the track.

Part 6 starts with the sound of guitar, with each plucked string echoing. It sounds almost like a Hawaiian guitar. Swirling thin synth sounds occupy the background. The guitar playing has a yearning and hauntingly beautiful quality to it. This is a very sparse, yet gorgeous section of *DSOTM 4*.

Part 7 will put your speakers to the ultimate test with slow, reverberating gong sounds that resonate for several seconds and have a deeper and deeper bass quality with each sounding of the gong. This will shake the walls, bookshelves or ceiling panels of the music store or your home, if you turn up the volume and use a subwoofer.

Part 8 sees the tempo go up and then stop for some sparkling effects. Rapid fire percussion sounds that are again brilliantly recorded take center stage for a while, backed by Klaus' Minimoog masquerading as guitar. The track ends with more marvelous sounding percussion, which sounds like tom-toms played at inhuman speed; this is just plain fun to listen to!

Part 9 starts out like a Moog sound demo disk. It then picks up the theme of Part 8 with some great crisp percussion; the gong from Part 7 sounds one more time, and the CD ends.

The Dark Side of the Moog 4 is a very good to excellent CD. A wide variety of sonic textures are involved, and the whole feels like a major success!

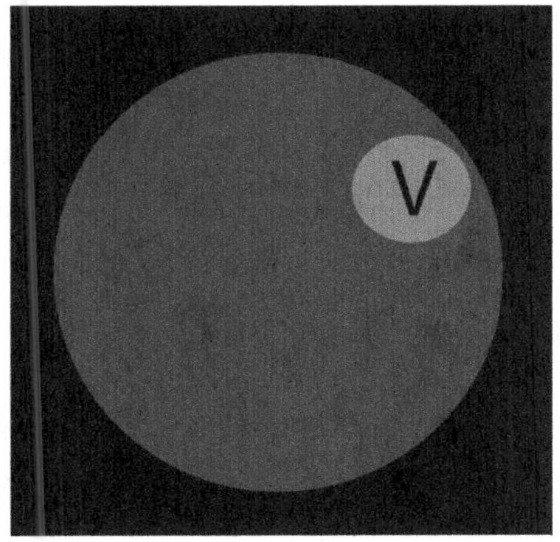

1996 *The Dark Side of the Moog 5* (with Pete Namlook and Bill Laswell)

From a review by Jim Brenholts, *All Music Guide* at http://www.artistdirect.com/nad/store/artist/album/0,,252957,00.html

"One of the coolest things on this disc is a 14-second intro by Robert Moog himself... [T]his CD features the sequences, atmospheres, and ambience associated with this trio. The soundscape elements flow seamlessly within the intricate sound design. Namlook, Schulze, and Laswell are always at the top of their game."

The following is adapted from David Law' original review at http://www.synthmusicdirect.com/moog5aw.cfm:

"The album is introduced by none other than Bob Moog himself, before rich textures emerge to occupy the first five minutes. Part 3 is a pulsating piece...And lastly, but by no means leastly, we are treated to part 8 - and 'treated' is the key word. This is a completely brilliant piece with oscillating sequences twisting around a deep bass rhythm. Mellotron voices are added to the mix to really put the finishing touches to a masterpiece."

From http://www.ambientmusicguide.com/pages/S/schulze.php:

"*Dark Side Of The Moog V* finds the pair at their most mystical and trippy and boasts some exquisite passages of ambient trance."

A review by Matt Howarth (CD on Fax Records in Germany):

"This time the ongoing collaboration between these two electronic musicians results in 60 minutes of cohesive instrumental tunes (seven of them, with an eighth track being a spoken word intro by Robert Moog giving his e-mail address and welcoming the listener to this *Dark Side* outing). Rich sequencing and pinnacle drones... the pieces range from ambient (not unlike Namlook's solo work) to dynamic (with remarkably strong Schulze influences). The CD's final piece bears a surprising distinct similarity to the sound of Delerium (aka Bill Leeb and Rhys Fulber, aka Front Line Assembly).

"Add Bill Laswell to two tracks and you get a solid and highly recommended dose of superb electronic music."

My review of *Dark Side of the Moog 5*:

This CD is notable for the spoken introduction by Dr. Moog. It makes for a pretty exciting start to have his dramatic words preceding the sounds of his instrument in a proud and bold musical intro.

After Dr. Moog, multiple Moog sounds are heard, a typical winding and twisting, "thinner" sound and a supporting, smoother synth pad. The music sounds "spacy" at the beginning. It brings to mind interplanetary space travel in somewhat the same way the completely different sounds of Hawkwind do. The first two parts are over fairly quickly.

The music shifts to pulsating sequencer sounds that echo about as Part 3 of the eight-part CD begins. Drums enter and then pause, leaving the synths to strut their stuff. The drums return to form a heavy beat above the quivering, resonating synths. Bill Laswell appears on this track.

Chiming bells suddenly take over the soundscape, sounding very nice. More-restrained drums enter, along with a few phaser shots from the synth. Emphasis shifts to a crashing bass beat which isn't really the best, in my opinion. However, the synths that have been forming the backbone for a while sound better when the drumming stops. Frankly, that's one section of drumming that I didn't like much.

Part 4 starts with smooth, shimmering synth pads that have a haunting, yet lovely sound. The synths emote, unabated, during the nearly 4-minute course of Part 4. This is a truly beautiful section of music.

Part 5 starts with bass synth, combined with the sound of "rattlesnakes." The rhythm is slow and plodding. Sounds of shaking, reverberating percussion echo about. Higher, bell-like sounds enter the mix at about 2:00, followed by intermittent deep resonating bass pulses that sound very good. In the background, slowly evolving, higher pitched yet slightly dark sounding synths contribute to the mood of this part. Part 5 has an almost relaxing quality to it.

The song meanders along for over 13 minutes and is kept interesting by the synth sounds in the background, a sort of Moog synthesized form of "Frippertronics." The ending is subtle, very spacy, and extends longer than I thought it would. It's another very creative and satisfying musical idea.

Part 6 starts with pulsating pads, phaser like synth shots and drumming. There are mysterious voices in the background, then even more authoritative drumming. The mixture of sound elements is attractive, including spacier Moog effects and pads in the second half of the song.

Part 7 begins with a cosmic sounding drone that alternates between a lower tonal character and a higher one which seems to emerge and reverberate from the lower synth. This droning section is very deep space music – a very fine passage. This is dreamy, hypnotic and ethereal "space drone" at its best.

Part 8 starts out with bouncy, lively yet spacy sounding synths that echo about, joined by an evolving sequencer line and then impacted greatly by a bold bass line. The Moog synthesizer shows off a multitude of creative capabilities combined with emotionally rewarding changes in the music.

With lots of sequencing and rhythm, this is an exciting musical idea, executed superbly. When it seems it can't get much better, it does. Some fantastic sounding choirs enter the mix for another audio thrill! The choirs yield to some sharply textured synth, well recorded and used boldly in the stereo spectrum. Drumming re-enters, followed by re-entry of the choirs, and the synth "jabs" continue in the background. Part 8 ends in a slowly bending drone.

Part 8 is everything an electronic music fan could want; the same can be said for the whole *DSOTM 5* CD. The five *DSOTM* CDs that I own (4-7, 9), are very consistent in their quality level, which is very high.

Klaus Schulze Rebuilds His Studio

KDM: "In 1996, Klaus Schulze rebuilt completely his studio, incorporating new digital technologies but still keeping part of his analog keyboards, including the Alesis Andromeda 6 voice synthesizer, two EMS Synthi A synths, the Memory Moog and two Minimoogs."

1996 *Trance Appeal* (Wahnfried)

From Jim Brenholts, *All Music Guide*, at http://www.allmusic.com:

"*Trance Appeal* is the best Richard Wahnfried album. Collaborating with Joerg Schaaf, Klaus Schulze has crafted a far-reaching space music CD...[T]he result is, well, a trance symphony. From the composer of the world's only e-music opera, that makes sense. The 11 'movements' are held together by the dark atmospheres."

My review of *Trance Appeal*:

Derek Sheplawy of SPV North America was kind enough to send me the re-release, as I already owned the original.

KS talks about *Trance Appeal* and *Are You Sequenced?* being more techno-related in the re-release booklet and also mentions that the reason the tracks are short for Schulze tracks is because Joerg Schaaf likes to get to the point quicker. Since Wahnfried is a democratic project with equal say for all the musicians, Klaus didn't force the longer intros (my paraphrase of what is in the re-release booklet). I found the re-release interview that Klaus gave in early 2007 to be quite entertaining. He says some funny things that had me laughing out loud. I also find the aesthetics of the CD cover and booklet artwork quite appealing. The recording quality of the CD is excellent.

On to the music!

The first track, "Suspense," starts with wind sounds, then some starkly appealing synth in magnificent sound and stereo separation. The sounds are thin and short as well as quick. Synth pads drift in joined by a siren-like sound. One thing I can say about this CD is that Klaus and Joerg use a wide array of sounds, many unusual, and they seem to have a lot of fun with it!

Track 2, "Bizarre" has some strange vocal sounds entering and leaving the mix quickly. At some points it sounds like some of the sounds I've heard in *The Dark Side of the Moog* series. Female choir comes in and out. No sounds continue for very long in this track. Its just a whole series of odd sounds entering and leaving quickly, backed the whole time by Klaus' slow synth pads.

Track 3 is "Rubbish." By the way, there is no space between the tracks, but they are not cross-faded. A strange voice, sequencer patterns, phaser shots and bell-like synth sounds all take turns in the mix.

"Angel Heart" is next, starting with thumping like a heartbeat. Various quick synth jabs combine with hazy synth pads that become more musical and with a backing beat to form a very lovely sound. Then, of course, in true Schulze fashion, the song shifts completely to sequencer. There are layers of sequenced sounds which sound quite good. This is the best track (and the longest) on the album so far.

"So What?" (another Miles Davis song title!) starts with hard, quick synth pulses, heavy bass and drumming. There is a building of the song that one might hear in the dance club as the music climbs to prime time levels. The pace is quick and the sounds are unusual. Choir sounds enter at just past 2:00. This track, while short, is pretty compelling and entertaining.

"Towarisch" starts in a *DSOTM* style. Synth sounds hinting at human voices enter the mix more than once, sounding different each time. Glossy, bright, short and repeated synth sounds in glorious stereo play for a bit and then soaring synth pads yield to some spectacular choirs, some of the best I've heard in Klaus Schulze's music.

"Das Mädchen mag es" is next and once again begins startlingly like a *Dark Side of the Moog* CD. In fact, these sounds are strikingly similar to sounds used on a *Dark Side of the Moog* CD I own. I'm leaning toward saying this is the same song – perhaps re-done in a slightly different way?

"A Chilly Fiesta" is up next, emphasizing non-drum percussion and *In Blue*-style synth playing, along with occasional bass notes. The song pace and style match the title. In this song cowbell-like sounds are the percussive centerpiece.

"Esprit sans fronti res" starts with rapid middle- to high-pitched sequencer and bass, progressing to a much more emphatic sequencer line fattened up by another sequencer pattern and backed by a beat that is almost a four-on-the-floor trance beat. In this track, as throughout *Trance Appeal*, the synth pads occasionally rise into a sound that sounds starkly like *DSOTM*. This track is sequencer heaven, as several different sequenced patterns take turns at establishing a temporary groove. "Esprit" is a very good offering, full of changes and great sounds that somehow all come together to provide a creative and very gratifying listening experience.

"Psychedelic Clubbing" starts with a potpourri of sounds as if the musicians are getting paid by the number of unique sounds they include in the mix! This is a wild one with rapid fire sequenced sounds, a quick backbeat, and then the familiar synth pads that have permeated *Trance Appeal*. A voice chants "do do do do"; it may be computer generated. The voice changes pitch from high to low to lower and then high again. A female choir sound enters at about 5:00. Synth pads dominate for a few minutes, giving a rest from the intensity, the aural assault.

"Le Sleep des Animaux" is the last track from the original CD. Percussive sounds in exaggerated stereo start off, yielding to some choir-like pads and percussion-like synth hits, again in full stereo.

The bonus track is "Marooned" from the tapes that didn't make it onto *Contemporary Works II*. It starts with what sounds like a demo for a hot new synthesizer. There is a synth sound that sounds like crackling, a fascinating sound which I have never heard from a synthesizer before. At one point it sounds like the grand finale of a fireworks display. This outburst evolves into a sound like an accelerating motorcycle, then tornado siren or air raid siren-like synth sounds emerge and drift across the soundscape in a grandiose way. This piece is insanely creative. And it was consigned to the reject pile and never released! It's mind blowing!

Only incredibly talented and creative musicians could possibly have conceived of and executed this piece of music. This bonus track is inspired and inspiring. There are some twittering sounds and more sharply rising and falling synth sounds (reminiscent of some sounds made by Keith Emerson in Emerson, Lake and Palmer's music) along with very dramatic middle- to low-pitch pads.

Sweeping, very moving synths enter towards the end, causing a swelling feeling of partial chills and emotion sweeping through my body in a wave, resulting in a trace of tears.

I wonder how much other really great music Klaus has created that is unreleased – I'll bet a lot. You need to read his comments in the booklet to see how he might alleviate that situation!

Wow! What a CD! I'm almost at a loss for words after reviewing *the Crime of Suspense, Vanity of Sounds* and *Trance Appeal* all in one day. What an experience! I feel the rush of the greatness of all this music even as I type and again a swelling of emotion resulting in moist eyes. I'm truly moved to tears.

Joerg Schaaf Interview with Greg Allen

GA: Did your interest in synthesizers start with programming or playing or perhaps from listening to synthesizer music?

JS: Until 1975 I had no relation to electronic music at all - all that I listened to was music from my parents. I was about 12 or 13 years old when I listened at the door of my sister who played a tape with the Pink Floyd *Wish You Were Here* album. That had a big impact on me and from that day, enjoying the music of my parents was not possible anymore!

I also realized that there are electronic instruments out there producing sounds that I had never heard before, and I spent hours in record shops searching for synthesizer based music. My first record ever was the Pink Floyd *Animals* album. I can't recall how often I played that record, but I am still enjoying that masterwork today.

However, after buying a couple of Pink Floyd albums over the months (the money I had to spend for records was very limited), I found a bunch of Tangerine Dream records in a record store. That was the time where every single instrument they were using was listed in the back cover of the record. That blew me away instantly. My first TD record was *Stratosphere. Stratosphere* came with that Moogish staccato sequencing sound; that formed my personal sound taste a lot.

Synthesizers were too expensive for pupils like me. So I started some electronic experiments and built up simple oscillators and filters and made some sound experiments. My biggest wish was getting at least one of these instruments. But that was a dream for years, and the first synth I was able to buy was this little MS-20 from Korg. That was better than nothing but it was not possible to realize the sounds I was looking for.

Beside typical electronic music I listened to all this progressive stuff. I enjoyed Manfred Mann's *Nightingale and Bombers* album for his Moog Solos, Genesis, Yes, Saga, etc. and I formed my first band with other freaks. We played a kind of "progressive rock for the poor man" because our playing skills were very limited. I had a Crumar Multiman String Synthesizer, an MS-20, a badstone phaser and a WEM copycat that I borrowed from another band.

That was a funny time, but the day came, where the band was split. I first searched for other musicians but realized shortly later that I want to do my own stuff independent from other musicians, who mostly came into the practicing room to make some jam sessions.

In the beginning I used multiple tape recorders to create my noisy ambient-like music. The recording quality of this music was already fascinating, but a dramatic step forward was the appearance of the C64 computer and the C-Lab sequencing software. That was the starting point of everything. For the first time it was possible to record some music with superb sound quality.

I used to work in a music shop and managed the synthesizer department. I had the opportunity to use all the stuff I was selling there: Synthesizers, FX-Boxes, DAT recorders. I was sitting in a wonderland the whole day. And when no customer was in the shop, I produced my music. My practicing room was the synthesizer department. I lived directly above this shop, on the second floor and stayed there very often, even in my spare time.

GA: When were you first aware of Klaus Schulze and his music?

JS: In 1978/79 a Klaus Schulze song reached the top twenty in a Frankfurt radio station, HR3. They played "Georg Trakl" from the *X* album. That was a very relaxed mood and this earthshaking bass sequence attracted my ears and my body. My next record was the *X* album from Klaus. Klaus produced a completely different sound than Tangerine Dream. All these orchestra loops and the real drum playing gave this album a completely other atmosphere.

My interests in strange sounds like the EMS self-resonating filter drones, the pitch-shifted feedback delay sounds (directly at the beginning of the album) in combination with the mellotron choirs was for me the real out[er] space sound.

Beside that, the Klaus Schulze sound has this kind of urban character - it was sounding different from contemporary music but not completely electronic. It had much more emotions and never even touched pop music. So, Kraftwerk invented electronic Pop Music, Klaus Schulze invented Ambient Music, and TD did something between both extremes.

GA: How did you meet Klaus for the first time? How did it happen that you came to collaborate with him?

JS: After my music shop job I was hired by Quasimidi. As the product manager I visited Klaus Schulze in 1994 for the first time. He heard the Quasimidi Quasar synthesizer and was interested in this instrument. I came to his studio showing him some secrets of the machines and we had a good time. After presenting him some of my demos he invited me to use his studio for a night. Because of my work in the shop it was easy for me to manage all that gear he was using there and I presented him with my studio production the next day. Well - he was very impressed especially by a flutish Shakuhashi solo I played on one of his EMU samplers. He asked me to do a Wahnfried album together with him. Wow! What a chance!

GA: Was your performance on the Wahnfried album, *Trance Appeal*, your first released recording where you played synthesizer?

JS: I only made some demo CD's for music synthesizers for Quasimidi and produced my own music just on my personal DAT tapes but the Wahnfried *Trance Appeal* was my first real music production.

GA: What form did your computer programming take on *Trance Appeal* and how did it influence the sound? One thing I noticed about the album is that it seemed that you both were having fun with a wide variety of bold and unusual sounds. That seemed to give the album a unique identity. Is there anything else you can mention about the creation of some of these interesting sounds?

JS: We are always having fun with unusual sounds. We can spend hours just with an EMS synth, inserting some of the pins and listening to the forever evolving sound it creates.

For *Trance Appeal* both of us made pre-production demos in advance. I spent some extra nights in his studio as well, to create the basic structure of songs and sounds, and we produced the stuff based on these ideas later together.

The first track of the album was nearly completely produced with my MS-20. I made tons of samples of my little synth. For me it was a big thank you to an instrument I never loved but which made all other things possible. It was my starting point in creating electronic music. So I made all these MS-20 samples and recorded a demo on the Atari Notator software. I loved the groove quantize function of the Notator software.

So my electronic beebs and drones started to groove. Some people reported that they first thought their CD player was broken when the first track started. This high bleeb sound of the MS-20 jumped between the speakers but reminded a little bit of a CD player error sound that usually becomes audible, when the laser is scanning crazily back and forward on the CD.

In contrast I put [in] this very deep sounding bass drum. I always love to mix extremes in my arrangements. This very high bleep sound together with this booming bass drum, and then this special FX sound from the MS-20 was controlled by a step sequencer with the activated glide function. From the beginning I planned this track as an opening scene of the album.

Nearly the whole album has a very dark atmosphere and always changes the musical direction - sometimes from one bar to another. For that reason it is not a typical Klaus Schulze work. Wahnfried for Klaus always was a project, where different musicians are creating something new beside the Klaus Schulze solo work. Each musician has to bring in his own ideas and depending on who is appearing on an album, the music can be very different.

GA: How did you and Klaus come up with the compositions for *Trance Appeal*?

JS: We both more or less composed them independently from each other and brought them together in Klaus' studio. Only one track – "Towarisch" – has been completely composed and produced together. "Suspense", "Rubbish", "Angel Heart", "So What" and "Le sleep des Animaux" was my part, and "Bizarre", "A Chilly Fiesta", "Esperit sans fronti res" and "Psychedelic Clubbing" was Klaus' part.

GA: When you were invited to accompany Klaus to the Duisburg concert, did you know ahead of time that you would be performing or was the plan more to have you there to offer support with programming and your knowledge of the instruments (due to being a programmer at Quasimidi who built the modular system for Klaus)?

JS: It was from the beginning planned as a concert with both of us. The concert was much longer than the CD *Dosburg Online*. Before the "Art of Sequencing" started, we did a lot of atmospheric ambient stuff with our synths that did not come onto the CD. I was not on stage from the early beginning - I just came up with the atmospheric intro of the "Art of Sequencing". I programmed the grooves and sequences on the Quasimidi gear for the "Art of Sequencing," but in general, nothing was exactly planned in that concert.

The big QM rack system was introduced for the first time for this concert, and we had only a couple of hours between finishing the setup and delivering it to the stage. If I remember correctly, we only practiced about half an hour with the system after I finished the sequences and before it was shipped to Duisburg.

GA: How much playing did you actually do during that concert (which became *Dosburg Online*)? Do you have any other memories about that concert?

JS: Sure, I have a lot of memories about that concert. For me, it was a completely new experience to play for such a big crowd of people. Because the whole concert was more improvised, I always kept an eye on Klaus' fingers and I mostly had to react to what he was doing.

Sometimes I confused him a little bit, by triggering atmospheric SFX (special effects) sounds on my sampler, at the same time he was playing and tweaking his EMS. In this situation all the different sounds are just streaming through the speakers and no one can say which noise was caused by whom. The mélange of everything is what makes these sound escapades very surprising, not only for the audience but also for the two players. That is really fun.

GA: "Schruer Der Vorwelt" (from *Ballett 3*) is mentioned as an outtake from *Contemporary Works II*, although you're not listed in the credits for *Contemporary Works II*. In what context was that piece recorded?

JS: Hmm - Greg - I am sorry to say that I have no bloody idea. I do not even know that title!

GA: How did the name "Subsonic Affair" come about on the track you recorded for *A Tribute to Klaus Schulze*? Is there anything you can mention about how you were invited to play on the tribute album or about the track itself?

JS: I know Mario Schönwälder because he did the catering at our radio station concert just two days after the *Dosburg Online* concert. By the way, that radio concert was much longer than *Dosburg Online*. We played there for three hours or so.

I can't remember exactly who asked me for the track, Klaus or Mario but I was proud to produce one track for this album. I had not much time doing the track - if I remember correctly I just recorded the track in one late afternoon. I made my special version of "Georg Trakl" because it was the first track I ever heard from Klaus Schulze.

GA: What can you tell me about the *Keys Magazine* Demo in 1996, "Dreieinhalb Stunden," which ended up on *Ultimate Edition* as Track 7 on CD 50?

JS: It was a funny production. The guy from the *Keys* magazine was sitting behind us, and we just did it. He was surprised that we just started the machines and instantly started recording some motifs and finished the whole track in about three and a half hours or so!

GA: It looks like the last released piece of music where you and Klaus played together was "Trance 4 Motion." Unfortunately, this is one of the four CDs from *Contemporary Works I* that I haven't heard. What can you tell me about how it was agreed that you would perform on it, the process you and KS used to create it, and how it came out?

JS: This track is also a long improvisation. I created some drum patterns and prepared some sounds, and then we just decided to start the recording with some sound textures. When we did it, I never thought that it would be published on a record. Unfortunately for me, Klaus added some vocal tracks on it, which I don't really like because for me they disturb the minimalist, evolving rhythm we made in the studio.

GA: Can you give an overall description of what it's like for you to work with Klaus?

JS: For me it is fun and a kind of relaxation from my work. When I visit Klaus, I am leaving my normal life behind me and dive into music and sounds. We both are music "night workers." So normal night and day rhythms are not equal to my normal living, either.

Elfi does a perfect catering job when I am there. I am usually waking up a little bit earlier than Klaus and start with a good breakfast. Then I normally step out for an hour or so and enjoy the countryside around the studio. We never start our work earlier than about 6:00 p.m.

Klaus says, the sun is too loud in the early afternoon. Before starting to record anything we enjoy some talking about everything - from Monty Python to Angela Merkel! We are doing that until we burn to tweak the knobs again.

We both know that not every day is the perfect day for a studio work. Sometimes you start all the machines and with the first sound you are triggering you instantly realize that nothing will sound good in your ears this day. Then it is better to keep talking and start the work one day later. No one forces us to finish something the other day. But when we started tweaking and playing nothing stops us. After a couple of days we are totally drifted in. Sometimes we are playing until the sun is becoming too loud again.

GA: This is a question that I've asked some others – what is it about Klaus Schulze that makes him such a special musician?

JS: Klaus is very good in creating a working atmosphere that just lets the creativity flow. There is no deadline or hurry. He sometimes sits just behind you for a couple of hours and lets you do what you want to do.

Sometimes he gives some tips, but he lets you do what you want to do. I think he made his selection of that musician before they come into his studio for a recording. As soon as he made a decision to work with someone, he is more interested in what this musician can bring into the music instead of wanting to form someone into another direction. He knows what he wants to get, but he also knows that he only will get it if he does not disturb the creative process.

Klaus' own music is a non-compromise thing. He is interested in a lot of other music, but he is not so much influenced by this music. He found his own style, and he works on developing this style further. His music often sounds very dramatic and hypnotic. Sometimes it sounds like it's from outer space and other times it sounds just like Klaus is talking through his instruments to the listener. This combination makes it very special, in my opinion.

GA: Have you kept in touch with Klaus since the year 2000?

JS: Sure. I was very busy during the last couple of years because of my synthesizer hardware project and Klaus had a lot of other trouble, but we are staying in contact. It was limited to some phone conversations for a couple of years, but we are planning to record a new Wahnfried album together. It will be the first Wahnfried production with my Spectralis Synthesizer. The Spectralis is the synthesizer for doing live electronics. It's like a modular synth plus a sampler plus a sequencer in one little box. I am quite sure that this unit will play a major role in the next Wahnfried album.

GA: I also came across *Another Strange Day in Gonxa* by the Dutch Multimedia Project, Wave World. It's mentioned that there is a Klaus Schulze remix of the track "Biosphere" from the Solipsist Paradise album *Aware* in 1996. It mentions Klaus as having played percussion and you contributing the bass line. What can you tell me about that project?

JS: That was a remix contest from Akai and the German magazine called *Keyboards*. The winner [got] one day at Klaus Schulze's studio, and Klaus asked me to attend in his studio for this production. It is funny that they are still mentioning this bass line. It was nothing special. Just a few notes I replaced the original bass line with. I also improvised some chords in the beginning of that track, if I remember correctly, but that has nothing in common with my personal music.

GA: What are your thoughts and memories about recording "Tradition and Vision" (I'm listening to it as I write these questions; it's very hypnotic and addicting!)?

JS: "Tradition and Vision" has been recorded for a radio special at Klaus' 50th birthday. It was played live in the studio but air streamed later from a radio station (if I remember correctly).

GA: Did you and Klaus plan the almost 24-minute slower paced period of interesting and experimental type sounds to be followed by a long hypnotic, compelling groove ahead of time, or did it just develop that way as you composed the song?

JS: It was an improvisation from the first to the last bar.

OK - as always when we record these kinds of improvisations, we are usually programming some rhythms and sequences to trigger them later in our improvisation.

On "Tradition and Vision" we had multiple sequences and rhythms running and muted them. We then started with the atmospheric SFX landscapes and chords and added more and more of the rhythmic tracks by un-muting them or fading them in. At the beginning they get faded in from time to time, and later they are becoming the main element. From time to time we played some rhythmic elements live on the keyboards to get more variations.

GA: Was "Tradition and Vision" done in basically one take or was it a longer process?

JS: We just started the DAT recorder and enjoyed our playing. We made no additional overdubs later, and we kept all mistakes in there. So it is a very authentic live session.

Near the end there is a chord theme Klaus or I played on the JD-800 synthesizer with a sequence from a polymorph in the background. The polymorph was not set up correctly so it did not receive the transposed keys from the second keyboard. At the third reprise it finally transposed correctly. That is one of the failures on that recording that shows that everything has been recorded in one go!

GA: If you had just a paragraph or two to describe Klaus Schulze, what would you say?

JS: In my opinion Klaus Schulze stands for passion and addiction. He is now almost 60 years old, but his heart for his very special own music still burns in the same way like back in the seventies, when everything began.

GA: Do you have any interesting stories about your time working with and knowing Klaus Schulze -- or anything else you'd like to add?

JS: When I was about 19 years old, Klaus gave a concert in my hometown and I visited that concert. I was very impressed by the big caravan that was standing behind the concert hall. I instantly thought - Wow, what a luxury. Later I heard from Klaus that it was a very sad time, and that there was not even enough money to rent a room in a hotel back at that time.

1997 *Dosburg Online*

From B22 at http://www.synthmusicdirect.com:

"It was never the easiest of albums to get your hands on first time around... It's certainly an album of highs, lows and inconsistencies that will frustrate some listeners and fascinate others... Roelof Oostwoud['s]... operatic voice adds an interesting deviation in the live set. The vocal performance is excellent... [T]he problem lies with poor lyrical content... decidedly coarse, juvenile and ill conceived, not much thought gone into it... With a sprinkling of musical masterpieces across the set, *Dosburg* simply has to be a highly recommended listen; it's Achilles heel being those two vocal efforts."

Here's Matt Howarth's review (CD on Eye of the Storm Records in Germany):

"Continuing to produce modern electronic music of the finest quality, Schulze delivers 79 minutes this time of snappy tempos and a tasty synthetic balance of drama and hypnotics. Joining Schulze this time is Joerg Schaaf, the pair producing sinuous E-perc, fluting keyboards and dreamy treble tonalities that cavort with a hybrid of swelling orchestral strings. Two songs feature the operatic in English vocals of Roelof Oostwoud. This CD's compositions are strong, and heavy with a new groove and sensational sequencing."

(© Matt Howarth, reprinted from www.soniccuriosity.com with permission.)

My thoughts on *Dosburg Online*:

This is an album that I missed the first time around; the re-release is my first exposure. I've had mixed feelings.

I like the first song, "L'age core," quite a bit with its "Crystal Lake"-style bell sounds, floating synth pads and synthesized flute. This flute has magnificent clarity and presence in the stereo spectrum. "L'age core" is a very striking start to *Dosburg Online*.

The second track "Requiem für's Revier" also impressed me a lot. This was my first exposure to Roelof Oostwoud and perhaps my first exposure to real operatic singing in Klaus' catalog. "Opera Trance" (from *Jubilee Edition*) has singing but no words. I was surprised at how much I liked and enjoyed Roelof's voice. Klaus' synthesizer accompaniment behind Roelof's vocals is just right, a very pleasing combination.

Now, we come to the issue mentioned by B22 in the Synth Music Direct review, "poor lyrical content... decidedly coarse, juvenile and ill conceived, not much thought gone into it." Interestingly, Klaus mentions in the interview for the re-release that Roelof made up the lyrics as he sang the final song "Primavera."

It's "Requiem für's Revier" that first jolted me with its lyrics, however. I grew up on rock 'n roll and have never really been exposed to opera. So I was listening to an opera singer, feeling moved and surprised that I can get into such serious music. The tone of the singing denotes passion, feeling, and a sophisticated air. Then I heard Roelof sing, "Who gives a shit about the common man?" What? Is this a serious song or is it meant to be camp?

I felt conflicted about this because I still really liked the singing, Klaus' backing synth pads, and Wolfgang Tiepold's cello. I think the lyrical contents are actually of some substance.

Starting with "Groove 'n' Bass," I have a different feeling practically every time I listen to the middle tracks. Sometimes "Groove 'n' Bass" feels like a throwaway track; other times, it sounds good. This time, it registers favorably. It's a building track with sampled human voice, a little flute and very nice sounding percussion (think *Transfer Station Blue*!).

Track 4, "Get Sequenced," continues uninterrupted from "Groove 'n' Bass" but soon morphs a bit with synth soloing by Klaus, the beat continuing unchanged. This track also has a nice feel as it progresses. The sequenced portion quickens some, with synth sounds floating about the panorama between the left and right speaker.

A metallic sound announces the arrival of "The Power of Moog," which is a smooth continuation in beat and style from the previous two tracks. It reminds me a little bit of *Are You Sequenced?*, except not as laid back in rhythm. Sounds evocative of the punchy synth sequencer in Jean Michel Jarre's *Equinoxe* alternate with sounds reminiscent of KS' Minimoog in *Body Love*.

As "Up, Up and Away" takes over, the backing, sequenced beat quickens even more to a four-on-the-floor trance-type beat. An intense Minimoog solo by KS sears the soundscape in the first couple of minutes; in fact, the Minimoog is the signature sound of the piece.

The song's energy level accelerates with great sequencing, wailing Minimoog, and high-pitched sounds fluttering and almost shrieking through the mix.

I think I've identified why the middle songs were previously unremarkable to me. They are basically one continuous track with a musical identity similar to *Are You Sequenced?* but dissimilar in style to the rest of the songs on *Dosburg Online*.

I've liked "Dawn till Dusk" every time, so I'm expecting it and the following "Art of Sequencing" to be good.

"Dawn till Dusk" is mellow, with a hint of melancholy, yet beautiful. It very smoothly evolves into "The Art of Sequencing," the highlight of the album. The transition from the gorgeous "Dawn till Dusk" to "The Art of Sequencing" is downright exciting! Sequencers layer one on top of the other, the first starting slower, and the second quickly, with a third layer somewhere in the middle. They all have a different tonal characteristic. This is an incredible beginning to this song. It's some of the most seductive and compelling sequencer I've ever heard!

The sequencing, somewhat hypnotic, almost makes for a good dance rhythm. Drum-like sounds enter with intermittent thumps starting around the 7:00 mark. A whip-like sound follows; a little funk!

Klaus invents countless ways to delight us, and we never know what's next, but it's an enchanting journey to take!

Woodwind type sounds appear past the 10:00 mark. A deep bass synth alternates with choir. This is fantastic stuff!!! The choirs remind me of the choir organs on Genesis' *Selling England by the Pound*. "The Art of Sequencing" is packed with musical pleasure! The beat is ever strong and still a bit funky. This would sound great on a club system! It's an absolutely great song, another astounding highlight in a career full of indescribably rewarding heights.

As the "Art of Sequencing" evolves into "Primavera", let's see how made up these lyrics seem (remember Klaus' comment that the lyrics for Primavera had been improvised)! Long, sensuous synth pads open the song before Roelof's entrance. His singing evokes emotions irrespective of the lyrics and thus can be considered another musical instrument.

My original attraction to "Requiem für's revier" was that it sounds serious and heartfelt, thus moving me emotionally. I feel less like the lyrics are improvised in "Primavera." The backing synthesizer and possibly cello are exquisite in their complementary role to the tenor Roelof. His singing is powerful, as are the string sounds behind him, along with KS' trademark twittering sounds.

This CD is an excellent outing for Klaus (and Joerg Schaaf). I can't generally tell if one of his recordings is from a concert or produced in the studio, which is a plus. To think that this was a concert recording with no remixing is awesome! This rates as an upper echelon Schulze CD.

I like the picture (above) of Klaus, apparently after the last song, with his fists clenched and a big smile on his face. It's apparent that this was a magical night. I'm right there with Klaus on that high emotional plane as I listen to *Dosburg Online*.

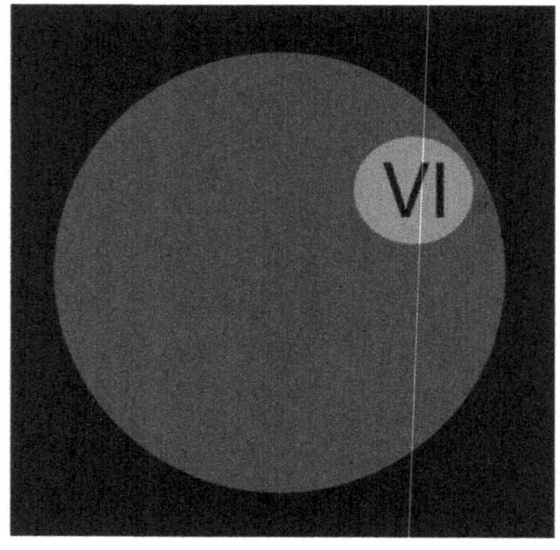

1997 *The Dark Side of the Moog 6* (with Pete Namlook and Bill Laswell)

From David Law at http://www.synthmusicdirect.com:

"Nice thick electronic tones mix with mainly unintelligible spooky vocal samples to get the first part of 'The Final DAT' underway...The rhythm becomes even more insistent. A superb sequence is added to it which morphs beautifully as the track progresses - absolutely fantastic!...Part 5 is the longest piece at twenty-four minutes. This is pretty much the centrepiece of the album and my favourite track here."

Brian Kirby, http://www.allmusic.com, writes:

"Like its predecessors, VI is a single song broken into six sections. After the moody first section of barely intelligible voices, the disc launches itself into a space rock/techno maelstrom that barely slows in tempo for the rest of its hour-plus length."

Another review by Matt Howarth (CD on Fax Records in Germany):

"This 64-minute CD has an awkward start with a vocal effects piece, but swiftly turns into a blinding explosion of truly awesome and highly rhythmic electronic music. This time, the collaboration between Pete Namlook and Klaus Schulze (with Bill Laswell on one track) produces a near perfect gene-splice of Namlook's dreaminess with Schulze's dynamics. This time, the music shines with an utmost brilliance--absolutely the gem of this collab series. Energetic keyboards and rushing pulses abound in this very melodic release."

My impressions of *The Dark Side of the Moog 6*

(this edition has six parts totaling 64:20; Bill Laswell appears on Part 4):

DSOTM6 starts immediately with thin, twisting and swirling Moog combined with a doctored human voice talking in the background. In fact there are probably as many as three voices, all seemingly giving a talk on some serious subject. The words are largely unintelligible, however, so it's all for effect. The entire first part – over seven minutes – features the synths and voices. Some of the words are distinguishable, and I have a feeling that on repeated listens, some might become clearer. I agree with Matt Howarth that this is the weakest part of *DSOTM6*.

Part 2 starts with a full synth pad, a Minimoog "lead guitar," and a slow beat in the background formed by percussion, with the off beat sounding like a tambourine. This is a very nice song!

Part 3 retains the same beat but soon features a fatter sounding synth with choirs. A quickened beat and a thin, high-pitched synth forming the melody give an entirely different feel, not that pleasant to me. Sequencer comes in forcefully and choirs enter; that part sounds great. I find Part 3 to be about half good and half not so good.

Part 4 has an atmospheric start with lots of percussion (an audio delight), some bubbly synth and then a four-on-the-floor-style beat. Very deep bass synth and myriad percussive sounds form a soundscape that sounds very nice. I imagine that for those with a subwoofer, this will shake the house, as I can detect very deep bass, even without a subwoofer.

Voices echo about the sound stage, at times understandable. A melody line leaning toward piano comes in, joined by another four-on-the-floor pounding rhythm. A resonating Hawaiian guitar style passage adds flavor to Part 4, which is my favorite on *DSOTM6* so far.

Part 5 starts out somewhat frantically, with a swirling mix of sounds including some juicy sounding synth jabs at times. Typical flowing Schulze "string" pads appear before sequencer floats in. This is another strong track.

This track sounds, perhaps, more like a Klaus Schulze solo album track than any of the other *DSOTM* tracks, hinting at *Body Love* synths as the track starts. Choirs enter just past 10:00, before Part 5 continues with surging energy and lots of electronic effects, including a persistent crashing sound. Bold, lush synth pads command attention past 14:00. The rhythm is formed largely by pulsating, bubbly lead. Part 5, over 24 minutes in length, is quite strong.

Part 6 begins with multiple lead synth sounds and a droning pad. Synth sounds "tap" the speakers lightly and repeatedly with a realistic presence; they sound like they are in the room. Part 6 puts on a brilliant display of synthesizer capabilities, like the dazzling finale of a fireworks show. All the stops are pulled out in this final section of *DSOTM6*, and the effect is outstanding!

Overall, *DSOTM6* is quite good, lacking some in Part 1 and portions of Part 2. The rest is spellbinding and elevates the CD to a very high status.

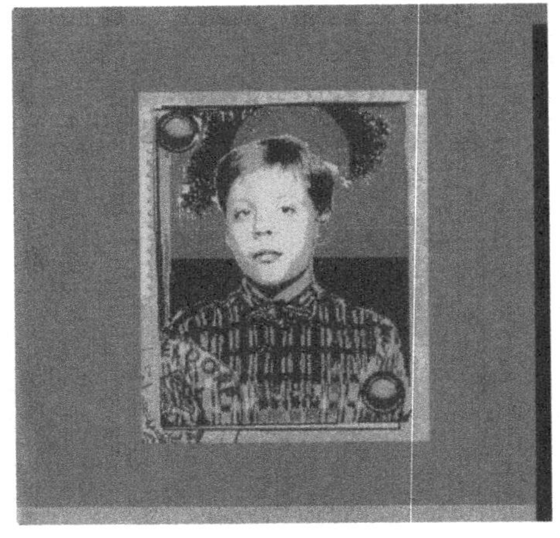

1997 *Jubilee Edition*

I will be reviewing CDs 1-10 of the *Jubilee Edition*, which I bought on eBay. This was my first exposure to the "boxed sets," and I was very pleasantly surprised at the quality of music on these ten CDs. That any recording artist could have a 25-year career with 40 or more released albums and have 45-50 CDs of quality unreleased material available is nearly unimaginable!. Even more astounding is that there seems to be a lot more strong material still unreleased. Klaus refers to the fact that he could have released an 80-CD set and makes a joking reference to possibly doing that when he turns 80. And, after hearing Klaus talk about deleting tracks from his computer, I would bet that many listenable tracks have been simply deleted.

Jubilee Edition CD 1

In any case, this first review will be of CD 1 of *Jubilee Edition* – which is CD 21 of *The Ultimate Edition*. The CD is named *Tradition & Vision* and is a nearly 79-minute track with eight subtitles. The track was finished on April 15, 1997 and features KS and Joerg Schaaf (already alluded to in Joerg's interview). They intended to make a recording "different than the rest" of the 25-CD *Jubilee Edition*.

Remembering the adventurousness of *Trance Appeal* with Schulze and Schaaf makes me think we're in for a barrage of creativity on this track. Note that there is only one track marker for this CD.

For a few minutes, *Tradition and Vision* becomes a sampling of a variety of unusual synthesizer generated sounds. Once again, this is a long track that sounds nothing like a song for the first several minutes. It sounds like it could have been a pre-1970 experiment in synthesized sounds. This first section is named "The Power of Myth" and is comprised totally of these "experimental" sounds.

The experimental sounds carry past "The Power of Myth" and then yield to some rather dark sounding synth pads at around 10:00. One of the pads sounds like a synthesized cello or perhaps a mellotron. For the first time in the piece, some genuine emotion-stirring synthesized "strings" are playing. These pads sound very good in contrast to the general "noise making" that has gone before.

At around 24:00, *Tradition and Vision* sounds a bit like *Trance Appeal* in some of the percussive sounds that are used.

Just after 25:00 a hint of a rhythm appears in the form of a bouncy bass sound. This sound starts to emerge more, giving the first hint at a song structure. Echoing percussive sounds and effects complement the bass line along with reverberating synth sounds. The piece is picking up steam around the 30:00 mark and now sounds like a very rhythm oriented track, even featuring an occasional drum roll.

This period sounds very creative and is more satisfying to listen to than the first ten minutes. No part of a Schulze track exists in isolation, however, as slow buildups set up more-rhythmic parts, and KS builds a piece up and down multiple times to create and maintain musical tension. This middle section is quite interesting and could last several more minutes without becoming boring.

Close to 37:00, the long percussion oriented section gives way, at least partially, to synth pads. The rhythm continues, coexisting with the synth pads. The synth pads drop out, and the rhythm takes over totally again. It's quite a hypnotic groove that has an almost addictive quality to it.

More and more effects begin to surround this steady groove that has been playing for close to 20 minutes. Dramatic synth pads overlay the beat, but thankfully, the groove continues right on – I'm not ready for it to end yet! The groove shifts via chord changes a few times, adding interest.

A sequencer enters at 50:00, ending the 25-minute period of uninterrupted rhythm. Multiple sequencers play, combining with other sounds to form a quickly assembled alternative rhythm. Surges of "wind" blow through as the sequencers playfully joust. It's quite a happy circumstance that one extended section of satisfying music has been replaced by one that is just as fascinating.

The sequencer patterns pick up velocity and are joined by Minimoog for a short time. At this point the composition has risen to the exceptional level. When KS does sequencers, he rarely if ever misses! This is a superb sounding section!

At close to 59:00, the Minimoog or a closely related instrument joins in (the CD notes mention Minimoog, Memorymoog and Rave-o-lution). The percussive sounds are ultra-clear. The last several minutes of *Tradition and Vision* are simply stunning in quality and put the capper on a run of at least 50 minutes of unrelentingly high quality music.

Jubilee Edition CD 2

The second CD is entitled *Avec Arthur.* Arthur Brown appears on the second long track of the CD. Klaus would play solo on the 1979 tour for the first half of the concert, then Arthur would appear with him in the second half.

The first song, just over 40:00, is "Re: People I Know." I know of all of them except the first, Eddie. The rest are Stomu, Harmut and Manuel, Michael S., Arthur and Marian Gold, of Alphaville.

The beginning is teeming with energy and quite spacy with voices in the background – lots of echoes. This is from the Düsseldorf concert on September 30, 1977. The piece is classic Schulze from the 1970s, which means it's very good - flowing synths and choirs with a majestic sound.

The mix evolves to synth and sequencer with a boomy sound. This quality seems to be due to the limitations of live recording. It may have something to do with the acoustics in the venue. So far the recording is decent and not really a distraction from the great music.

A buildup of energy takes place, featuring the shifting chords of the sequencer. It's joined in the background by a *Body Love*-like synth and then a second sequencer, producing an infusion of fun and delight.

At 26:00, the pace is frenetic with the sequencers and lead synth both supercharged.

The pace then slows down still featuring an explosion of synthesizer noise lasting three or four minutes. The pace slows further, featuring two sequencers, one played tentatively and the other ascending, soon joined by creeping synth pads. This is a relief after all the manic playing before.

The manic pace and wild synth sounds ruined the piece for me, given the potential it showed in the first 15:00 or so.

The second track, "Avec Arthur," starts with a jolting, primitive sounding synth assault. At this point the audio quality has become a factor in degrading the overall listening experience at times. Klaus employs his usual technique when Arthur sings with him, laying down a comfortable, nice sounding groove that is complementary to Arthur's singing style – this time featuring tom-tom and cowbell.

Arthur's vocals sound very slow and floating, blending with the rhythm.

A manic period for both the rhythm and Arthur's vocals follows until the 11:00 mark when Arthur moves into a period of nice vocals and Klaus slows the pace from manic to just a little quick. Arthur's voice sounds almost operatic during this period, as the song hits its stride.

Arthur's vocals become unremarkable until he lets out a loud shriek at about 22:00. After that his vocals sound clearer, more expressive. Now Arthur sounds much, much stronger, as is the accompanying music by KS. Somehow the recording seems better after 22:00. After a while Arthur seamlessly changes his vocals to French.

A significant, all-instrumental interlude follows by Klaus, sounding very good.

Overall, "Avec Arthur" has its strong moments, but weak passages and a subpar recording mar the performance. The crowd's response at the end of the CD seems to indicate that they liked it a lot!

Jubilee Edition CD 3

CD 3 is from a concert in Budapest on October 24, 1982. Rainer Bloss plays keyboards, mostly electric piano, according to the liner notes.

The first section, "Ludwig Revisted," is another interpretation of the classic track from *X*. The track lasts 21:27 and has four subtitles: 'Cozy Ludwig,' 'Watchful Ludwig,' 'Marching Ludwig' and 'Spooky Ludwig.'

"Ludwig Revisited" seems to start about where the track picks up on the *Dziekuje Poland Live '83* album. The string synthesis sounds strong. As in the Poland Concert, the tape loop section has lively piano and other instrumentation that is likely to maintain interest more than just the loop.

The electric piano playing by Rainer sounds great in this section. The recording seems superior to the one on "Avec Arthur," even though both are live performances. After a while the tape loop seems distinctly in the background, and Klaus and Rainer both solo on their respective instruments. The piano playing has a jazzy feeling to it. I'm guessing that this live version was longer and a cut in was done just prior to the loop to make it shorter. The pulse of the loop is accentuated by sequencer.

When the grandiose full orchestral passage emerges after the loop, Klaus' synthesis of orchestral sounds is very realistic. I thought for many years that it was Klaus' synthesizers rather than an orchestra on the original "Ludwig II von Bayern" from *X*. I was always so impressed at how well he had created an orchestral sound with synthesizers!

"Ludwig Revisited" sounds pretty familiar, but it's well done here. I don't mind having three versions of "Ludwig" by now. It's such a great song and the different interpretations are fun. Besides, if Klaus could have as many versions of "Ludwig" as Monet had of water lilies, he would still be allowed about 45 more interpretations!

The second track, "Peg Leg Dance," lasts 39:18 and is very well recorded. Fifteen seconds into the song, a hypnotic beat starts and will not let up for most or all of the track. In fact it just gradually intensifies from this point.

There have been times where I have really heavily gotten into this track – drawn in by the rising, relentless intensity of the addictive repeating rhythm. The Minimoog is already present at the 7:00 mark, adding to the frenzied pace. This is an all out romp! String refrains from *Audentity* are played repeatedly, interestingly, because this track could be compared to "Spielglocken" for its similar driving rhythm pattern.

I try to imagine what it would have been like to have been at this concert and felt this much energy emanating from the stage. Around the 15:00 mark, certain sounds conjure up images of Jarre, perhaps from *Equinoxe*. This is an especially brilliant and compelling portion of the song.

"Peg Leg Dance" is definitely a standout track in the Schulze catalog!

The activity around the lead sequencer gets especially manic around the 27:00 mark. It's just an all-out, no holds barred assault! An additional deep bass sequencer joins in with the lead and intense Minimoog soloing to create an even wilder atmosphere.

The track backs down in pace near the end, as the crowd breaks out into extended, raucous applause.

Klaus speaks to the crowd between Tracks 2 and 3. The third track was given the name "Die spirituelle Kraft des Augenblicks." A plodding type rhythm takes hold of the song, surrounded by various synth improvisations. It sounds kind of like a jam that may not have been composed all that much beforehand. The synth soloing sounds a little shrill, for some reason.

As B22 from Synthmusicdirect.com observed, there are no bad songs for true Schulze fans – only good, better and great songs. "Die spirituelle Kraft des Augenblicks" grows on me, possibly due to lowered expectations based on the early part of the song. The last two minutes return to classic KS synth pads in the *Timewind/Moondawn* vein. A nice way to end.

Jubilee Edition CD 4

The next two disks form a "Trance Opera sans lyrics" (this expression from the CD cover notes). The operatic voice is sampled and never sings actual lyrics. Sometimes the pitch of the voice is changed, occasionally in bizarre ways. This is actually a three-part Opera, since the bonus disk on *Are You Sequenced?* now contains "Vat Was Dat." The recording was to be part of the soundtrack for the American-Hungarian movie *Living on Borrowed Time,* although not much of the music was used in the movie. I'll review all three CDs here – CD 4 and 5 of *Jubilee Edition* and the bonus CD to *Are You Sequenced*?, "Vat Was Dat?".

CD 4, *Borrowed Time,* is one continuous 77-minute piece of music.

The first five minutes develop slowly with a wide assortment of samples (some human voices), crystal clear acoustic guitar, and other "instruments".

The first indication of trance in *Borrowed Time* comes with an initially subdued sequencer. Each time the chorus sings "Zoom," the sequencer gathers a little steam or there is a chord change.

The recording quality on *Borrowed Time* is excellent – on a par with a very good studio recording. The "buildup period" of the piece continues to use lots of voice and "choir" samples, stretching to over 17 minutes at the same moderate tempo. There is a tension building; the pace has been moderate but is beginning to accelerate.

A drum pounds into the mix at about 18:30, but the tempo is pulled back. Bass lines, very interesting percussion and a nearly "FM Delight"-like piano add interest to the still restrained track.

Huge crescendos take place around the 29:00 mark and for the first time, we hear our "star singer" warming up his voice amidst the cacophony. In another surprise turn, the music reverts back to where it was maybe 20 minutes ago, with just sequencer and various sampled voices, still at a quite moderate and restrained pace

Virtually the entire disk is a long buildup. As a standalone disk, I don't think it would hold up but in the context of a longer Opera, it could be well placed. The main male operatic lead makes increasingly frequent appearances in the mix, as the CD winds toward the 77:00 mark.

Due to the "buildup" feel of this piece, it seems clear that it should be considered the first segment of the full Trance Opera.

Klaus in his studio.

Jubilee Edition CD 5

Opera Trance starts with a tenor voice, surrounded by massive musical confusion in the form of crashes, crescendos and all kinds of surging sounds.

The first time this voice becomes a bizarre, high pitched "wail" is the 2:00 mark. It sounds almost like a voice from "Alvin and the Chipmunks." I've wondered whether Klaus included this voice in keeping with the principle that he has expressed regarding beauty only being able to be appreciated as a contrast to ugliness.

In any case, the piece starts toward full motion with a lilting pace. The operatic voice sings (no words) and sequencer starts at about 5:00. The first drumming enters with a steady but fairly slow beat. Other sampled voices are plentiful as *Opera Trance* moves toward the 10:00 mark.

Amazingly, the sense of a full orchestra is created quickly and tastefully, as several elegant sounding orchestral layers are revealed in a short period of time.

The opera tenor again takes over, joined at times by a second operatic voice. The lead voice is very expressive at times, changing octaves periodically.

The trance beat quickens, with operatic singing in full swing at 16:00, making it about 94 minutes for this multi-track opera to get into full swing. There are still brief but frequent orchestral crashes or bursts that are thrown into the mix, with other sampled voices and occasionally, the bizarre sounding chipmunk voice. The beat backs off to allow an enjoyable sequencer to play for a short time before the pulsing trance "drum" returns.

The persistent beat, crashes, other sampled voices including the chipmunk and the lead singer are all featured up to the 38:00 mark.

The instrumentation for the next several minutes is very creative and enjoyable providing a refreshing change. This is a magnificent musical bridge back to the main theme. Well rested, the opera singer returns at 43:00 with as much vigor as ever.

At 49:00, the trance beat revs up noticeably. A fast sequencer cuts in and solos for a bit, adding a very unexpected and stimulating treat! More sequencers are added in, and the trance beat takes off, faster than ever.

At 137 minutes into the "opera", it still holds my interest.

At 60:00 (into *Opera Trance*), powerful orchestrations yield to an even more emphatic beat, joined by a very brisk piano after a while. It seems whenever the sampled lead singer re-enters the mix, an interlude makes his return more interesting, even exciting.

I'm curious to see how "Vat Was Dat" holds up as the third part of this "opera". In a quote from the liner notes for CD 5 of *Jubilee Edition*, (presumably) KDM states, "There exists a third (77- minute-long) part called 'Vat Was Dat,' done in a similar, almost danceable style. This part is not included here, because it just repeats the same phrase, over and over again, which is okay for, say, five or ten minutes. But 77? Always the same? You would call me a lunatic."

At the risk of being thought a lunatic, I will next review "Vat Was Dat" - all three parts of the opera in the same review session!

"Vat Was Dat" – Bonus Disk from *Are You Sequenced?* (Part 3 of the Trance Opera)

The marathon continues as I play and review the third disk of the Trance Opera. It starts out sounding purely like a continuation of *Opera Trance* (CD 2 of the three). The mastering of the recording sounds a bit different, with more bass and perhaps a little less emphasis on the high end. With this coming from the re-issue set rather than the *Jubilee Edition*, it's not a shock that the sound would be a bit different. Perhaps the "lunatic" moniker will have to be applied because this CD is virtually identical in content to the previous, with only an earlier appearance of rhythm differentiating the two.

If you don't own *Opera Trance* of *Jubilee Edition*, this would be a nice bonus disk for *Are You Sequenced?*. I would have preferred receiving the original second CD with the Snap! remixes.

I recommend "Vat Was Dat" only for those who don't have the *Jubilee Edition* version, which I prefer. Listening to all three in a marathon session has turned out to be too much!

Jubilee Edition CD 6

The title of CD 6 is *Real Colours*. The first track, "Real Colours in the Darkness," has already been discussed in the review of *Inter*Face*, but I'll listen to it again and write any additional impressions if they add to the discussion of this track.

Within the first minute, I'm in awe of "The Real Colours", and feel lifted to a place that only the best Schulze songs can take me.

From the liner notes: "The newly found 11:59 version seems to be the 'original' and first choice for release because the music fits much better to the title, and the length fits to the duration given on the LP cover. How and why a completely different piece – in mood and in duration – found its way onto the actual 1985 album is another one of those mysteries. Neither KS nor I remember. *Man weiss so wenig.*"

The second song, "Hitchcock Suite," lasts just over 40 minutes and is subtitled in three parts with names of actresses who appeared in Alfred Hitchcock movies ('Tippi Hedren', 'Janet Leigh' and 'Karen Black [into:] Barbara Harris').

"Hitchcock Suite" begins, as you might expect from the title, in an ominous, almost scary, minor key reminiscent of "Velvet Voyage" - at least in the first couple of minutes. The liner notes mention that Part 3 of "Hitchcock Suite" is a "very 'Velvet Voyage'-like track." This first subtitle, 'Tippi Hedren,' features a drifting, droning sound backed by choirs and synth. Does this sound familiar?

'Janet Leigh,' the second subtitle, consists of drifting and droning synth textures combined with higher pitched sounds. It's distinctly more ominous than the first track and may be the only one of the three tracks that doesn't much resemble "Velvet Voyage."

'Karen Black (into:) Barbara Harris' starts out very much like "Velvet Voyage" with Klaus speaking in a voice that echoes and is more "up front" than any of the voices in *Mirage*'s "Velvet Voyage". This sounds almost like another version of "Velvet Voyage." The first take would be the original, the second version would actually be this one, and the third would be the version on the re-release of *Mirage*.

Within the first five minutes, I'm feeling that this version is very good - better than the version on the re-release of *Mirage*. The majestic sound of the choirs stands out in this version.

This version is very well recorded and in general, just superb; a spectacular version well worth seeking out, if at all possible.

The third track, recorded in 1975, is named "Semper idem" (11:35). It starts with a wavering synth that sounds like a cross between accordion and bagpipes. The next passage sounds like *Timewind*, with long, drifting synth pads mixed with *Body Love* and its Moogy synth. The essence of *Timewind* predominates.

The last song, from the same recording session in 1975, is "Semper idem is Wann soll man springen?" A large Moog-like sound comes boldly into the soundscape and resonates, morphing into more Moog sounds that aren't quite as brazen.

"Wann soll man springen" is a little spacier than "Semper idem," with the accordion/bagpipes sounding more like accordion tinged sequencer and lasting much further into the track. Combined with the grandiose synth notes, this is a truly awesome piece of music! It's marred only by an out-of -place and strange period of noise in the last four minutes.

Real Colours, the sixth CD of *Jubilee Edition*, is a real treasure trove of sonic delights! It's a strong CD – not perfect but close.

Jubilee Edition CD 7

CD 7 is entitled *Cyborg's Faust*. The first track, "Cyborg's Traum", has nothing to do with the actual *Cyborg* album. The second track is "Ballet pour le Docteur Faustus." So, it seems the title of the CD is a combination of the two titles. This was recorded in 1972 or earlier, with equipment similar in its primitive nature to that used on *Irrlicht*.

In the first 8:00, "Cyborg's Traum" delivers a pronounced drone (which holds for six minutes), organs and very clear sounding semi-twitters bouncing around in the stereo spectrum. The organs drop out and the song begins to sound much less musical, like an experiment in noises.

This should probably be considered a historical document of Klaus' early experimentation. As "Cyborg's Traum" passes 23:00 with lots of starkly non-musical noises, I wonder if this is worth a total listen.

Intense twittering reveals hints of the organ re-entering, giving the piece more of a creative quality and causing me to feel moved by the music. It's one of the first times in this song that I've felt emotionally involved. The organ soloing here is actually a bit better than the intense organ playing on *Irrlicht*'s "Satz: Ebene."

"Cyborg's Traum" doesn't measure up to the quality of most Schulze material.

Next is "Ballet pour le Docteur Faustus," recorded in 1978. It starts out resembling "Velvet Voyage" just a little – it's interesting from the start. The "Velvet Voyage" resemblance doesn't last very long, yielding to layers of synth pads that are very expressive sounding, conveying a feeling of deep emotion. It's a really nice stretch of about five minutes of classic sounding Schulze synth.

String pads and sequencer play together, sounding very good. The strings have a very buoyant, lively, springy sound, one of the signature sounds in this piece. Piano-like sounds like those of the first few minutes of "Friedrich Nietzsche" on *X* drop into the mix. These instantly recognizable sounds from *X* are used liberally for several minutes.

This is a far superior track to "Cyborg's Traum," a top notch Schulze composition, slowly evolving and filled with interesting, exciting sounds and changes.

Listening to this 38-minute track leads to the thought that Klaus has been better able to express himself musically, at least at times, with the advent of the CD.

The sounds fade into a drone; then the synth rises again. A middle range sequencer begins to gather a lot of energy and kick up the tempo to its most driving level yet. All around the rest of the sound field, higher-pitch pads play the recurring bouncy, springy melody of "Ballet pour le Docteur Faustus."

High-register sequencers join in for a dazzling combination of rhythms, sequencers and pads.

This is really an excellent piece of music, among the best on the 10-CD set. The audio quality is very good to excellent. The last few minutes are purely spacy sounding material, still of high quality.

Jubilee Edition CD 8

CD 8, *Vie de reve*, consists of three tracks, the longest being the title track at nearly 49:00. "L'affaire Tour" (over 19:00) and "There was Greatness in the Room (Fragment)" complete the disc.

The title track was recorded on the 21st of April in 1976 at a concert in Reims, France. The last two songs were recorded in Brussels on October 24, 1979. Apparently the second and third tracks represent the two encores, with the second encore being cut off due to technical reasons. *Vie de Reve* is divided into six subtracks on the CD cover listing but not broken up with track markers on the CD.

White noise and soaring electronics start *Vie de reve*, sounding a bit like a desert sandstorm with air raid sirens going off. Droning organs yield to *Timewind*-style, more sensuous full synth with the "sandstorm" still active.

This sounds good; its classic '70s Schulze, after all, with a twist. Twittering sounds along the way add to the mid-to-late-'70s feel. Very stark, industrial sounding synths come in, louder than anything else in the sound field by far. Their thinner, twangy character gives them a sound like a Moog solo from *Body Love*.

Vie de reve, played in front of a French crowd, is about as strong a reflection of the power of KS' albums from this time frame as you could want. It seems fitting that the French crowd got to hear this classic extended "sound collage," since they were the strongest original lovers of Klaus Schulze's music.

I experience this as a great piece of music and look up to the CD player to see that just over 16 minutes have elapsed. I wonder how Klaus can extend this idea for 49 minutes and keep the quality up.

There is an amazing intensity in the music as it approaches the 20:00 mark. There's a lot of the twangy, fast soloing (sometimes higher pitched and other times a deeper pitch) played over the long, sweet sounding synth pads a la *Timewind*. It's a lot of *Body Love* meets *Timewind*, with hints of *Moondawn* thrown in.

It's significant that Klaus had at least three classic albums behind him by the time of this concert. This experience allowed him to play this music with a boldness, flair and confidence that gives it the unmistakable stamp of the highest-quality, most innovative electronic music ever created circa 1976 – the music of Klaus Schulze.

A bright and sparkly sounding sequencer comes in over a long held synth note adding even more intrigue and excitement to a song that seemed to have already touched the pinnacle. Twin sequencers are joined by even sharper and deeper sequencer sounds that echo about the soundscape. These are really unusual sounds that Klaus plays with for a few minutes.

It's like Klaus was a kid in a candy store, with all these new sounds to experiment with from these wonderful "new" synthesizers. A whole new world opened up and Klaus embraced it and exploded into it with historic impact. I'm reminded of Klaus' quote from the main interview (repeated in all the re-release booklets) about getting his first Moog and how that was for him, like having all the Christmases come at once!

Around *Vie de reve*'s 33:00 mark, a distinctly *Moondawn*-ish passage occurs, reinforcing the high quality of this track, which has everything that was exciting about KS' music up to 1976 thrown in, plus a little bit more. It sounds like there may be a few "dropouts" in the tape, but that doesn't affect the experience at all, except maybe to remind me that the recording is an older concert recording. The audio quality is actually quite strong. *Vie de reve* is a track that can easily blow you away if you're a hardcore Schulze fan.

"L'affaire Tournesol" starts out with raucous crowd applause which didn't come from the Reims concert (which contains Vie de reve) – but could have. It starts off with a bright sequenced piano-like sound, playing in an irregular pattern. Soon, cowbell, drumming and a high-pitched drone are part of the song. This all happens quite quickly in the first two-plus minutes of the song.

A classic, melodic Schulze synth pad joins in, followed by a fairly intense KS Minimoog solo.

Once the Minimoog stops, there is just cowbell and a methodical, thumping beat. Little two note synth phrases play repeatedly.

After a time, an organ comes in, followed by a deep drone in the background, supporting some elegant classic Schulze synth pads. The last 5:00 of the song contain non-stop "string" synth pads.

As KS comes out for the second encore in Brussels, the crowd is going berserk. How I wish I had been able to experience this from closer up, instead of observing KS' career from afar in the U.S. I never had the money to travel to Europe when I was younger. On the other hand, I think I can appreciate Klaus more at this point because the availability of his CDs is at an all time high, the boxed sets are all out there, he is still producing great music (Kontinuum!) and I own more of his CDs than ever before.

"Greatness" includes droning synths, singing through the vocoder, classic choirs, and then the appearance and singing of Arthur Brown. Choirs back Arthur's singing the whole time. Arthur starts to sing some of "Shadows of Ignorance" as the music in the background is straight out of *X* (including choirs and the same piano line described before from the first few minutes of "Friedrich Nietzsche"), quite an interesting combination.

This is overall a very good CD that has a lot of highlights.

Jubilee Edition CD 9

Der Welt Lauf is the title for CD 9 of The Jubilee Edition.

The first track, "Goodwill" is described in the liner notes as "one track from a handful of poppy experiments that Klaus did as a kind of a research exercise on popular music." Let's give it a listen!

"Goodwill" starts with a wide variety of samples; what sounds like someone running up steps, human utterances, crowds cheering, a door shutting. Hazy synth and bass give the song a musical component as more samples play - spacy female vocal, a male wailing, a motorcycle starting. At 2:36, the track takes off, with a fairly brisk bass beat, drums and heady sequencer. A synth blast changes the direction around the 4:00 mark as "Goodwill" continues its peppy pace. Another blast at 6:30 ushers in pulsating synth and a spirited sequencer pattern.

This piece stays interesting via a wide variety of sounds and tempos and by never staying in the same framework for very long before the next switch to a new tempo and set of instruments. There are myriad changes signaled by blasts of sound, more than on any other Schulze track, perhaps. This could be because the running time -- just over 13:00 -- is shorter than a typical KS piece.

The second track, "Whales," was planned as a soundtrack for a film about whales. The movie was never done, however. The song starts with a huge bassy, heavy wave of synthesizer sound. Soon the sound of a whale calling out several times combines with sweeping synth pads. Alluring choir effects are also a prominent part of the early mix.

It's a tumultuous soundscape, if for no other reason than the presence of the alarmingly intense and frequent cries and piercing shrieks of the whales.

The track is split up into two parts, the first, described above, called 'Pas de deux.' The second part of "Whales" is 'Whale Hunting.'

The reason I mention the divide is that there is a stark change in the tone of the song when 'Whale Hunting' begins. The whale shrieks have been replaced by synthesized female voice, male choirs, other various samples, and an overall slowed pace in a minor key.

The third track on CD 9 of *Jubilee Edition* is "Experimentelle Bagatelle," a short song at 4:06. KDM warns in the liner notes to "expect what the title does promise."

The song starts out with pulsating synth, soon partially evolving to a harsh metallic sound. Suffice it to say that this is a totally "experimental sounds" oriented track. This is one song that would obviously never make it onto a "regular KS solo release."

The last track is the title track, "Der Welt Lauf," pairing Manuel Göttsching and Klaus Schulze. Manual plays Gibson guitar and synthesized guitar, sounding similar to Klaus' Minimoog (so says

KDM in the liner notes). This live performance was recorded from Klaus' European tour (in the Dutch town of Leiden) in November of 1981.

"Der Welt Lauf" starts with lots of crowd chatter, followed by vibrating chimes. Reverberating guitars and synths dominate for the next few minutes. "Der Welt Lauf" is marred by marginal recording quality.

A percussive-type sound, like steady whipping or crashing, is a constant presence for the next several minutes, surrounded by light sequencer and synth solo (Manuel's synth guitar?).

This same song form continues past the 17:00 mark; "Der Welt Lauf" is really about Klaus and Manuel playing in a no-holds-barred jam session, a raucous romp.

An almost total cessation of music occurs at 26:00, with some crowd cheering (and even coughs), followed by a much more floating, soothing soundscape featuring guitar and synths. This sounds very good, and after the wild ride of the last several minutes, I find myself enjoying this part more.

The pace picks up again with sequencer and synth guitar solo reaching a manic level fairly quickly.

My opinion of "Der Welt Lauf" might be significantly upgraded by a better recording. I simply don't know what the piece of music would sound like if it were recorded in the studio or if it possessed audio quality similar to most KS' recordings (live or studio).

Jubilee Edition CD 10

My final review of the *Jubilee Edition* set is of *[Die Kunst...]*. It features a very short track of :29 at the start of the CD (interestingly, on the liner notes, this is listed as the third of four songs). This was the trailer for the announcement of a German TV film, recorded on July 21, 1993.

Following is an 8:00 track and a 64:00 track which is a very early experimental piece. KDM warns, "This early document should be taken as just this, a document of an experiment anno 1971-1972, that was never intended for release then." The final "cut" on this CD features interview fragments from KS in 1982.

On to the music! The beginning seconds feature a choir burst as in "Velvet System" from *En=Trance*; it evolves into a few seconds of very nice synth and then stops at :29.

"Les Jockeys camoufles" begins with two distinct sounds, one in each stereo channel. "Bayreuth Return"-style twittering and the conga/tabla sound used on *Blackdance* are prominent. This more strongly evokes thoughts of *Blackdance*, even though most of the other sound elements that accompanied the conga and tabla playing on *Blackdance* are missing. "Les Jockeys" is an interesting listen, in that it shows Klaus experimenting and foreshadows some of his early- to mid-seventies work.

"Die Kunst, hundert Jahre alt zu warden" (64:05) is next and starts out sounding like no other piece than *Irrlicht*. The music is eerie with similar experimental sounds to those on *Irrlicht*, yet with their own interesting character (KS didn't use a synthesizer here, just as with *Irrlicht*). The instruments used as described by KDM in the liner notes are the damaged Fender guitar amplifier, the Teisco organ, guitar, drums (played by KS), an echo machine and various tape speeds.

"Die Kunst..." features pulsating organ and lots of active percussion - a nice soundtrack as it approaches 10:00. The organ and percussion played at varying tempos carry the piece up to the 25:00 mark.

At around 27:00, the sound changes to an even more experimental, ethereal and almost contemplative sound. This is an emotionally rewarding section of the track. The music evolves into a drone with sparkling synth sounds surrounding it and then back to a rapidly pulsating synth.

Grandiose organ strains play over a drone as the track hits 40:00.

This piece is filled with experimental sounds throughout its 64 minutes. The final section sounds similar in parts to the organ playing passage in "Satz: Ebene."

"Die Kunst..." is a nice historical document. It takes me back to the time where Klaus was just starting to find a style with this new music that he was so motivated to create. I can feel passion and interest coming from Klaus via this music. He had to be very motivated and passionate to take these instruments and create the kind of music heard here and on *Irrlicht*. Aside from being a historical document, there are moments in the music that cause that feeling of elation we all get when Klaus creates magic with his music. So, "Die Kunst..." is very worthwhile!

The final track is literally called "From an Interview with KS in 1982 (with many thanks to John Diliberto)."

He first talks about how they were trying to find something new at the time of *Electronic Meditation*; he says they went over the top with it. He also talks about the people at the radio station saying to check the turntable, it seems like it's broken, because they [Tangerine Dream] were always repeating. He mentions how the radio people were afraid to look straight at them.

Klaus also talks about how the synthesizer was not available yet and how he took an organ that a friend gave him and modified it. He mentions that there was no harmony any more [after modifying it] but when he touched the keys he would think "what a great sound."

Klaus also talks about the desire to get away from the pressure of playing Anglo-American music. There was a good feeling in saying "I created that -- it's not a copy." It was music standing on its own without a tradition.

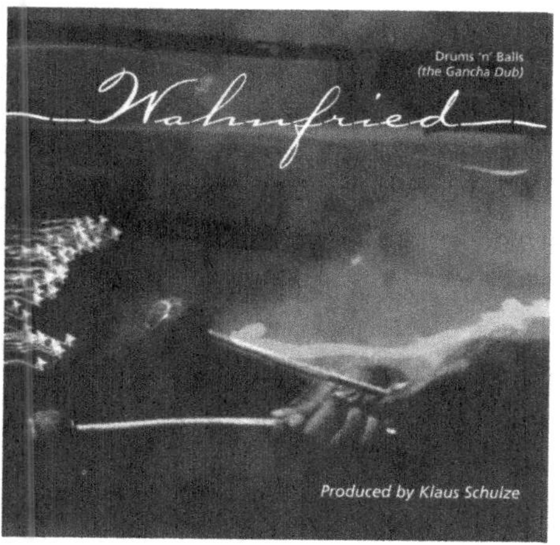

1997 *Drums 'n' Balls* (Klaus Schulze's Wahnfried)

The re-release version of *Drums 'n' Balls,* in effect, changes the name of the artist to "Klaus Schulze's Wahnfried" instead of the original version's "Wahnfried," since this really is more of a Klaus Schulze solo album. There are collaborators but they are either invented names for people who are not real or samples, some obtained from the group (Klaus' friends) Snap! ("Rhythm is a Dancer").

This is, then, actually an album Klaus made all by himself, which is why I find it heartening that the cover says, "Klaus Schulze's Wahnfried." I would have preferred that all the Wahnfried albums had carried the Klaus Schulze name. True, he had collaborators, but he also had collaborators such as Harald Grosskopf, Michael Shrieve, and Wolfgang Tiepold, on his solo albums. One of the stated reasons all along for using the Richard Wahnfried or Wahnfried pseudonym was that Klaus would not offend his fans with some music that was different from his usual solo fare. It doesn't matter to me if Klaus adventures into non-typical realms under his solo name. He has even done that more and more as the years have gone on.

It's understandable, though, in the context of the time in which the "Wahnfried" monikers were used, that the music might upset fans who were used to a certain Schulze style. So this is not a criticism of the way it was handled, but more my personal opinion of how I react to the use of the pseudonym.

From François Couture, *All Music Guide* at http://www.artistdirect.com/nad/store/artist/-album/0,,3861527,00.html:

"*Drums 'n' Balls* was credited to a number of musicians, including percussionists Joe 'Dum Dum' Loevenstone and Sloto Olatunye, and bassist Venus Dupond, but those turned out to be bogus names... The drum machine occupies a central role throughout, as does a synth bass, the prime mover of the whole album... *Drums 'n' Balls* is not a bad album per se (if anything, it still bears Schulze's craftsmanship), but it quickly runs out of ideas."

My impressions:

Drums 'n' Balls has four tracks plus a bonus track.

It starts with the title track, which begins with a pulsing, bass-laden synth line and lots of remarkable percussive sounds. The initial minutes are striking for the sensational recording and the absolutely magnificent percussive sounds. It's a real sonic treat!

Occasional vocal samples mix with the relentlessly stunning percussion. This may be the best audio recording ever put down on a Klaus Schulze album. It's hard to determine whether my liking for the song "Drums 'n' Balls" is more because of the music or the audio quality, but added together, they make the title track an absolute winner!!!

"Percussy" starts with more deep bass and remarkable percussion. The song picks up some lingering synth pads along the way and a bit of a funky beat. The outstanding feature continues to be the sensational recording, showing off red-hot percussion.

The first two cuts are simply spellbinding. I would call them the single greatest display of superior audio recording and percussion that I've ever heard on an album.

"House of India" is next, with samples of an Indian female singer (Katarina Nevaseynewa) culled from the archives of Luca Anzilotti and Michael Münzing of the group Snap!.

After a period of Katarina's sensuous, floating vocals, a rhythm takes shape built on a rapidly pulsating sequencer and accompanied by synth that approximates a brass sound. Occasional resonating bass drum is integrated before the return of Katarina's vocals. "House of India" is a nice track, led by the sequencer and vocals.

"Bass of Orion" is the last of the original *Drums 'n' Balls* songs. It starts with monk-like singing, synthesized strings, and a lazy sounding bass that sounds like the bass used on the old Glen Campbell song "Galveston" (for anyone who remembers that song!). Striking, superbly recorded percussion returns, but it's not used as much as in the previous two tracks. Past 9:00, plucky, pongy-sounding synth blurbs are introduced, adding another intriguing sound to a CD that's full of them. "Bass of Orion" has an overall very laid back feeling to it.

The bonus track, "Chicken Biryani," uses Katarina Nevaseynewa's voice again. The track was recorded the year before *Drums 'n' Balls* was released. Klaus had the track laying around with no use for it on any of the albums he was working on at the time (he preferred "House of India"). With the re-release he decided to share it with the fans, since he thought of it as a wonderful piece of music (so Klaus said in the interview in 2005 with Albrecht Piltz for the re-release of *Drums 'n' Balls*).

"Chicken Biryani" features a moderate pace with Katarina's vocals, some thunder, other spliced-in vocals and occasional snappy, popping synth sounds. There is another sound that made me think of a ping pong ball being hit with full force in an echo chamber. "Chicken Biryani" is a decent but not spectacular ending to the *Drums 'n' Balls* re-release.

I rate it as a very fine album, spectacular at times; containing some of the best recorded and intriguing music that KS has ever put down on recorded media.

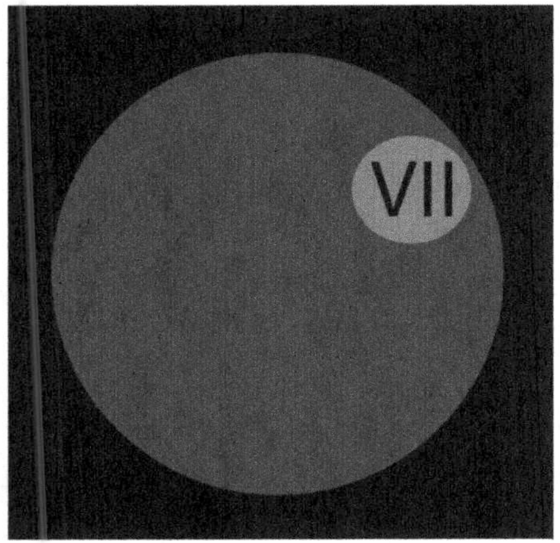

1998 *The Dark Side of the Moog 7* (with Pete Namlook and Bill Laswell)

From David Law at http://www.synthmusicdirect.com:

"Part three is the longest at nineteen minutes and for the most part is a real floater taking us to the outer regions of space, complete with cosmic winds and solar flares... Part four... very dynamic track and I loved every second of it."

Review by Damon Capehart at http://datacide.com:16080/aw032/:

"A little shorter than the others, and even then, it stretches out a bit. [Don't most FAX releases?] It's still quite good, though. Almost as good as *DSOTM V,* (my personal fave)... With *DSOTM V* being a 10, this is a 9 (for brevity only)."

My review of *The Dark Side of the Moog 7*:

DSOTM7 is 50 minutes long, broken into six parts. Bill Laswell's duties are on Part 3 this time.

The CD starts with pulsing synths in both speakers, slowly resonating classic Moog lead and long synth pads. A female voice, reminiscent of *Beyond Recall,* appears. *The Dark Side of the Moog* disks are darker and more "ambient" in sound than Klaus Schulze's releases. Klaus' solo albums can be dark but can also be infinitely upbeat (e.g., *En=Trance*).

Part 2 starts with a strong, solid sequencer and drums, reminding me of 1980s electro funk. Upbeat sequencer and lead synth melody precede choirs and drumming. This is a very rewarding section. More drumming and even more elaborate choirs follow. The sequencer parts have a nice strong, authoritative feel to them. Part 2 is a stimulating and fun section of music – a standout track!

Part 3 has a soothing, dreamy characteristic with a long, gentle pad and hints of light choir intonations. The first 7:00 have a very tranquilizing, laid-back feel, featuring chord changes in the pads. A slightly building tension based on increased activity occurs around 8:00, only to yield to more synth pads combined with occasional vocals creating a very otherworldly quality; a slow and floating feeling takes over for several minutes. At the end, a sequencer buildup leads seamlessly into Part 4.

Part 4 continues restrained yet solid sequencer sounds. Very soon, strong sequencer rhythm erupts, backed by drums and spacy vocals. A whipping sound again reminds me of electro-funk – it's pretty danceable at this point. Part 4 also has a flavor of electronic playfulness that reminds me of Kraftwerk. All in all, it's an up-tempo groove but not quite as good as Part 2.

Part 5 starts with violin-like synth sounds enveloping the whole stereo spectrum. Chord changes provide interest as synth pad and "violin" carry the whole track.

Part 6 starts with slow, bass producing synth pads along with a few treated voices. A soft piano-like sound plays gently with the synths as vocal whispers emanate out of the piano playing.

Part 6 is comprised of multiple synth pads, sounding very sweeping and sumptuous with a very slowly played piano (sounding a little like a Harold Budd album) - a stellar track!

The Dark Side of the Moog 7, like the other editions I've heard or seen reviewed, is a success.

1998 *A Tribute to Klaus Schulze*

This CD contains one track apiece from ten electronic musicians, plus a track from Klaus himself, "The Schulzendorf Groove," performed by The Schulzendorfer Groove Orchestra (KS). This KS track is about 14:00 long. Also noteworthy is one track by the group called Subsonic Affair, "Remember *X*." Subsonic Affair is really Joerg Schaaf.

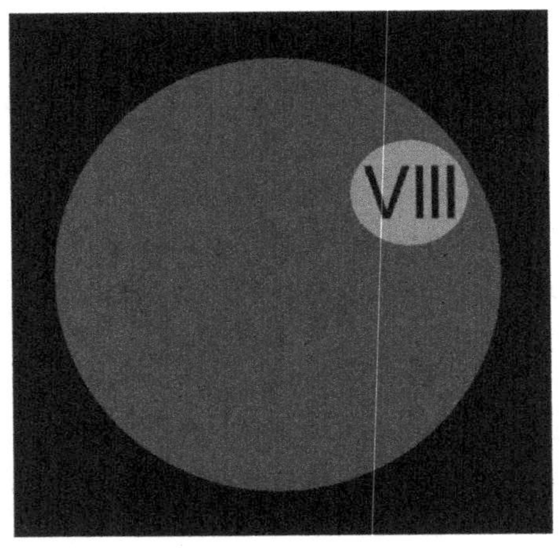

1999 *The Dark Side of the Moog 8* (with Pete Namlook)

Review by Damon Capehart at http://datacide.com:16080/pk146/:

"So, overall I give this an 8.5/10, mostly because of (IMO) Klaus' limitations performing live... If you're a big Klaus Schulze fan, on the other hand, you will love this release. In this case, the album gets 12/10, and if you don't get a copy somehow, then you're REALLY missing out."

From Heather Phares, *All Music Guide*, at http://www.answers.com/dark+side+of+the+moog+8%3A?cat=entertainment

"Though it might not be the most immediately engaging volume of the series, another *Dark Side of the Moog* album is always welcome."

From David Law at http://www.answers.com/topic/dark-side-of-the-moog-8:

"Half way into the 25-minute opening section the pace quickens and the sequence becomes louder, the drums really start to kick and another typically Schulzian sequence is tossed into the pot, incredible! Turn up loud. This must have got the audience in rapture, absolutely amazing!... The final section, effectively the encore, is an intense floater with a mournful Schulzian lead. A superb track to finish a superb album."

From http://www.ambientmusicguide.com/pages/S/schulze.php:

"Bill Laswell joins them for *Dark Side VIII*, which proves a fine showcase for their more upbeat excursions."

1999 *Trailer*

From David Law at http://www.synthmusicdirect.com:

"Most of the tracks from this CD are taken from the just issued *Ultimate Edition* and as such acts as a sort of promotional release for that massive project but it is also of interest because three of the tracks contained on it don't appear on that set or any where else for that matter... So to sum up, there are some fine tracks here and it will no doubt be snapped up by Schulze completists because of the three otherwise unavailable numbers but it would also be a good purchase for those fans who can't quite afford any of the *Ultimate Edition* boxes."

Chapter 12 Klaus' Solo Career and Collaborations 2000-2004

2000 *Ultimate Edition*

Combining *Historic Edition* (10 CDs), *Silver Edition* (10 CDs), *Jubilee Edition* (25 CDs) and five extra CDs compiled specifically for this edition, the *Ultimate Edition* has long been sold out and has been an occasional item on eBay and even Eurock.com. All of the material is set to be re-released by sometime in 2008, according to the Official Klaus Schulze Website. By the time you have this book, that re-release may already be started.

I first became intrigued when I started to read some of the reviews with effusive praise on the KS website. I felt like I was definitely missing something important in the Schulze catalog. As I've mentioned before, I did buy CDs 21-29 of the set on eBay and, as you can see from my Jubilee Edition reviews, I found a lot of worthwhile material.

2000 *Contemporary Works I*

Six of the 10 CDs from *Contemporary Works I* have been a part of the re-release series. It appears the other titles will not be re-released, giving those who bought the limited edition some exclusivity.

From http://www.starsend.org/ContemporaryWorks.html:

"[W]ithin Contemporary Works the listener will find the interesting techno rhythms, classical harmonics and tribal timbres that Schulze has been recently exploring."

The following reviews of the CDs from *Contemporary Works* I (10 CD set on Rainhorse/Manikin Records), which were not involved in the re-release series, come courtesy of Matt Howarth:

"Each of these ten CDs comes in a cardboard sleeve, most of which sport rather impressive computer art. These sleeves are packaged in a wooden box with a design burned into the cover. A metal clasp holds the box shut. Also included is a 60 page glossy booklet full of color pictures and exhaustive data (which, unfortunately, is all in German)."

CD 3: Wahnfried: *Trance 4 Motion*

Traditionally, the Wahnfried band has been Schulze's opportunity to explore collaborative efforts. These releases tend to feature a more relaxed form of Schulze's music, one that has been heading in a decidedly trance direction. These 79 minutes are no exception; the track features Joerg Schaaf, who has been Schulze's Wahnfried partner now for a few releases.

This trance inevitably adopts stronger attributes, injecting the atmospheric mood with livelier sensibilities that cavort and whirl with clever effect. Despite the increase of complexity and swifter rhythms, this music retains a calming quality that [soothes] as it relaxes.

There is a short (15:00 is short for Schulze's music) remix by Solar Moon System that carries the music into definitely peppier territory, with more prominent percussives, searing guitar, and sneaky vocal snippets.

CD 4: *U.S.O.: Privee*

For this 65-minute disc, Schulze joins U.S.O. (being Uwe Lehr, aka Razoof Lear, on drums, and Olli Finken, aka O'Finken, on guitar). The result is a tasty dose of dreamy synthesizer music heavily flavored by more traditional instruments, giving the pieces a remarkably earthy sound.

A thick bass presence excellently compliments the flowing melodies.

The guitar alternates between obvious guitar notes and tortured string effects. The drumming, although enhanced at its edges with subtle tempos, maintains a solid beat that refuses to wax or wane.

CD 5: *Klaus Schulze vs. Solar Moon: Docking*

For this 77-minute disc, Schulze goes head-to-digital-head with Solar Moon System (being Tom Dams and George Boskamp) in the "Versus" style of remix dueling popular among techno bands. The result is quite a departure from Schulze's normal output.

Complexity is replaced with cyclic repetition as a foundation. This sonic platform does reach further than Schulze's music, with the constant presence of organic dub-style vocals (not to be confused with the use of sampled vocal snippets). The application of E-perc is far more sedate than Schulze's stylings, being regular and languid instead of surging and dynamic.

The overall mode of this music is deeply rooted in modern techno and trance genres: establishing a model that remains generally untampered throughout. Additions are employed as enhancements that add to the existing music, but they rarely embellish it.

CD 10: *Klaus Schulze: Adds & Edits*

This final disc in the set features a selection of shorter pieces averaging three and five minutes each. These tracks are collaborations between Schulze and the others found in this box set, although there are four pieces by Schulze in solo mode (including a 10-minute composition that gives an example of his epic slow burn quality in a briefer, more compressed composition).

Solar Moon System

From the Solar Moon System Logbook '94_'00 -- Klaus Schulze on Solar Moon System (from https://www.forcedexposure.com/artists/solar.moon.system.html):

"How could this happen after being a musician for over 30 years -- I get a self-produced CD single from a band I don't know about -- and it makes me freak out completely! I wish you all the same amazement and uplifting silence that I felt listening to Solar Moon's music." -- Schulze.

From Lothar Lubitz, SynGate, January 2001, at http://www.syngate.net/008%20manikin/Manikin_Rainhorse_200011.html:

"Solar Moon System is a musician/DJ collaboration from Cologne, Germany and consists of Tom, George, O´Finken [Olli Finken] and Razoof [Uwe Lehr]. They call their trip hop downbeats and dub sounds just moon pop. The above mentioned CD single 'Outer Canal Street' is included in the *Logbook* album, a retrospective of their works between 1994 and 2000."

Archie Patterson, Eurock, March 2001, at http://www.syngate.net/008%20manikin/Manikin_Rainhorse_200011.html:

"This is the first solo release on Klaus Schulze's Rainhorse Records label, and I can see why Klaus loves Solar Moon System. Their sound combines long spatial soundscapes, loops, and sequences, with sampled voices and effects. The result is futuristic space music that conceptually and sonically will transport your mind to other realms of listening."

A further description of Solar Moon System, from http://www.solarmoon.com/solar/index.html:

"Solar Moon is a production collective from Cologne/Germany, operating live and in the studio since the mid-nineties... over the years, Solar Moon bred various party concepts including deejaying, live visuals and light design. With their trademark sound incorporating dub, midtempo breakbeat and deep house, Solar Moon has delivered remix work for bands and projects."

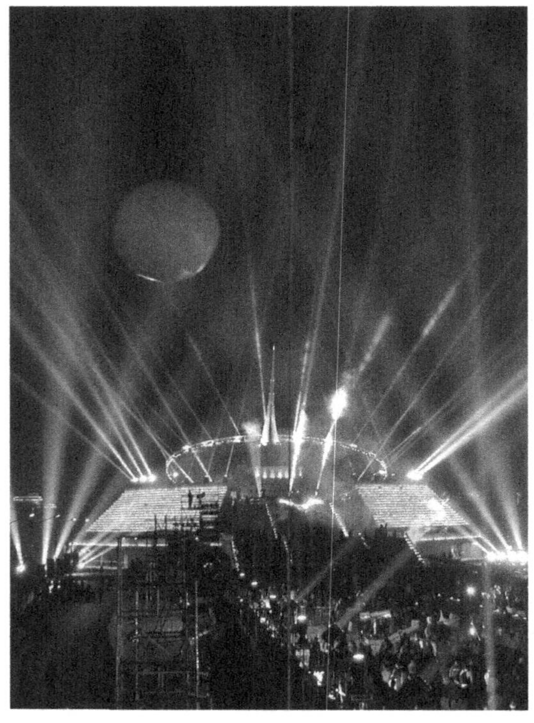

2000 The Millenium Event in China

KDM describes the Millenium Event in China and Klaus Schulze's involvement in it through his music:

"KS was asked to do the official music for the real Millenium Event on the 31st of December 2000 into the 1st of January 2001. It happened in Beijing, China: Thirty minutes KS music for the main event New Millenium New Beijing, an exciting light show from 23:40 to 00:10. This was not a live concert but the music was specially composed, played and recorded before by Klaus and then used as playback. The event was shown (at least) on all Chinese TV programmes, and therefore the music of Klaus was heard by approximately one billion people. The artistic director of the event, the light artist Gert Hof, does also the visuals for the German pop group Rammstein, and he did last year's Millenium Party in Berlin with Mike Oldfield."

2000 *Friendship* (with Ash Ra Tempel)

From Edgar Kogler http://www.amazings.com/reviews/review0790.html:

"Göttsching is in charge of the guitars, whereas Schulze is the one who deals with the synthesizers, sequencers and effects. Throughout the album the style nearest to Schulze predominates in a special manner."

2000 *Gin Rosé at the Royal Festival Hall*

From Edgar Kogler at http://www.amazings.com/reviews/review0789.html:

"Schulze and Göttsching performed a large suite with experimental passages, whereas others were symphonic. A work not lacking in rhythm…."

2001 *Live @ KlangArt CD 1*

From David Law at http://www.synthmusicdirect.com/:

"People who thrill at seeing a musician surrounded by bank upon bank of knobs illuminated by LED's will love the artwork as you get page after page of it (24 full glossy ones to be precise). Both pictures and music are taken from his recent KlangArt Festival performance in Osnabrück.

[Regarding the first track "Breeze to Sequence",] "[e]thereal pads provide a tranquil backdrop to the pulsations as they mutate. The style will be familiar to what you will find on his recent works but there are frequent moments which take me back twenty years.

[Impressions of the last track on CD 1, "'I Loop You Schwindelig':] "...a track that is full of energy and yet the host of pulsations and beats are kept under tight control giving a feeling of space rather than clutter which adds to its subtle beauty still further. After a bit the mind becomes mesmerized as you are taken into a state of trance. More detail is added during the last ten minutes of this twenty eight minute monster, but even so I did think that it went on a tad too long but this is only a minor quibble and I know that many a Schulze fan could listen to this sort of thing forever."

Here's my review of *Live @ KlangArt CD 1*:

CD 1 comes with a 24-page booklet with color photos of the concert (this is not the re-issue, since it wasn't available at the time of this writing).

In the beginning minute of "Breeze to Sequence" (15:08), voices reminiscent of *The Dark Side of the Moog* albums, combine with phaser-like synth pulses, which at times have a glissando effect. A crash of thunder ushers in a pair of sequencers, choirs and drum machine. The choirs have a purposeful, almost religious sound to them as they sing in a semi-chant style. Minimoog surfaces at close to the 6:00 mark, playing a lead that is very much in tune with the rest of the fairly brisk rhythm.

It's noteworthy that on this CD, the back cover shows four tracks, but both my CD player and Windows Media Player show only two. The first track is shown on the players as a combination of "Breeze to Sequence," "Loops to Groove," and "From Church to Search." This forms a track a little over 42 minutes (a track with no name!).

As the beat picks up energy around the 11:00 mark, the searing nature of Klaus' Minimoog ascends.

"Loops to Groove" (12:58) begins with a throaty human voice before restrained drumming picks up the pace just slightly over long, slow KS pads. The piece provides a pronounced breather from the previous sizzling tempo. The slow pace never changes as we move into "From Church to Search" (14:06).

Interplay between a male and female singer singing in the style of chanting monks introduces the song. The beat picks up just a bit, and things are getting more interesting again as the pads take on more diversity and passion.

A hint of percolating sequencer emerges, signaling what may become the first significant rhythm since around the 15:00 mark (of the nameless 42-minute track). Wolfgang's cello plays in the background while the beat is still at a fairly slow pace.

Beyond Recall-style samples emerge. Choirs and stunning, rising synths bring about a very intense and emotionally charged stirring passage. The first time I heard it, I was blown away by it. These last three minutes are one of the highlights of CD 1.

The final track on CD 1, "I Loop You Schwindelig," starts with synth pulses that sound tentative but seem to be the harbinger of increased intensity to come. Musical tension is present right from the start.

Sharp sounding percussion at around 2:40 instantly leads to thoughts of Michael Shrieve. A moderate paced sequencer starts, building the tension a little more. Reintroduction of the percussion indicates that we're in for a wild and fun ride!

Bubbling sequencers and the "doo doo doo doo" sample that Klaus occasionally uses add more spice to the mix. Surprisingly, despite some nice percussion riffs, the pace of "I Loop You Schwindelig" never picks up. The last 7 minutes are filled with interesting sounds.

Live @ KlangArt CD 1 is a pleasant CD. Without giving too much away about CD 2, it seems that this CD represents a buildup in this concert which is analogous to the way Klaus builds up his songs (the beginning can often be slower and less intense than later sections of a KS composition). From that point of view, I can't downgrade this CD for being too laid back, because it may be merely serving its role well in the context of the overall "musical piece" that consists of all the music played that evening.

2001 *Live @ KlangArt CD 2*

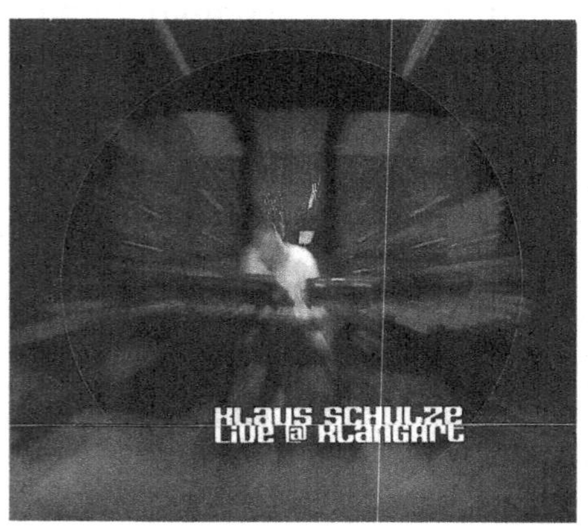

From David Law at http://www.synthmusicdirect.com/:

"This CD is even better than the first one in the series... This is awesome stuff -- so much is going on. Yet another sequence enters at the 6:00 mark -- a high-register one. Then the drums come in. How on Earth he manages to control the maelstrom and then construct a scorching lead line over the top I will never know. It's all extremely exciting and Klaus sounds as if he is having fun... At 9:00 their second track together, 'Tracks of Desire,' is the shortest over both CDs, but it is a stunning little piece beginning with solo cello which becomes very deep at times then at almost two minutes in it is joined by soft synth pads. For the rest of the track both pads and cello weave rather sad sounding Picture Music. The feeling of sadness is emphasized still further during the last minute by choral effects which can just be heard very low in the mix."

My review of *Live@KlangArt* CD 2 (24-page booklet included)

The early moments of "La Fugue Sequenca" (21:59) are sprinkled with synth pads and echoing flute notes. The unique (for KS) synth pads and flute play together for a very different KS sound. The lightness of the beginning gives way to a darker tone for a bit. Following some sampling, a lively, playful sequencer enters and is joined by a second, causing me to experience a soaring emotional feeling.

Deep bass notes, "drumming" and other percussion work their way into the mix. The concert consists of only Klaus and Wolfgang Tiepold.

A Minimoog solo rips into "La Fugue Sequenca," its electric guitar quality combining with active sequencing to form a great sound.

Engrossed in Klaus' Minimoog solo, I became oblivious to the fact that this is a very rhythm oriented track until the return of drums re-enforced it. The multiple sequencers are fantastic! I never tire of hearing Klaus create sound tapestries with sequencers.

Close to the 15:00 mark, the sounds all intensify, with a deeper sequencer and a Minimoog solo that takes flight even higher than before.

How remarkable it must have been for the concertgoers at KlangArt to hear this multitude of mind blowing sounds coming from one and only one man playing on stage! I'm marveling at it myself. It's amazing that Klaus can play a one man band with the stunning results that he gets. And, as usual, I'm amazed at how Klaus can compose these intricate and delightful pieces of music time after time.

"La Fugue Sequenca" is a very auspicious beginning to the concert!

Wolfgang Tiepold plays cello near the end of the piece, continuing into "Cavalleria Cellisticana" (21:51) and blending with Klaus' very long and minor key synth pads for a very beautiful sound which I experienced as very moving. The cello elicits a feeling of deep longing, yearning; an expression of a deep need unfulfilled.

An occasional manipulated deep human voice is mixed in. This is an exquisite, very engaging period of expression – making me feel that I'm listening to something very special. This may be the best Klaus and Wolfgang ever sounded together!

Awe-inspiring, yet subtle choirs join Klaus and Wolfgang – combining to make a magical period even more overwhelmingly wondrous.

A more buoyant feeling arrives with sequencers and drums re-joining the mix. The sequencers play at rapid-fire tempo as the sound joyously and rapturously spirals upward.

The last 17:00 or so represent a microcosm of the human experience - joy and exhilaration followed by a down period characterized by yearning and sadness. This period of struggle is followed again by a feeling of being wholly alive. And the cycle repeats.

Wolfgang Tiepold's solo cello plays very compellingly coinciding with the start of "Tracks of Desire" (9:13). Klaus' synth pads join after a couple of minutes. The cello sounds spectacular at times, filling my speakers with a full sound. During the times the cello produces the most bass, it sounds as if it's ready to expand beyond the limits of my speakers. Eight minutes into "Tracks of Desire" the gentle, yet stirring choir sings again (this sounds like a choir filled with angelic female voices).

Mid-register sequencer and dramatic pad followed by percussion and drums usher in "Last Move at Osnabrück." Soon, a slashing percussive downbeat develops - mixing very well with the rising tide of sequencers and drums. A very interesting rhythm has been formed. Without warning, an overwhelmingly, indescribably beautiful surge of synths pads elevates the experience of the music further than I dreamed possible. This CD is one of the most stunning pieces of music that I've ever heard anywhere. It is all the more impressive for its relentlessly high quality that is sustained for approximately 66 minutes.

Now I know why Klaus has the reactions that you will see in the last several pictures of this concert, which I pulled out of the huge selection he sent me.

Klaus used the choirs on this CD differently than on any other album, fitting in with the grandeur of this musical achievement very well.

Only occasionally will a person experience art at this level! I can use every superlative that I can think of but this CD seems to be beyond that!

Photos from Live at KlangArt:

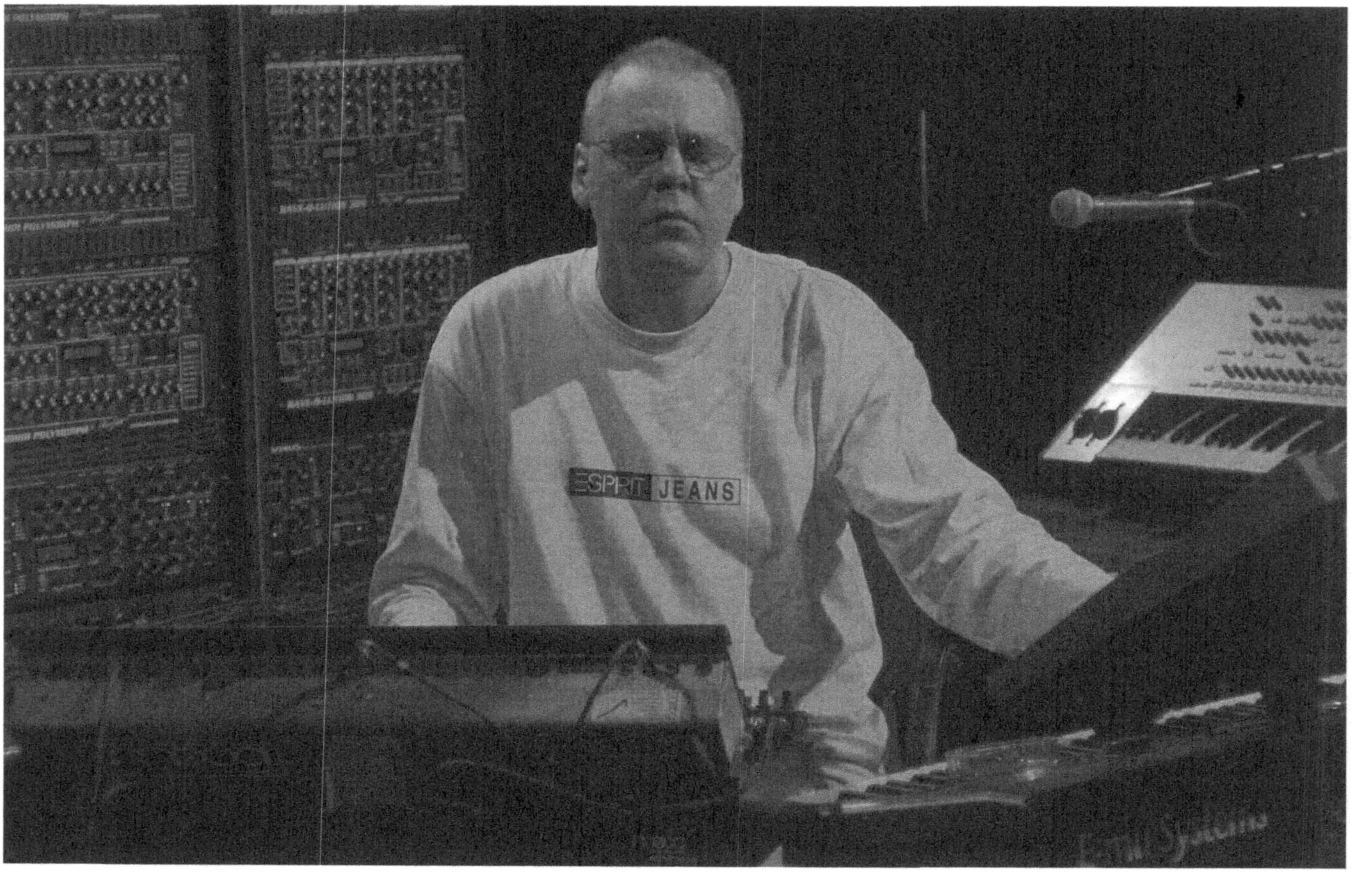
ESPRIT JEANS

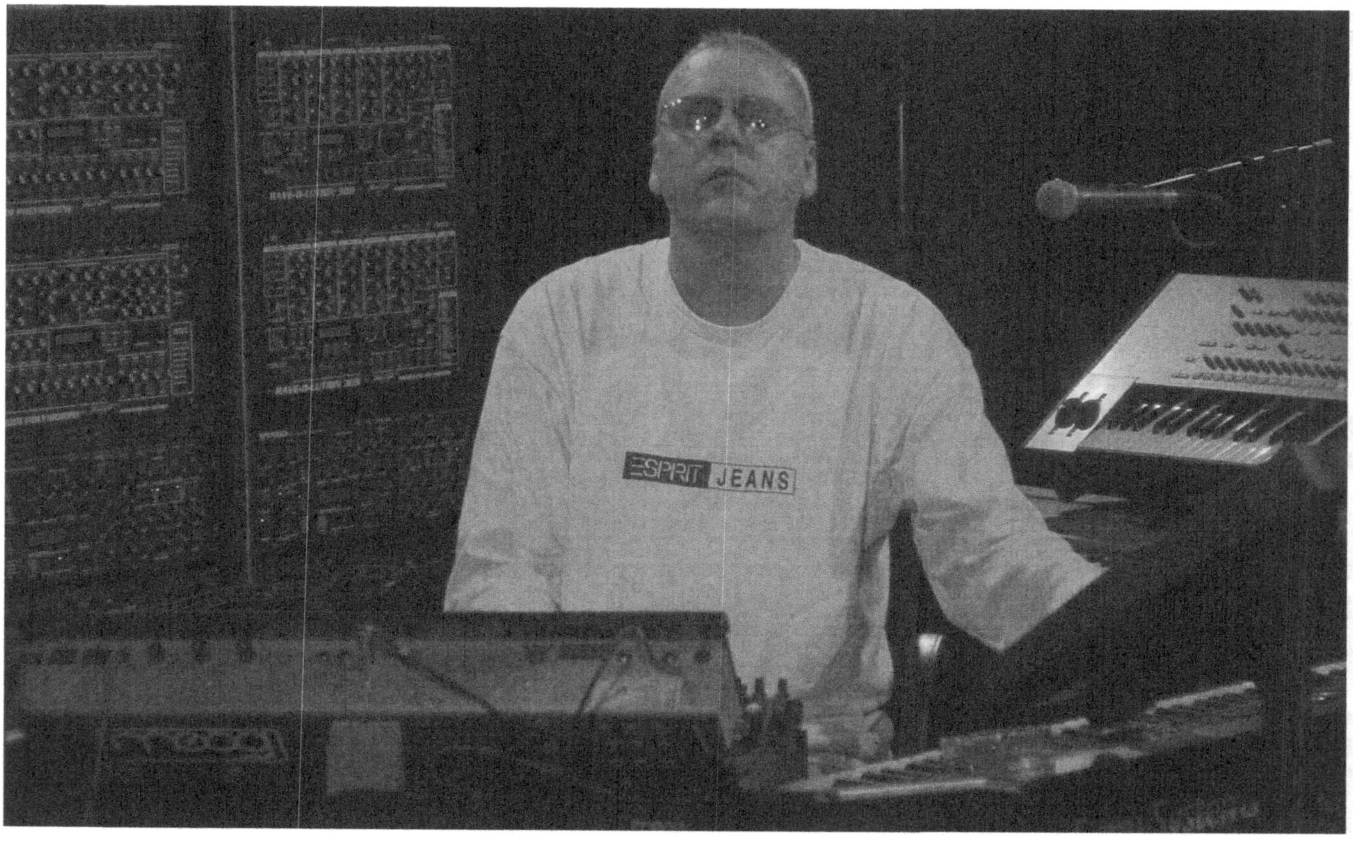
ESPRIT JEANS

2001 Supergroup Appears on TV Channel SAT1 singing "Those Were the Days" in Criminal Movie *Klassentreffen*

From http://www.faithfulandtrue.de/sputnikr.htm:

"An all-star-band consisting of Marian Gold, Klaus Schulze, Toni Nissl, F.J. Krüger and 'Fredi Schnitzel' are 'the wondering stars' to be shown with a classical song by Mary Hopkin, 'Those Were the Days' on the 20th of February 2001 in TV channel SAT1 in the criminal movie *Klassentreffen*".

In an interview for Radio Eins, which you can download also on the Sputnik Roadhouse website, Marian said (among other things):

"Oh yes, it was very funny... during our careers from time to time we met and in various productions we also worked together. Because of this soundtrack for the criminal movie we had the possibility to make something together in the combination of these musicians and finally we had the chance to leave a bit the genre in that we work normally and do something completely different together. And this was quite good. We had a lot of joy.

"Fred Schnitzel plays the bass. And the person with this nickname is nobody else than the legendary Florian Schneider from the band Kraftwerk".

I've seen this video, and it's a real treat. I especially like Marian's singing. Here is what I wrote to KDM after initially seeing the video:

"In doing my research, I of course came across the video with Florian Schneider, Marian Gold and KS on keyboards performing 'Those Were the Days.' I like the version by Mary Hopkin many years ago and though it may be considered cheesy by some, I like this version. I like Marian Gold's voice; it reminds me of that certain commanding quality that Johnny Cash and Ernest Tubb had, along with Brendan Perry of Dead Can Dance, even Bryan Ferry on certain songs. It is also so cool to see KS in the background playing keyboards. Talk about some legendary players in a 1:25 video!"

A picture of the supergroup performing in the movie Klassentreffen.

Klaus in Poznan.

Klaus on vocoder.

Paris 16 November 1978.

2002 *Contemporary Works II*

Contemporary Works II consists of five disks and a booklet which contains a description of the process of putting together *Contemporary Works II.* Klaus had intended a 10-CD set but later decided on five. A couple of good tracks by Marian Gold were cut but will likely still be used in a future release.

KDM then goes on to give a description including his impressions of each of the CDs. There are, of course, photographs of Klaus and his studio, as well as a comic strip, "Contemporary Walks," by Matt Howarth. There is also a fairly lengthy article by Georg Abts (who contributed photographs for this book) on "The Making of Electronic Music". This includes "A Visit to Klaus' Studio" and "The Wizard of EM, How Klaus Works Today." Finally, there is an article by Klaus D. Mueller entitled "In Concerts."

The artists listed for *Contemporary Works II* are KS (electronics, keyboards, guitar), Wolfgang Tiepold (cello), Thomas Kagermann (Arabian flute, violin, vocals), Audrey Motaung (vocals), Julia Messenger (altered vocals, Julia told me her voice had been used on *Contemporary Works II* but it was unrecognizable as her), Tobias Becker (oboe, English Horn), Mickes (guitar), Tom Dams (some groove loops). Also of note, I believe that all five of these CDs will be re-released as part of the massive re-release series on SPV. The first is scheduled to be *Virtual Outback*, which will likely have been released by the time this book is published.

Contemporary Works II CD 1 – *Virtual Outback*

Virtual Outback consists of one song, "The Theme: The Rhodes Elegy" at 65:00 (no subtitles!). It starts with slow, resonating Fender Rhodes piano-like notes, followed by a very slowly evolving oboe note. A very slow pace in the first few minutes, make this sound like music that could be used for meditation.

After 3:00 string pads enter, accompanied by oboe. These first minutes are very nice!

Trance Appeal-type synth sounds, percussion, and booming "drums" reveal the first stirrings of rhythm at about five minutes, while the oboe continues to solo as the centerpiece. A quickened tempo prevails through 15:00. After that, the track evolves into a mid-tempo pace for a while.

The recording quality is quite good. Cello or violin joins in between 13:00 and 14:00. As I retreat from the laptop back to my listening position at the apex of the "listening triangle", I appreciate the recording even more. The booming drums have a very satisfying bass quality, and the percussion sounds very crisp, with excellent stereo separation.

At the 20:00 mark, it occurs to me that the sound of the piece could be described as sensual, especially as the oboe takes on a much fuller, breathy sound.

Two heavily altered voices come into the mix. Occasional light choirs surface from time to time. This is a very nice, soothing, yet intriguing piece of music to listen to. What else would we expect from the master? Klaus' post-2000 work is revealing itself as being on a very high plane.

Choir voices sing over sparse instrumentation, that sparseness accentuating the effect of the choirs. Soon, a reverberating, fabulous sounding electric guitar gets center stage. The longer the song plays, the more I think that it's a fantastic piece of music.

The piece slows down past the 40:00 mark to the point where the drum beat sounds like a heart beating by itself. Just when it seems it might be getting a little long and monotonous, the subtle beauty of the soft, distant choirs and the elegance of an understated electric guitar create an elevated feeling, yet again.

The choir "members" sound as if they are conducting their own choral symphony in the far off distance, and "Elegy" takes on a peaceful, ethereal, almost blissful, ambient character.

"The Theme: The Rhodes Elegy" is a very strong start to *Contemporary Works II*!

Contemporary Works II CD 2 – *Timbres of Ice*

On the inside of the front insert of the CD is a face shot of Klaus. It's noteworthy that each *CW II* CD has a different color swath on the front of the insert and the face image of young Klaus Schulze on the inside of the insert is in that same color -- for all except CD 5, which has no face shot on the insert.

Timbres of Ice consists of three songs, "The Lonely Dead of Midnight" (10:51), "They Shut Him Out of Paradise" (41:41), and "Die Prophezeiung erfüllt sich" (23:15). On to the music:

"The Lonely Dead of Midnight" starts with very crisp, clean, resonating acoustic guitar possessing a plaintive, yearning quality. Dramatic, minor key synth provokes a deeply emotional feeling from within me. Oboe-like sound enters at close to 7:00 as the soundscape is, again, sparse – yielding a beauty born of elegance and simplicity.

"They Shut Him Out of Paradise" (41:41) begins as a continuation of "The Lonely Dead," with an echoing, highly treated male voice – but, wait, KDM mentioned in the booklet that comes with *CW II* that this is a high female voice, treated in such a way that it sounds like a male voice.

Deep bass and drums form an evolving rhythm, together with an indecipherable throaty vocal. The highly treated vocals serve as another instrument in the mix.

Percolating, bubbling synth plays along with a mysterious sounding lead that adds a lot to the track. At first it sounds like Minimoog, then more like a smooth, high-register synth pad.

The treated vocals are a dominant part of the song. They are creative, with an interesting texture but at times sound disturbing. Klaus is forever taking risks, daring to try something different!

The sound becomes almost ambient approaching 20:00. Klaus' approach in *CW II* seems so creative that I imagine that a Frippish sounding guitar may be formed with human vocals altered so radically, that they are playing distinguishable and believable guitar notes. I have no basis in fact for that but mention it only to point out how daring and creative the music on *CW II* can be.

The highly unusual vocals bear the mark of the grand adventurer Schulze!

Actually, this is just what I want from *Contemporary Works II* – a fresh approach and a challenging yet highly rewarding listen. The growth of Klaus as a musician has obviously continued, and in many ways his music is grander and more mature than ever! *Contemporary Works II* sounds fresh and alive with the joy that is so typical of KS' music.

"Die Prophezeiung erfüllt sich" (23:15) consists of Klaus' mellow synth pads throughout, forming a gentle backdrop for the main element of the song – cryptic human voices which have a very interesting texture and are recorded very well, in sensational stereo. These voices are the centerpiece of the track, the main instrument involved.

"Die Prophezeiung" is a nice track.

Contemporary Works II CD 3 – *Another Green Mile*

KDM mentions in the booklet notes that, although the CD has five track markers, it can also be experienced as one piece. He also refers to the fact that some of the loyal Klaus Schulze listeners like it that way. Count me in that group! I think I talked about it elsewhere in this book, but I enjoy seeing a CD with one track of 65 minutes (such as "The Theme: The Rhodes Elegy of Virtual Outback") or even over 70 minutes (such as "My Ty She").

This may go back to the special feeling that came with owning *Timewind* with its two long tracks, creating a special feeling that I was onto something new, different and cool! So, to this day, I would prefer that longer tracks such as those on *In Blue*, for example, would simply be listed as a single track with no subtitles. Another CD in that category would be *Royal Festival Hall Vol. II.* I would much prefer that the subtitles be left out.

Luscious synth pads and oboe start "Between Twilight and Dawn" (13:20), a very gentle, almost tentative piece of music, with just pads and oboe. The oboe sounds synthesized to me. "Between Twilight and Dawn" has a very peaceful, potentially relaxing feel.

"In the Street, in the Rain" (4:33) continues without a break, marked by the introduction of strong female vocals soaring over the synth pads. My best guess is that this is Audrey Motaung, whose vocals are very appealing, fitting in beautifully with the flow of the piece. An occasional drum thump and increasingly steady percussion end the track.

"The Wisdom of the Leaves" (12:27), the third track, begins as all instrumental with very soothing sounds and a very satisfying bass backing – a little jazzy but in a very KS sort of way! Cello and violin alternate to form a very pleasing mix. Percussion forms a very steady, yet soft and gentle rhythm, around which the various solos play.

Audrey sings again at the outset of "The Story Does Unfold" (12:05). The percussive rhythm, now having played for several minutes, forms a stylish groove. This strength of *Another Green Mile* became apparent almost imperceptibly at first, but once fully realized, becomes a very strong part of the composition. Meanwhile Audrey's voice has a power and expressiveness which is very impressive.

This CD would make an excellent choice when you're feeling stressed and need some very peaceful music to sooth your soul.

A very rhythmic quality, starkly different from the rest of *Another Green Mile*, ushers in the last track, "Follow Me Down, Follow Me Down" (28:46). For the first time on *Another Green Mile*, sequencers are present, adding a lot to the listening experience. The first 3:00 are very exciting, stimulating, fun and rewarding!

The sequencers trickle in around a very steady backbeat, formed possibly by a drum machine, becoming the centerpiece of "Follow Me Down". Floating, spacy sounding violin enters the mix past the 5:00 mark, adding a glorious new element to an increasingly impressive track. A very slow, space-guitar sound adds even more.

Around 8:00, much – but not all – of the beat suddenly drops out; replaced by muffled, treated voices.

This is a more complex Schulze composition, with a wide variety of tempos and instruments. A very steady, hypnotic beat is joined at the 11:00 mark by treated guitars and at times just the treated voices. This beat continues unabated for the next 20:00. The treated guitars sound excellent, with an ethereal, floating quality.

Another Green Mile is a pleasant, relaxing CD overall, with rhythm taking over for the last 20:00 or so. The highlights are the repetitive percussive groove in Track 3, "The Wisdom of the Leaves;" the beat and the sequencers in "Follow Me Down"; and Audrey Motaung's singing.

Contemporary Works II CD 4 – *Androgyn*

“In the Dimness of Light” (12:47) starts with cello and gurgling synth sounds, soon joined by bass and drums and a downbeat that says “funk.” Treated, indecipherable reverberating vocals solo for a time. One of the most noteworthy aspects of *Contemporary Works I* and *II* is Klaus’ use of the human voice as an instrument in so many pieces of music.

Cello follows the vocals with its very interpretive sound, adding a lot to the track, which has a very impressionistic feel.

“Back to the Future” (28:02), the second track, features “Klaus playing the guitar in a cosmic slide guitar technique, such as used in Ash Ra Tempel, 32 years before” (from KDM, in the *CWII* booklet).

The track opens in a heavenly way with glorious, imaginative stirring pads and probably the slide guitar referred to above. This is truly blissful music, an absolutely superb slice of musical nirvana.

Both the piano-like notes and the slide guitar reverberate once they sound, creating a very relaxing and spacy atmosphere. Drums and other percussion enter after 7:00; the spacy slide guitar continues playing as before.

“Back to the Future” is a stunning piece of music, reminding me of the genius of Schulze.

Audrey’s voice starts Track 3, “There’s No Mystery” (4:37), again showing power and surprising softness or gentleness at the same time. It’s also moved back and forth between the left and right speakers, to great delight. Slow synth pads and emotionally charged violin playing alternate with her voice to form another winning piece of music.

“There’s No Mystery” blends seamlessly into the fourth track, “Don’t Ask the Question Why” (5:08). The tempo picks up, with percussion forming a quickened rhythm, supported by drums and oboe.

The brisk rhythm of this piece continues straight through “The Passion Burns” (4:22) and on into the final song, “This House Full of Shadows” (20:43). The same driving, funky rhythm persists for upwards of 30:00. Audrey sings in a background role in “The House of Shadows.” The groove is especially addictive, it’s grown on me over the course of these three songs - I’m hoping it doesn’t stop. It’s another KS groove that can go on for a long time without being boring. In fact, it’s been accompanied by nothing for the last several minutes, and that has been a treat!

Androgyn is a great CD, pure and simple!

Contemporary Works II CD 5 – *Cocooning*

Cocooning consists of eight tracks, the longest at 26:11 ("Easy Listening") and three tracks of 2:17 or less!!!

"Easy Listening" (26:11) starts out very peacefully, layering several instruments, including acoustic guitar, percussion, pads and what sounds like a treated piano or softened guitar. The acoustic guitar has the lead for a long time.

This is definitely a different sound for KS - very slow, laid back and gentle - but very nice. For the first 13-14 minutes, "Easy Listening" changes less than just about any Klaus Schulze song I can think of.

"And She is Kind and Gentle" (12:01) refers to Blanche (presumably Klaus' French girlfriend at the time of *Body Love*); according to KDM in the *CW II* booklet. The song starts with oboe and pads. The oboe plays quite expressively, while the pads gain more authority than they had in "Easy Listening."

The pads become predominantly minor in key and laden with bass. The piece becomes much more emotion provoking as it progresses, moving into the category of a strong piece of music.

"I Just Have to Sing My Hymns" (20:03) starts with another heavily altered voice (which sounds male). A rhythm forms rather quickly, along with pads and the altered voice. By the 2:00 mark, there is a soulful and funky beat developing. The voice can be considered strictly another instrument.

Since Klaus is so playful with the sounds in this set, using lots of alterations, it's difficult to identify the instruments being played.

After the 9:00 mark, a distinguishable voice sings fairly passionately, with resonance, as it morphs between a female and male sound. A second altered male voice is intertwined with the morphing voice. All along, there's a very hypnotic groove. Nobody but KS could have created something like this! It's incredibly creative and most astoundingly, it really works as a very enjoyable piece of music. Several sound elements are involved in propelling the groove and in making it sound very interesting.

The music blends smoothly into the fourth song, "I Just Have to Sing My Hymns," which has a much mellower tempo. It's basically an oboe solo leading to the fifth song, "Blowin' thru the high grass," which starts out with light electric guitar playing in front of the same soft tempo. The guitar plays in a soulful, almost bluesy way.

"Many dreams have faded in" takes over from "Blowin'," with oboe re-entering the mix. This time the oboe has a sharper sound.

"Many dreams" (1:29) continues the mellow, almost jazzy quality, melding soon into "Many fears have vanished" (9:36), which reintroduces the bluesy electric guitar. This is the fourth consecutive song with the same continuous backbeat, very slow and lazy. The guitar becomes quite expressive and even reverberates (close to an echo effect), at times. It sounds quite a bit more interesting than in "Blowin' Thru the High Grass."

"Many fears" is all about the soulful lead guitar, which makes the song one of the better pieces on *Cocooning.*

The guitar takes on a slide guitar sound for the final track, "As the Years Went by."

Cocooning has just enough high points to give me a good feeling about it. Another excellent CD to listen to when you're stressed out. I think it could be either background music or a more serious, focused listen.

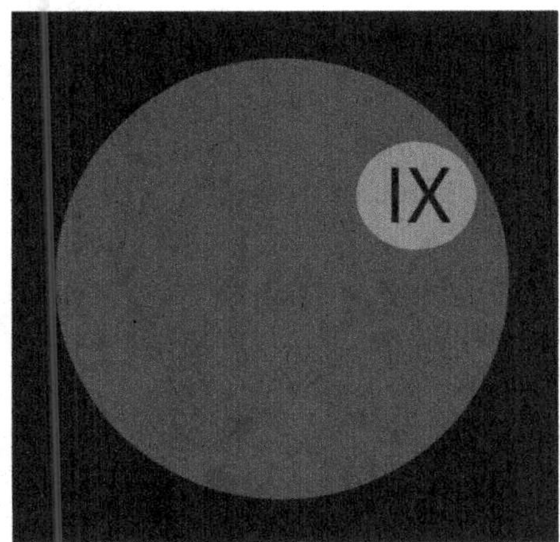

2002 *The Dark Side of the Moog 9* (with Pete Namlook)

The following is from a review by Chuck van Zyl/STAR'S END on May 2, 2003 (at http://www.starsend.org/DarkSideOfThe-Moog9.html):

"On this album, the music's trajectory rises immediately into low-earth orbit...powered with the pulse of layered analogue percussion cycling softly beneath the wandering counterpoint of electric piano and vintage synth leads...rhythmic element comes from steadfast sequencer driven synth tones."

From David Law at http://www.synthmusicdirect.com/moog9.cfm:

"When number VII of this series was released I thought it was the best so far and yet to these ears each volume since then has scaled even greater heights. Volume IX is simply stunning."

From Glenn Swan http://www.allmusic.com:

"Part[s] one and three are melodic tapestries of soft sequencers and shuffling percussion à la Tangerine Dream... Part two.... [and] part four... are a welcome sorbet for the ears, adding an element of mystery without being abrasive... [The] disc closes with part five and six.... reminiscent of an Equinoxe-era Jean Michel Jarre."

From http://www.ambientmusicguide.com/pages/S/schulze.php:

"*Dark Side IX* is exquisite tone colour music in the best Berlin-school tradition, muted and gently rhythmic, mournful yet beautiful, perhaps the best album the pair have recorded together."

My impressions of *The Dark Side of the Moog IX* (the FAX CD, consisting of one track (54:32) divided into six parts).

Part 1 starts with atmospheric noises and deep rumblings. Arising from this soundscape, a piano-like chime plays, resonating and sounding very soothing. Very spacy sounds are all around, including choirs in the background. A somewhat funky beat develops amidst the chimes and choirs. The beat continues to develop to the point that it becomes an endearing and central part of the track. Exquisite sounding Minimoog is introduced in the late phases. This is a smooth, soaring, dreamy sounding Minimoog that is interwoven with the rest of the music.

Towards 15:00, when it seems this track couldn't possibly get any better, a fantastic sounding sequencer thrusts into the mix, joined by a very authoritative beat. This sequencer has a progressing sound that matches the rest of the track. The moment that the sequencer and beat came into the song was one of pure musical delight and awe. I am totally into this piece of music – it's a master stroke from Schulze and Namlook. It's music that's about as good as it gets!

Part 1 is silky smooth, sophisticated, funky, jazzy, rhythmic, spacy, hypnotic, atmospheric and nearly trance inducing, all at once. In short, it's an absolutely stunning piece of music!

The effect of Part 2 is, again, very spacy with notes reverberating, dying and then powerfully and energetically surging again. Part 2 is captivating and does nothing to take away the feeling of greatness that *DSOTM IX* has conveyed so far.

Part 3 starts with the same kind of chime sounds as Part 1 but a little more like a piano sound. A sense of anticipation and excitement are fueled by the addition of distinct bass notes and synth pads mixed with the chimes, as the song begins to pick up momentum. A very soulful sequencer provides a fantastic beat, which continues to build an upward sense of momentum. I'm reaching for superlatives for this section, but I can't find the words. It's beyond awesome! One of the greatest electronic songs ever recorded! Everything fits together in such a heavenly way that it's hard to believe. Part 3 is elegant, cohesive, stimulating – a totally spectacular track. It's really hard to think of anything better in the history of electronic/space music, at least while I'm so absorbed and in love with this song at the moment!

Part 4 enters with little or no pause, with white-noise/wind-like sound. It's simply a transitional musical phrase leading into Part 5, which begins with flowing synth pads. A bouncy sequencer rhythm emerges from the droning synth pads, sounding just a little like the signature sound from *Picture Music*'s "Totem." A rapidly pulsing sequencer enters, transforming the song, bringing an electric feeling with its ever increasing speed and hard hitting sound, before backing off almost totally. Thunder crashes repeatedly in the background, while a poignant sounding Minimoog plays along.

The rapid sequencer weaves its way in and out of the soundscape, at times producing a feeling of exhilaration. A dreamy, floating female voice adds to the very enchanting feeling of Part 5.

Part 6 starts with the same rapid, bouncy, hard edged sequencer of the previous section. At the start of Part 6, it fires up to its most intense level yet and then leaves. In its wake are plaintive, yearning synth pads and synth solo. This is very moving music; in fact I'm feeling a welling up of emotion, some chills, perhaps imminent tears. This is a powerfully emotional section of music.

The Dark Side of the Moog IX has just completely bowled me over, blown me away and stunned me. It's an absolute masterwork for Namlook and Schulze! It has to be the best in the series, even though the series has many triumphant moments.

2002 *The Evolution of the Dark Side of the Moog*

From Jim Brenholts at http://www.allmusic.com: "almost perfect space music for cadets and even for casual fans. It is essential even for collectors with the entire set on hand already."

2003 *"Andromeda"* (Promo CD)

"Constellation Andromeda" is the bonus track on the *Dreams* re-issue, clocking in at 23:52.

2004 *"Ion"* (Promo CD for Alesis at the Frankfurt Music Fair, April 2004)

"The Ion Perspective" is the bonus track on the *Le Moulin De Daudet* re-issue.

Chapter 13 Klaus' Solo Career and Collaborations, 2005–2007

2005 *Moonlake*

From Ras Bolding and Jannik Juhl Christensen at http://www.geiger.dk/english/reviews/:

"*Moonlake* is an album for people who really like electronic sound - the music is rich in sonic details... You could say Klaus Schulze is basically doing what he has always been doing and that is true... [H]e has managed to find a balance between updating his sound and doing what he is best at... *Moonlake* is definitely the best album from Schulze in many years. An album which should appeal to the old fans but also introduce new ones. Highly recommended!"

From B22 at http://www.synthmusicdirect.com:

"'Playmate in Paradise' (30.07) soon lunges forward from a sedate beginning into a rhythmic backbeat that romps over the first half of the track sounding very contemporary and 'of the moment'... Indian hand drums open up the second piece, "Artemis in Jubilee" (17.49)... [T]he mood [is] intensified a little more by additional ethnic drums played in unison prior to even more contemporary drum sounds being added pushing things along into an upbeat groove.... [On] Track 3.... we find ourselves in Jean Michel Jarre/Equinox mode... "Mephisto" (15.23) [is] [a]gain a live recording, again an excellent recording... You know I think this album could just sneak into my top five favourite Schulze albums of all time truth be known... Here we have a CD of music that allows me to go to someone who has never heard of Schulze and may not even be remotely interested in the electronic music scene and say here, listen to this."

My review of *Moonlake*:

"Playmate in Paradise" (30:07) carries the same semi-funky groove throughout most of the piece. The singing of Thomas Kagermann enhances it, giving the breakdown sections of the song a very spacy feel. Thomas' voice is free, with an ethereal quality. I've become a fan since listening to the other KS albums he's been on and doing the interview and exchanging e-mails with him. He seems like a really nice guy.

The groove serves as a foundation for Thomas' violin and vocals. It lightens some, and Thomas' vocals become more pronounced as the track approaches the very spacy sounding middle section at around 14:00. The middle portion almost sounds a bit like a mini "Velvet Voyage." It's a very slowly unfolding, floating, dreamy passage. I didn't know what to make of it at first, but if nothing else, it's Klaus being adventurous, as usual. I think he's found a musical soulmate in Thomas Kagermann.

The journey out of the middle passage starts with the groove building up slowly but surely. Before it can hit full stride, though, Thomas gets in some very nice floating, non-lyrical vocals. Whether in the foreground or background, they add to the intrigue of the song.

The energy then rises, featuring synth with more bass and Minimoog solo. I've come from not enjoying Minimoog solos before writing this book to really enjoying them now. The surging of synths combined with the track-long groove behind the Minimoog makes for an invigorating and strong stretch run for "Playmate in Paradise."

A funky mixture of sounds featuring bongo-like drumming starts "Artemis in Jubileo," forming a fantastic groove quite different from the previous piece. This one gets very percussion oriented around the steady and brisk pulsing rhythm. Synth pads add another sonic pleasure to an already tasty mix. The rhythmic beat of "Artemis" ranks as one of the best ever in a Klaus Schulze song! This is a song to turn up the volume and just enjoy!

Soaring, spirited strings mix with the groove to give the piece a majestic, triumphant and joyous sound. It's one of the great Schulze tracks of any decade!

"Same Thoughts Lion" starts tentatively and then, delightfully, "Totem"-like synth splashes form the basis of a rhythm. The song quickens around these splashes, with a building sequencer line and various other sounds taking the song to a higher energy level. Of course, just as the energy level peaks, KS takes it down and starts to build it back up. Around the 5:00 mark the percolating synth sounds have sharpened a bit and come rampaging back into the mix to help form a driving rhythm. Perky percussion helps add to the feeling of a driving groove.

"Mephisto," the last track, starts out sounding like the middle of "Playmate," very spacy with echoing sounds. Suddenly, a totally seductive sequencer pattern starts. A mind blower! Another jangly sequencer pattern starts in concert with the original one. This is heady territory! Throw in some pads, and we have an astonishing sound. I'm experiencing this as one of Klaus' better albums for the first time during this listen!

"Mephisto" grows a little funky as it approaches the 6:00 mark, with drumming becoming a more prominent element. Gentle choirs add to the sound at around 8:30, followed by the first wails of the Minimoog. The Minimoog soloing and choirs carry the day, over the active and relentless beat, until the end.

Moonlake rates as a very good album which has a high "ceiling" with repeated listens.

2005 *Vanity of Sounds*

(re-release of CD 1 from the deleted box set *Contemporary Works I*)

From B22 at http://www.synthmusicdirect:

"[R]est assured that this is a CD that's gonna be snapped up like discount thermal underpants at the South Pole by Schulze devotees...The title track... I have to say that it's all a little un-Schulze-like, maybe he'd picked up some minor influences from his collaborative friends along the way!!! In any case, a 'sound' compositional piece, building very subtlely to an intense level that just gradually creeps up on you... 'The Wings of String" (14.47) is without a doubt gonna be the highlight of the album for most all of you SMDers (and if not, why not? What's wrong with you?)... And there you have it, a Schulze album, but almost not a Schulze album. It's truly magnificent in places; a little protracted in others."

My review of *Vanity of Sounds*:

I'm reviewing this one right after reviewing *The Crime of Suspense*. It seems like a good time to do it while *The Crime of Suspense* is still fresh in my mind for comparison purposes. So, here we go!

The title track starts with an instant cacophony which quickly recedes to just Klaus' synth and then entertains more drum, bass explosions and mangled voices. A synthesized flute is a little reminiscent of some of the sound textures on *Royal Festival Hall Vol. 2*.

Klaus ramps up a crisp sequenced sound for just a short time. Echo-laden synth sounds pulsate for a while before a very bassy crash occurs. The sequencer seems to be ramping up, but slowly; the mix is filled with all kinds of disparate and unusual sounds - only Klaus Schulze could give this mix direction and coherence! This is another CD with top flight recording quality.

"Vanity of Sounds" gradually intensifies, and I'm struck by the thought that all these sounds could be experienced as a mess but, on the contrary, they combine to make a very interesting piece of music. And I'm left even more in wonder as to how Klaus can pull this off. The reality is that it makes the track even more appealing and leaves me even more in awe than if conventional instrumentation had been used.

This is another Klaus original; no one else could create a piece like this, which is becoming thrilling! There is even a trace of '80s funk in the mix, with an inserted whip-like drum crash that repeats many times. As I listen, I'm thinking I've never heard a song that was so compelling and yet so complicated! The second track, "Sacred Romance", is cross-faded in.

"Sacred Romance" begins with choir sounds and searing synth that sounds like a wailing Eric Clapton blues style guitar, as sequencer and synth pads occupy the background.

The relentless sequencer is joined by drums as the track picks up energy. The synthesized guitar stays front and center for quite a while, sounding very good. The guitar drops out at about 11:00 - the sequencer is now central with some synth blurbs popping in.

"The Wings of String" is cross-faded in from "Sacred Romance," starting with a variety of gurgling sounds, male choir, a strange voice and, of course, a sequencer pattern. A rapid string and bass hit comes in repeatedly, sounding very good over the sequencer. Some brilliantly recorded short synth stabs enter the mix. The song is off to a very stimulating and encouraging start! The sequencer picks up the pace and sounds positively exhilarating!

The pace backs off around 8:00, and synth pads combined with very well recorded percussive sounds take the lead. A short time later, the slow pace is altered by the return of the sequencer. This is simply a thrilling piece of music from Klaus Schulze! Nothing else can be said or felt in the presence of the intoxicating sequencer line that appears, entrances, then leaves. A choir, sounding like chanting monks, enters at around 14:00 and finishes the song, as "From Words to Silence" fades in over them.

This piece starts with a vocoder enhanced voice. Crisp, clean percussive sounds seem like they are right in the room with me. Even some of the instrumentation takes on the vocoder tinge. The pace is slow - even past the 5:00 mark, the vocoder treated voice is present. This might be the most extensive use of the vocoder since *Death of an Analogue* – but sounds nothing like it.

For the next several minutes, there is just the laid-back beat and Klaus' slow synth pads, until sudden and startling thunderous crashes and noises come in and disappear around the 11:00 mark.

Suddenly, only the slow synth pad and some choir drones remain at a much reduced volume. Eventually, just Klaus' synth soloing and a few other sounds remain as "From Words to Silence" takes on a slower, more meditative pace. Only synth pad and ocean side sounds remain, waves crashing gently.

At the end, only twin synth pads at a very slow and healing pace remain. The composition is striking in the way it's conceived and carried out. My emotions are affected, as is so often the case with Klaus' music. This is extraordinarily mature music from Klaus Schulze.

Vanity of Sounds is a very satisfying album. It almost inspires reverence for Klaus' talents and the place he has arrived at as a creative genius. Yes, he is only human, but there is something awe inspiring in experiencing someone realizing his potential in this way - especially in the realm of art and creativity.

2005 *The Dark Side of the Moog 10* (with Pete Namlook)

From David Law at http://www.synthmusicdirect.com/moog10.cfm:

"Well, some people have told me that this will be the last in the series so that alone would make it special but musically I wouldn't really go along with the claim. That isn't to say it is a bad album, there isn't really anything wrong with it and indeed some of it is excellent, it is just that I enjoyed volumes seven, eight and nine more. Still wouldn't stop me wanting it in my collection if I owned the rest of the series though!"

2006 *The Crime of Suspense*

(re-release of CD 2 from deleted box set *Contemporary Works I*)

From B22 at http://www.synthmusicdirect.com:

"So, a change of modus for Mr. Schulze, as we hear him drifting into a style that suits the aptly named *Contemporary Works* title to a tea. Think Enigma, Deep Forest, System 7 and you won't be far wrong. It's one of those occasions where only you the listener can decide at what stage ambient becomes chill out/trance, where dance stops and world music starts...I'm left at the end of it thinking that so much more could have been done with these great long tracks. As it is Klaus gets into a groove early on in each of the pieces and sticks with it throughout, providing intricate solos that never really break free of the basic rhythm and flourish. A slow burner of an album it might be, but does it ever really ignite?? It's over to you, Schulze fans, to make up your own minds."

My review of *The Crime of Suspense*:

"Good Old 4 On The Floor" starts out, with the echoing heavenly voice of Julia Messenger, wordless, her voice drifting in front of Klaus' throbbing synthesizer pulse. It's a sensational beginning to the CD!

Beyond the central pulsing synth, Klaus works in other synth sounds, and the rhythm intensifies. Julia's vocals start to include words. Some great high percussion hits drift about the sound spectrum. Finally, the four-on-the-floor beat, which is the closest I've ever heard Klaus to a bonafide trance sound.

The four-on-the-floor subsides, giving way to the pulsating synth sequence as the main rhythm. The combination of this great sounding sequencer pattern with Julia's superb vocals, the four-on-the-floor beat (which comes and goes), and the striking percussion sounds make for a top flight song!

The sonic quality of the CD is excellent. Following a period of the steady trance beat and a swell of escalating percussion, Julia rejoins and the track forges ahead at about 10:30. In the last two- plus minutes, Julia's voice occasionally floats dreamily in the mix. This is an excellent track!

Thomas Kagermann's flute slides in to start "J.E.M." even before "Good Old 4 On The Floor" has ended. The flute is playing solo and echoing; the transition is superb!

Klaus' sequenced rhythm climbs into the mix as the flute continues. This is a new sound in KS' music, and it is exquisite. The rhythm strengthens and eventually quickens to a choppy, almost funky character. The flute continues playing - gradually with a little more vigor. Thomas' vocals can be heard, beginning close to the 11:00 mark. "Overchill" fades in over the end of "J.E.M."

"Overchill" starts out in a dub fashion, with bubbling synth and percussion playing over a bass. The percussion hits echo and cross between the speakers, as in a dub reggae song. A classic Schulze synth pad drifts into the mix, orchestrating a background to the "dub track." Julia's voice floats in over the moderately paced dub beat.

This track is a testimony to the growth of Klaus Schulze's music. In the new millenium, he is clearly still innovating. He is moving into new and exciting territory. These are the new classics and Klaus' choice of collaborators and compositions are first rate! Julia Messenger and Thomas Kagermann are both very creative and spirited musicians. They are very well used in the albums they appear in, adding a stunning new dimension to Klaus Schulze's music.

The Crime of Suspense is a very good CD, bordering on brilliant, that invites liberal doses of additional listening and has the potential to rate as a Schulze classic (with all the others!). "Overchill" is over 29:00 and due to its laid back pace and sense of sameness after a while, it may run too long.

The bonus tracks are from the promo CD, given only to those who pre-ordered *Contemporary Works I* -- as Klaus describes them, his most loyal fans.

"Ruins," the first bonus track, is very impressive. An up-tempo sequencer is surrounded by synth jabs and smooth string pads. Drumming and other various synth sounds give the track a lot of energy and interest. Although short at 4:34, it's one of the best bonus tracks of the re-release series.

"Castles" finishes the CD. Long synth pads and flute start the piece and then a sequencer rhythm begins. Drumming and some throaty vocal sounds add to the gradually rising energy. The track fades out at 4:15, making it sound like we've just heard a sample of a longer song.

Overall, *The Crime of Suspense* is a top flight album. There is a temptation to call it an astonishing album. There is no doubt that it contains many dazzling moments.

My interview with Julia Messenger starts on the next page.

Julia Messenger Interview with Greg Allen

Julia contributed vocals to *The Crime of Suspense, Ballett 3* from *Contemporary Works I* and also "vocal instrumentation" on *Contemporary Works II*:

GA: How did you first meet Klaus Schulze? What were the circumstances that lead to your working with him?

JM: I first met Klaus Schulze in 1999. It was after a "Summer Jam" concert in Cologne where I was singing some of my tunes as a special guest to Solar Moon Sound System. "Summer Jam" is Europe's biggest reggae festival. Afterwards there was a dinner with a small group of people. As it happened I was seated near Klaus and was able to chat. I was immediately struck by his charisma – he is a man who is larger than life. He held a presence from then on which I have never seen waver. I also noticed the respect he commanded and the power he exuded– the same power that I believe is inherent in his personality and emanates from his work. At an appropriate level he was also very loving and supportive, and we took to each other pretty much from the start.

GA: Was your work in the sessions for *Contemporary Works I* designed for a specific song or CDs known in advance? Did you know, for example that "My Ty She" was destined for *Ballett 3* and "Good Old 4 On The Floor" was set for *The Crime of Suspense*?

JM: For "Good Old 4 On The Floor," I actually recorded the vocal track in my own studio without having heard any of the music first. Klaus rang me, and asked if I'd be interested in collaborating with him. He requested that I sing at a certain tempo in a certain key, and just improvise. So I created a backing track for myself, in the Key of C minor at the tempo he'd requested. I quickly produced something that sounded quite inspirational to myself, as I wanted to sing in the studio for as long as it took. I recorded only the one take. I then put that vocal recording on a CD and sent it to Klaus. As it turned out he was really happy with what I'd done – I recall he said, "It's murder!" He ended up using the take exactly as I'd sung it.

At this stage, I had no idea that the improvised singing I'd just sent him was going to appear in a track called "Good Old 4 On The Floor". It was such a pleasant surprise when I received the Klaus Schulze 10-CD box set months later and heard the track for the first time. I was happy also that he had used the vocal take as it was, and as I'd felt it. I actually heard the context and style of the music for the first time and I loved it. I think he really did it justice. It's a beautiful piece that I'm very grateful to be part of.

For "Overchill" it was the same process. I recorded it on the same evening as "Good Old 4 On The Floor." Again I made a backing track for myself (this time in Bb minor), recorded the vocal take and sent it to Klaus. As this was the second take I'd done for the evening, I feel it was more relaxed and in my flow. In this track lyrics start to flow out of me during my improvisation in a manner that at the time does not feel conscious.

In *Ballett 3,* however (or "My Ty She"), I had more of an idea of the project Klaus was working on, as this was one of the later tracks to be recorded for the 10-CD box set. For me the difference with this track is that Klaus had already composed the backing, and I was able to sing to it.

GA: Was there any difference in your approach or the feeling you felt in working on the more groove oriented "Good Old 4 On The Floor" as opposed to the very atmospheric "My Ty She"? In some ways the vocals sound similar even though the instrumentation is so much different.

JM: The approach to singing the vocal takes for "Good Old 4 On The Floor" and "Overchill" was very different to "My Ty She". The main difference was that for "Good Old 4 On The Floor" and "Overchill" I'm actually singing to a track that I had created (which you don't hear of course), and with "My Ty She" I'm actually singing to the music of Klaus.

GA: Was your work on *The Crime of Suspense, Ballett 3* and *Adds & Edits* all done in the same sessions? How long did the work take?

JM: The tracks are all improvised, and all created in one take. The length of time it took to sing is roughly the same length of time as on the finished track.

GA: How did you feel when you heard the finished products (the songs you were involved in) that would become *The Crime of Suspense* and *Ballett 3*?

JM: I really love the depth of *Crime of Suspense* and what we achieved with "Good Old 4 On The Floor". There's a beauty and atmosphere to it that's of an ethereal quality, and for me there's a special silence you can hear in the music. If I can put it into words, it's as if it expresses our connection to the Universe.

I feel the same about "Overchill", and it's always intriguing for me to discover at what point I was at in my life through the lyrics that appear in the improvisation. So I enjoy listening to this one. I feel that Klaus captures the mood of the vocals extremely well.

In "My Ty She" or *Ballett 3,* however, I actually don't feel I'm expressing myself the way I would have liked to have. This was recorded as a completely different set up. Klaus gave the track he had composed to myself, Thomas Kagermann and Tom Dams, and requested that we "do our thing" on it.

So we all set ourselves up in a studio setting to record our takes at the same time. However, we were all in separate rooms and couldn't see each other. I'd also never heard the music before to which I was going to sing. I remember standing at the microphone in that room with headphones on and having no idea how long the track was or what it was going to be like. I didn't realize that it would be much more than half an hour. Hence there is a lot of apprehensive guesswork on my part, and I can feel that when I listen to it.

I remember it was actually quite difficult, as I was trying to do my thing, but also leave space for the others. However, as I couldn't see them, we couldn't queue our start and end points off each other very easily. What I didn't realize at the time was that Tom knew exactly how long the track would go for. He was in the room with the computer and track recording. So he was aware he was going to pitch in at the end, and for most of the 75 minutes I was being too tentative. I was over-cautious so as not to take away from his artistic space - and 75 minutes of hesitation and waiting for another artist is a long time!

So for me with this track, I'm not as in my body as I'd normally like to be. The focus and presence that I'd usually like to have during a session was unfortunately distracted.

GA: Do you have any feeling about the way yours and Thomas Kagermann's voices work together on "My Ty She"?

JM: I love singing with Thomas Kagermann. Now that I live in Australia again, it's one of the things I miss most about being in Germany. We sang a few times together in a purely improvisational group called "Papalagi" that Thomas had formed. Papalagi was special in that we would put ourselves on stage in front of an audience and let the music of that moment come to us. Most of these gigs were recorded. The audiences often couldn't believe that it was improvisation. I would make up songs on the spot that sounded rehearsed and previously conceptualized. It was some of the best fun I've had in my musical career. There is something very special and spiritual about playing music in front of an audience this way. I often lost myself and let another part of me do the singing and lyrics.

People would say that it was like the voices of Julia and Thomas were 'in love'. Our voices interwove, blended and respected each other. They fed off one another and were also inspired and challenged by each other. Personally, I don't feel like Thomas and I quite nailed it on "My Ty She" like we could have. Our usual mode of "feeling" each other was not there on this evening. We were in our separate vocal booths with headphones on, were unable to see and gauge each other, and therefore I don't feel we interacted the way we could have.

Looking back, it would have been preferable to see the other musicians during the recording, and either perform with them, or to have sung the parts separately. On the other hand the piece has its own beauty - the beauty of being that it 'is what it is'.

GA: Can you tell me a little about what it's like to work with Klaus? Is there anything interesting you could relate about your experience working with him? Was there something about working with him that brought out the best in you creatively?

JM: I love being able to improvise and just sing. It's been one of my favorite things to do ever since I can remember. However, there is unfortunately not such a great demand or platform for this in my career as it stands today. I generally write lyrics, songs and music, and then produce them in my studio, or work on them with other producers.

This is a different way of working for me, and I love it. It's a very special gift to be able to connect with other people in an atmosphere where the aim is to just feel the present moment as is, let it be, and actually record it and have it put onto a Klaus Schulze record! It's a lovely way to share and connect with other musicians and listeners, and I feel very blessed and grateful to be in this position.

I think the fact that Klaus loves my voice is also a reason that he is able to bring out the best of me creatively. I am honored that he has called me his favorite singer.

GA: What is the atmosphere like when arriving at and recording at Klaus' studio? I'm talking not only about the studio itself but also the setting of his home in Hambühren, which Thomas described as being in a forest setting.

JM: For the first and second CD box sets of Klaus', I actually wasn't in the studio with him, I recorded in my own studio. However, in 2003, when I was back living in Australia, Klaus invited me to Germany to sing on something else he was working on. I had been at Klaus's studio before, but this was the first time I was going to sing in it.

For this particular recording, I stood in a little vocal booth Klaus had had built, and looked through the glass doors to the studio monitor so that I could see where we were at in the track, and if there were any changes coming up. This was quite easy to see, as his studio monitor is on a huge projector screen on the wall – very cutting edge!

"Moldau" (the name Klaus gives his studio), is a very special place, and also because it's the place Klaus spends most of his time.

Off the main road (which is not a busy one, as it's in a small town), you drive for quite a while down a dirt track with the mystical Germanic forest enveloping you on either side. The looming trees almost take away your vision of the sky as you drive down the track, so it becomes quite dark. I remember in winter driving into mist and a beautiful hue of an almost blue/olive green. When you do arrive at Klaus' abode, it feels like the road has ended.

It's a place far away from civilization and a sacred space that Klaus has created for his work. The studio is connected to the house, but when you close the studio door, however, you feel you are in another world. It's a surprisingly small studio for a man that's larger than life.

At either end of the studio, sliding doors lead you on one side to the road that brought you there, and on the other side, a little garden - that Elfi, his wife, tends to. Past the garden, you get the sense that there is endless forest. It feels comfortably secluded, cozy and almost mysterious.

Back inside the studio, another wall houses all of Klaus' equipment – including the large studio monitor! The back wall has an all too comfortable sitting area, where a couch and coffee table are nestled and set between a vocal booth on one side, and a bar on the other – of course!

The color scheme is a deep red and the musical equipment is housed and orderly in well-carpentered wood. The fittings and the furnishings are of top quality. The large coffee table is also wooden and very beautiful. A great atmosphere is created when sitting around it, having a few drinks and listening to music with people. The sound system of course is awesome, and we've had a couple of great little parties there.

I remember one great night in particular was Elfi's 40th birthday. Klaus had surprised her and taken her to the local Italian restaurant (which is one of his favorite places to go – the food there is delicious!). When she arrived, there was a group of us waiting to have a lovely dinner and help her celebrate. We then continued on our celebrations back at Moldau until all hours of the morning - listening to music and drinking very expensive champagne in honour of the occasion. Klaus can be a lot of fun, and Elfi is one of the sweetest people you'll ever meet.

When I went to record at Klaus', Elfi had shopped for me and remembered that I liked soymilk, fruit and yoghurt! She was so thoughtful. This and many other small gestures she made helped me to feel very welcome and at home when I stayed at Moldau for a couple of days.

GA: Had you used your voice in an almost instrumental way before *Ballett 3*? How does that make you feel when you are able to use your voice as a musical instrument versus singing prepared lyrics? If there's a difference you feel, could you elaborate on that?

JM: There is definitely a difference I feel using my voice as a musical instrument as opposed to singing prepared lyrics. It feels very comfortable connecting with my inner being when I'm using my voice as an instrument. There is no concentration involved, as I don't have to remember lyrics. In this way I can just concentrate on expressing what I feel like saying at the time. I feel very lucky to be able to use my voice in this way. Often lyrics flow out of me at these times anyway, and it's later on that I understand what I was saying.

I've been using my voice in an instrumental way ever since I can remember. It's always something I've enjoyed doing, and I'm grateful that people like to hear it. As a teenager I created and sometimes recorded very similar musical nuances to what you hear on these CDs. I loved improvising, and I remember being inspired by the improvisational singing I'd heard on Pink Floyd's *Dark Side of the Moon*. I felt an affinity with that type of singing and music. However, there hasn't been a huge opportunity for it professionally in my music. Hence I was really happy to have the chance to sing with Klaus, and let another part of my soul come out.

GA: This is the same question I asked Thomas Kagermann: do you have any other stories, feelings or anecdotes about your work with Klaus that you'd like to share?

JM: Yes, I have a lovely story from my first visit to Klaus' studio.

I had previously been on a trip to Paris, where I visited a cute, authentic and very Parisian eatery. On the wall hung an old fashioned type of phone incased in wood, with an old black receiver, big buttons for dialing and a silver, round speaker phone. When I was sitting on the couch in Klaus' studio for the first time, I was looking around and taking in the space around me. I turned to the wall near Klaus, and there was the same type of telephone.

I enthusiastically exclaimed "Oh! You have one of those phones! I don't believe it, I just saw one in a café in Paris! I love it!"

And Klaus looked at me and said in a Clark Gable type voice (or perhaps more Lauren Bacall!): "You like it?.... You can have it.." And he proceeded to take it off the wall, disconnect it and hand it to me!

After some resistance, I realized he was serious, and he wanted me to have this phone. My joy, was his joy, and to this day, that phone has hung on my studio wall!

GA: What was your contribution to Disc #10, *Adds & Edits* on *Contemporary Works I*?

JM: *Adds and Edits* is actually an excerpt taken from "Good Old 4 On The Floor."

GA: Are there any plans for or possibilities of working with Klaus Schulze again?

JM: I'd love to work with Klaus again, but at present there are no plans.

GA: Which direction do you see yourself moving musically in the next few years? What is your real passion musically, or do you have a fond place in your heart for multiple musical styles?

JM: It's hard to answer what my real passion is musically as it changes from day to day. I do love to write a good song, and I love to write not only the music but the lyrics as well. I don't sing anything unless I've written at least the melody and lyrics, as that way I am assured an honesty and connection to what I'm singing.

I have written books and books of poetry and words, and I love to edit and cut up bits for songs. I also love to create lyrics from the moment. Sometimes the songs you hear of mine are songs where I've improvised the vocals and come up with lyrics immediately, and sometimes it's more thought out. Either way I feel passionate about it. I always aim to create the best piece I am capable of at that time.

At the moment I'm working on my live act, as I've been more studio focused the past few years. Singing again for audiences is something I'd like to experience more of. It's quite a job, though, as I'm producing a live act, which incorporates a balance between electronic music and organic instruments. Playing my songs with other people is for me where it's at, and fusing my electronic productions into a live act with real musicians is no mean feat!

I have a fond passion for multiple musical styles, and I am open to all possibilities. In the very near future, I have been asked to work with people in the dance/trance music scene, so that will be something totally different and something I'm very much looking forward to.

Another desire of mine is to further explore my voice. At the moment, as well as performing my own songs, I also perform jazz - to enhance my knowledge of both song and voice. I also have fun singing classical and musical comedy with my old singing teacher (we have soirees when we can!), and I'd also like to further experiment with different vocal sounds - to delve deeper into myself.

Either way, it's all about just loving what I do, and keeping myself consistently interested.

GA: Can you talk about some of the diverse projects and various styles you've worked in, including Solar Moon System, Klaus Schulze, Ruby Fruit Jungle, rock and jazz groups, classical voice training and live performances at raves, festivals and clubs? Now that's diversity! Your vocal talent seems to lend itself well to a number of genres.

JM: Thank you for doing your homework!

As a teenager I sang with my older sisters in a group we called "The Messenger Sisters." We would sing all of our own material mixed with a few cover songs. The style was either acoustic guitar and three part harmony, or *a cappella*. It was at this stage that I discovered my voice could sing '60s type soul songs, and for the next few years I also played in many bands covering both soul and jazz. At the same time I also explored the improvisational style of singing I talked of earlier. By the age of eighteen I was earning good money with some good bands and other outfits around Melbourne.

Following high school, I went on to the Melbourne Conservatorium of Music, where four years later I topped my year in Classical singing and earned a Bachelor of Music. At the Conservatorium I studied under Jacques Pottier, who had been the principal tenor of the Paris Opera from 1957 –1972. During University, I supported myself mainly through singing gigs – both corporate and public.

After University I was the lead singer of an all girl band called "Ruby Fruit Jungle." We were extremely popular in our hometown of Melbourne, as well as around the country. Internationally we toured Hong Kong, Scotland, Ireland and Germany. "Ruby Fruit Jungle" explored world music mixed with pop and electronica. As well as singing, I played djembe and other hand percussion.

Our music found a niche throughout a broad spectrum. We played festivals, clubs, raves and pub gigs. The shows were usually highly energetic, entertaining and easily relatable. I believe this was due to the element of world percussion, as well as singable melodies and our use of electronic samples. Inadvertently, through the introduction to various electronic producers, these performances led me to further my solo career as it stands today.

In 2003 I was asked by a Californian record label to produce my first solo album, which I wrote and produced in my studio in Melbourne. Since then many tracks and collaborations have eventuated, including the release of two more albums, one of which is a solo album entitled *And We Danced*, and the other being a collection of my "productions and collaborations" of the same title.

GA: I listened to your singing on the song with Klaus Schulze on your Myspace site along with the other three songs. They seem to range from very atmospheric and dreamy (with Klaus) to quite funky with "Stripped." Even though the musical styles are so different, is there a common emotion or feeling that you bring to each kind of music?

JM: The common theme for me when I'm writing and creating melodies and vocal lines in particular, is to honor the track that I'm singing on – whether I've produced it myself, or another producer has given me their music to create on. Hence the styles I write and sing in are often worlds apart and not recognized as the same artist. My job is simply to hear the track, and to be the channel for what I believe it's trying to say. I'm not exclusive at all in my musical tastes, and hope never to be.

Nor am I exclusive in the way I like to create music. I'm very happy to do the production myself. I derive a lot of pleasure in creating songs from the ground up, including the creation of beats, bass lines, and so on. I'm equally as happy to just write the melody and lyrics over someone else's music if I feel it speaks to me.

Different types of music make me feel different things. Klaus' music, for instance, makes me feel reflective, deep, personal, exposed and vulnerable in the most empowered way. Singing on a dance track, however, can bring out a totally different part of me – it can be cheeky, sexy and often very tongue-in-cheek. With other music I may take a more intellectual approach, and at other times it may just be that I'm keeping to a particular genre that is appropriate for the music.

When I write my own music and songs, it's often very melodic (although sometimes it's spoken word), and I let the lyrics just flow from me. Usually the music and the lyrics occur simultaneously.

A lot of my songs are in a very diverse style, as on different days I tap into different parts of myself - or perhaps of those around me. Sometimes I think: "Oh dear, the fans will be very confused now!" However, it's all me. This is the only way I could be happy and stay grateful and challenged in what I choose to do.

GA: Have you sung in the style that you used on *The Crime of Suspense* and *Ballett 3* (the dreamy, floating, atmospheric sound where your voice needs no words) on any other recorded music? If so, which albums or singles?

JM: The only other recordings I have where I sing in a similar style are those that I still have from my teenage years! I also have some recordings of live improvisational gigs with Papalagi.

GA: Have you sung Trance? With the really great trance records, such as *Burned with Desire* by Armin van Buuren, featuring outstanding female vocals with an ethereal quality, you would seem well suited for that!

JM: It's funny you should ask, as I'm currently talking with Ferry Corsten about working with him for his next album. He's one of the biggest Trance producers in the world, and his last album was number one on iTunes Dance Charts in the USA for two weeks.

GA: Can you talk just a bit about your classical training? How important was that in the way you have been able to use your voice in a wide variety of styles since then?

JM: My Classical training has been invaluable to me as a singer. As I mentioned earlier, at the Melbourne Conservatorium of Music, I studied under Jacques Pottier, who had been the principal tenor of the Paris Opera from 1957 –1972. Having taught many classical and famous popular singers in France, Jacques had developed his own technique, which was the only technique I'd found that related to all the styles of singing I was versed in. It was also the only technique I'd found that I understood and enjoyed.

I'd struggled a lot with learning classical before I met Jacques. My voice didn't take to singing scales without a clear focus, and most of the techniques I'd learned felt old-fashioned and unhelpful. Hence, I usually found singing lessons to be confusing, difficult and a tiring waste of time! Thus it was truly a blessing to meet Jacques.

For the first time I related to a technique that felt honest and easy. Suddenly I had a clarity in the exploration of my voice. I still enjoy a lesson from him from time to time today.

Jacque's technique is so good, that at 77 years of age he can still sing Tosca and other such difficult pieces of music better than a 30-year-old! He still sings regularly for audiences. He is extremely passionate about what he does and in furthering his technique into the world. To me he is very inspirational in his desire and passion for voice.

GA: Besides the Klaus Schulze *Contemporary Works I* project, what musical projects have creatively stimulated you the most (feel free to name as many as come to mind!)?

JM: I enjoy collaborating with numerous people in various styles from down-tempo, to electro-pop, to dance, pop, ambient and so on. I've never been exclusive as to a style, however the main genre I've found a niche in can be broadly termed as "electronic." If I like it and find inspiration in it, I'll do it.

There are a few people I work with that stimulate me or have stimulated me creatively in the past. These situations are usually always fleeting, as I sing, write and record in less than a day with these people, and then move on. The music however, stays with me.

The list of people I'm recording with at present is almost too broad to mention. However, presently I'm enjoying working with PFL, a dub/down-tempo project. I also like some recent music I've created with Frank Elting in Berlin - which is more electro pop orientated and very fun to listen to.

I've also written a few lovely tracks with Lutz Boddenberg, one in particular that I love called "A Space in my Heart."

There are always numerous people I'm working with at any given time, from all over the globe, and I hope to always find more people to work with and create with.

However, I'm also extremely stimulated by producing my own solo albums, and although they are always the most challenging, time consuming and exhausting, I definitely find them in the end the most rewarding! I really feel I am able to express myself in not only a vocal way, but also through the music. I've recently released my second solo album *And We Danced* in a digital format.

2006 *Ballett 1*

(re-release of CD 6 from deleted box set *Contemporary Works I*)

From B22 at http://www.synthmusicdirect.com:

"*Ballett 1* is not the most jovial of recordings given the thought behind the music presented here...[It] is quite a collaborational achievement, Tiepold's Cello work exaggerating the fact. It's a sedate, mournful affair and as such not an album that leaps out and grabs you, but one which grows on you. As is so often the case with the music of Schulze...I'm still left with a sense of anticipation awaiting the release of *Ballett 2*. With Tiepold taking joint command for a better part of the album repeated listens reveal different aspects of the music that may have been missed first time around."

My review of *Ballett 1*:

The CD features KS and Wolfgang Tiepold, with Tiepold developing his contribution to the track "Agony" himself. The CD has a classical feel, especially right at the beginning.

"Getting Nerr" (10:43) begins with choir crescendos and a high female voice. There is some strange chattering, and then the cello fires up with rapid strokes. This spirited, up-tempo section of cello playing is absolutely astonishing! It's one for the ages, a highlight passage in the Schulze *oeuvre*. At times I've heard just a hint of "Eleanor Rigby" in this piece. There appear to be two cellos – or possibly Wolfgang on one and KS synthesizing the other. One is in a minor key and the other higher. "Getting Nerr" provides an enthralling first 10-11 minutes for the CD!

Minor key synth pads and a wailing cello, playing in a somewhat somber or pensive way, start the second song, "Slightly Touched" (29:32). A slow sequencer works its way into the mix, quite unobtrusively, at around 4:00. Not long after that, the sequencer starts to come to life more.

As if not to be overtaken, Wolfgang's cello gains a little in energy. The sequencer and pads play a little more optimistic melody as Wolfgang's cello stays slow and somewhat mournful. The sequencer continues a steady ascent as the cello plays on passionately. This ascent levels off as sequencer and cello intermingle for quite some time.

"Slightly Touched" is a very mellow piece of music and may vary in its impact according to one's mood. I didn't feel it much this time. It could be another one of those songs that sounds better and better, in the context of the CD, with repeated listens.

"Slightly Touched" moves seamlessly into Agony, the third and final track, with solo cello. For some reason the cello sounds much more urgent and compelling in this song. Klaus' synth pads join in, so the formula at this point is about the same as in "Slightly Touched." It just seems that Wolfgang's cello has an extra sharpness or "bite" to it here. Klaus plays throughout this CD in a way that allows Wolfgang to be showcased. Klaus' contribution is largely limited to drifting synth pads that complement the cello playing.

Around 8:00 into "Agony," I noticed the clarity and force of Wolfgang's cello playing. The recording really helps, as virtually every nuance in his playing can be heard and appreciated. The cello playing is of a higher pitch as a deeper bass sound is playing. That sound is like a deep drone but occasionally seems to have some texture to it, like the cello.

I noticed that if I move back away from the desk where my laptop and speakers are and listen at the recommended listening point (where a triangle forms with imaginary lines drawn from my chair to each speaker and then from one speaker to the other), the sound is improved, and the whole experience is changed.

I think I'll listen to this again in that position and then write a little more about it.

My notes from the second listen:

I noticed that "Slightly Touched" benefited quite a bit from my being away from the speakers. There is a definition in the cello playing that is better experienced. I also noticed that there are myriad passages with deep, rich, satisfying bass sounds – and I'm not using a subwoofer! Just this evening, I played the whole track again and started to really appreciate it more.

For some reason, this CD has drawn me in more than any other. It's challenging music for me. It's ironic, in that I love the sound of the cello. I really want to like this CD, especially "Slightly Touched," which was most difficult for me at first.

2006 *Ballett 2*

(re-release of CD 7 from deleted box set *Contemporary Works I*)

From B22 at http://www.synthmusicdirect.com:

"*Ballett 2* features both Wolfgang Tiepold on cello and to a somewhat larger extent Thomas Kagermann on flute, violin and vocals adding a sense of eastern/Arabic spice...The material presented on *Ballett 2* comes across as being much more animated than that of *Ballett 1* with a more prevalent use of sequencers, though their use still seems to be something which is kept in check, only being spooned out in very limited doses. Once more it's a relatively somber sounding set of tracks that fill the disc...So what of *Ballett 2*? Well this one has been very easy to review actually as it's the most consistent of the discs I have yet encountered from the *Contemporary Works* set...A highly recommended and very enjoyable album, I think you'll find."

My review of *Ballett 2*, with KS on electronics, Wolfgang Tiepold (cello on one song), and Thomas Kagermann (flute, violin and vocals):

"Atmosphere Concrete" (7:32) starts with lots of bass, echoing flute, and vocals from Thomas, plus a deep roaring sound that recalls the strength and sometimes fury of nature. It's a very interesting and creative mix, with wind-like sounds, deep rumbling, bird-like sounds, chanting by Thomas, and a flute that reminds me of Native American music. Mixed in with all this are periods of droning. The first song is powerful, stormy and tumultuous.

As the music switches to "Kagi's Lament," a 30-minute piece, the sound changes totally, with KS playing long, emotion charged synth pads and Kagi playing a very poignant and sonorous violin. The changeover is quite strong and, in fact the whole CD up to this point is remarkably good.

Sequencer starts just 3:00 into the piece, as Thomas' violin continues to play with passion. Thomas enters with vocals, singing a near-chant and playing his breathy, resonant flute. At times, it sounds like Thomas' voice is layered twice. Again, I'm reminded of Native American music – from Thomas' vocals to his flute playing. Klaus' synth stays active, playing with a bubbly texture.

This is a piece of music that comes together well in so many ways. With Thomas Kagermann and Klaus Schulze together, we're dealing with some major creativity and twin dynamos of talent! When they get together, expect something really imaginative, unusual and of a very high quality. Thomas' violin sounds absolutely fantastic in this piece of music. This style that Schulze and Kagermann have formed really allows Thomas' violin to shine in a magical way. The song picks up some increased impetus at around 21:00, with Kagermann's violin playing more forcefully and Klaus' synths increasing in volume for a short time.

Once again, Kagermann's violin soars majestically, inspiring awe, like a seagull mystically and effortlessly floating through a blue sky above the ocean water. Thomas' violin playing is a real highlight of "Kagi's Lament."

The third track is "Wolf's Ponticelli," featuring – you guessed it, Wolfgang Tiepold.

The song surges with bold synth pads in the first few seconds before Wolfgang's cello comes in. The cello playing is so clear that you can hear the bow's movement against the strings, emitting an almost creaking sound at times.

Sequencers and drumming join in to give a very strong beat in the background. For a while, Wolfgang's cello drops out, and the beat is very much in the foreground. The beat here sounds a tad funky, with the added effect of strings being plucked at times on either the cello or violin. All of the playing around this beat, including Klaus' synth creations, sounds really good. At close to 12:00, the song drops back to some very nice percussion, and the cello re-enters. "Wolf's Ponticelli" is constructed with a very nice beat that is sustained by a variety of interesting, fun-to-listen-to sounds. It's a very plucky beat at times.

Klaus' Minimoog-that-sounds-like-electric-guitar solo begins around 17:00.

The sounds from Kagi's Flute reverberate strikingly to start the fourth song, "The Smile of Shadows." It plays with strength, a sense of confidence, spirit and vigor that is riveting and dominates the track in the early going. Thomas Kagermann is simply a splendid and versatile flutist.

Once again, on "The Smile of Shadows," the beat and flute playing is accompanied at times by some simply marvelous percussive type synth playing, the synth blurbs literally smacking the soundscape, but in a very pleasant way. As the flute playing gathers intensity, the percussive synth-based sounds are simply spectacular. This is another extremely strong piece of music – I absolutely love it! On top of everything else, it's a great source for an audio demonstration. It sounds like the microphone is even picking up the sound of Thomas' lips making sounds in contact with the flute as he gathers for the next series of notes. Wow! What a piece of music!!!

The bonus track is "Trance 4 Motion," 5:42 in length. Despite its name, this song is like the cool-down song that might be played at the end of a vigorous aerobics class.

Notwithstanding the rather bland (compared to the rest of the CD) bonus track, *Ballett 2* strikes me as an absolutely marvelous musical experience!

Thomas Kagermann Interview with Greg Allen

Thomas contributed vocals, violin and flute on *Moonlake*, (only violin and voice on *Moonlake's* Playmate in Paradise), *Contemporary Works I* and *Contemporary Works II*.

Thomas' initial reply to my invitation to interview included this:

"I enjoy working with Klaus very much - he is a unique musician. It is my pleasure, answering your questions about our musical cooperation."

GA: When did you learn to play the violin and flute?

TK: I had classical flute and violin lessons from my seventh birthday on.

GA: How did you come to be a guest musician with Solar Moon System? Who was with the collective then? What was the first music/album you worked on with them? Did you strictly play music or did you do some production work with them also?

TK: I met Tom Dams on a free musicians-session in the beginning of the nineties. We instantly realized that we have a fantastic resonance with each other concerning free improvising music.

We then formed a music-collective named Papalagi (see www.papalagi.net) which was a pool of musicians from Solar Moon System and musical friends of my own projects. As far as I remember, Morgenrot was the first Papalagi album, which was as always in the history of Papalagi, a direct-to-DAT-recording of a concert. On the Solar Moon album guestbook, the guys invited me to play some violin parts.

GA: When did you first meet Klaus Schulze? Can you describe the circumstances?

TK: I met Klaus Schulze in his fabulous studio in the middle of the forest. From the first glance on, this man was sympathetic to me. Klaus is a man with a big heart. He had prepared some sequences for me to play for the *Ballett* albums (*Contemporary Works I*). We did not talk about what kind of violin should be played now.

I remember when he said: "play". So I plugged in my violin and played on a 45-minute piece of wonderful electronic music. And when he stopped the recording machines we knew that we are "from one family". We realized that Klaus' way of shaping and modulating a tone is very similar to my way of doing this on the violin, the flute and with my voice. There seems to be some "familiar pre-experiences" which I can't explain.

GA: How did it happen that you were asked to work with Klaus on the *Contemporary Works I* material?

TK: Tom Dams, who worked with Klaus Schulze, had told Klaus about "this free-playing violin player from the westerwald" and this awakened his interest in what I was doing with my instruments.

GA: I saw that you were described as a multi-instrumentalist for Fiedel Michel and that the band was described as Germany's #1 folk band. It looks like Fiedel Michel released several albums between 1972-1980. How did you come to join the group? How was the band formed? Could you describe the music Fiedel Michel made and what the experience was like?

TK: Fiedel Michel was the first band I played with. It was pure German folk. Acoustic violin, acoustic guitar, mandolin and three voices. No mikes, no technique, nothing. Our idea of forming Fiedel Michel touches a very sensitive point in German music. In the early seventies, nobody of the young, music-interested people played or listened to German folk music. German folk music was absolutely OUT because of the Nazi past where German folk songs had been abused for Nazi agit-prop.

So we normally played Irish or English songs or Bob Dylan songs or whatsoever but NO German stuff. We decided to break this bad history and started singing German folk songs - with the consequence that a couple of years later we had a huge German folk revival that lasted till the beginning of the eighties. So you can say we brought back a piece of German culture to the kids that seemed to be lost forever.

GA: Was folk music your first love in music? How did you come to develop your love of folk music? When did you first start playing it?

TK: I discovered folk music after I was fed up with classical music. Deep in my heart I am a free playing, free breathing man - a traveling man, a gypsy. The atmosphere around classical musicians was always too dull for me, not relaxed, not natural, too bourgeois for my soul. I love freedom in playing and not, "you have to play a piece so and so otherwise it's wrong." This is too narrow for me.

In folk music was more freedom, more gypsyness, more fun. This moved my heart.

GA: When did you first meet Julia Messenger? Was it through Solar Moon System or when you both worked together with Klaus?

TK: I met Julia through Tom Dams just before they got married.

GA: Was your voice treated in some way on parts of your singing on *Moonlake*? It sounds like a slight echo effect or some other treatment to give it a more ethereal sound.

TK: I love working free with my voice. So on *Moonlake*, I sometimes shift my voice into overtone areas. I learned just by listening to world music and I realized that the human voices on this planet open a wide horizon for vocal experiments; much wider than a folk singer could imagine (LAUGH).

GA: How were the parts arranged for you and Julia on *Ballett 3*? Your voices both have a kind of spacy feel and intertwine and complement each other so well. It's one of the most mesmerizing vocal performances by a male and female combined that I've ever heard.

TK: Julia's and my voice are melting together as though we were singing together for a million years. I can't explain why. I am a very, very intuitive musician and so is Julia, I think, too. You can also hear our melting together voices on my solo album *Kyrios* and especially on the Papalagi album *Stadtraum Februar.*

GA: How did your involvement in the *Moonlake* session come about? I assume your work on *Contemporary Works I* and *Moonlake* were done at different times, with the *Moonlake* recordings being separate.

TK: Yes, the *Moonlake* recordings were made 2 years after the *Contemporary Works*. We made the *Moonlake* recordings in my wonderful music dome, which we built next to my house. It's a wonderful place for music. Tom Dams brought Klaus' playbacks to the dome here and he recorded my violin, flute and vocals here, then took it back to Klaus' studio and mixed it together there.

GA: For *Moonlake*, was the instrumental already conceived and recorded when you sang your vocals? Did you create your own vocal interpretations in "Playmates in Paradise" or did Klaus have it pretty much conceptualized what he wanted in the vocals?

TK: Klaus always lets me work free, because he knows about the obviously higher musical magic of free played stuff. He takes what he needs and leaves the rest - a wonderful way of producing, which is closely connected to the wide horizon of the person Klaus Schulze.

GA: You mentioned to me in your e-mail that you enjoy working with Klaus very much and that he is a unique musician. What is it, in your opinion, that makes Klaus such a unique musician?

TK: Klaus simply doesn't consider any other possibility of playing music than his own. You know, how many musicians on this planet try to find a way of being a 'successful' musician by thinking: "This or that guy has success with this and that. So, I will do also this and that, then I will be successful too." I think this is the reason why we have so much uninspiring music on this planet.

When I stop comparing myself with others, the whole thing starts to become interesting, because then I show character, and that inspires. Klaus once told me that he never thought about 'success' but only in the development of music. For me he is the prototype of what this American singer sang about: "I did it my way."

GA: Sometimes I hear you singing in a mid to high range and then a much lower register voice in the background on Klaus' material. Are those both your voice? If so, is one treated, perhaps or is that just you changing octaves?

TK: Sometimes Klaus uses a voice processor for our voices, which change the formant of the vocal, so it sounds like octave jumps too.

GA: What song is that playing on your website (http://www.kagermann.com) when you first enter, before you click on 'weiter'? It only plays for a short time but it sounds very appealing!

TK: It is a little part of the song "Krystos Anesti" from my album *Kyrios*.

GA: Did you record the vocals for *The Crime of Suspense* song "J.E.M." and the *Ballett* CDs all in the same sessions? How long did they last? Were you and Julia present at the same time for *Ballet 3*?

TK: Yes, all in the same sessions. It took us two days of relaxed recording with a lot of pause. Julia and I were not present at the same time for recording.

GA: The flute playing at the beginning of "J.E.M." sounds so breathy, natural and clear with a nice resonance. How did you feel that came out?

TK: I don't think before and when playing. I just let myself be carried by inspiration. The flute on that mentioned beginning came out very gentle.

GA: What language are you singing in near the end of "J.E.M."?

TK: I improvise on languages, like we improvising musicians always did on tones. I said to myself: when improvising on tones is possible, then improvising on language should also be possible! And, as we can hear, IT IS.

GA: It seems that your involvement in Klaus' albums was the most on the 75-minute piece, "My Ty She," where your vocals are a major part of the song, as well as violin and flute. The combination of your ethereal vocals with Julia's makes it an extraordinary work! Was that the most gratifying of your work with Klaus? Can you talk about the formation of the piece and how you felt during its creation and afterwards as well, when you heard the completed work?

TK: *My Ty She* is really a great, fundamental *oeuvre* of the cooperation with Klaus, where all registers are pulled. I am always wondering, how simple it is creating good music, when you meet good musicians like Klaus Schulze and Tom Dams and Julia Messenger, for example. It is like you never feel exhausted, stressed or tired. On the contrary: after and during sessions I feel fresh, awake and well.

GA: Do you have any other stories, feelings or anecdotes about your work with Klaus that you'd like to share?

TK: Meeting Klaus and his wonderful wife Elfi in his studio right in the middle of the forest is always like traveling to another planet. When I come into the "normal world" again, I always feel like leaving a petrol station where they sell human-energy-light-petrol. So, no wonder that Klaus, Tom and I call our new project where we are just in the middle of beautiful recordings "Die von der Tankstelle."

GA: Is *Ocean Vol. 1 – Nature in Concert* your most recent album? What can you tell me about that album?

TK: I have a live project here in Germany that is called "Deep Blue & Violunar," i.e., I play live with various loops and samples to that great BBC film *Deep Blue* (original soundtrack turned down). It is a wonderfully deep optical and acoustic trip. The music on *Ocean* consists mainly of the soundtracks I created for this project. The audience is always deeply impressed with this general beauty. I'll send you a little film impression by mail.

GA: How did you hook up with Broekhuis, Keller and Schönwälder? How many albums have you done with them? Is the music you made with them similar to any other projects you've worked on?

TK: I once met these guys on a liquid sound festival and we instantly improvised together and had a lot of fun, which was recorded live on the *Liquid Sound* album.

GA: Which album of theirs do you like the most? Can you talk just a little about *Liquid Sessions* and *Live @ Dorfkirche Repelen*?

TK: They invited me to play on their annual Repelen live concert in that church. This is always a very well prepared concert event with full house and beautiful light installations. They are no "professionals," but they love and enjoy their music, which is of course very influenced by Klaus Schulze.

2006 *For Barry Graves* Video (appears on German TV station WDR)

The Klaus Schulze video *For Barry Graves* was originally broadcast on German TV station WDR, on a special broadcast on August 12, 2006 and August 13, 2006. The video was filmed in 1977. It is also presented in the *Ultimate Edition* on Disc 42, where the running time is a little less than on the video. The video shows Klaus sitting on the floor surrounded by many synthesizers and facing a mirror. The music starts out sounding a little like "Velvet Voyage" from *Mirage* and gradually changes into a very good sequencer section. The camera first shows Klaus reflected through the mirror, and only as the camera backs away does one realize that they have been watching Klaus' reflection.

The video was broadcast on the second night of a two night special that featured not only Klaus but Popul Vuh, Kraftwerk, Tangerine Dream, Amon Düül II, Can, Guru Guru, Scorpions, Kraan, Eloy, Embryo and others.

Many Klaus Schulze fans have probably seen this on YouTube. I watched it innocently enough before realizing the implications of possibly pirated music on YouTube. It seems it has been taken down recently.

Here's the story of Klaus' situation with the video, as told to me by KDM:

"The rights of that *Barry Graves* film are owned by a huge German TV station. And the rights [to] the music [are] owned by KS (and by me because I'm the music publisher). The film was shown on German TV recently, in a series of similar films with early German music by Tangerine Dream and others. Which means that many German fans have it recorded on video or DVD, and of course they make copies (see: YouTube), and therefore, the record company was NOT interested anymore. Of course, and before, they were eager to release this old footage on a bonus DVD, as they did with the Ars Electronica concert on *Dig It*. But the public performance on TV (and even more the private recordings and the YouTube availability) made the film worthless for the label."

From my perspective, this is the single best video footage I've ever seen of Klaus Schulze. I wish it had become available on one of the re-releases. It would have been really nice to own that video to watch at home on a large TV screen.

RadioGoethe.com Klaus Schulze Two Hour Special Program

This two-hour radio program on San Francisco radio station KUSF features some excellent Klaus Schulze selections interspersed with interview segments with Klaus. The link is http://www.radioGoethe.com. Once there, click on "Audio/Video" in the menu to the far left. In the submenu, choose "Shows." You will then see a listing that includes "Radio special about Klaus Schulze." If you choose that and wait a while for the download, then you're in for a treat. Hopefully, this link will be left on the website for quite some time to come!

Here's KDM's explanation of how a radio show like this is put together:

"It was surely one of the many, many telephone interviews that KS gave since we do these re-releases (and before). There was a man in the record company who just was doing the work with the press. Since early 2005 he also arranged for KS many interviews, with larger and smaller magazines, newspapers, radios, and one TV.

With the radio it works always like this: A certain date and time is arranged before. At this date the radioman calls then KS in his studio, and KS is already prepared. He knows: So-and-so from a radio from this town (or country) will call at five o'clock. And the radioman is prepared technically, to record the whole. A specialty with a radio interview is that KS is mostly asked, after the actual interview is finished: 'Please could you say a personal hello to our listeners?' And the artist (and KS too) is doing so in most cases. Any interim talks or advices ('could you please say...') are of course deleted when the shaped interview is broadcast later on, similar to an interview for a magazine, which is also 'brought into shape' before print, so that it can fill a certain space, and all sentences are understandable."

2007 *Ballett 3*

(re-release of CD 8 from deleted box set *Contemporary Works I*)

Since receiving my copy of *Ballett 3*, I've been really struck by its beauty. It has grabbed my attention as a very good album, possibly one of Klaus' best even though it's in a far different style from his "classics" of the '70s.

I've become a bigger Klaus Schulze fan in the last few years than ever before. I think it's because KS' body of work has built to such a mind boggling level in terms of quantity and quality.

So back to *Ballett 3*. Klaus wrote the series as a tribute to his mother, who was a ballet dancer, mostly before Klaus was born. As Klaus tells it, she was a real prima ballerina, but when she married Klaus' father at age 19, he asked her to quit. It seems she didn't quit permanently until Klaus was born in 1947, following his brother's birth in 1944.

The music is stunning! Wolfgang Tiepold on cello, Tobias Becker on oboe, Thomas Kagermann on vocals, flute and violin combine with Julia Messenger on vocals to create this fascinating album.

The CD starts with one very long piece of music, "My Ty She", which runs 75:40. There are no subtitles, just one long piece of music.

The CD starts out with Klaus' synth playing in a lower register for just a few seconds before being joined by Wolfgang Tiepold's cello, which sounds magnificent. This cello playing evokes strong emotions immediately and is joined by oboe quite quickly. It's very plaintive, almost mournful in its sound.

The first several minutes have a classical music feel. Klaus' subtle and slow synth pads in the background are a perfect complement to the traditional instruments. A softly sequenced synth rhythm joins in at close to the 6:00 mark. Cello and violin are still prominent, and synth pads and rhythm, while complementary, still allow the cello solo to stand out.

At about 13:30, the real heart stirring part of "My Ty She" begins with Julia Messenger and Thomas Kagermann alternately singing ethnic sounding vocals. Their singing is a revelation, certainly the best I've heard on a KS album. The orchestral instruments communicate a deep yearning feeling, stirring my heart and soul.

Julia's voice simply floats above the music without words as does Thomas' voice; this is music and expression at its most sublime. As the violin joins in with the dreamy synth and floating vocals, the composition is very coherent. It feels like all the parts are combining perfectly, creating a feeling of wonder within me.

It's easy to get carried away by this piece of music and indeed, I have. As I listen to it, I'm sure this is another masterpiece in the sprawling collection of released Schulze music.

At the 30:00 mark, it's long since become obvious that this is a very special track – but there are still 45 minutes left!

The music possesses a drifting quality, with its steady backbeat provided by Klaus' dual synths. A slow to medium tempo allows orchestrations to emerge majestically. After a while violin joins, playing with aching emotion. Julia and Thomas again alternate vocally.

Thomas begins to sing in a deeper, almost throaty sound, then reverts back to his normal voice. The two singers complement each other splendidly. At around 39:00, Julia's voice takes on a treated sound and then is usurped by an elegant alternating duet with Thomas and Julia's untreated voices, a nice touch.

The oboe enters with an extremely plaintive feel, expressing the hunger of the human soul compassionately for those who feel deeply. I close my eyes and luxuriate in this sublime state guided by the music.

Close to the 70:00 mark, Thomas begins a recitation in a very deep voice for a short time, the oboe returns and the track winds towards its conclusion. I thought I heard a *Beyond Recall*-like seagull floating through on a few occasions. The wind-up of this piece is very creative, almost blissful. Julia sings softly, the seagull cries out in the distance. This work contains absolutely spellbinding performances by several of the artists and is supported by a wonderful musical idea.

The bonus track, the 3:30 "Schauer Der Vorwelt," starts with a driving beat. There are repeating screams of a somewhat disturbing quality. A sample plays, followed by a suddenly enthralling sequencer and again spoiled by a similar scream and then more sequencer. Much of it sounds bland or even ugly and then out of the ugliness a few moments of beauty will emerge.

The greatness of *Ballett 3* derives from the stellar track, "My Ty She."

2007 *Kontinuum*

I just received my copy of Kontinuum in the mail from Eurock yesterday, so this will be a chance to get a first impression of this new 2007 release.

"Sequenzer [From 70 to 07]" starts with dual sequencers, one with a higher pitch than the other. The lower-pitched sequencer at times becomes so blunted as to almost disappear and then morphs into a sound exactly like the higher-pitched sequencer. This happens a few times before the track moves on.

This first part must represent the 70 (of "70 to 07"), as it does sound more like something Klaus would have done in the 1970s. At around 4:00, I can tell that the song is evolving but very slowly. A repetitive sounding sequencer plays in stereo and then combines with another sequencer which is more melodic, sounding almost like a music box. Gradually, traces of synth pads drift in so slowly that a sense of mystery is added to the piece.

Swirling synth sounds become more active, taking away from the dominance of the sequencers a little by the 10-11:00 mark. This song has a classic feel – something like "Crystal Lake." If I just close my eyes and get lost in the sound, I feel like I could listen to this track for a long time.

A deep bass laden sound emerges at around 12:00, stimulating some classic KS synth pads. More active sounds are layered on top of the long, soft and soothing synth pads; all the while the sequencer patterns continue. This does sound like a retro Klaus Schulze piece of music. Not particularly like any of his 1970s albums, but with a sound decidedly unlike anything he's been doing since 1980, for the most part.

At around 18:00, the sequencers disappear in favor of synth pads that feel more like something from *Timewind* or even *Moondawn*.

The last 7:00 do not see the return of the sequencer but more a spacy *Moondawn*-like purely electronic vibe.

Surprise! Klaus Schulze returned to a very classic "electronic music" sound for *Kontinuum*.

"Sequenzer" melds into "Euro Caravan" with no pause. The initial stages are deep, bassy, slowly evolving synth with some very sparse atmospheric sounds. A sampled, softly singing, echoing voice sneaks into the mix. This is very, very spacy. I wasn't expecting something like this but it's quite welcome. It actually feels great to have Klaus Schulze making music like this. It goes back to his roots, while benefiting from all his years of growth and maturation as a musician.

The background singing sounds like some of the very atmospheric singing Thomas Kagermann has done, yet the overall atmosphere of "Euro Caravan" is very minimalist electronic. Finally, at 9:00, a pair of sequencers start, initially sharing the sound stage with the singer and the gentle pads but becoming more emphatic with time and giving the song a beat where it had none. Some ping-pongy synth sounds reverberate around like pinballs in a pinball machine. This track gets the best of both worlds by starting with such a slow, spacy sound and then picking up some springy, rhythmic sounds. Hints of the former sound persist even as a groove has formed with the sampled voice still weaving in and out of the soundscape.

Although I said that KS had returned to a very classic "electronic music" sound for *Kontinuum*, I think that the rhythmic part of "Euro Caravan" sounds more like it came from *Moonlake*. So we have *Moondawn*-like sounds and *Moonlake*-like sounds on the same CD!

"Euro Caravan" blends into "Thor [Thunder]" with a thunderous boom. After a couple of booms, a drone takes hold, accompanied by music that's again quite spacy sounding. Another sampled voice takes part in the drifting, ethereal character of "Thor" in its early stages. A muted thunderclap provokes longer synth pads and a near choir sound in the background. "Thor" is changing, and at close to 8:00 a bold sequencer bursts onto the scene, sounding very exciting. Other sequencers join in and the sonic ride still feels very satisfying!

The quality and content of *Kontinuum* so far is a shock! It's not what I expected at all but is so fresh and just downright astonishing! No more evidence of the artistic genius of Klaus Schulze was necessary, but *Kontinuum* only emphasizes it more. Add to that the fact that KS is a very mature artist, and there is an unbelievable concurrence of talent and experience that is revealed fully by this album.

"Thor" continues to gather energy along the way, retaining all the same ingredients of sequencer, choirs, and occasional floating, sampled voice. The intensity of the rhythm builds slowly as the halfway point passes. "Thor" has evolved from an introspective, meditative piece of music in its beginnings to a virtual toe tapper in the middle sections. I'm betting on a return to the unearthly, space sounds in the later stages.

The sequencer and rhythm pattern stop at around 23:00, fulfilling my prediction. Choir sounds linger with reverberating sampled voice and multiple synth pads, including a droning, deeper sounding pad. The track becomes more and more subdued as it nears conclusion. Finally a thunderclap sounds, some wind blows, and the album concludes.

Kontinuum is a first class album and actually could enter the competition for best Klaus Schulze album ever. That is an accolade that I've never been willing to consider because there are too many first rate albums from KS to choose a "best."

The Second Klaus Schulze Classic Period?

After listening to much of Klaus' work from 2000-2007, I have had the thought many times that this is KS' second "Classic Period." The first, of course, was the 1970s with brilliant albums such as *Picture Music*, *Timewind*, *Mirage* and *X*. I think that since 2000, Klaus has been in a particularly creative and high quality period of releases. The music has been very diverse and stretched beyond anything Klaus had done prior to 2000. The use of collaborators only enhances the devastating power of many of the albums released post-2000. I'm inclined to say, at this point, that the 2000 and beyond "classic" period has gone beyond even the quality of the original classic period. The only difference is that this second great period can probably never carry the same surprise factor as the first. For me, even the surprise factor has become fairly even. I've been delighted, shocked, astounded, awe-struck, by this period in Klaus Schulze's career in which he has performed at such a high level.

Chapter 14 More Klaus Schulze Career Information

Pink Floyd Connection

Again from KDM:

"During two nights in August, Klaus had some wonderful private meetings with Gilmore, Wright and Mason of Pink Floyd, who were touring Germany at this time. It came out that all three know, have, and value all of Klaus' records. Most funny for everyone was that KS called the keyboard player Rick Wright erroneously 'Tony Banks.' What laughter!"

Billy Bob Hargus at http://www.furious.com/PERFECT/kschulze.html quotes KS: "When I started to do my music, and before, I was listening to Jimi Hendrix and Pink Floyd, before to the Spotnicks and Ventures."

The Use of the Term "Krautrock"

From KDM's interview with Archie Patterson of www.Eurock.com:

Q: From your perspective, what was the reaction of the German people in general to this new phenomenon called "Krautrock"?

KDM: No one in Germany called this music "Krautrock" then. Ash Ra Tempel or TD was called "Ash Ra Tempel," or "Tangerine Dream," or "those crazy people"! The nationalistic British music press put the label "Kraut" or "Krautrock" on some of the bands, if they noticed them at all (after '73 and mostly because Virgin released some of them and paid for advertising). Of course, the Brits meant "Kraut" spitefully.

[He continues:] The Germans as a whole didn't react at all. Some journalists mentioned the names; some people bought the records. As said above, it was a minority. German rock music was not highly regarded. Apart from the albums I got for free from the people I worked for, I never bought a record by a German artist or group! It was just not cool. Pink Floyd WAS better than TD. Hawkwind WAS better than A.R.T. And the Stones WERE and ARE much better than all the hundreds of German copies. The exception was in 1973 when Kraftwerk hit it big with *Autobahn.*

I've wondered how "Krautrock" could come into such common usage when the word "Kraut" seems to be a derogatory term." At http://www.wasistdas.co.uk/FAQs.htm#racist, this question was addressed (these are among the frequent questions answered by the author of the article):

Q: Isn't the term "Krautrock" a bit racist?

A: Don't know. It's certainly not politically correct, but is that enough to make it racist? I think the term was coined in a derogatory sense by a British music journalist. Some Germans referred to the music as “Kosmische,” which means “cosmic.”

However, I believe the term “Krautrock” was adopted and reclaimed by bands such as Faust (who recorded a song called “Krautrock”) and re-used in a more positive way, much like the re-appropriation of racist terms by many black musicians.

It is a tricky one. I have always believed the term “Kraut” to be an unpleasant, abusive word and not one that I would like to use in reference to musicians and people I greatly admire and respect.

The Re-release interviews

Here’s some insight into the inner workings of the interviews that KS gave in conjunction with the massive re-release project.

From one of my many e-mail exchanges with Klaus Mueller:

“In 2004 and until spring 2005, KS did plenty of interviews, mostly arranged by the record company (and a few by me) because of the re-releases, and we had many, many articles and reviews in German and international papers. He did all these interviews by e-mail, on telephone, or they came to his studio (if it’s TV or radio), but he was not interested in the results, after.

“The record company collected all this stuff and I collected all this stuff. If there was one or another really FUNNY or extraordinary article, or remark, I show it to Klaus, as always. But generally, we never speak much about these press things; because we know the history, we know the questions, we know the answers, we know the press. Also I have seen many books with a longer or shorter mention of KS, and not just once: mostly not quite correct.”

Miscellaneous observations

- KDM: “Klaus is ALWAYS very enthusiastic, if he did something good. Or, even if it's just a new toy, I mean: instrument or effect. He can rave about it as if he's newly and heavily in love.”
- KS: “I am still no keyboard player. In comparison, say, to Oscar Peterson, I am an amateur. Because my craft is not playing the keyboard, but finding and combining sounds, building and using the structure to create emotions with sounds.”

Why Klaus Schulze Album Sales Figures Are Not Published

From the 2001 interview with Archie Patterson of Eurock:

AP: In the early days what was the record industries reaction to the music of KS? Over the years what was the largest selling KS album and how many copies did it sell?

KDM: Why and how should the record industry react? There was no such reaction. Sales figures? Recently I discussed with KS if I could publish such figures in "The KS Circle", the monthly publication about Klaus. I have fascinating statistics that I made in the late seventies and in the early nineties. We agreed that these figures are still nothing for outsiders. Because: any statistic would be misinterpreted by most readers because they don't know, or forget: a record that is for 20 or 25 years available, sold of course more than one that is on the market for just the last six months. An album that is distributed worldwide by a huge label (for instance: *Timewind*, *Mirage*, or *Babel*), would sell automatically more than an album released only in Germany. This says nothing about the quality of an album. Readers would only see the figures – and not what's the reality behind them. Also people are used to (and seem to believe) exaggerated figures that other artists tell them. And IF I would print our figures, I would be honest. Therefore, we NEVER published sales figures of KS' albums."

Chapter 15 Additional Interviews

Robert Rich Interview with Greg Allen

Robert Rich is a prominent electronic musician who started building synthesizers at a fairly young age and then moved on to an active career as a published electronic musician. He's known, in part, for his "sleep concerts" in San Francisco in the early 1980s where concertgoers would bring their sleeping bags and be lulled to sleep by Robert's slow, trance inducing music. Robert would play through the night, attempting to play appropriate music for the various stages of sleep. He's also known for his study of just intonation and his application of it in his music. Wikipedia has this to say about just intonation:

Just intonation is any musical tuning in which the frequencies of notes are related by ratios of whole numbers. Any interval tuned in this way is called a just interval; in other words, the two notes are members of the same harmonic series.

Some of Robert's better albums include *Gaudi* (a brilliant album), *Yearning* (with Lisa Moskow on sarod and RR playing slowly unfolding, spacy electronics) *Strata* (with Steve Roach), *Soma* (with Steve Roach) and early works such as *Trances and Drones*.

Robert is also known for his use of lap steel guitar within electronic compositions, an absolutely stunning sound that he has used fairly liberally in his works. You can check out Robert's website at www.robertrich.com.

Here's my interview with Robert, who told me when I first contacted him that he had listened to a lot of Klaus' music in the late '70s.

GA: In your first e-mail reply to me, you mentioned that you listened to Klaus a lot in the late '70s but not much since. Do you remember the circumstances surrounding your first being exposed to Klaus' music? Do you remember which albums you heard first and how they made you feel?

RR: I learned about Klaus a few years after I discovered some of the more mainstream electronic music of the time. After hearing Vangelis, Kraftwerk, Tangerine Dream, Jarre and others when I was about 12 or 13, I started thumbing through the import bins and buying records that had cool looking covers or synths listed on the back. I lived near a university bookstore, and they must have had a very astute buyer at the time, because they had an amazing import section and very low prices. So I discovered Klaus by random search along with some other amazing (and sometimes very obscure) music. This would be around 1977, I think. The first album I found of his was either *Blackdance* or *Timewind* (probably *Timewind*). I listened to this the same way I listened to other great spacemusic - late at night I would turn off the lights, lay down and listen with my eyes closed, floating away to an internal visual place. I could actually use the music to trigger out-of-body sensations. I remember, later on, I wrote Klaus a few letters, and he always replied politely with a short note and a printed list of past concerts he had performed. I think he understood that his American audience was small and rather intense. I respected the fact that he took the time to answer letters from a 16-year-old.

GA: Also, did your experience with synthesizers begin before you began listening to Klaus' music?

RR: Actually I started building synthesizer kits about a year before I heard Klaus' music, but it was all part of the same process of discovering a sound that seemed to exist in primordial form inside me. As my homebuilt modular system slowly grew, I was certainly aware of his music, and I remember several attempts at creating sequences with the same melodic flow as he could obtain, with frustrating results because my PAIA kit sequencer was so unstable that the pitches would drift and warble.

In part, my inability to emulate his sound (and of other artists using good equipment) led me into my own more personal style using the electronics to trigger slow, atonal environmental noises. By the time I could have come close to the richness of his sequencer style, I felt that he and others had defined it so completely that I needed to express something very different, to map out my own terrain. Trying to veer away from the German spacemusic vocabulary that Klaus helped define, for me came from a conscious decision out of respect for the source.

GA: I'm interested in your reference to "discovering a sound that seemed to exist in primordial form inside me." What do you think it is about electronic music that is so special that it has caused you to follow an extended course that leads you toward that sound?

RR: I would have to clarify that the "sound" isn't specifically from electronic instruments. I was also attracted to Indian classical music, Indonesian gamelan, Harry Partch, Tibetan Buddhist ritual, Annea Lockwood's nature compositions, Terry Riley's minimalism and such, all of which share a psychoactive or ethereal component.

Pauline Oliveros' phrase "Deep Listening" captures the idea best: music that gets the listener to slow down and go inside, music that taps into the ritual and shamanistic uses of sound to guide altered states of consciousness, something primordial, something deeply internal. I consider the German spacemusic scene and some electronic music as part of this continuum. It's not the synthesizers themselves that make this music psychoactive, it's the act of using the instruments for certain trance-conducive musical purposes. All you need to do is contrast '70s European space/electronic music with dryer sounding synth composers like Wendy Carlos, or synth ditties like "Popcorn" to see that synths don't always make psychedelic music.

GA: Is there a form of satiation that is involved that is fulfilled when you compose a great song from the heart and yet still need to continue the search in the form of more songs and compositions?

RR: Perhaps you mean hunger rather than satiation? It's really a lack of satiation. Certain sounds percolate up from the depths and want to make themselves heard. Once you are done helping to bring that sound into the world, a new sound makes itself known. It's not so much a hunger/satiation metaphor as much as a metaphor of servitude, performing a duty that calls out to you from deep inside.

GA: Do you think this is related to why electronic music artists such as yourself, Klaus Schulze (and others) have made this journey over such extended periods of time and been so prolific?

RR: I'm sure we all have personal motivations that can't be lumped so easily together; but I suspect that many of us share some sort of siren's call that comes from a hermetic place. This isn't the sort of music that people make to get rich or popular. The social motivations inherent in pop music don't function so well in trance music - it's a private world that calls out from silence. Those of us who have long careers would probably be doing this regardless of whether or not an audience existed for it. We keep plugging away for other reasons.

GA: Where do you see Klaus Schulze in the history of electronic music?

RR: Perhaps as a consistent voice for the vocabulary of spacemusic, certainly as an innovator and a pioneer, if not perhaps as a somewhat obsessive creator within the narrow vocabulary that he has charted for himself.

GA: Do you have any sense of what it is about Klaus Schulze's music that is so special?

RR: Perhaps, his single-mindedness and persistence. I think because he continues to represent these ideas of music as a trance-formative experience, unlike some of the peers in his generation who became hungry for more mainstream recognition and lost that psychoactive energy.

Robert Rich

Exclusive Klaus Schulze Interview with Greg Allen

GA: I'm interested in the unique, delightful and even mysterious sound that forms the propulsive centerpiece of the track "Totem" and "C'est Pas La Meme Chose" from *Picture Music*. Can you describe the process that you used to come up with this almost legendary (among KS fans) sound or rhythm? How did you feel once you had put together this sound and after completing "Totem"? Were you excited? Also, how did you feel once it was decided to put "C'est Pas La Meme Chose" on the re-release of *Picture Music*?

KS: The rhythm of *Picture Music* was done with the ARP Odyssey and I used the filter resonance, synchronized by sample and hold. That's the reason it sounds a bit groovey – because the drum machine and other rhythm generators didn't exist and therefore this was the kind of basic rhythm that sounds sometimes like Indian drums or tablas.

That was probably the first thing where I used rhythm again because after I stopped playing drums, I didn't like rhythm at all. Then I made just this kind of pad orientated music like *Irrlicht* or *Cyborg*. That's probably where people thought that this represented another attitude or approach towards electronic music and that probably fascinated the people.

For me I would say it was not a special feeling and I did not feel good or bad after that - it was just doing music normally; it was a lot of fun I had with that. I think you always have to have fun with music or doing music - otherwise it is the wrong piece that you did.

When you asked me, "How did you feel once when you decided to put a bonus track on *Picture Music*?" - How should I feel? I mean I made some music, so for me it is just normal that if there is space on a disk and people want to have some extra music, to put another track (consistent with *Picture Music*) on the disk. It was not a special feeling after that. It was just normal for me to add some extra music there.

GA: I believe also that you said that The Orb sampled this sound (from "Totem"). Did Alex Paterson contact you around the time he decided to sample your music? If so, did he express any general admiration for your music? Do you know which Orb album the sample appears on?

KS: I believe that you said the Orb sampled the sound from "Totem"; this is the wrong information you got. The Orb never sampled from me. It was the people from German Spoons, they sampled some of this rhythm. And also Future Sound of London sampled from me and they even paid for the samples. So, as far as I know, the Orb never sampled from "Totem" or any other part of my music.

GA: Klaus, KDM mentioned to me that you had been satisfied with "George Trakl" as a 5:20 piece on the Brain release of *X*. I never thought anything was wrong with "George Trakl," but once I heard the re-release version, I was blown away! How have your thoughts evolved about this piece of music? How excited, if at all, were you when it was decided to include the longer version, first on *Ultimate Edition* and especially on the re-release, where so many people discovered it anew?

KS: When you say "satisfied," of course I'm always satisfied with the music when I release it, otherwise I would not release it. When you said that I used the long piece, it was just through the limitation of vinyl records. There were just about seven minutes left on the original vinyl, so I just shortened it because I liked the music very much but there was not enough space.

Now, on a CD where we have 80 minutes instead of 50 minutes and since "Trakl" couldn't be complete on the record, we used the opportunity to include the entire piece that I originally made. It was not a case of being excited, like you always say; after that, for me, it was just a longer version which could now be heard by people who never heard it before.

GA: In one of my e-mails with KDM, he wrote that you had admired the music of Johnny and the Hurricanes and the Ventures. Did your liking for these instrumental groups influence your path in any way once you decided to go solo and virtually all instrumental?

KS: Yes that's true, it was not only Johnny and the Hurricanes and the Ventures, it was also especially the Shadows, which was the backing band for Cliff Richard, and also the Spotnicks, a Scandinavian band.

It was at the time when I started to play electric guitar. I had the classical training with acoustic guitar when I was five years old. When I was around nine or ten, I liked the electric guitar more, which I think is quite understandable, it's a nicer toy than the acoustic guitar! I also used delays at this time from the tape machine, which was an old telefunken that I used when I recorded *Irrlicht*.

So, I just copied the Shadows and the Ventures. *Walk Don't Run*, for example, was one of their albums and so it made for a lot of fun, but it was not creative. It was just to play like they already had composed and I wanted to just sound like them. I had none of my own spirit of composing - not in these years.

Then, later on I stopped playing guitar and at this time I stopped listening to these bands and musicians. I switched over to drums and then, of course, I heard Art Blakey and Ginger Baker and similar artists.

GA: You've spoken before about the fact that beauty can't be experienced without ugliness to contrast with it. Do you make a conscious attempt to employ that in your compositions? If so, could you elaborate on how you bring out beauty by contrasting it with "ugliness?"

KS: Yes, this is the same thing with major and minor chords. When you play music or you paint a picture, there would be no black without white and no green without red. It's the same in music, when you always play in minor, your ears and your brain get used to these chords, which doesn't allow for a changing in moods. That's the reason I use only short major chords, to allow the listener to hear how beautiful minor sounds.

Also, in the same spirit, I use somehow disharmonic atmospheres and also a bit disharmonic vocals just to show how nice, how comfortable you feel when you hear the pure harmony. But if you always play in harmony, it is the same thing. You get used to it and when you get used to something, you get easily bored by it. I don't want to bore people and that's the reason why I use this kind of tension between beauty and ugliness, as you say here (in a musical sense).

GA: How did working with Michael Shrieve influence you or affect how you used percussion in your work, if at all? Are there any specific albums where you applied techniques or concepts learned as a result of working with Michael?

KS: Yes, the strange thing that led to working with Mike was we got to know each other through the *Go* recording sessions. Also, through the concert in Paris when we played in the Palais Des Sports. We gave an encore, just Mike and me - Michael and me, he doesn't like the shortening to Mike, he prefers Michael. So that suddenly, we realized that we could play very well together. That was the reason that I called him when *Go* was finished and asked him whether he would like to play on my records. He actually played on Wahnfried and also on the *Trancefer* album.

And you know, he taught me that rhythm is a part of physical movement. When I was playing my sequences, he listened to it and then he said, "Klaus, stand up and try to walk with it". In the beginning, it didn't really work so then he said, "adjust the speed." So then I was adjusting and then suddenly I had the kind of speed which fits to my body movements.

Now, we always work on the computer with BPM, but with a normal sequencer in the early days we never knew which beat-per-minute speed we had.

So, in coordinating with my body movement, it came out to 95 beats per minute exactly. Even if I play slower or faster sometimes, he taught me that rhythm is only good if your body feels well with it. Then you don't have to artificially match the rhythm. That was a most impressive thing that I learned from him. Of course I learned a lot about drums and about percussion from him and he's a real nice guy anyway, so it was really a lot of fun. It's a pity that we haven't met after all this time, but now I'm more on drum machines and drum loops anyway.

GA: How did you meet Pete Namlook? You've described the process you use in putting together your solo albums. Could you describe the process you and Pete (and sometimes Bill Laswell) employed when creating *The Dark Side of the Moog* series?

KS: I had an interview with a guy from Frankfurt. He was coming to my house to do the interview and he brought Pete with him, because they knew each other and Pete wanted to meet me. He just said he'd like to bring the friend (Pete) with him and so I said "OK, no problem".

Then, when we were here after the interview, we [Pete and Klaus] had all the small talk. We were talking about various things and we finally decided that we liked each other very much and to do some music together.

It worked very well. The special thing with this meeting, which was for me also very funny, was that Pete said, "Klaus you have here all the Moogs. They're old instruments for us, they're just dreams

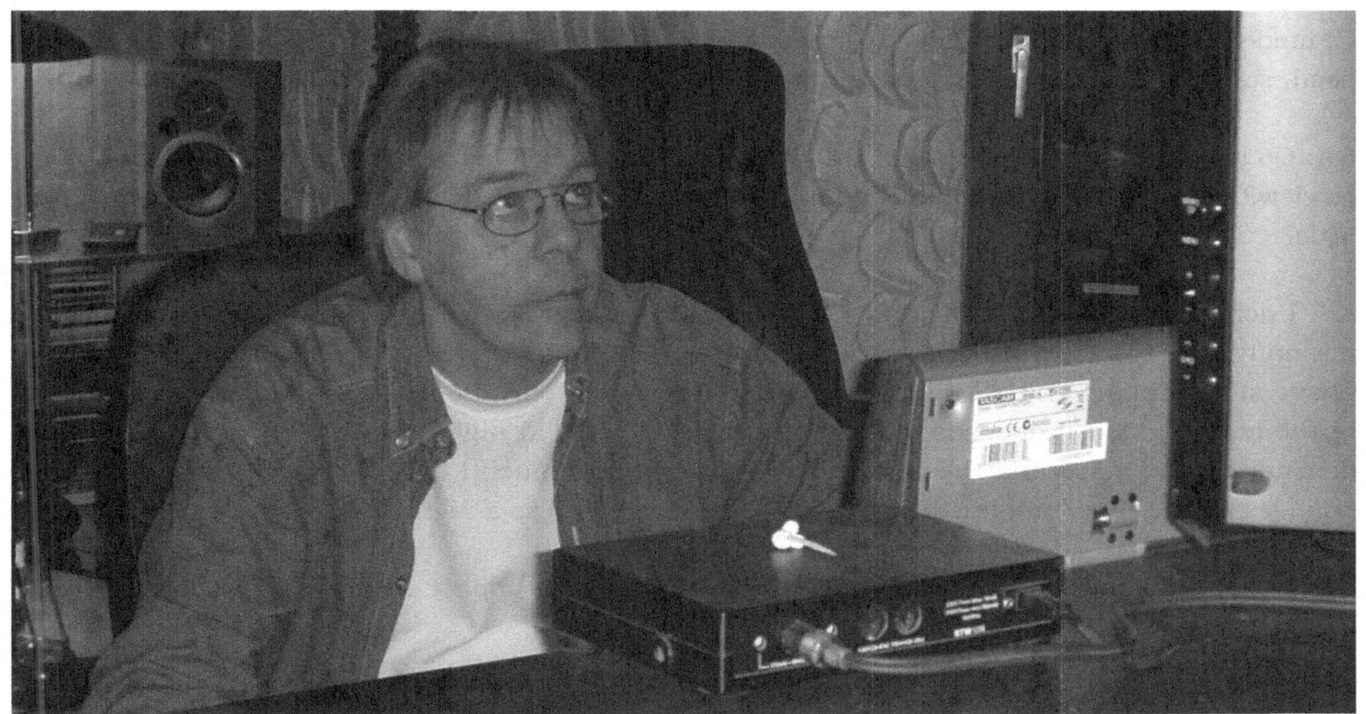

and you have them here and you don't use them. What do you think about using them, especially for our *Dark Side of the Moog*?" So, they used the old instruments and I said, "OK, why not?" and I was myself surprised because I hadn't used them for ten years.

We came also to the name, when I started to play the Moogs again. We said, "OK" and we made a kind of a joke about Pink Floyd's *Dark Side of the Moon* and *The Dark Side of the Moog.* And always on the project, *Dark Side of the Moog,* we used modified Pink Floyd titles. That was just a game. The music has nothing to do with Pink Floyd.

So, we started [unintelligible] live together. We did a concert together and then through his connection to Bill Laswell, Pete said once, "Let's add a bass player to that." It was Bill Laswell and I said ,"OK, no problem". We made about three or four records together, but I never saw this guy. It was all sending the tapes backwards and forwards or via computer.

This is the story of *The Dark Side of the Moog,* which is not any more existing. We stopped the project. We just thought after 10 CDs, it's enough. Probably we will start a new project but we will see. It will probably be called "Brothers in Arts." We want to do a new project but how that will look or sound, nobody knows yet. It will be a surprise also for us.

GA: What was the reason for the track *For Barry Graves* being named after Barry Graves? I've read that he was a German journalist, author and radio moderator (DJ). Is that right?

KS: Yes, the reason that we gave this name was just to honor him because in the early days he was very much concerned about electronic music, which was very rare in Germany at the time. He also was a guy who announced at my concert, before the concert. Then it was filmed by the TV which he made the connection to. That's the reason we call it *For Barry Graves*. Since ages ago, he's been dead, so that's the reason we named it *For Barry Graves* - kind of to honor him.

GA: Do you still work at night after your wife has gone to bed, as you mentioned in a previous interview? Is it still something like 10 p.m. to 5 a.m. on a regular basis, or have you scaled it back a little?

KS: I don't know who told you that I started making music when my wife is going to bed, but I normally have started at 8:00 in the [evening]. Around the time when it's getting dark and the telephone stops ringing and all the business is done more or less. So, I start to do music 'till mostly in the morning, but it depends. Sometimes I stop at 11:00 at night or I work the next morning. It depends on the mood and the power you've got and how much I have to say in music. And so it changes all the time, and it is just true that I am more or less a night worker, like you say.

GA: Does your illness of a couple years ago still have some impact on the way you work on your music?

KS: No, it doesn't have any influence, and the illness is more or less forgotten. I don't care about the past. I look rather to the present and the future.

GA: How is your health now? How do you feel?

KS: I feel well, everything is OK.

GA: KDM told me (in writing) that you still use the EMS Synthi A immensely. It looks like you first acquired this instrument around 1973-74. Do you still use the very same Synthi A that you acquired back then, or have you gotten newer models?

KS: That is not really the case. I use it live very much but in the studio I rather don't use it. That's because it's a special instrument for me, which is responsible for the abstract intros and sounds. I need this on stage just to make bridges from one set to another set.

I also needed the Synthi A when I had to change the synthesizer sound. There, I cannot make a minute of silence and just say, "Hold on a second, I just want to change my sound". So, that's the reason why the EMS is so connected. It's always running through sample and hold and modulation so that it sounds like it would be always developing itself.

And that's the reason why I use it very much on stage but in the studio I don't use it so much. There I can stop the recording, change the sound and go on with recording - so it's not really immensely used, the EMS. Even if the sound is very special and I like it very much - I still use it, and I will use it in future concerts.

GA: Does the Synthi A have more diverse sound making capabilities than the Minimoog, which you have referred to as having certain strengths but also having limitations?

KS: Now, of course, I mean that the Minimoog has more or less kind of a lead sound. And maybe a little bit of atmosphere if you use the noise generator, but then it's finished. The EMS is more or less made for atmosphere sounds - because you can hardly play it [tonally], because it's definitely out of tune every second. So, it's just made to be an atmosphere sound source for me.

GA: In researching for this book, I noticed that *Irrlicht* got overall good reviews, some calling it a classic. I read an interview in 1978 where you mentioned the artistic and commercial success of *Irrlicht* was near zero. Has your opinion of *Irrlicht* changed with the perspective of passing years?

KS: I think the artistic thing was not like zero. I was joking - otherwise I wouldn't have released it. I think they just misunderstood it in the interview, that it was just more or less commercially no success.

OK, artistically you can say I made better albums afterwards like *Timewind* or *X* or *Mirage* but it's a development also of technology. Also, that at this time when I made *Irrlicht*, I had no synthesizer yet. *Irrlicht* is kind of a break in the music feeling of the time but not so much influenced by technology. It's more influenced by intellectual mood, whatever it is.

At this time, it's kind of a milestone in musical history but not from an electronic music point. It's more or less a broken organ and kind of a filter feedback modulation. And that's all that is done, but it's still worth being mentioned because it was the beginning of my solo career. Also, it was the beginning of a new kind of music, which wasn't possible before. Later on, I went on to make new music, but the first step is also the most important step.

GA: How did you feel when the track "But Beautiful" was chosen as the bonus track for *Cyborg*? That is such a great track, in my opinion, with traces of a few of the '70s Schulze classics evoked.

KS: I answered already with *Picture Music;* it's the same story.

GA: You have flirted with a Trance sound on some of your tracks like "Opera Trance" and "Peg Leg Dance," even some of the Wahnfried material (even "Spielglocken"). Have you ever seriously considered releasing some Trance that would fit within the genre as done by DJs like Armin Van Buuren, Tiesto, Markus Shulz, Paul Van Dyke, etc.?

KS: Well, I don't know about whether I flirted with somebody or with some music styles. I just always do music which I like in the moment and if I come nearer to a fashion or not to a fashion it has nothing to do with my going to a special commercial attitude. It's just at this time I feel like doing this, and next time I feel something else. And like you said, I'd say I don't even know these people. I heard something of Paul van Dyke and that's all that I know about this scene. I'm not so much interested in it. It's very refreshing stuff that they do but it's not my cup of tea, like we say.

GA: Did it surprise or even hurt you that there were complaints or criticism about the use of repeated samples around the time of *Beyond Recall, Royal Festival Hall Vol. 1 and 2* and *The Dome Event*? It sounds like you might have re-evaluated the use of samples yourself, as I recall reading that you mentioned samples should only be used once. Could you comment on how you feel about the use of samples now and how your feelings have changed since the early '90s?

KS: No, I'm never touched by critics, you know. It's just that I make the records the way I like them, and of course I hope that all my fans like the music too. But if they like this or if they don't like it, it's no reason for me to change the music or to even stop the music. It's always a question of taste, and that's the reason why some people like a certain kind of music on my records and other people like different things.

Sometimes people like *Picture Music*, other people liked *Moondawn* and other people liked *X* or *Are You Sequenced?* or whatever. So, I think it's quite useless to think about critics because if you make an album and you play it to a hundred people they will all have a different attitude towards it. And different complaints or praises about the album. What can you do? The only measurement, measuring point, you can have is your own responsibility for the music. That's the reason I don't care so much about this.

GA: Are there any plans to include the original "Velvet Voyage" on a re-release for the benefit of people that might have discovered your music recently and don't have that original version?

KS: I don't know. All these bonus tracks and the selection of them is more up to Klaus Mueller, who has done this kind of job because I'm really too lazy to listen to all my other tapes.

It's always material from the past, and I'd rather make a new record than to work with old stuff. Mueller is quite fit with it with the knowledge about these old tapes. So this is a job that I don't do so much. I don't even really think - I just trust him that he will choose the right piece.

GA: How did it feel to be invited to parties with King Albert of Belgium and President Francois Mitterrand of France as a result of the film score for *Le Moulin de Daudet*? Do you remember anything about those experiences that you could relate?

KS: Again, always you ask, "How do you feel!"

You answered it yourself. It was a result of the fact that I did some music for *Le Moulin de Daudet*. Daudet is like Goethe for children in France. And in Belgium they speak also French. The premier of the movie was in Brussels and in Paris, so after the show we met and then we had a couple of drinks and it was very funny.

So with Mitterrand, I saw the movie in his Palace where his Government is sitting in Hotel Deville. After that, we had a small dinner and we talked a lot about just politics and things like that, but it was not a special feeling.

I think I don't know whether I understand your word "feel," but it's that in your career you have always different people you met. You have no special feelings there when you met them - then it's just a nice evening or it's a boring evening. You never can say that you have this special feeling with that, you know?

GA: Klaus, *Ballett 3* really struck me with its beauty, especially with the use of the human voices almost as additional instruments. Did you have this piece largely composed ahead of time or did it arise from experimentation and adjustments among you, Wolfgang Tiepold, Tobias Becker, Thomas Kagermann, Tom Dams and Julia Messenger? Could you talk about how this long, stunning piece of music was put together?

KS: (Reading question) Klaus, *Ballett 3* really struck me with its beauty... "that's nice for you!"

I never compose ahead of time. It's just like all my music is just composed in the moment where I play it. Afterwards, I try to arrange it to a piece of music, which then sounds like it's been composed. I don't compose any music before I play any keys. The reason is that I play the keys before I compose and during the playing back, I compose. In the arrangement, I do the final mix and then the record is finished. I call it improvisation and you called it composition, which sounds more serious, of course, but it's...just music.

I think when I met all these people that played on *Ballett 3*, it was a time frame of some weeks. Actually the music always, hopefully you're not disappointed, but the music was made in the same time as other longer pieces. We started with the recording, we finished with that recording and the piece was finished. So if, say, *Ballett* is 70 minutes long - we need 70 minutes for that piece of music.

It's like *Timewind*. When I composed *Timewind*, like you can read in the booklet as well, it was done between 10 and 12 o'clock in the night. Let's say within two hours I made *Timewind*.

It depends because when you are in a good mood you can make it in two hours, and if you are in a bad mood, you throw away 100 hours. So, when it works it works, when it doesn't work, it doesn't work. I don't want to compose intellectually because then it is too artificial. It has to kind of flow out of me and it should then be OK on the tape or the hard disk, wherever you recorded, and there will be no question of being calculated music. It's not my way of doing music.

GA: You've talked often about how the music you create is meant to stir emotions. Many of your compositions have had that effect on me, stirring deep emotions. Is there anything you do to ensure that your music is the type where deeply felt emotion is evoked in the listener? Could it just be your belief that music can mainly do one thing, which is to stir emotions?

KS: I think I said that already. That I do the music emotionally, especially in so-called contrast to electronic instruments, [which]...people say sound cold and work mechanically. Like every instrument, I think it's up to the man who makes music with the instrument.

Then the instruments sound like the man. If the man is very cold and let's say rational, the instrument will sound like that. And also the same is true with the violin. I mean, a violin doesn't grow on a tree, you know, so it's also made in a very sophisticated way. There are people who play it in a very emotionless way, and other people just play it very emotionally.

The same is true with synthesizers. Instruments are just tools. The reason they sound the way they do depends on how you treat them. That's the reason that music, for me, has to be always emotional. Which art form can be considered rational? I mean, therefore we have science.

Music is art just like painting, like sculptures, like whatever. They have to be emotional because that's a counterpoint to, let's say, science, you know. And even if everybody thinks that electronic music is just a piece of [equipment] that seems like science – no, you can use an instrument like everything else. You can drive a car, you can kill people with a car and also you can save people with a car by bringing them to the hospital very quickly. So, they (cars and synths) have both capabilities. It's always up to the user or to the man who is working with them.

GA: Are you a person who feels emotion very deeply? When I listen to an album like *Timewind* and I feel this deep passionate, yearning quality in the music, I feel that the creator of the music feels emotions on a very deep level.

KS: Yes, of course, otherwise I couldn't make music like this. What you feel is right, so the question is really answered. It is of course different because deep feelings could be different for everybody. The only thing that is important is that you can feel that you are open to this kind of music. If you are open to this kind of music, you have all the spectrum of emotions you want. Everybody has different emotions, but at least they are all deep. And that's the reason why I do this kind of music: because I don't want to be a kind of wallpaper musician, you know - so it is too boring for me.

GA: Klaus, how did it come about that Bob Moog opened *Dark Side of the Moog 5*? How much did that mean to you to have him start the album off with his introduction?

KS: Yes, you have to know that I know Bob Moog personally and we are - we have been friends. We met a couple of times and the main thing is that through Bob Moog I was able to make my music. So, it was a very big honor for me that he even spoke on the CD, when he opened *The Dark Side of the Moog*. I like him very - I liked him very much. I like him still, even though he is not anymore with us - but it is very important. Robert Moog was for me, I don't know, of the same importance as the 220 volts of electricity which makes it possible to record and to have a studio.

GA: Are there any other videos of you in concert that might be available for release in the future (besides the *For Barry Graves* and Ars Electronica)?

KS: No, there is nothing else because at that time when I made my live shows, it was more or less too expensive to get a film crew. And the technique was not so advanced, like today, where you have a camera that you can film everything for cheap money and also with a very high quality. At that time, nothing like that existed.

As of today, it is planned that we will probably do a DVD with my record company next year during my concerts with a real film crew and post production, everything. However, up until now, there are only the two things which are available in normal quality.

Steve Roach Interview with Greg Allen

Steve is one of the preeminent space music musicians of the period beginning in the early 1980s. My top three (excepting Klaus, of course, who is in a different category but was definitely influential to the next "generation") would be Steve, Robert Rich, and Jonn Serrie.

Steve's music first caught my ear when I was in the car in the '80s and heard this dreamy, spacy music playing which I really liked. I didn't retain the artist's name very well, and when I went to the record store, I saw Steve Reich and thought maybe he was the artist I'd heard. So I bought that, but it was nothing like Steve Roach's music.

I eventually caught up with Steve's music since I was an avid listener to the *Hearts of Space* radio show. My first two purchases were *Quiet Music* and *Structures From Silence*. *Quiet Music* was and is a CD to play when you really want to slow down and relax. Other top CDs from Steve that I purchased from the early to middle '90s are *Strata* (with Robert Rich; *Strata* has two fantastic electronic music pieces back-to-back – "Forever" and "The Grotto of Time Lost"); *Soma* (with Robert Rich); *World's Edge* (containing a 60-minute piece of music, "To the Threshold of Silence," which is well named); and *The Magnificent Void* (which impressed me a lot the last couple of times I listened to it).

I haven't kept up with Steve's recent output, which has been quite prolific overall. Visit www.steveroach.com to learn more. There is also a picture of Steve and Klaus meeting after a concert that Steve had played.

One other thing that Steve is noted for is his playing of the didgeridoo (check out this link: http://en.wikipedia.org/wiki/didgeridoo). I saw Steve play a concert at a Goth festival in Chicago about 10 years ago, and he started off with long held single notes on a very long and large didgeridoo. Those resonating notes eventually lead to a spacy synth note that just sort of sustained and evolved over a whole hour. It was a fantastic treat!

The interview:

GA: Do you recall when you heard your first Klaus Schulze album, which album it was and your feelings about it at the time?

SR: *Timewind* was the first LP I heard. In Early '78 I was working in a small import record shop in La Mesa, California. Once a week new shipments would come in from JEM imports, a stateside importer of all of the Euro electronic, progressive and beyond.

I was already in the deep end with Tangerine Dream, Kraftwerk, Can, and much of the German and European electronic and progressive music. I still remember cracking open the box to stock the shelf and pulling *Timewind* out, amazed at the cover right off. At first play I was taken over; things were different, changed forever after that one.

As I was expanding into musical and creative horizons and feeling the urge to create with sound, I was looking for extended pieces and zones that held a feeling for a longer period. *Timewind* hit that nerve directly. And the fact that it was created by one person, with a handful of synths, spoke deeply to me.

GA: I think that Klaus was breaking ground with many of his first ten releases. Can you recall which albums you heard and felt that "Wow!" feeling?

SR: Well as I mention *Timewind* was the one for me but then went to *Picture Music*, the track "Totem" in particular. And then I was on board with the succession of classic period releases. *Mirage*, *X*, *Body Love* - these along with *Timewind* and *Picture Music* were and still are my favorites and the ones that had this kind of connected sense between them all.

GA: You also wrote at least one review that I know of about KS, I believe back in the 1970s. Did you interview Klaus for that article? If so, what were your impressions as you approached it and did the interview?

SR: The article was for *Synapse* Magazine, one of the first magazines in the States for Electronic Music. I did not interview Klaus for this. I wrote him back then and he sent a several page bio which I drew from, along with some info I had found in some articles at the time. I knew the editors of *Synapse*, and it was a natural way to share what I was feeling passionate towards. While they were more into the academic side of electronic music, they were quite open to the entire Berlin school, and I was always flying that flag in their presence.

GA: When did you get your first synthesizer and begin to play? Was that acquisition inspired by Klaus Schulze and/or Tangerine Dream, or was there another inspiration?

SR: It was inspired by the feelings I was tapping into both without and with music. The experience of Klaus' music along with the early classic Tangerine Dream and selective progressive music such as *Yes* was all vital in helping to ignite the inner fire. As I mention in the first question, because it was clear that Klaus was working from a solo place, that in itself was very inspiring for me and gave me a further confirmation for the path I was on.

GA: If any of Klaus' first ten albums were of inspiration to you in starting your career (I'm noting that your very first release was in 1979, about the time *Dune* came out), which ones and how did they affect your developing sound leading up to your first major work *Structures From Silence* (feel free to insert Tangerine Dream or others into the equation, if appropriate)?

SR: *Structures From Silence* was created around 1982. While I was still immersed and addicted to sequencer based music, I was at the same time exploring a kind of sound that was a direct response to wanting to get off sequencers so to speak; to move away from the impulse to stay working in that form of using sequencers and that mode of expression.

Along with this I was becoming more aware of the longer standing influence, that of the deserts and natural areas I grew up in. This was also a period where I was doing a lot of inner work and tuning into the breath and breathing as a fundamental awareness tool. *Structures from Silence* is really about this process more than anything.

Like any artist, be it Klaus to the members of TD, there is music and art that feeds the artist's soul in the formative years and helps to get you off the ground so to speak. So much of the late '70s electronic and progressive music was an important part of the process in tapping into the current for my own creative life. It was impossible to not feel that something really amazing and powerful was occurring in technology driven music during that time.

For me, nothing was taken for granted, and at every turn it was exciting to hear the music coming out; to be creating it and to see the development of the technology at the front lines of the time. At the same time, one can never underestimate the other non-musical episodes in life at that time that are impossible to translate into the picture you're asking about.

GA: Can you pick a favorite Klaus Schulze album from the '70s or is that too difficult to do for you like it is for me?

SR: *Timewind.*

GA: Is the motivation behind *Structures from Silence* and *Quiet Music* traceable back to Klaus Schulze and/or Tangerine Dream -- or was there another primary impetus for their creation?

SR: As I mention above, *Structures from Silence* and *Quiet Music* were conscious departures [a]way from these roots. When *Structures* was created, it was really without any agenda to release it. It might have been a year before that idea came around.

GA: When I acquired *Stormwarning,* it was a new Steve Roach sound to me but I really liked it because it had the intense sequencing that was reminiscent of parts of *Phaedra,* Michael Hoenig's *Departure from the Northern Wasteland* and maybe especially *Ricochet* by Tangerine Dream. What inspired you to make an album with that decidedly up-tempo sound?

SR: By that time my dual personality of deep-quiet pieces like *Structures from Silence, Quiet Music* and the raging sequencer style was at its peak. The combination of the live setting and living in the Los Angeles fast lane during the '80s was fully realized here. These concerts were well attended and no one was really doing this kind of music live at this level in the LA area at the time. It really brought out the electronic music listeners from all over, and the energy was high at these concerts. This was about pure energy and creating that sound from a place that is intensely focused; a kind of martial arts approach to being fully present and going for it with the pure analog approach. The sound system was provided by Gary Raymond, a kind of cult figure in the sound reinforcement world in southern California. The sound systems were big and loud, Voice of Theater, classic '70s-'80s stacks with unreal folded subwoofer energy as well, which was vital in shaping what you hear on *Stormwarning.*

GA: Have you personally met Klaus and/or played with him?

SR: We met briefly after my concert at 1991 KlemDag in Holland. That was a great feeling indeed if only brief. There is a photo of this moment at my website, he is wearing all white, and I am wearing all black.

GA: Have you continued to follow his career since his '70s heyday? Was there ever a period for you where his albums became more difficult to obtain?

SR: I still check in but not so closely over the years, and I am still updating my collection with the recent released versions of the early classics.

My respect will always be held in the highest place for the accomplishments in Klaus' music and the inspiration it still provides. He is without question a pinnacle in the landscape of technology based music and beyond.

Chapter 16 Extra Pictures

prost
JEANS

Appendix A Klaus' Concerts

Recollections of concerts by Klaus D. Mueller: "I just remember some small things from some concerts, but mostly I even don't remember WHICH concert it was: a supporting group that played 45 minutes longer as agreed. A concert where I am falling asleep backstage, because KS played so long and peaceful (today they would call it maybe: "new age music"). A concert that had to be cancelled because there was a VERY bad electricity, so we had to pack in the already built-up equipment when there was already some audience in the hall. A concert where we could not use our (small, home-made) laser show because the local promoter had announced it as a HUGE light show. A concert in Spain with seven professional TV teams in the hall; and no one had informed us before. I was so angry that I only gave KS on stage very dark (blue) light, so that those TV cameras cannot film much. In general, those Spain concerts were lousy organized, very lousy. See, I mostly remember some happenings that were disturbing the concert, because it was MY job that concerts did happen, that they happen undisturbed and that they happen in time.

"Many concerts were great. Some concerts that were not so great. The one I still remember very well was in February 1973 in Paris. The first big concert for all artists, in front of a sold-out auditorium of raving fans who wanted to see the new sensations from Germany. First played Tangerine Dream, then Ash Ra Tempel (with KS, and with me making first the announcement and then some eerie sounds with a frequency generator). And then played KS as soloist, on the new Farfisa organ, prerecorded tape (his drumming), echo machine, and an EMS synthesizer. It was a huge success. And all the coming French successes came from here."

The following list shows which concerts can be found on what CD. A complete list of all Klaus Schulze concerts is available in "The Works":

Date	**Location**	**Album**	**Track**
05/19/71	Berlin, West Germany	The Private Tapes 2	4
05/19/71	Berlin, West Germany	The Private Tapes 3	5
09/10/71	Berne, Switzerland	The Private Tapes 6	4
02/28/73	Cologne, West Germany	The Private Tapes 4	5
02/28/73	Cologne, West Germany	The Private Tapes 5	5
1975	West Germany	*Silver Edition* 3	3
1975	West Germany	*Silver Edition* 9	1
04/28/75	France	*Historic Edition* 8	2
05/30/75	Munich, West Germany	*Historic Edition* 3	1-3
1975	Germany	*Silver Edition* 10	1
10/04/75	Furth, Germany	*Ultimate Edition* 48	
10/24/75	Munich, West Germany	*Historic Edition* 5	3
1976	France	*Historic Edition*	6
04/20/06	Rouen, France	*Historic Edition* 2	2
05/09/76	Rotterdam, Netherlands	*Historic Edition* 6	1
06/12/76	Paris, France	*Go Live from Paris*	1-14
10/05/76	Berlin, West Germany	*...Live...*	2

11/04/76	Brussels, Belgium	*Silver Edition* 3	1+2
11/07/76	Oberhausen, West Germany	*Historic Edition* 2	3
11/07/76	Oberhausen, West Germany	*Historic Edition* 8	1
10/17/77	Brussels, Belgium	*Historic Edition* 1	2
10/17/77	Brussels, Belgium	*Historic Edition* 2	1
10/27/77	Amsterdam, Netherlands	*...Live...*	4
11/13/79	Paris, France	*...Live...*	1+3
09/08/80	Linz, Austria	*Jubilee Edition* 24	1
11/22/81	Leiden, Netherlands	*Historic Edition* 1	1
11/22/81	Leiden, Netherlands	*Historic Edition* 5	1+2
07/02/83	Katowitz, Poland	*Dziekuje Poland Live '83*	1
07/08/83	Lodz, Poland	*Dziekuje Poland Live '83*	3
07/09/83	Warsaw, Poland	*Dziekuje Poland Live '83*	2
07/10/83	Gdansk, Poland	*Dziekuje Poland Live '83*	4+5
08/05/89	Dresden, East Germany	*Dresden Performance*	1+4
05/11/91	Cologne, Germany	*The Dome Event*	1
09/10/91	London, Great Britain	*Royal Festival Hall Vol. 1*	1
09/10/91	London, Great Britain	*Royal Festival Hall Vol. 2*	1+2
05/27/94	Paris, France	*Das Wagner Desaster*	1-3
05/31/94	Rome, Italy	*Das Wagner Desaster*	4-6
09/27/96	Derby, Great Britain	*Are You Sequenced?* (1)	1-11
11/24/97	Duisburg, Germany	*Dosburg Online*	1-9
04/31/99	Hamburg, Germany	*The Dark Side of the Moog 8*	1-8
06/09/01	Osnabrück, Germany	*Live @ KlangArt 1*	1-3
06/09/01	Osnabrück, Germany	Live @ *KlangArt 2*	1-4

Appendix B Film Scores

There are many movies, documentary films, radioplays, etc. in which music from KS' albums is used (for a quite complete listing, please refer to "The Works"), but only a few for which KS composed original music.

Which soundtracks did Klaus compose?

Year	Title and Country	Type
1973	Das grosse Identifikationsspiel (Germany)	Radio Play
1975	*Leben am seidenen Faden* (Germany)	Documentary
1976	French Movie (never produced)	Movie
1976	*Chromengel II* (Germany)	Short Movie
1976	*Nachtwache* (Germany)	Short Movie
1976	*Götterdämmerung* (Germany)	Short Movie
1976	*Schau ins Land* (Germany)	Short Movie
1976	*Selig* (Germany)	Short Movie
1976	*Lichtblick* (Germany)	Short Movie
1976	*Wolkenpfad* (Germany)	Short Movie
1976	*De beste van de klas* (Netherlands)	Movie
1976	*Kriester* (Germany)	Documentary
1976	*Body Love* (Germany)	Movie
1976	Schwanensee (Germany)	Ballet
1978	*Barracuda* - The Lucifer Project (USA)	Movie
1983	*Next of Kin* (Australia)	Movie
1984	*Angst* (Austria)	Movie
1985	*Walk the Edge*	Movie
1985	*Havlandet* (Norway)	Movie
1985	Dr. Faustus elektrisiert (Germany)	Radio Play
1992	*Le Moulin de Daudet* (France)	Movie
1992	*Gegenwart* (Germany) (music was not used)	
1992	A Film About Whales	Documentary
1992	*Planetens spejle* (Mirror of the Planet) (Denmark)	Movie
1993	Aktiv (Germany)	TV Magazine
1993	*Burgen und Schlösser* (Germany)	Documentary
1993	Zwischen Himmel und Erde (Germany)	Radio Program
1994	***Potsdamer Platz*** (Germany)	Documentary
1994	*Kölcsönkapott idö* (*Living on Borrowed Time*) (Hungary)	Movie
2000	New Millenium New Beijing	Event

Which soundtrack recordings are released on CD?

Year	Title and country of movie	Album	Track
1976	*Body Love* (Germany)	*Body Love*	1-3
1976	*Body Love* (Germany)	*Body Love* Vol. *2*	1+3
1976	Schwanensee (Germany)	*Historic Edition* 9	1+3
1978	*Barracuda* (USA)	*Historic Edition* 4	4
1984	*Angst* (Austria)	*Angst*	2-5
1985	*Havlandet* (Norway)	*Historic Edition* 9	2
1992	*Le Moulin de Daudet* (France)	*Le Moulin de Daudet*	1-21
1993	*Burgen und Schlösser* (Germany)	*Silver Edition* 1	1-4
1993	Zwischen Himmel & Erde (Germany)	*Back to the Universe*	5
1994	*Potsdamer Platz* (Germany)	*Silver Edition* 4	1
2000	New Millenium New Beijing	*Contemporary Works 2* bonus CD	1-4